State-Space Models with Regime Switching

State-Space Models with Regime Switching
Classical and Gibbs-Sampling Approaches with Applications

Chang-Jin Kim and Charles R. Nelson

The MIT Press
Cambridge, Massachusetts
London, England

This book was set in Times Roman by Windfall Software using ZzTEX.

Library of Congress Cataloging-in-Publication Data

Kim, Chang-Jin, 1960–
  State-space models with regime switching : classical and
Gibbs-sampling approaches with applications / Chang-Jin Kim and
Charles R. Nelson.
    p.   cm.
  Includes bibliographical references and index.
  ISBN 978-0-262-11238-3 (alk. paper), 978-0-262-53550-2 (pb)
    1. Economics—Mathematical models. 2. State-space methods. 3.
Heteroscedasticity. 4. Sampling (Statistics) 5. Econometrics. I.
Nelson, Charles R. II. Title.
  HB135 .K515 1999
    330′.01′5118—dc21   98-44193
                                                   CIP

To Young-Ho and Kate

Contents

Preface and Acknowledgments

State-space models and Markov-switching models have both been highly productive paths for research in econometrics because they address primary issues in our attempts to understand the economy. Unobserved variables are important actors in our stories about consumption behavior, unemployment, inflation dynamics, indices of economic activity, monetary policy, and financial markets. In these situations the state-space framework, made operational by the Kalman filter, is the only one we have for making statistical inference in the time series context. There is also compelling empirical evidence that economic systems exhibit occasional jumps from one regime to another. When such a switch occurs the distribution of the data seems to change. For example, the macroeconomy periodically switches from boom to recession and back again, and dynamics differ between these two regimes. Financial markets periodically switch from a low-volatility regime to a high-volatility regime, and then back again. It is attractive to model such transitions as a Markov process.

The problem of marrying state-space modeling, employed to make inferences about unobserved variables, with a Markov process, employed to make inferences about the timing and nature of switches in regime, is not a trivial one. This becomes clear when we think about the fact that the timing of switches between regimes is unknown, and inference is conditional, in principle, upon all possible combinations of such dates. Recently, it has yielded to two lines of attack. One is from the classical perspective of maximum likelihood estimation, in which an approximation is used to reduce the dimensionality of the problem to manageable proportions. The second approach casts the problem in the Bayesian framework and uses Gibbs-sampling methodology to break the problem down into a sequence of steps that involve only Monte Carlo simulation. An advantage of the latter is that it permits exact inference in finite samples, demonstrating that the computer is not just a tool but is fundamentally changing how we do inference in econometrics. Subsequently, the range of applications for these methods has expanded much faster than we have been able to investigate them, and we felt that it was clearly time to gather results in this area together, along with computer programs, to make these tools generally available to research workers.

This book grew out of lecture notes developed for courses in econometrics taught by Chang-Jin Kim at Korea University and at the University of Washington, Seattle. The students in those courses were the source of numerous helpful comments, questions, and corrections. We have debts to more individuals than we can acknowledge here, but we will try to mention a few. Andrew Harvey is responsible for introducing state-space models to econometrics and developing inference for them. James Hamilton convinced the profession that Markov switching captured important features of the dynamics of the economy and showed how to do inference. We were also influenced particularly by the work of Siddhartha Chibb, Francis X. Diebold, James Stock, and Mark Watson. We have a special debt to Arnold Zellner, who suggested the Gibbs-sampling approach in a letter to Chang-Jin Kim and has been an invaluable source of wisdom and encouragement to Charles Nelson throughout his career. We are also grateful to our coauthors on papers that form the background for this book: Myung J. Kim, Richard Startz, and Charles Engel. James Morley, Chris Murray, and Young-Sook Lee read drafts of the manuscript carefully and provided corrections and suggestions. Finally, we are grateful to Terry Vaughn of The MIT Press for giving us the freedom to prepare the manuscript of this book in accordance with our instincts.

One of the guiding principles of this book is operationality, and we felt that it would be incomplete without ready access to the computer programs we used in its preparation. These are available from a web site at the University of Washington with the address

http://weber.u.washington.edu/~cnelson/SSMARKOV.html

If that address ceases to be available, please contact one of the authors by email at cjkim@kuccnx.korea.ac.kr or cnelson@u.washington.edu. Use of the programs in published work should be acknowledged by citing this book.

State-Space Models with Regime Switching

1 Introduction

This book aims to introduce to a wider audience of researchers in economics and finance recent advances in the estimation of state-space models in which switching between regimes occurs stochastically according to a Markov process. These are systems in which there is an unobserved or state variable that we would like to estimate through time, but we also want to allow for periodic shifts in the parameters that describe the system's dynamics or volatility. For example, we may have a vector of economic indicators measured monthly and would like to extract an index or common factor reflecting the state of the economy today. At the same time, we have reason to believe that dynamics and volatility differ between recessions and expansions, so we would like to allow for switching in parameters between these two regimes. Until recently, it was feasible to address either the state variable problem or the regime-switching problem, but not both at the same time. With the methods presented in this book, this and many other previously intractable models in economics and finance become operational.

Part I of the book discusses the classical approach to the estimation of state-space models with Markov switching in the maximum likelihood framework, then part II presents, in parallel, the Bayesian approach using Gibbs-sampling, a computation-intensive methodology that simulates joint posterior densities of parameters, state variables, and regimes. The methodology is illustrated at each step by examples, including time-varying regression coefficients with heteroskedasticity, fads and time-varying volatility in financial markets, a model of the business cycle that allows for asymmetry between expansions and contractions, extraction of an unobserved index of economic activity from a set of indicator variables with regime switching at turning points, decomposition of heteroskedastic exchange rates into permanent and transitory components, and testing for mean reversion in asset prices when returns are heteroskedastic. Actual output from programs and data sets available to the reader accompany each example.

Although more familiar to economists, the classical approach poses special difficulties in this context because of the potentially very large number of evaluations of the likelihood function required. Fortunately, the approximation method due to Kim (1994) makes maximum likelihood estimation feasible. However, two shortcomings of the classical approach motivate interest in the Bayesian alternative. First, the degree of approximation in any paticular case is unknown, though comparison with exact results in examples of interest suggest it may be small. Second, and of perhaps greater practical importance, in the classical approach estimation of state variables is conditional on maximum likelihood estimates of the parameters. In constrast, treatment of state variables, parameters, and regimes as jointly distributed random variables means that with the Bayesian approach, estimates of each appropriately reflect uncertainly about the others.

1.1   State-Space Models and Markov Switching in Econometrics:
A Brief History

The state-space model and Markov switching are not new in the statistics and econometrics literatures. But a growing number of published papers that employ them demonstrates their usefulness and widening application. In essence, a state-space model is one in which an observed variable is the sum of a linear function of the state variable plus an error. The state variable, in turn, evolves according to a stochastic difference equation that depends on parameters that in economic applications are generally unknown. Thus, both the path of the state variable through time and the parameters—describing the dynamics of the state variable, its relationship to the data, and the covariance structure of stochastic disturbances—are to be inferred from the data. Harvey, in his influential 1981 book and a series of early papers, introduced to economists the use of the Kalman (1960) filter for obtaining maximum likelihood estimates of parameters through prediction error decomposition was introduced. It became clear from Harvey's work and others' that a surprising range of econometric models, including regression models with time-varying coefficients, autoregressive moving average (ARMA) models, and unobserved-components time series models, could be cast in state-space form and thus be rendered amenable to the Kalman machinery for parameter estimation and extraction of estimates of state variables.

Economists have long recognized the possibility that parameters may not be constant through time but rather that structural shifts may occur, dividing the period into distinct regimes with different parameter values. In the regression model context, Quandt (1972) studied the case of independent switches in regime, then Goldfeld and Quandt (1973) extended the analysis to regime-dependent-switching probabilities according to a Markov chain. Dynamic models with Markov switching between regimes are relatively new. However, since James Hamilton introduced them in his seminal 1989 paper as a tool for dealing with endogenous structural breaks, the number of published papers that apply Markov-switching models has been enormous. An important appeal of these models is their ability to account for the accumulating evidence that business cycles are asymmetric, as discussed in a literature in which the work of Neftci (1984) is particularly influential. Furthermore, they suggest an alternative to the autoregressive conditional heteroskedasticity (ARCH) model of Engle (1982) and its extensions for modeling conditional heteroskedasticity, an important feature of asset returns.

Though models that incorporate both state variables and regime switching seem a natural extension of these literatures and have many obvious potential applications, their estimation posed serious computational barriers. However, with the algorithm for approximate maximum likelihood estimation developed by Kim (1993a, 1993b, 1994), a broad class of models becomes operational that could not be handled before. Applications discussed in this book include a time-varying parameter model of monetary uncertainty with heteroskedasticity, transient fads and crashes, Friedman's (1964, 1993) "plucking model," which accounts for a number of features of business cycle asymmetry, and construction of an index of coincident indicators where Markov switching occurs between business cycle regimes. Thus, the state-space model with Markov switching may be considered a general approach to dealing with endogenous structural breaks.

As mentioned above, the necessity of approximation for obtaining a computationally feasible algorithm for estimation and the treatment of parameter estimates as fixed when estimating state variables in the classical framework lead us to consider the Bayesian approach as an alternative. To make the latter point clear, an index of coincident indicators for the economy is obtained in two steps: In the first step, the parameters of the state-space model are estimated via approximate maximum likelihood; then, in the second step, we condition on those estimates so we can run the Kalman filter to extract the estimate of the index from the observed indicators. Similarly, inferences about which regime, recession or expansion, the economy is in at each point in time condition on the maximum likelihood estimates of the parameters.

Bayesian methods have a long history in econometrics; the classical reference work is Zellner 1971. Gibbs-sampling methods, originally introduced by Geman and Geman (1984), turn out to be the key to feasible estimation of the state-space model with Markov switching in the Bayesian framework. Albert and Chib (1993) introduced Gibbs-sampling in the context of Markov switching, and Carlin, Polson, and Stoffer (1992) and Carter and Kohn (1994) introduced Gibbs-sampling in the context of state-space models. Kim and Nelson (1998) make Gibbs-sampling operational for the state-space model with

Markov switching and construct an experimental index of coincident indicators that encompasses both comovement among economic variables and nonlinearity in the evolution of the business cycle. Gibbs-sampling exploits these models' conditioning features to break the problem down into feasible steps. The additional empirical examples presented in this book demonstrate both the operationality of the Gibbs-sampling approach in a wide range of applications and the empirical relevance of treating state variables, regime switches, and parameters as jointly distributed random variables. Thus, in the example of an index of coincident indicators, uncertainty about whether the economy is in recession or expansion at a particular date is appropriately reflected in the estimate of the state variable, the index of coincident indicators, for that date.

Looking to the future, we think that the most exciting prospect that this methodology holds is for dealing with evolution and change in economic systems. The empirical literature from many areas seems to convey the same message: Relationships between variables as well as dynamics evolve over time or shift abruptly, and disturbances are heteroskedastic. We find that predictability in asset returns varies across subsamples, as does volatility; money demand functions are notoriously unstable and heteroskedastic; and the dynamics of recessions differs greatly from that of expansions. The case for modeling change is compelling, and we hope that its feasibility becomes more apparent with this book.

1.2 Computer Programs and Data

All computations presented in this book can be replicated using programs written in Gauss © by C.-J. Kim and data sets that may be downloaded from the web site

http://econ.korea.ac.kr/~cjkim/

Readers who use the programs in published work are asked to acknowledge their use and cite this book as the reference.

References

Albert, James H., and Siddhartha Chib. 1993. "Bayes Inference via Gibbs Sampling of Autoregressive Time Series Subject to Markov Mean and Variance Shifts." *Journal of Business and Economic Statistics,* 11(1), 1–15.

Carlin, Bradley P., Nicholas G. Polson, and David S. Stoffer. 1992. "A Monte Carlo Approach to Nonnormal and Nonlinear State-Space Modeling." *Journal of the American Statistical Association*, 87(418), Theory and Methods, 493–500.

Carter, C. K., and P. Kohn. 1994. "On Gibbs Sampling for State Space Models." *Biometrica*, 81, 541–553.

Engle, R. F. 1982. "Autoregressive Conditional Heteroskedasticity with Estimates of the Variance of UK Inflation." *Econometrica*, 50, 987–1007.

Friedman, Milton. 1964. "Monetary Studies of the National Bureau." *The National Bureau Enters Its 45th Year*, 44th Annual Report, 7–25; reprinted in Milton Friedman, 1969, *The Optimum Quantity of Money and Other Essays*, chap. 12, 261–284. Chicago: Aldine.

Friedman, Milton. 1993. "The 'Plucking Model' of Business Fluctuations Revisited." *Economic Inquiry*, April, 171–177.

Geman, Stuart, and Donald Geman. 1984. "Stochastic Relaxation, Gibbs Distributions, and the Bayesian Restoration of Images." IEEE Transactions on Pattern Analysis and Machine Intelligence, 6, 721–741.

Goldfeld, S. M., and R. E. Quandt. 1973. "A Markov Model for Switching Regression." *Journal of Econometrics*, 1, 3–16.

Hamilton, James D. 1989. "A New Approach to the Econometric Analysis of Nonstationary Time Series and the Business Cycle." *Econometrica*, 57, 357–384.

Harvey, Andrew C. 1981. *Time Series Models*. Oxford: Philip Allan and Humanities Press.

Kalman, R. E. 1960. "A New Approach to Linear Filtering and Prediction Problems." *Transactions ASME Journal of Basic Engineering*, D82, 35–45.

Kim, Chang-Jin. 1993a. "Unobserved-Component Time Series Models with Markov-Switching Heteroskedasticity: Changes in Regime and the Link Between Inflation Rates and Inflation Uncertainty." *Journal of Business and Economic Statistics*, 11, 341–349.

Kim, Chang-Jin. 1993b. "Sources of Monetary Growth Uncertainty and Economic Activity: The Time-Varying-Parameter Model with Heteroskedastic Disturbances." *Review of Economics and Statistics*, 75, 483–492.

Kim, Chang-Jin. 1994. "Dynamic Linear Models with Markov-Switching." *Journal of Econometrics*, 60, 1–22.

Kim, Chang-Jin, and Charles R. Nelson. 1998. "Business Cycle Turning Points, A New Coincident Index, and Tests of Duration Dependence Based on A Dynamic Factor Model with Regime-Switching." *Review of Economics and Economic Statistics*, 80, 188–201.

Neftci, S. N. 1984. "Are Economic Time Series Asymmetric over the Business Cycle?" *Journal of Political Economy*, 92, 307–328.

Quandt, R. E. 1972. "A New Approach to Estimating Switching Regressions." *Journal of the American Statistical Association*, 67, 306–310.

Zellner, Arnold. 1971. *An Introduction to Bayesian Inference in Econometrics*. New York: John Wiley & Sons.

I THE CLASSICAL APPROACH

2 The Maximum Likelihood Estimation Method: Practical Issues

Part of the attraction of the ML theory is that it does offer estimator and test proce-dures that are technically almost universally applicable, provided one has a reasonably precise model. . . . There is a much better reason for using likelihood theory in that it provides a coherent framework for statistical inference in general.
—Cramer 1986, p. 8

The maximum likelihood estimation method is a way of obtaining estimators of a model when a specific distributional assumption is made about the vector of sample observations. Unlike least squares methods which use only the first two moments, maximum likelihood incorporates all the information in a model by working with the complete joint distribution of the observations.

Since the classical inferences for the models in chapters 3 through 6 depend heavily on maximum likelihood estimation, we provide a review of the method with a focus on related practical issues. For a more complete analysis of the maximum likelihood estimation method, readers are referred to Cramer 1986, Judge et al. 1982, Davidson and MacKinnon 1993, and Harvey 1990, from which this chapter draws.

2.1 Maximum Likelihood Estimation and the Covariance Matrix of $\hat{\theta}_{ML}$

A statistical model with a k-dimensional vector of parameters, θ, specifies a joint distribution for a vector of observations $\tilde{y}_T = [y_1 \quad y_2 \quad \ldots \quad y_T]'$:

Joint Density Function: $p(\tilde{y}_T | \theta)$, (2.1)

which, in the discrete case, provides us with the probabilities of obtaining a particular set of values for $\tilde{y}_T$, given θ. The joint density therefore is a function of $\tilde{y}_T$ given θ.

In econometric practice, we have a realization of the $\tilde{y}_T$ vector, or the sample data, and we do not know the parameter vector θ of the underlying statistical model. In this case, the joint density in (2.1) is a function of θ given $\tilde{y}_T$, and it is called the likelihood function:

Likelihood Function: $L(\theta | \tilde{y}_T)$, (2.2)

which is functionally equivalent to (2.1). Different values for θ result in differ-ent values for the likelihood function in (2.2). The likelihood function specifies the plausibility or likelihood of the data given the parameter vector θ. In the maximum likelihood estimation method, we are interested in choosing pa-rameter estimates so as to maximize the probability of having generated the observed sample, by maximizing the log of the above likelihood function:

$$\hat{\theta}_{ML} = \text{Argmax} \ln L(\theta|\tilde{y}_T), \qquad (2.3)$$

where $\ln L$ refers to the log likelihood function.

Maximizing the log likelihood function instead of the likelihood function itself enables us to estimate directly the asymptotic covariance matrix, $\text{Cov}(\hat{\theta}_{ML})$, of the maximum likelihood estimate, $\hat{\theta}_{ML}$. The expectation of the second derivatives of the log likelihood function provides us with the information matrix $I(\theta)$:

$$I(\theta) = -E \left[\frac{\partial^2 \ln L(\theta|\tilde{y}_T)}{\partial\theta\partial\theta'} \right], \qquad (2.4)$$

which summarizes the amount of information in the sample. The inverse of this information matrix provides us with the lower bound for the covariance matrix of an unbiased estimator $\tilde{\theta}$, known as the Cramer-Rao inequality:

$$\text{Cov}(\tilde{\theta}) - I(\theta)^{-1} \quad \text{is positive semidefinite.} \qquad (2.5)$$

In addition, it can be shown that the maximum likelihood estimator $\hat{\theta}_{ML}$ has the following asymptotic normal distribution:

$$\sqrt{T}(\hat{\theta}_{ML} - \theta) \longrightarrow N(0, (\bar{H})^{-1}), \qquad (2.6)$$

where

$$-\frac{1}{T} \frac{\partial^2 \ln L(\theta|\tilde{y}_T)}{\partial\theta\partial\theta'} \to \bar{H} = \lim \frac{1}{T} I(\theta).$$

For an easy proof of the Cramer-Rao inequality and the asymptotic normality of the maximum likelihood estimator, refer to Harvey 1990. Equation (2.6) suggests that the maximum likelihood estimator is consistent and asymptotically efficient in the sense that its covariance matrix reaches the Cramer-Rao lower bound. Equation (2.6) also provides us with an idea of how to estimate the covariance matrix of the maximum likelihood estimator, using the inverse of the negative of the second derivative of the log likelihood function (Hessian) evaluated at $\hat{\theta}_{ML}$:

$$\text{Cov}(\hat{\theta}_{ML}) = \left[-\frac{\partial^2 \ln L(\theta|\tilde{y}_T)}{\partial\theta\partial\theta'} |_{\theta=\hat{\theta}_{ML}} \right]^{-1} \qquad (2.7)$$

2.2   The Prediction Error Decomposition and the Likelihood Function

For maximum likelihood estimation, we need to derive the joint density function or the likelihood function (they are functionally equivalent) for the vector $\tilde{y}_T$, given a statistical model. For independent observations, its derivation is straightforward:

$$L(\theta \mid \tilde{y}_T) = \prod_{t=1}^{T} p(y_t \mid \theta), \tag{2.8}$$

where $p(y_t \mid \theta)$ is the marginal density of an individual observation. For dependent observations, products of the conditional densities allow us to achieve the same goal:

$$L(\theta \mid \tilde{y}_T) = \prod_{t=2}^{T} p(y_t \mid \tilde{y}_{t-1}, \theta) p(y_1 \mid \theta), \tag{2.9}$$

where $\tilde{y}_t = [\, y_1 \quad \ldots \quad y_t \,]$, $p(y_t \mid \tilde{y}_{t-1}, \theta)$, $t = 2, 3, \ldots, T$, is the conditional density, and $p(y_1 \mid \theta)$ is the marginal density of y_1. Notice that for the first observation, we have no information on which to condition.

However, the derivation of the conditional densities used in (2.9) for dependent observations may not always be straightforward. Consider, for example, the following unobserved-components model with normality assumptions:

$$y_t = x_t + e_t, e_t \sim \text{i.i.d.} N(0, \sigma_e^2) \quad t = 1, 2, \ldots, T, \tag{2.10}$$

$$x_t = \delta + \phi x_{t-1} + v_t, v_t \sim \text{i.i.d.} N(0, \sigma_v^2), \tag{2.11}$$

where e_t and v_t are independent and $\mid \phi \mid < 1$. The conditional density $p(y_t \mid \tilde{y}_{t-1}, \theta)$ is not directly obtained from the statistical model, where $\theta = [\delta \quad \sigma_e^2 \quad \sigma_v^2 \quad \phi]'$ in the present case. Taking advantage of the normality assumption, the vector of observations $\tilde{y}_T$ can be represented by the following multivariate normal distribution:

$$\tilde{y}_T \sim N(\mu, \Omega), \tag{2.12}$$

with the likelihood function:

$$L(\theta \mid \tilde{y}_T) = (2\pi)^{-\frac{T}{2}} \mid \Omega \mid^{-\frac{1}{2}} \exp\{-\frac{1}{2}(\tilde{y}_T - \mu)'\Omega^{-1}(\tilde{y}_T - \mu)\}, \tag{2.13}$$

where all elements of μ and Ω are complicated functions of δ, σ_e, σ_v^2, and ϕ. Even when μ and Ω can be specified explicitly, maximizing the log of the likelihood function with respect to unknown parameters would be troublesome because of the inversion of the $T \times T$ matrix Ω. Harvey (1980) provides a solution to these difficulties, based on the prediction error decomposition obtained from applying the triangular factorization of the Ω matrix in (2.12).

Note that, for the $T \times T$ positive-definite, symmetric matrix Ω, there exists a unique triangular factorization of the following form:

$$\Omega = AfA', \tag{2.14}$$

where f is a diagonal matrix with positive elements and A is a lower triangular matrix with the following forms:

$$f = \begin{bmatrix} f_1 & 0 & 0 & \dots & 0 \\ 0 & f_2 & 0 & \dots & 0 \\ 0 & 0 & f_3 & \dots & 0 \\ \vdots & \vdots & \vdots & \ddots & \vdots \\ 0 & 0 & 0 & \dots & f_T \end{bmatrix}, \quad A = \begin{bmatrix} 1 & 0 & 0 & \dots & 0 \\ a_{21} & 1 & 0 & \dots & 0 \\ a_{31} & a_{32} & 1 & \dots & 0 \\ \vdots & \vdots & \vdots & \ddots & \vdots \\ a_{T1} & a_{T2} & a_{T3} & \dots & 1 \end{bmatrix},$$

and where $f_t > 0$ for all t. Substituting (2.14) into (2.13), we have:

$$\begin{aligned} L(\theta \mid \tilde{y}_T) &= (2\pi)^{-\frac{T}{2}} \mid AfA' \mid^{-\frac{1}{2}} \exp\{-\frac{1}{2}(\tilde{y}_T - \mu)'(AfA')^{-1}(\tilde{y}_T - \mu)\} \\ &= (2\pi)^{-\frac{T}{2}} \mid f \mid^{-\frac{1}{2}} \exp\{-\frac{1}{2}\eta' f^{-1}\eta\} \\ &= (2\pi)^{-\frac{T}{2}} \prod_{t=1}^{T} f_t^{-\frac{1}{2}} \exp\{-\frac{1}{2}\sum_{t=1}^{T} \eta_t' f_t^{-1}\eta_t\} \\ &= \prod_{t=1}^{T} \left[\frac{1}{\sqrt{2\pi f_t}} \exp\{-\frac{1}{2}\frac{\eta_t^2}{f_t}\} \right], \end{aligned} \tag{2.15}$$

where $\eta = A^{-1}(\tilde{y}_T - \mu)$ and η_t is the t-th element of the $T \times 1$ vector η. Because A is a lower trangular with ones in its diagonal elements, one can easily show that the t-th element of η can be rewritten as:

$$\eta_t = y_t - y_{t|t-1}, \tag{2.16}$$

where $y_{t|t-1}$ is the prediction of y_t conditional on $\tilde{y}_{t-1} = [\, y_1 \quad \cdots \quad y_{t-1} \,]'$, which is information up to $t - 1$, since we have:

$$y_{t|t-1} = \sum_{i=1}^{t-1} a_{t,i}^* y_i, \quad t = 2, 3, \ldots, T, \tag{2.17}$$

where $a_{t,i}^*$ is the (t, i)-th element of A^{-1}. Notice that the argument in the bracket of the last line in (2.15) is a normal density function of y_t conditional on past information:

$$y_t \mid \tilde{y}_{t-1} \sim N(y_{t|t-1}, f_t), \tag{2.18}$$

where f_t is intereprted as the variance of the prediction error $\eta_t = y_t - y_{t|t-1}$.

To summarize, equations (2.15) and (2.18) suggest that when the observations are normally distributed, insofar as we have the prediction errors and their variances, the log likelihood value can be easily calculated. Thus, the success of maximum likelihood estimation for a complicated dynamic time series model with dependent observations may depend on the availability of the prediction errors and their variances. For the unobserved component model specified in equations (2.10) and (2.11), for example, the Kalman filter introduced in chapter 3 provides us with η_t and f_t used in the last line of equation (2.15). With normality assumptions, equation (2.15) is a general approach to deriving the likelihood function for dependent observations of a dynamic time series. For a multivariate case, it is easy to see that (2.15) is replaced by:

$$L(\theta \mid \tilde{y}_T) = \prod_{t=1}^{T} \left[\frac{1}{\sqrt{(2\pi)^n |f_t|}} \exp\{-\frac{1}{2} \eta_t' f_t^{-1} \eta_t\} \right], \tag{2.15'}$$

where n is the dimension of y_t, η_t is $n \times 1$, and f_t is $n \times n$.

2.3 Parameter Constraints and the Covariance Matrix of $\hat{\theta}_{ML}$

2.3.1 Constrained Optimization

The maximum likelihood estimator, $\hat{\theta}_{ML}$, can be obtained by setting the first derivative of the log likelihood function to 0:

$$\frac{\partial \ln L(\theta \mid \tilde{y}_T)}{\partial \theta} = 0. \tag{2.19}$$

In most cases, however, a closed-form solution for $\hat{\theta}_{ML}$ is not available. Thus, in general, we resort to a nonlinear numerical optimization procedure to maximize the log likelihood function. Given initial estimates (θ^{j-1}) of the parameters, new estimates (θ^j) are obtained using the information provided by the first derivatives (and sometimes, depending upon the algorithms employed, the second derivatives) of the log likelihood function evaluated at θ^{j-1}. New estimates are obtained such that the log likelihood value evaluated at the revised estimates is larger than that at the initial estimates. This process may be iterated until convergence is achieved to obtain the value of the parameters that maximize the log likelihood function. In some cases, the maximum may not be unique. For specific and easy expositions of various algorithms for numerical optimization, readers are referred to chapter 4 of Harvey 1990.

When numerical optimization is employed to maximize the log likelihood function with respect to θ, the computer searches over the parameter space that ranges between negative infinity and positive infinity. But some of the parameters may have to be constrained to lie in an interval. For example, if one of the elements in θ is a probability (p), then it must be constrained such that $0 < p < 1$. In general, such constraints may be imposed by the following transformations of a vector ψ that ranges between negative infinity and positive infinity:

$$\theta = g(\psi), \tag{2.20}$$

where $g(.)$ is a continuous function. Then the log likelihood function may be considered a function of ψ:

$$\ln L(\theta \mid \tilde{y}_T) = \ln L(g(\psi) \mid \tilde{y}_T) = \ln L(\psi \mid \tilde{y}_T), \tag{2.21}$$

and the unconstrained numerical optimization may be applied with respect to ψ.

For example, if θ_j, the j-th element of θ, represents a variance, then $\theta_j > 0$. Then we may use the transformations

$$\theta_j = \psi_j^2 \quad \text{or} \quad \theta_j = \exp(\psi_i).$$

If θ_j represents a probability term, then $0 < \theta_j < 1$. The transformation we may employ is

$$\theta_j = \frac{1}{1 + \exp(\psi_j^{-1})}.$$

If θ_j represents an autoregressive parameter in an AR(1) model, then we may want to constrain the parameter within the stationary region $-1 < \psi_j < +1$:

$$\theta_j = \frac{\psi_j}{1+|\psi_j|}.$$

If $\theta = [\phi_1 \quad \phi_2]'$, where ϕ_1 and ϕ_2 are the autoregressive coefficients of the model in an AR(2) model, we may want to constrain the values of ϕ_1 and ϕ_2 within the stationary region (roots of $(1 - \phi_1 L - \phi_2 L^2) = 0$ lie outside the unit circle). In this case, we may employ the transformation

$$z_1 = \frac{\psi_1}{1+|\psi_1|}, \quad z_2 = \frac{\psi_2}{1+|\psi_2|},$$

$$==> \phi_1 = z_1 + z_2, \quad \phi_2 = -1 * z_1 * z_2.$$

Notice, however, that the recommended procedure in fact imposes the further restriction that the roots of the AR(2) polynomial are real. Finally, consider the following generalized autoregressive conditional hetereskedasticity (GARCH)(1,1) model:

$$h_t = a_0 + a_1 e_{t-1}^2 + a_2 h_{t-1}.$$

We generally want $a_1 > 0$, $a_2 > 0$, and $0 < a_1 + a_2 < 1$. The following transformations achieve this goal:

$$a_1 = \frac{\exp(\psi_1)}{1 + \exp(\psi_1) + \exp(\psi_2)}, \quad a_2 = \frac{\exp(\psi_2)}{1 + \exp(\psi_1) + \exp(\psi_2)}.$$

2.3.2 Constrained Optimization and the Covariance Matrix of $\hat{\theta}_{ML}$

In section 2.3.1, we noted that applying *unconstrained* optimization to the log likelihood function in (2.18) with respect to ψ is equivalent to applying *constrained* optimization with respect to θ, the parameter of interest to us. Unconstrained optimization then results in $\hat{\psi}_{ML}$ and $\text{Cov}(\hat{\psi}_{ML})$, the maximum likelihood (ML) estimate of ψ and its covariance matrix. But we actually want the parameter estimates and the covariance matrix for θ. As $\theta = g(\psi)$, the ML estimate for θ is easily obtained by

$$\hat{\theta}_{ML} = g(\hat{\psi}_{ML}). \tag{2.22}$$

We can also obtain $\text{Cov}(\hat{\theta}_{ML})$ based on $\text{Cov}(\hat{\psi}_{ML})$ and $g(.)$ in the following way:

$$\text{Cov}(\hat{\theta}_{ML}) = \left(\frac{\partial g(\hat{\psi}_{ML})}{\partial \psi}\right) \text{Cov}(\hat{\psi}_{ML}) \left(\frac{\partial g(\hat{\psi}_{ML})}{\partial \psi}\right)'. \tag{2.23}$$

The following provides a proof of equation (2.23). Differentiating the log likelihood function $\ln L(\theta) = \ln L(g(\psi))$ with respect to ψ, we get

$$\frac{\partial \ln L(g(\psi))}{\partial \psi} = \frac{\partial \ln L(g(\psi))}{\partial \theta}\left(\frac{\partial g(\psi)}{\partial \psi}\right), \tag{2.24}$$

and then differentiating again,

$$\left(\frac{\partial^2 \ln L(g(\psi))}{\partial \psi \partial \psi'}\right)$$

$$= \left(\frac{\partial g(\psi)}{\partial \psi}\right)' \frac{\partial^2 \ln L(g(\psi))}{\partial \theta \partial \theta'}\left(\frac{\partial g(\psi)}{\partial \psi}\right) + \frac{\partial \ln L(g(\psi))}{\partial \psi}\left(\frac{\partial^2 g(\psi)}{\partial \psi \partial \psi'}\right). \tag{2.25}$$

As

$$\frac{\partial \ln L(g(\psi_{ML}))}{\partial \psi} = 0,$$

(2.25) is written as

$$\left(\frac{\partial^2 \ln L(g(\hat{\psi}_{ML}))}{\partial \psi \partial \psi'}\right)$$

$$= \left(\frac{\partial g(\hat{\psi}_{ML})}{\partial \psi}\right)' \frac{\partial^2 \ln L(g(\hat{\psi}_{ML}))}{\partial \theta \partial \theta'}\left(\frac{\partial g(\hat{\psi}_{ML})}{\partial \psi}\right) \tag{2.26}$$

Multiplying both sides of (2.26) by -1 and then taking the inverse of both sides, we have

$$\left(-\frac{\partial^2 \ln L(g(\hat{\psi}_{ML}))}{\partial \psi \partial \psi'}\right)^{-1}$$

$$= \left(\frac{\partial g(\hat{\psi}_{ML})}{\partial \psi}\right)^{-1} \left(-\frac{\partial^2 \ln L(g(\hat{\psi}_{ML}))}{\partial \theta \partial \theta'}\right)^{-1} \left(\frac{\partial g(\hat{\psi}_{ML})}{\partial \psi}'\right)^{-1}.$$

(2.27)

Arranging the terms in (2.27) and noting that

$$\text{Cov}(\hat{\theta}_{ML}) = (-\frac{\partial^2 \ln L(\hat{\theta}_{ML})}{\partial \theta \partial \theta'})^{-1}$$

and

$$\text{Cov}(\hat{\psi}_{ML}) = (-\frac{\partial^2 \ln L(\hat{\psi}_{ML})}{\partial \psi \partial \psi'})^{-1},$$

we get equation (2.23).

References

Cramer, J. S. 1986. *Econometric Applications of Maximum Likelihood Methods*, Cambridge: Cambridge University Press.

Davidson, Russell, and James G. MacKinnon. 1993. *Estimation and Inference in Econometrics*. Oxford, UK: Oxford University Press.

Harvey, Andrew C. 1981. *Time Series Models*. Oxford: Philip Allan and Humanities Press.

Harvey, Andrew C. 1990. *The Econometric Analysis of Time Series*. 2nd ed. Cambridge: MIT Press.

Judge, G. G., R. C. Hill, W. E. Griffiths, H. Lutkepohl, and T.-C. Lee. 1982. *Introduction to the Theory and Practice of Econometrics*. New York: John Wiley & Sons.

3 State-Space Models and the Kalman Filter

State-space models, which typically deal with dynamic time series models that involve unobserved variables, have a wide range of potential applications in econometrics, since economic theory often involves unobservable variables— for example, permanent income, expectations, the ex ante real rate of interest, and the reservation wage. Engle and Watson (1981) apply them to modeling the behavior of wage rates; Garbade and Wachtel (1978) and Antoncic (1986) apply them to modeling the behavior of ex ante real interest rates; Burmeister and Wall (1982) and Burmeister, Wall, and Hamilton (1986) apply it in estimating expected inflation; and Kim and Nelson (1989) apply it to modeling a time-varying monetary reaction function of the Federal Reserve. Stock and Watson's (1991) dynamic factor model of coincident economic indicators is a recent application of state-space models. For more surveys and applicability of state-space models, refer to Engle and Watson 1987; Harvey 1985, 1989, and 1990; and Hamilton 1994a and 1994b.

The basic tool used to deal with the standard state-space model is the Kalman filter, a recursive procedure for computing the estimator of the unobserved component or the state vector at time t, based on available information at time t. When the shocks to the model and the initial unobserved variables are normally distributed, the Kalman filter also enables the likelihood function to be calculated via the prediction error decomposition discussed in chapter 2.

This chapter reviews the state-space model and the Kalman filter with reference to applications, beginning with the time-varying-parameter model in section 3.1. We then discuss general state-space models in section 3.2, with a focus on the unobserved-components model. Sections 3.3 through 3.5 deal with specific applications of the state-space models and the Kalman filter to actual economic problems.

3.1 Time-Varying-Parameter Models and the Kalman Filter

Consider the following regression model, in which the regression coefficients are time varying with specific dynamics:

$$y_t = x_t \beta_t + e_t, \quad t = 1, 2, 3, \ldots, T \tag{3.1}$$

$$\beta_t = \tilde{\mu} + F\beta_{t-1} + v_t, \tag{3.2}$$

$$e_t \sim \text{i.i.d.} N(0, R), \tag{3.3}$$

$$v_t \sim \text{i.i.d.} N(0, Q), \tag{3.4}$$

where y_t is 1×1; x_t is a $1 \times k$ vector of exogenous or predetermined variables; and e_t and v_t are independent. We further assume that β_t is of dimension $k \times 1$; F is $k \times k$; and Q is $k \times k$. For example, with $\tilde{\mu} = 0$ and $F = I_k$, each regression coefficient in β_t follows a random walk. If F is a diagonal matrix, and the absolute values of its diagonal elements are less than 1, each regression coefficient follows a stationary AR(1) process. An extension of the model to a more general case is straightforward once one is acquainted with the general state-space model presented in section 3.2.

In sections 3.1.1 and 3.1.2, we consider two alternative ways of making inferences about β_t conditional on information available up to time t, assuming that all the hyperparameters of the model ($\tilde{\mu}$, F, R, and Q) are known. In section 3.1.1, we show that a sequence of generalized least squares (GLS) regressions enables us to achieve our goal. However, this method may be extremely inefficient in terms of its computational burden. This motivates us to consider making inferences about β_t by employing the Kalman filter in section 3.1.2. If some of these hyperparameters are not known, however, they have to be estimated first before making inferences on β_t. Section 3.1.3 discusses maximum likelihood estimation of the model's unknown hyperparameters.

3.1.1 GLS Estimation of β_t

For simplicity of the analysis, assume that $\tilde{\mu} = 0$. Then, from equation (3.2), we get

$$
\begin{aligned}
\beta_t &= F\beta_{t-1} + v_t \\
&= F^2 \beta_{t-2} + F v_{t-1} + v_t \\
&\quad \cdots \\
&= F^{t-2}\beta_2 + F^{t-3}v_3 + F^{t-4}v_4 + \ldots + F v_{t-1} + v_t \\
&= F^{t-1}\beta_1 + F^{t-2}v_2 + F^{t-3}v_3 + \ldots + F v_{t-1} + v_t.
\end{aligned}
\tag{3.5}
$$

Using the above equation, we can solve $\beta_1, \beta_2, \ldots, \beta_{t-1}$ as functions of β_t and $v_t, v_{t-1}, v_{t-1}, \ldots$.

$$
\begin{bmatrix} \beta_1 \\ \beta_2 \\ \vdots \\ \beta_{t-1} \\ \beta_t \end{bmatrix} = \begin{bmatrix} F^{-t+1}\beta_t - (F^{-1}v_2 + F^{-2}v_3 + \ldots + F^{-t+1}v_t) \\ F^{-t+2}\beta_t - (F^{-1}v_3 + F^{-2}v_4 + \ldots + F^{-t+2}v_t) \\ \vdots \\ F^{-1}\beta_t - F^{-1}v_t \\ \beta_t \end{bmatrix}
$$

$$
= \begin{bmatrix} F^{-t+1}\beta_t \\ F^{-t+2}\beta_t \\ \vdots \\ F^{-1}\beta_t \\ \beta_t \end{bmatrix} - \begin{bmatrix} (F^{-1}v_2 + F^{-2}v_3 + \ldots + F^{-t+1}v_t) \\ (F^{-1}v_3 + F^{-2}v_4 + \ldots + F^{-t+2}v_t) \\ \vdots \\ F^{-1}v_t \\ 0 \end{bmatrix} . \tag{3.6}
$$

From (3.1) and (3.6), we get:

$$
\begin{bmatrix} y_1 \\ y_2 \\ \vdots \\ y_{t-1} \\ y_t \end{bmatrix} = \begin{bmatrix} x_1 F^{-t+1} \\ x_2 F^{-t+2} \\ \vdots \\ x_{t-1} F^{-1} \\ x_t \end{bmatrix} \beta_t
$$

$$
- \begin{bmatrix} x_1 F^{-1} & x_1 F^{-2} & \ldots & x_1 F^{-t+1} \\ 0 & x_2 F^{-1} & \ldots & x_2 F^{-t+2} \\ \vdots & \vdots & \ddots & \vdots \\ 0 & 0 & \ldots & x_{t-1} F^{-1} \\ 0 & 0 & \ldots & 0 \end{bmatrix} \begin{bmatrix} v_2 \\ \vdots \\ v_{t-1} \\ v_t \end{bmatrix} + \begin{bmatrix} e_1 \\ e_2 \\ \vdots \\ e_{t-1} \\ e_t \end{bmatrix} . \tag{3.7}
$$

Writing equation (3.7) in matrix notation, we have:

$$
\tilde{y}_t = \tilde{X}_t^* \beta_t + \tilde{\epsilon}_t, \tag{3.7'}
$$

where

$$
E[\tilde{\epsilon}_t \tilde{\epsilon}_t'] = A_t (I_{t-1} \otimes Q) A_t' + R I_t = \Omega_t, \tag{3.8}
$$

and where

$$
A_t = \begin{bmatrix} x_1 F^{-1} & x_1 F^{-2} & \ldots & x_1 F^{-t+1} \\ 0 & x_2 F^{-1} & \ldots & x_2 F^{-t+2} \\ \vdots & \vdots & \ddots & \vdots \\ 0 & 0 & \ldots & 0 \end{bmatrix} .
$$

One could apply GLS to the model (3.7)′ for $t = k + 1, \ldots, T$, where k is the dimension of β_t. A major difficulty, however, is that each GLS application requires an inverse of a $t \times t$ matrix: simple

$$\beta_{t|t} = (\tilde{X}_t^{*\prime} \Omega_t^{-1} \tilde{X}_t^*)^{-1} \tilde{X}_t^{*\prime} \Omega_t^{-1} \tilde{y}_t, \qquad t = k + 1, k + 2, \ldots, T, \qquad (3.9)$$

where $\beta_{t|t}$ refers to an estimate of β_t conditional on information up to time t.

The Kalman filter approach discussed below can easily be implemented without having to invert such large matrices.

3.1.2 The Kalman Filter and Estimation of β_t

The Kalman filter is a recursive procedure for computing the optimal estimate of the unobserved-state vector β_t, $t = 1, 2, \ldots, T$, based on the appropriate information set, assuming that $\tilde{\mu}$, F, R, and Q are known. It provides a minimum mean squared error estimate of β_t given the appropriate information set. Depending upon the information set used, we have the *basic filter* and *smoothing*. The basic filter refers to an estimate of β_t based on information available up to time t, and smoothing to an estimate of β_t based on all the available information in the sample through time T.

Throughout this book, we use the following notation:

ψ	the information set.
$\beta_{t|t-1} = E[\beta_t | \psi_{t-1}]$	expectation (estimate) of β_t conditional on information up to $t - 1$.
$P_{t|t-1} = E[(\beta_t - \beta_{t|t-1})(\beta_t - \beta_{t|t-1})']$	covariance matrix of β_t conditional on information up to $t - 1$.
$\beta_{t|t} = E[\beta_t | \psi_t]$	expectation (estimate) of β_t conditional on information up to t.
$P_{t|t} = E[(\beta_t - \beta_{t|t})(\beta_t - \beta_{t|t})']$	covariance matrix of β_t conditional on information up to t.
$y_{t|t-1} = E[y_t | \psi_{t-1}] = x_t \beta_{t|t-1}$	forecast of y_t given information up to time $t - 1$.
$\eta_{t|t-1} = y_t - y_{t|t-1}$	prediction error.
$f_{t|t-1} = E[\eta_{t|t-1}^2]$	conditional variance of the prediction error.

$$\beta_{t|T} = E[\beta_t | \psi_T]$$

expectation (estimate) of β_t conditional on information up to T (the whole sample).

$$P_{t|T} = E[(\beta_t - \beta_{t|T})(\beta_t - \beta_{t|T})']$$

covariance matrix of β_t conditional on information up to T (the whole sample).

Assuming that x_t is available at the beginning of time t and a new observation of y_t is made at the end of time t, the Kalman filter (basic filter) consists of the following two steps:

1. *Prediction:* At the beginning of time t, we may want to form an optimal predictor of y_t, based on all the available information up to time $t - 1$: $y_{t|t-1}$. To do this, we need to calculate $\beta_{t|t-1}$.

2. *Updating:* Once y_t is realized at the end of time t, the prediction error can be calculated: $\eta_{t|t-1} = y_t - y_{t|t-1}$. This prediction error contains new information about β_t beyond that contained in $\beta_{t|t-1}$. Thus, after observing y_t, a more accurate inference can be made of β_t. $\beta_{t|t}$, an inference of β_t based on information up to time t, may be of the following form: $\beta_{t|t} = \beta_{t|t-1} + K_t \eta_{t|t-1}$, where K_t is the weight assigned to new information about β_t contained in the prediction error.

To be more specific, the basic filter is described by the following six equations:

Prediction

$$\beta_{t|t-1} = \tilde{\mu} + F\beta_{t-1|t-1}, \tag{3.10}$$

$$P_{t|t-1} = F P_{t-1|t-1} F' + Q, \tag{3.11}$$

$$\eta_{t|t-1} = y_t - y_{t|t-1} = y_t - x_t \beta_{t|t-1}, \tag{3.12}$$

$$f_{t|t-1} = x_t P_{t|t-1} x_t' + R, \tag{3.13}$$

Updating

$$\beta_{t|t} = \beta_{t|t-1} + K_t \eta_{t|t-1}, \tag{3.14}$$

$$P_{t|t} = P_{t|t-1} - K_t x_t P_{t|t-1}, \tag{3.15}$$

where $K_t = P_{t|t-1} x_t' f_{t|t-1}^{-1}$ is the Kalman gain, which determines the weight assigned to new information about β_t contained in the prediction error. Given the hyperparameters of the model, $\beta_{t|t}$ in equation (3.14) is the same as that in equation (3.9).

Derivation of the four equations in (3.10)–(3.13) is straightforward. To derive the smoothing equations in (3.14)–(3.15), we consider the following arguments. Let Z_1 and Z_2, conditional on ψ_{t-1}, be normally distributed as follows:

$$\begin{matrix} Z_1 \\ Z_2 \end{matrix} \mid \psi_{t-1} \sim MVN \left(\begin{pmatrix} \mu_1 \\ \mu_2 \end{pmatrix}, \begin{pmatrix} \Sigma_{11} & \Sigma_{12} \\ \Sigma_{21} & \Sigma_{22} \end{pmatrix} \right). \tag{3.16}$$

Then the distribution of Z_1 given Z_2 and ψ_{t-1} is given by

$$Z_1 | Z_2, \psi_{t-1} \sim N(\mu_{1|2}, \Sigma_{11|2}), \tag{3.17}$$

where

$$\mu_{1|2} = \mu_1 + \Sigma_{12}\Sigma_{22}^{-1}(Z_2 - \mu_2), \tag{3.18}$$

$$\Sigma_{11|2} = \Sigma_{11} - \Sigma_{12}\Sigma_{22}^{-1}\Sigma_{21}. \tag{3.19}$$

Thus if we let $Z_1 = \beta_t$ and $Z_2 = y_t - y_{t|t-1} = \eta_{t|t-1}$, then we have $\mu_1 = \beta_{t|t-1}$, $\Sigma_{11} = P_{t|t-1}$, $\Sigma_{22} = f_{t|t-1}$, and $\Sigma_{12} = P_{t|t-1}x_t'$. Therefore, equations (3.14) and (3.15) result. For more details on the derivation of the Kalman filter, refer to Hamilton 1993 and 1994a,b.

In equation (3.10), an inference on β_t given information up to time $t-1$ is a function of an inference on β_{t-1} given information up to time $t-1$, due to equation (3.2). Thus uncertainty underlying $\beta_{t|t-1}$ is a function of uncertainty underlying $\beta_{t-1|t-1}$ and Q, the covariance of the shocks to β_t. This is shown in equation (3.11). The prediction error in the time-varying-parameter model consists of two parts: the prediction error due to error in making an inference about β_t (i.e., $\beta_t - \beta_{t|t-1}$) and the prediction error due to e_t, a random shock to y_t in (3.1). Thus in equation (3.13), the conditional variance of the prediction error is a function of the uncertainty associated with $\beta_{t|t-1}$ and of R, the variance of e_t.

The updating equation in (3.14) suggests that $\beta_{t|t}$ is formed as a kind of weighted average of $\beta_{t|t-1}$ and new information contained in the prediction error $\eta_{t|t-1}$, the weight assigned to new information being the Kalman gain, K_t. Examining the Kalman gain more carefully, we notice that it is an inverse function of R, the variance of e_t; and given x_t, it is a positive function of the uncertainty underlying $\beta_{t|t-1}$. For simplicity, assume that β_t and x_t are 1×1. Then the Kalman gain can be rewritten as

Model: $y_t = \beta_t x_t + e_t, \quad e_t \sim \text{i.i.d. } N(0, \sigma_e^2)$
$\qquad\quad \beta_t = \mu + F\beta_{t-1} + v_t, \quad v_t \sim \text{i.i.d. } N(0, \sigma_v^2)$

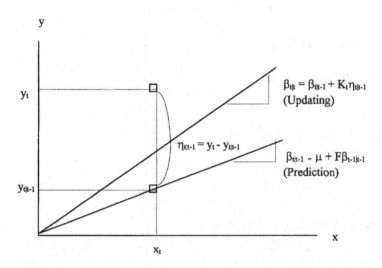

Figure 3.1
The Kalman filter: TVP model

$$K_t = \frac{1}{x_t} \frac{P_{t|t-1}x_t^2}{P_{t|t-1}x_t^2 + R}, \tag{3.20}$$

where $P_{t|t-1}x_t^2$ is the portion of the prediction error variance due to uncertainty in $\beta_{t|t-1}$ and R is the portion of the prediction error variance due to random shock e_t. We can easily see that

$$\left| \frac{\partial K_t}{\partial (P_{t|t-1}x_t^2)} \right| > 0,$$

suggesting that as uncertainty associated with $\beta_{t|t-1}$ increases, relatively more weight is given to new information in the prediction error, $\eta_{t|t-1}$. This is quite intuitive, since an increase in uncertainty in $\beta_{t|t-1}$ may be interpreted as a deterioration of the information content of $\beta_{t|t-1}$, relative to that of $\eta_{t|t-1}$.

The above prediction and updating steps of the Kalman filter may be understood more intuitively with the help of figure 3.1. The horizontal axis in the

$$\beta_{0|0}, \quad P_{0|0}, \quad l(\theta) = 0$$

$$\Downarrow$$
$$\Downarrow$$

$$\beta_{t|t-1} = \tilde{\mu} + F\beta_{t-1|t-1}$$

$$P_{t|t-1} = FP_{t-1|t-1}F' + Q$$

$$\Downarrow$$

$$\eta_{t|t-1} = y_t - y_{t|t-1} = y_t - H_t\beta_{t|t-1} - Az_t$$

$$f_{t|t-1} = H_t P_{t|t-1} H_t' + R$$

$$\Downarrow$$

$$l(\theta) = l(\theta) - \frac{1}{2}\ln((2\pi)^n \mid f_{t|t-1}\mid) - \frac{1}{2}\eta'_{t|t-1}f_{t|t-1}^{-1}\eta_{t|t-1}$$

$$\Downarrow$$

$$\beta_{t|t} = \beta_{t|t-1} + P_{t|t-1}H_t'f_{t|t-1}^{-1}\eta_{t|t-1}$$

$$P_{t|t} = P_{t|t-1} - P_{t|t-1}H_t'f_{t|t-1}^{-1}H_t P_{t|t-1}$$

$$\Downarrow \qquad \qquad t - 1 = t$$
$$\Downarrow$$

$$l(\theta) = -\frac{1}{2}\sum \ln((2\pi)^n \mid f_{t|t-1}\mid) - \frac{1}{2}\sum \eta'_{t|t-1}f_{t|t-1}^{-1}\eta_{t|t-1}$$

Figure 3.2
Flowchart for the Kalman filter

figure represents the x variable available at the beginning of each period, and the vertical axis represents the y variable realized at the end of each period.

Given the initial values, $\beta_{0|0}$ and $P_{0|0}$, the six equations in the basic filter can be iterated for $t = 1, 2, \ldots, T$. (Refer to figure 3.2) This provides us with a minimum mean squared error estimate of β_t, $t = 1, 2, \ldots, T$, given information up to time $t - 1$ or t. For stationary β_t in equation (3.2), the unconditional mean and covariance matrix of β_t may be employed as the initial values, $\beta_{0|0}$ and $P_{0|0}$. The unconditional mean of stationary β_t is derived as

$$E[\beta_t] = \tilde{\mu} + F E[\beta_{t-1}] + E[v_t], \qquad (3.21)$$

$$\beta_{0|0} = \tilde{\mu} + F\beta_{0|0} \quad \text{(At Steady State)}, \qquad (3.21)'$$

$$\beta_{0|0} = (I_k - F)^{-1}\tilde{\mu}. \qquad (3.22)$$

The unconditional covariance matrix of stationary β_t is derived as

$$\text{Cov}(\beta_t) = F \, \text{Cov}(\beta_{t-1})F' + \text{Cov}(v_t), \qquad (3.23)$$

$$P_{0|0} = F P_{0|0}F' + Q, \quad \text{(At Steady-State)}, \qquad (3.23)'$$

$$\text{vec}(P_{0|0}) = \text{vec}(F P_{0|0}F') + \text{vec}(Q), \qquad (3.24)$$

$$\text{vec}(P_{0|0}) = (F \otimes F)\text{vec}(P_{0|0}) + \text{vec}(Q), \qquad (3.25)$$

$$\text{vec}(P_{0|0}) = (I - F \otimes F)^{-1}\text{vec}(Q), \qquad (3.26)$$

as $\text{vec}(ABC) = (C' \otimes A)\text{vec}(B)$.

For nonstationary β_t in equation (3.2), the unconditional mean and the covariance matrix of β_t do not exist. In this case, $\beta_{0|0}$ may be set at any arbitrary $k \times 1$ vector (wild guessing). But in order to assign very large uncertainty to this wild guess, we must assign very large values to the diagonal elements of $P_{0|0}$. For example, if $P_{t-1|t-1}$ is a very large positive definite matrix, most of the weight in the updating equation (3.14) is assigned to new information contained in the forecast error for y_t, and the information content in $\beta_{t|t-1}$ is treated as negligible. Alternatively, if we assume that $\beta_{0|0}$ is a vector of unknown constants, we can treat the elements of $\beta_{0|0}$ as additional parameters to be estimated. In this case, $P_{0|0}$ should be set equal to a $k \times k$ matrix of 0s when estimating the hyperparameters of the model via MLE, because $\beta_{0|0}$ is not a random variable. Once these parameters are estimated along with other hyperparameters of the model, we can run the Kalman filter again by setting $\beta_{0|0} = \hat{\beta}_{0|0,\text{MLE}}$ and $P_{0|0} = \text{Cov}(\hat{\beta}_{0|0,\text{MLE}})$ for inferences on β_t, $t = 1, 2, \ldots, T$.

Smoothing $(\beta_{t|T})$ provides us with a more accurate inference on β_t, since it uses more information than the basic filter. The following two equations can be iterated backwards for $t = T - 1, T - 2, \ldots 1$, to get the smoothed estimates:

Smoothing

$$\beta_{t|T} = \beta_{t|t} + P_{t|t} F' P_{t+1|t}^{-1} (\beta_{t+1|T} - F\beta_{t|t} - \tilde{\mu}), \tag{3.27}$$

$$P_{t|T} = P_{t|t} + P_{t|t} F' P_{t+1|t}^{-1} (P_{t+1|T} - P_{t+1|t}) P_{t+1|t}^{-1}{}' F P'_{t|t}, \tag{3.28}$$

where $\beta_{T|T}$ and $P_{T|T}$, the initial values for the smoothing, are obtained from the last iteration of the basic filter. Equations (3.27) and (3.28) can be derived in the same way as the updating equations (3.14) and (3.15).

3.1.3 Maximum Likelihood Estimation of the Model Based on the Prediction Error Decomposition

The discussion in the previous section assumes that the model's parameters are known. However, some of these parameters are usually unknown. In this case, we need to estimate the parameters first; then the estimate of β_t, $t = 1, 2, \ldots, T$, is conditional on these estimated parameters. In chapter 2, we discussed the evaluation of the likelihood function based on the prediction error decomposition. That is, when the observations are normally distributed, insofar as we have the prediction error and its variance, the log likelihood value can be calculated easily. For given parameters of the model, the Kalman filter provides us with prediction error ($\eta_{t|t-1}$) and its variance ($f_{t|t-1}$) in equations (3.12) and (3.13) as by-products. In addition, if β_0 and $\{e_t, v_t\}_{t=1}^{T}$ are Gaussian, the distribution of y_t conditional on ψ_{t-1} is also Gaussian:

$$y_t | \psi_{t-1} \sim N(y_{t|t-1}, f_{t|t-1}), \tag{3.29}$$

and the sample log likelihood function is represented by

$$\ln L = -\frac{1}{2} \sum_{t=1}^{T} \ln(2\pi f_{t|t-1}) - \frac{1}{2} \sum_{t=1}^{T} \eta'_{t|t-1} f_{t|t-1}^{-1} \eta_{t|t-1}, \tag{3.30}$$

which can be maximized with respect to unknown parameters of the model.

For nonstationary β_t in (3.2), the log likelihood function is evaluated from observation $\tau + 1$ ($\tau \gg 1$):

$$\ln L = -\frac{1}{2} \sum_{t=\tau+1}^{T} \ln(2\pi f_{t|t-1}) - \frac{1}{2} \sum_{t=\tau+1}^{T} \eta'_{t|t-1} f_{t|t-1}^{-1} \eta_{t|t-1}, \tag{3.31}$$

where τ is large enough. Notice that we start the Kalman filter with an arbitrary initial value $\beta_{0|0}$ and $P_{0|0}$, with large diagonal elements for nonstationary β_t. Iterating the filter starting from $t = 1$, then evaluating the log likelihood function from $t = \tau + 1$ minimizes the effect of the arbitrary initial value $\beta_{0|0}$ on the log likelihood value.

3.2 State-Space Models and the Kalman Filter

3.2.1 State-Space Models

State-space models, which were originally developed by control engineers (Kalman 1960), are useful tools for expressing *dynamic systems that involve unobserved state variables*. The reader is referred to Harvey 1989 and Hamilton 1994a and 1994b for other expositions. A state-space model consists of two equations: a transition equation (sometimes called a state equation) and a measurement equation.

Measurement Equation: An equation that describes the relation between observed variables (data) and unobserved state variables.

Transition Equation: An equation that describes the dynamics of the state variables. The transition equation has the form of a *first-order difference equation* in the state vector.

Consider the following representative state-space model:

Measurement Equation

$$y_t = H_t\beta_t + Az_t + e_t, \tag{3.32}$$

Transition Equation

$$\beta_t = \tilde{\mu} + F\beta_{t-1} + v_t, \tag{3.33}$$

$$e_t \sim \text{i.i.d.}N(0, R), \tag{3.34}$$

$$v_t \sim \text{i.i.d.}N(0, Q), \tag{3.35}$$

$$E(e_t v_s') = 0, \tag{3.36}$$

where y_t is an $n \times 1$ vector of variables observed at time t; β_t is a $k \times 1$ vector of unobserved state variables; H_t is an $n \times k$ matrix that links the observed y_t vector and the unobserved β_t; z_t is an $r \times 1$ vector of exogenous or predetermined observed variables; $\tilde{\mu}$ is $k \times 1$; v_t is $k \times 1$. Elements of the H_t matrix may be either data on exogenous variables or constant parameters. The positive-definiteness of R and Q in (3.34) and (3.35) is not always guaranteed. A usual practice is to write equations (3.33) and (3.35) alternatively as:

$$\beta_t = \tilde{\mu} + F\beta_{t-1} + Gv_t^*, \tag{3.33}'$$

$$v_t^* \sim \text{i.i.d.} N(0, Q^*), \tag{3.35}'$$

where G is $k \times g$; and v_t^* is $g \times 1$ $(g \leq k)$. In this representation of the transition equation, the positive definiteness of Q^* is guaranteed, and the relationship between Q in (3.35) and Q^* in (3.35)$'$ is given by $Q = G Q^* G'$.

In econometrics, the state-space representation of a general dynamic linear model includes autogressive integrated moving-average processes and classical regression models as special cases. Examples include

An AR(2) Model

$$y_t = \delta + \phi_1 y_{t-1} + \phi_2 y_{t-2} + w_t, \quad w_t \sim \text{i.i.d.} N(0, \sigma^2), \tag{3.37}$$

Measurement Equation

$$y_t = \delta^* + [\, 1 \quad 0 \,] \begin{bmatrix} \beta_{0t} \\ \beta_{0,t-1} \end{bmatrix}, \tag{3.38}$$

Transition Equation

$$\begin{bmatrix} \beta_{0t} \\ \beta_{0,t-1} \end{bmatrix} = \begin{bmatrix} \phi_1 & \phi_2 \\ 1 & 0 \end{bmatrix} \begin{bmatrix} \beta_{0,t-1} \\ \beta_{0,t-2} \end{bmatrix} + \begin{bmatrix} w_t \\ 0 \end{bmatrix}, \tag{3.39}$$

where

$$\delta^* = \frac{\delta}{1 - \phi_1 - \phi_2}.$$

An ARMA(2,1) model

$$y_t = \phi_1 y_{t-1} + \phi_2 y_{t-2} + w_t + \theta w_{t-1}, \tag{3.40}$$

Measurement Equation

$$y_t = [\, 1 \quad \theta \,] \begin{bmatrix} \beta_{1,t} \\ \beta_{2,t} \end{bmatrix}, \tag{3.41}$$

Transition Equation

$$\begin{bmatrix} \beta_{1,t} \\ \beta_{2,t} \end{bmatrix} = \begin{bmatrix} \phi_1 & \phi_2 \\ 1 & 0 \end{bmatrix} \begin{bmatrix} \beta_{1,t-1} \\ \beta_{2,t-1} \end{bmatrix} + \begin{bmatrix} w_t \\ 0 \end{bmatrix}. \tag{3.42}$$

An Unobserved-Components Model   A typical application of the unobserved components model would be to decompose the log of real GDP into two
independent components: a stochastic trend component and a cyclical component:

$$y_t = y_{1t} + y_{2t}, \tag{3.43}$$

$$y_{1t} = \delta + y_{1,t-1} + e_{1t}, \tag{3.44}$$

$$y_{2t} = \phi_1 y_{2,t-1} + \phi_2 y_{2,t-2} + e_{2t}, \tag{3.45}$$

$$e_{it} \sim \text{i.i.d.} N(0, \sigma_i^2), \quad i = 1, 2, \qquad E[e_{1t} e_{2s}] = 0 \quad \text{for all } t \text{ and } s, \tag{3.46}$$

where the roots of $(1 - \phi_1 L - \phi_2 L^2) = 0$ lie outside the unit circle.

Usually, there exists more than one way of writing a dynamic system in
state-space models. In the current example, depending on which one of y_{1t}
and y_{2t} (or both) may be treated as the state variable(s), we have at least three
different representations. (Alternative representations of a time series imply the
same observable moments of the time series.)

REPRESENTATION 1   Suppose we want to treat y_{2t} as an unobserved state
variable. In this case, we may want to transform the model so that y_{1t} does
not show up in the model. This is done by taking a first difference of y_t in
(3.43). Then we could design the measurement and transition equations based
on the transformed model:

$$\Delta y_t = \Delta y_{1t} + \Delta y_{2t} \implies \Delta y_t = \delta + \Delta y_{2t} + e_{1t}, \tag{3.47}$$

Measurement Equation

$$\Delta y_t = \delta + \begin{bmatrix} 1 & -1 \end{bmatrix} \begin{bmatrix} y_{2t} \\ y_{2,t-1} \end{bmatrix} + e_{1t}, \tag{3.48}$$

Transition Equation

$$\begin{bmatrix} y_{2t} \\ y_{2,t-1} \end{bmatrix} = \begin{bmatrix} \phi_1 & \phi_2 \\ 1 & 0 \end{bmatrix} \begin{bmatrix} y_{2,t-1} \\ y_{2,t-2} \end{bmatrix} + \begin{bmatrix} e_{2t} \\ 0 \end{bmatrix}. \tag{3.49}$$

REPRESENTATION 2   Suppose we want to treat y_{1t} as an unobserved state variable. In this case, we should transform the original model to eliminate the y_{2t} term. This is done by multiplying both sides of (3.43) by $(1 - \phi_1 L - \phi_2 L^2)$:

$$(1 - \phi_1 L - \phi_2 L^2)y_t = (1 - \phi_1 L - \phi_2 L^2)y_{1t} + (1 - \phi_1 L - \phi_2 L^2)y_{2t}, \quad (3.50)$$

$$\Longrightarrow \ y_t = (\phi_1 y_{t-1} + \phi_2 y_{t-2}) + (y_{1t} - \phi_1 y_{1,t-1} - \phi_2 y_{1,t-2}) + e_{2t}, \quad (3.51)$$

Measurement Equation

$$y_t = \begin{bmatrix} 1 & -\phi_1 & -\phi_2 \end{bmatrix} \begin{bmatrix} y_{1t} \\ y_{1,t-1} \\ y_{1,t-2} \end{bmatrix} + \phi_1 y_{t-1} + \phi_2 y_{t-2} + e_{2t}, \quad (3.52)$$

Transition Equation

$$\begin{bmatrix} y_{1t} \\ y_{1,t-1} \\ y_{1,t-2} \end{bmatrix} = \begin{bmatrix} \delta \\ 0 \\ 0 \end{bmatrix} + \begin{bmatrix} 1 & 0 & 0 \\ 1 & 0 & 0 \\ 0 & 1 & 0 \end{bmatrix} \begin{bmatrix} y_{1,t-1} \\ y_{1,t-2} \\ y_{1,t-3} \end{bmatrix} + \begin{bmatrix} e_{1t} \\ 0 \\ 0 \end{bmatrix}. \quad (3.53)$$

REPRESENTATION 3   Suppose we want to treat both y_{1t} and y_{2t} as unobserved state variables. In this case, we put both components in the state vector:

Measurement Equation

$$y_t = \begin{bmatrix} 1 & 1 & 0 \end{bmatrix} \begin{bmatrix} y_{1t} \\ y_{2t} \\ y_{2,t-1} \end{bmatrix}, \quad (3.54)$$

Transition Equation

$$\begin{bmatrix} y_{1t} \\ y_{2t} \\ y_{2,t-1} \end{bmatrix} = \begin{bmatrix} \delta \\ 0 \\ 0 \end{bmatrix} + \begin{bmatrix} 1 & 0 & 0 \\ 0 & \phi_1 & \phi_2 \\ 0 & 1 & 0 \end{bmatrix} \begin{bmatrix} y_{1,t-1} \\ y_{2,t-1} \\ y_{2,t-2} \end{bmatrix} + \begin{bmatrix} e_{1t} \\ e_{2t} \\ 0 \end{bmatrix}. \quad (3.55)$$

NOTE   When decomposing a nonstationary time series into a stochastic trend and a stationary component, one typically encounters the identification issue, which is carefully addressed in Nelson and Plosser 1982. In the preceding unobserved-component model, we assumed that the shocks to the two components, e_{1t} and e_{2t} are independent. How critical is this independence assumption? Let us address this issue in the simplest framework (a structural model) in which y_t is a sum of a random walk component and a white noise component:

$$y_t = y_{1t} + y_{2t}, \tag{3.56}$$

$$y_{1t} = y_{1,t-1} + e_{1t}, \tag{3.57}$$

$$y_{2t} = e_{2t}, \tag{3.58}$$

$$E(e_{1t}^2) = \sigma_1^2, \quad E(e_{2t}^2) = \sigma_2^2, \quad E(e_{1t}e_{2t}) = \sigma_{12}. \tag{3.59}$$

Suppose that the three parameters of the model, σ_1^2, σ_2^2, and σ_{12}, are not known. If the decomposed series y_{1t} and y_{2t} were observed, the parameters of the model could be easily estimated. However, only the sum of the two components, y_t, is observed. Thus, estimation of the parameters should be based on the observed series. We can easily show that y_t is an autoregressive integrated moving average (ARIMA)(0,1,1) process (a reduced-form model):

$$\Delta y_t = e_{1t} + e_{2t} - e_{2,t-1}, \tag{3.60}$$

$$\Longrightarrow \Delta y_t = \epsilon_t + \theta\epsilon_{t-1}, \quad E(\epsilon_t^2) = \sigma_\epsilon^2, \tag{3.61}$$

where θ and σ_ϵ^2 are functions of σ_1^2, σ_2^2, and σ_{12}. An identification problem arises because there exist more parameters in the structural model given by equations (3.56)–(3.59) than in the reduced-form model given by equation (3.61). We can estimate the parameters of the reduced-form model and then use these to indirectly estimate the parameters of the structural model. However, unless there is an identifying assumption in the structural model, leaving the same number of parameters in both models to be estimated, this is not possible. If the structural parameters are not identified, the decomposition is impossible.

The Time-Varying-Parameter Model The time-varying-parameter model that we discussed in section 3.1 is also a special case of the general state-space model in which H_t in the measurement equation (3.32) is replaced by a matrix of exogenous or predetermined variables. A specific example may be given by

$$y_t = \beta_{1t}x_{1t} + \beta_{2t}x_{2t} + \cdots + \beta_{kt}x_{kt} + e_t, \quad e_t \sim \text{i.i.d.} N(0, \sigma^2), \tag{3.62}$$

$$(\beta_{it} - \delta_i) = \phi_i(\beta_{i,t-1} - \delta_i) + v_{it}, \quad v_{it} \sim \text{i.i.d.} N(0, \sigma_i^2), \quad i = 1, 2, \ldots, k,$$

$$\tag{3.63}$$

$$E(e_t v_{is}) = 0, \quad \text{for all } t \text{ and } s, i = 1, 2, \ldots, k, \tag{3.64}$$

where $x_{it}, i = 1, 2, \ldots, k$, are predetermined or exogenous variables.

Measurement Equation

$$y_t = [\, x_{1t} \quad x_{2t} \quad \ldots \quad x_{kt} \,] \begin{bmatrix} \beta_{1t} \\ \beta_{2t} \\ \vdots \\ \beta_{kt} \end{bmatrix} + e_t, \tag{3.65}$$

$$(y_t = x_t \beta_t + e_t), \tag{3.65'}$$

Transition Equation

$$\begin{bmatrix} \beta_{1t} \\ \beta_{2t} \\ \vdots \\ \beta_{kt} \end{bmatrix} = \begin{bmatrix} \delta_1^* \\ \delta_2^* \\ \vdots \\ \delta_k^* \end{bmatrix} + \begin{bmatrix} \phi_1 & 0 & \ldots & 0 \\ 0 & \phi_2 & \ldots & 0 \\ \vdots & \vdots & \ddots & \vdots \\ 0 & 0 & \ldots & \phi_k \end{bmatrix} \begin{bmatrix} \beta_{1,t-1} \\ \beta_{2,t-1} \\ \vdots \\ \beta_{k,t-1} \end{bmatrix} + \begin{bmatrix} v_{1t} \\ v_{2t} \\ \vdots \\ v_{kt} \end{bmatrix}, \tag{3.66}$$

$$(\beta_t = \tilde{\mu} + F\beta_{t-1} + v_t), \tag{3.66'}$$

where $\delta_i^* = \delta_i(1 - \phi_i)$, $i = 1, 2, \ldots, k$. Comparing the measurement equations in $(3.65)'$ and (3.32), we notice that the time-varying-parameter model is a special case of the state-space model in which $H_t = x_t = [\, x_{1t} \quad x_{2t} \quad \ldots \quad x_{kt} \,]$. Here, x_t should be uncorrelated with e_t. If the observed z_t vector is included in the time-varying-parameter model, it may be correlated with x_t.

AN EXERCISE   Let us consider the following regression model, in which two of the regression coefficients are time varying (random walks) and the remaining coefficient is constant:

$$y_t = \beta_{1t} + \beta_{2t}x_{2t} + \beta_3 x_{3t} + e_t, \tag{3.67}$$

$$\beta_{it} = \beta_{i,t-1} + v_{it}, \quad i = 1, 2. \tag{3.68}$$

The state-space representation of the model is given by

Measurement Equation

$$y_t = [\, 1 \quad x_{2t} \,] \begin{bmatrix} \beta_{1t} \\ \beta_{2t} \end{bmatrix} + \beta_3 x_{3t} + e_t, \tag{3.69}$$

$$(y_t = H_t \beta_t + \beta_3 x_{3t} + e_t), \tag{3.69'}$$

Transition Equation

$$\begin{bmatrix} \beta_{1t} \\ \beta_{2t} \end{bmatrix} = \begin{bmatrix} \beta_{1,t-1} \\ \beta_{2,t-1} \end{bmatrix} + \begin{bmatrix} v_{1t} \\ v_{2t} \end{bmatrix},$$ (3.70)

$$(\beta_t = \beta_{t-1} + v_t).$$ (3.70)'

A Dynamic Factor Model   Suppose we have two stationary variables, y_{1t}, and y_{2t} with a common component c_t:

$$y_{1t} = \gamma_1 c_t + z_{1t},$$ (3.71)

$$y_{2t} = \gamma_2 c_t + z_{2t},$$ (3.72)

$$c_t = \phi_1 c_{t-1} + v_t, \qquad v_t \sim \text{i.i.d.} N(0, 1),$$ (3.73)

$$z_{it} = \alpha_i z_{i,t-1} + e_{it}, \qquad e_{it} \sim \text{i.i.d.} N(0, \sigma_i^2),$$ (3.74)

where e_{1t}, e_{2t}, and v_t are independent of one another. Stock and Watson (1991) employ a general version of the above dynamic factor model to extract an experimental coincident index from four coincident economic variables. A state-space representation of the above model is given by

Measurement Equation

$$\begin{bmatrix} y_{1t} \\ y_{2t} \end{bmatrix} = \begin{bmatrix} \gamma_1 & 1 & 0 \\ \gamma_2 & 0 & 1 \end{bmatrix} \begin{bmatrix} c_t \\ z_{1t} \\ z_{2t} \end{bmatrix},$$ (3.75)

$$(y_t = H_t \beta_t),$$ (3.75)'

Transition Equation

$$\begin{bmatrix} c_t \\ z_{1t} \\ z_{2t} \end{bmatrix} = \begin{bmatrix} \phi_1 & 0 & 0 \\ 0 & \alpha_1 & 0 \\ 0 & 0 & \alpha_2 \end{bmatrix} \begin{bmatrix} c_{t-1} \\ z_{1,t-1} \\ z_{2,t-1} \end{bmatrix} + \begin{bmatrix} v_t \\ e_{1t} \\ e_{2t} \end{bmatrix},$$ (3.76)

$$(\beta_t = F\beta_{t-1} + v_t).$$ (3.76)'

A Common Stochastic Trend Model   Suppose that we have two integrated series, y_{1t} and y_{2t}. If the two series are cointegrated, then there exists a common stochastic trend. A typical example would be the spot and forward exchange rates. Hai, Mark, and Wu (1996) consider the following common stochastic trend model for the spot and forward exchange rates:

$$y_{1t} = z_t + x_{1t}, \tag{3.77}$$

$$y_{2t} = z_t + x_{2t}, \tag{3.78}$$

$$z_t = z_{t-1} + \epsilon_t, \quad \epsilon_t \sim \text{i.i.d.} N(0, \sigma_\epsilon^2), \tag{3.79}$$

$$x_{1t} = \mu_1 + \phi_{11} x_{1,t-1} + \phi_{12} x_{2,t-1} + e_{1t} + \theta_{11} e_{1,t-1} + \theta_{12} e_{2,t-1}, \tag{3.80}$$

$$x_{2t} = \mu_2 + \phi_{21} x_{1,t-1} + \phi_{22} x_{2,t-1} + e_{2t} + \theta_{21} e_{1,t-1} + \theta_{22} e_{2,t-1}, \tag{3.81}$$

$$\begin{pmatrix} e_{1t} \\ e_{2t} \end{pmatrix} \sim \text{i.i.d.} N \left(\begin{bmatrix} 0 \\ 0 \end{bmatrix}, \begin{bmatrix} \sigma_1^2 & \sigma_{12} \\ \sigma_{12} & \sigma_2^2 \end{bmatrix} \right), \tag{3.82}$$

where z_t is a common stochastic trend and the stationary components x_{1t} and x_{2t} are assumed to be generated by a vector ARMA(1,1) process. A state-space representation of the above model is given by

Measurement Equation

$$\begin{bmatrix} y_{1t} \\ y_{2t} \end{bmatrix} = \begin{bmatrix} 1 & 1 & 0 & 0 & 0 \\ 1 & 0 & 1 & 0 & 0 \end{bmatrix} \begin{bmatrix} z_t \\ x_{1t} \\ x_{2t} \\ e_{1t} \\ e_{2t} \end{bmatrix}, \tag{3.83}$$

Transition Equation

$$\begin{bmatrix} z_t \\ x_{1t} \\ x_{2t} \\ e_{1t} \\ e_{2t} \end{bmatrix} = \begin{bmatrix} 0 \\ \mu_1 \\ \mu_2 \\ 0 \\ 0 \end{bmatrix} + \begin{bmatrix} 1 & 0 & 0 & 0 & 0 \\ 0 & \phi_{11} & \phi_{12} & \theta_{11} & \theta_{12} \\ 0 & \phi_{21} & \phi_{22} & \theta_{21} & \theta_{22} \\ 0 & 0 & 0 & 0 & 0 \\ 0 & 0 & 0 & 0 & 0 \end{bmatrix} \begin{bmatrix} z_{t-1} \\ x_{1,t-1} \\ x_{2,t-1} \\ e_{1,t-1} \\ e_{2,t-1} \end{bmatrix}$$
$$+ \begin{bmatrix} 1 & 0 & 0 \\ 0 & 1 & 0 \\ 0 & 0 & 1 \\ 0 & 1 & 0 \\ 0 & 0 & 1 \end{bmatrix} \begin{bmatrix} \epsilon_t \\ e_{1t} \\ e_{2t} \end{bmatrix}. \tag{3.84}$$

3.2.2 The Kalman Filter and MLE

Once a dynamic time series model is written in state-space form, the Kalman filter is readily available for inferences on the unobserved state vector β_t, conditional on the parameters of the model and the appropriate information set. The basic filtering and the smoothing algorithm are the same as those in section 3.1 with slight modification. For example, we have the H_t matrix in place of x_t of a time-varying-parameter model. The derivation and the intuition associated with the algorithms are the same. Treatment of the initial values, $\beta_{0|0}$ and $P_{0|0}$, is also exactly the same as in section 3.1.

Basic Filtering

Prediction

$$\beta_{t|t-1} = \tilde{\mu} + F\beta_{t-1|t-1}, \tag{3.85}$$

$$P_{t|t-1} = F P_{t-1|t-1} F' + Q, \tag{3.86}$$

$$\eta_{t|t-1} = y_t - y_{t|t-1} = y_t - H_t \beta_{t|t-1} - A z_t, \tag{3.87}$$

$$f_{t|t-1} = H_t P_{t|t-1} H_t' + R, \tag{3.88}$$

Updating

$$\beta_{t|t} = \beta_{t|t-1} + K_t \eta_{t|t-1}, \tag{3.89}$$

$$P_{t|t} = P_{t|t-1} - K_t H_t P_{t|t-1}, \tag{3.90}$$

where $K_t = P_{t|t-1} H_t' f_{t|t-1}^{-1}$ is the Kalman gain.

Smoothing $(t = T - 1, T - 2, \ldots, 1)$

$$\beta_{t|T} = \beta_{t|t} + P_{t|t} F' P_{t+1|t}^{-1} (\beta_{t+1|T} - F\beta_{t|t} - \tilde{\mu}), \tag{3.91}$$

$$P_{t|T} = P_{t|t} + P_{t|t} F' P_{t+1|t}^{-1} (P_{t+1|T} - P_{t+1|t}) P_{t+1|t}^{-1}{}' F P_{t|t}', \tag{3.92}$$

where $\beta_{T|T}$ and $P_{T|T}$, the initial values for the smoothing, are obtained from the last iteration of the basic filter. The procedure for the maximum likelihood estimation of the model's parameters is exactly the same as in section 3.1.

3.3 Application 1: A Decomposition of Real GDP and the Unemployment Rate into Stochastic Trend and Transitory Components

Nelson and Plosser (1982) suggest that the nonstationarity in economic activity should be removed by first-differencing rather than linear detrending, making the trend component of real GDP or GNP a random walk with drift rather than a deterministic function of time. Their analysis further suggests that most of the innovation variance in annual real GNP should be allocated to the nonstationary trend component, with little variance left over the stationary cyclical component.

Noting that annual averages blur the pattern of economic activity apparent in quarterly or monthly data, Clark (1987) applies a version of the unobserved components model discussed in section 3.2 to quarterly real GNP and the monthly index of industrial production in order to evaluate the relative importance of the stochastic trend and the stationary cyclical components of economic activity. In this section, we apply Clark's unobserved components model to quarterly real GDP for the period 1947:II–1995:III and measure the stochastic trend and the cyclical components. By taking advantage of a standard version of Okun's law, the univariate model is then extended into a bivariate unobserved components model of real GDP and unemployment rate, as in Clark 1989, and the unemployment rate is decomposed into trend and cyclical components as well.

To distinguish between time trend and stochastic trend models of real output, Clark (1987) considers the following unobserved components model:

$$y_t = n_t + x_t, \tag{3.93}$$

$$n_t = g_{t-1} + n_{t-1} + v_t, \quad v_t \sim \text{i.i.d.} N(0, \sigma_v^2), \tag{3.94}$$

$$g_t = g_{t-1} + w_t, \quad w_t \sim \text{i.i.d.} N(0, \sigma_w^2), \tag{3.95}$$

$$x_t = \phi_1 x_{t-1} + \phi_2 x_{t-2} + e_t, \quad e_t \sim \text{i.i.d.} N(0, \sigma_e^2), \tag{3.96}$$

where y_t is the log of real GDP, n_t is a stochastic trend component, and x_t is a stationary cyclical component; v_t, w_t, and e_t are independent white noise processes. In the presence of the decline in the U.S. productivity growth in the 1970s and reduction of labor force growth in the 1980s, we follow Clark (1987) in modeling the drift term (g_t) in the stochastic trend component as a random walk. As in section 3.2.1, we have at least three alternative state-space representations of the above model. We employ the following representation:

$$y_t = \begin{bmatrix} 1 & 1 & 0 & 0 \end{bmatrix} \begin{bmatrix} n_t \\ x_t \\ x_{t-1} \\ g_t \end{bmatrix}, \tag{3.97}$$

$$\begin{bmatrix} n_t \\ x_t \\ x_{t-1} \\ g_t \end{bmatrix} = \begin{bmatrix} 1 & 0 & 0 & 1 \\ 0 & \phi_1 & \phi_2 & 0 \\ 0 & 1 & 0 & 0 \\ 0 & 0 & 0 & 1 \end{bmatrix} \begin{bmatrix} n_{t-1} \\ x_{t-1} \\ x_{t-2} \\ g_{t-1} \end{bmatrix} + \begin{bmatrix} v_t \\ e_t \\ 0 \\ w_t \end{bmatrix}. \tag{3.98}$$

The unemployment rate is also assumed to have both a random walk component and a stationary component. By imposing a version of Okun's law, the unemployment rate may be specified as

$$U_t = L_t + C_t, \tag{3.99}$$

$$L_t = L_{t-1} + v_{lt}, \quad v_{lt} \sim \text{i.i.d.} N(0, \sigma_{vl}^2), \tag{3.100}$$

$$C_t = \alpha_0 x_t + \alpha_1 x_{t-1} + \alpha_2 x_{t-2} + e_{ct}, \quad e_{ct} \sim \text{i.i.d.} N(0, \sigma_{ec}^2), \tag{3.101}$$

where L_t is a trend component and C_t is a stationary component that is assumed to be a function of current and past transitory components of real output. Combined with the output equations (3.93)–(3.96), a state-space representation of the bivariate model is given by

$$\begin{bmatrix} y_t \\ U_t \end{bmatrix} = \begin{bmatrix} 1 & 1 & 0 & 0 & 0 & 0 \\ 0 & \alpha_0 & \alpha_1 & \alpha_2 & 0 & 1 \end{bmatrix} \begin{bmatrix} n_t \\ x_t \\ x_{t-1} \\ x_{t-2} \\ g_t \\ L_t \end{bmatrix} + \begin{bmatrix} 0 \\ e_{ct} \end{bmatrix}, \tag{3.102}$$

$$\begin{bmatrix} n_t \\ x_t \\ x_{t-1} \\ x_{t-2} \\ g_t \\ L_t \end{bmatrix} = \begin{bmatrix} 1 & 0 & 0 & 0 & 1 & 0 \\ 0 & \phi_1 & \phi_2 & 0 & 0 & 0 \\ 0 & 1 & 0 & 0 & 0 & 0 \\ 0 & 0 & 1 & 0 & 0 & 0 \\ 0 & 0 & 0 & 0 & 1 & 0 \\ 0 & 0 & 0 & 0 & 0 & 1 \end{bmatrix} \begin{bmatrix} n_{t-1} \\ x_{t-1} \\ x_{t-2} \\ x_{t-3} \\ g_{t-1} \\ L_{t-1} \end{bmatrix} + \begin{bmatrix} v_t \\ e_t \\ 0 \\ 0 \\ w_t \\ v_{lt} \end{bmatrix}. \tag{3.103}$$

Table 3.1 reports estimation results. As in Clark 1987, a significant portion of the quarter-to-quarter innovations in real GDP are cyclical from univariate and bivariate models. Figures 3.3 through 3.6 plot the log of real GDP along with its trend and cyclical components implied by the models. Figures 3.7 and 3.8 plot the unemployment rate and its trend and cyclical components implied by the bivariate model.

Table 3.1
Estimates of the unobserved components model of real GDP (1952:I–1995:III)

Parameters	Univariate model		Bivariate model	
σ_v	0.0056	(0.0013)	0.0049	(0.0006)
σ_e	0.0061	(0.0013)	0.0067	(0.0006)
σ_w	0.0002	(0.0002)	0.0003	(0.0002)
ϕ_1	1.5346	(0.1501)	1.4386	(0.0791)
ϕ_2	−0.5888	(0.1155)	−0.5174	(0.0569)
α_0	—		−0.3368	(0.0497)
α_1	—		−0.1635	(0.0310)
α_2	—		−0.0720	(0.0054)
σ_{vl}	—		0.0015	(0.0003)
σ_{ec}	—		0.0003	(0.0003)
Log likelihood	578.52		1566.99	

Note: Standard errors are in parentheses.

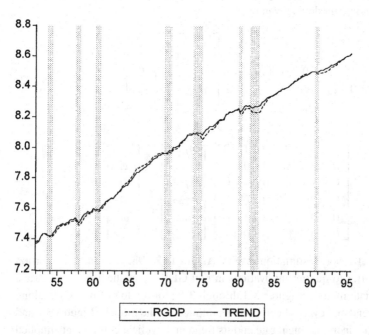

Figure 3.3
Real GDP and its trend component: univariate UC model

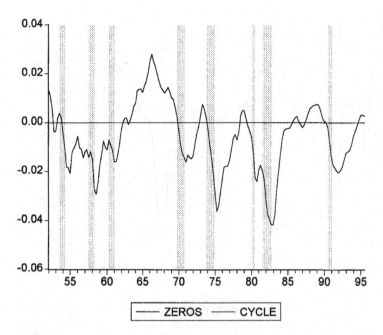

Figure 3.4
Cyclical component of real GDP: univariate UC model

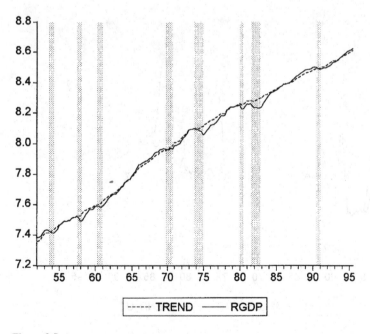

Figure 3.5
Real GDP and its trend component: bivariate UC model

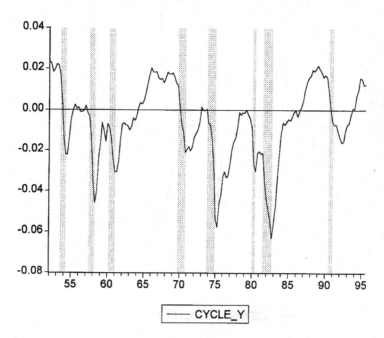

Figure 3.6
Cyclical component of real GDP: bivariate UC model

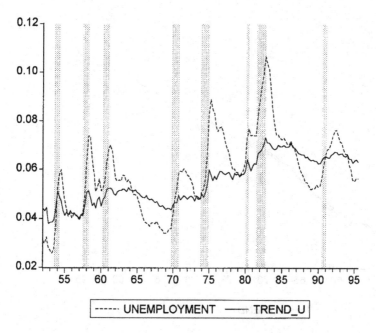

Figure 3.7
Unemployment rate and its trend component: bivariate UC model

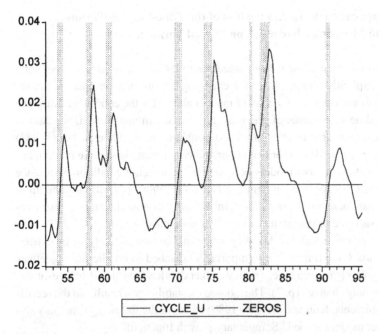

Figure 3.8
Cyclical component of unemployment rate: bivariate UC model

Note, however, that the sum of the estimated AR coefficients for the cyclical component is close to 1. We suggest that caution should be exercised in drawing inferences about the nature of the decomposition in the presence of a highly persistent stationary component. First, Nelson (1988) argues that the decomposition may be spurious, just as detrending by linear regression is known to generate spurious trends and cycles in nonstationary time series. His Monte Carlo experiment confirms that when data are generated by a random walk, the state-space model tends to indicate (incorrectly) that the series consists of cyclical variations around a smooth trend. Second, Perron (1990) suggests that the standard unit root tests are biased toward nonrejection of the null of a unit root when the data-generating process is stationary with a switching mean. Suppose that the mean of the stationary AR component of real GDP is subject to regime shifts. Even when the sum of the AR coefficients is significantly lower than 1, ignoring regime shifts would result in a highly persistent stationary component. Recently, Kim and Nelson (1997) considered this possibility by explicitly considering asymmetry in the cyclical component of real GDP.

3.4   Application 2: An Application of the Time-Varying-Parameter
Model to Modeling Changing Conditional Variance

Autoregressive conditional heteroskedasticity (ARCH), introduced by Engle
(1982), explicitly characterizes the changing conditional variance of the regression disturbances. This class of models allows for the conditional variance
to depend on the squares of previous innovations. In this section, we discuss
an alternative source of changing conditional variance. Whereas Tsay (1987)
and Bera and Lee (1993) show that parameter heterogeniety in the random coefficient autoregressive models is a source of changing conditional variance
such as ARCH, we focus on Kim and Nelson's (1989) application of the time-
varying-parameter model introduced in section 3.1 for modeling changing conditional variance or uncertainty in the U.S. monetary growth.

McNees (1986) states, "A policy reaction function is likely to be a frag-
ile creature. Over time . . . the importance attached to conflicting objectives
[of the policy] may change, [policy makers'] views on the structure of the
economy may change" (p. 7). Thus, based on stability test results on the regression coefficients, Kim and Nelson (1989) consider the following time-varying-
parameter model for the U.S. monetary growth function:

$$\Delta M_t = \beta_{0t} + \beta_{1t}\Delta i_{t-1} + \beta_{2t}INF_{t-1} + \beta_{3t}SURP_{t-1} + \beta_{4t}\Delta M_{t-1} + e_t,$$

$$\text{(3.104)}$$

$$\beta_{it} = \beta_{it-1} + v_{it},   \text{(3.105)}$$

$$e_t \sim \text{i.i.d.} N(0, \sigma_e^2),   \text{(3.106)}$$

$$v_{it} \sim \text{i.i.d.} N(0, \sigma_{vi}^2),   i = 0, 1, \ldots, 4.   \text{(3.107)}$$

In matrix notation, we have

$$\Delta M_t = x_{t-1}\beta_t + e_t,   \text{(3.108)}$$

$$\beta_t = F\beta_{t-1} + v_t, \text{ with } F = I_5,   \text{(3.109)}$$

$$e_t \sim \text{i.i.d.} N(0, \sigma_e^2),   \text{(3.110)}$$

$$v_t \sim \text{i.i.d.} N(0, Q),   \text{(3.111)}$$

where ΔM, Δi, INF, and $SURP$ stand for U.S. figures for the quarterly
M1 growth rate, changes in the interest rate as measured by the three-month

Table 3.2
Parameter estimates of the time-varying-parameter model of U.S. monetary growth (quarterly data, 1964:I–1985:IV)

σ_e	0.3712	(0.0633)
σ_{v0}	0.1112	(0.0627)
σ_{v1}	0.0171	(0.0341)
σ_{v2}	0.2720	(0.0607)
σ_{v3}	0.0378	(0.1634)
σ_{v4}	0.0224	(0.0375)
Log Likelihood	−97.0924	

Note: Standard errors are in parentheses.

T-bill rate, the inflation rate as measured by the CPI, and the detrended full employment budget surplus, respectively.

The Kalman filter is applied to make inferences on the changing regression coefficients. One nice thing about the Kalman filter is that it gives us insight into how a rational economic agent would revise his estimates of the coefficients in a Bayesian fashion when new information is available in a world of uncertainty, *especially* under a changing policy regime.

In an ARCH model, changing uncertainty about the future is focused on the changing conditional variance in the disturbance terms of the regression equation. As Harrison and Stevens (1976) state, however, a person's uncertainty about the future arises not simply because of future random terms but also because of uncertainty about current parameter values and the model's ability to link the present to the future. In the time-varying-parameter model above, uncertainty about current regression coefficients β_t results in changing conditional variance of monetary growth. This is well captured in an equation for the variance of the conditional forecast error in the Kalman filter:

$$f_{t|t-1} = x_{t-1}P_{t|t-1}x'_{t-1} + \sigma_e^2, \tag{3.13}'$$

where $P_{t|t-1}$ represents the degree of uncertainty associated with an inference on β_t conditional on information up to time $t-1$.

Table 3.2 reports parameter estimates of the model along with their standard errors for the sample period 1964:I–1985:IV (quarterly data). Figures 3.9 through 3.13 depict the Kalman filter inferences on the regression coefficients conditional on information up to time $t-1$. These show estimates of how the Federal Reserve has been changing its reaction to various macroeconomic variables in the presence of changing importance attached to potentially conflicting

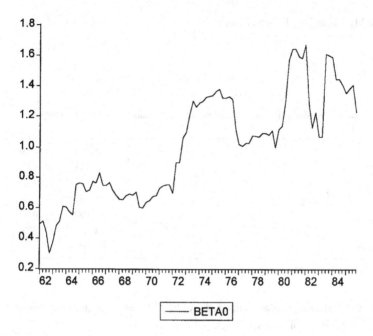

Figure 3.9
Time-varying regression coefficient: β_0

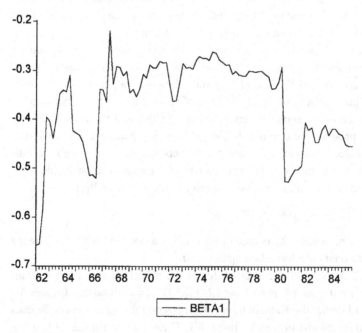

Figure 3.10
Time-varying regression coefficient: β_1

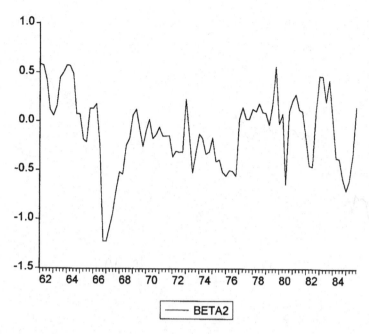

Figure 3.11
Time-varying regression coefficient: β_2

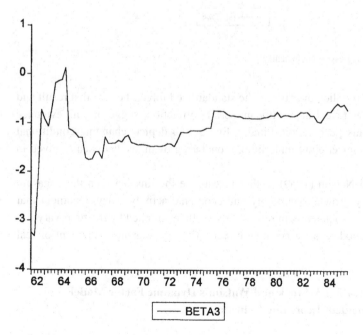

Figure 3.12
Time-varying regression coefficient: β_3

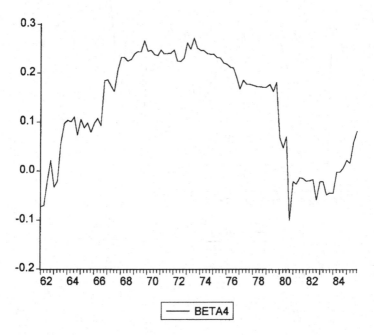

Figure 3.13
Time-varying regression coefficient: β_4

objectives of policy over time. The standardized forecast errors that result and
their squares reveal no significant serial correlation, suggesting no evidence
of model misspecification. Finally, figure 3.14 depicts changing conditional
variance or uncertainty underlying monetary growth, as analytically given in
$(3.13)'$.

Kim and Nelson (1989) further investigate the link between this measure
of monetary growth uncertainty and economic activity. They document that
uncertainty associated with monetary growth, as implied by the time-varying-
parameter model, has a negative effect on the permanent component of real
output.

3.5   Application 3: Stock and Watson's Dynamic Factor Model
of the Coincident Economic Indicators

Ever since Burns and Mitchell (1946), there has been consensus about a stylized fact of the business cycle: that is, the comovement of many macroeco-

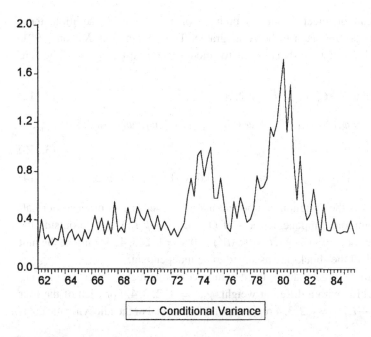

Figure 3.14
Conditional forecast error variance of monetary growth from a TVP model

nomic variables through the cycle. The index of coincident economic indicators issued by the Department of Commerce (DOC), developed for the purpose of summarizing the state of macroeconomic activity, is an example that exploits this stylized fact.

Recently, Stock and Watson (1991) developed a probability model of the coincident economic indicators, based on the notion that the comovements in many macroeconomic variables have a common element that can be captured by a single underlying, unobserved variable. As an appliction of the state-space model and the Kalman filter, this section focuses on Stock and Watson's (1991) dynamic factor model of the coincident economic indicators.

3.5.1 Model Specification and Identification Issue

Let Y_{1t}, Y_{2t}, Y_{3t}, and Y_{4t} be the logs of four coincident variables used to construct the coincident index: industrial production, personal income less transfer payments, total manufacturing and trade sales, and employees on nonagricultural payrolls. Unit root tests for each of these U.S. series suggest that one cannot reject the null hypothesis of a unit root. In addition, these four series do not seem to be cointegrated. Thus, Stock and Watson (1991) consider the following dynamic factor model in first differences of the four variables:

$$\Delta Y_{it} = D_i + \gamma_i \Delta C_t + e_{it}, \quad i = 1, 2, 3, 4, \tag{3.112}$$

$$(\Delta C_t - \delta) = \phi_1(\Delta C_{t-1} - \delta) + \phi_2(\Delta C_{t-2} - \delta) + w_t, \quad w_t \sim \text{i.i.d.} N(0, \sigma_w^2),$$
$$\tag{3.113}$$

$$e_{it} = \psi_{i1} e_{i,t-1} + \psi_{i2} e_{i,t-2} + \epsilon_{it}, \quad \epsilon_{it} \sim \text{i.i.d.} N(0, \sigma_i^2), \quad i = 1, 2, 3, 4, \tag{3.114}$$

where ΔC_t is the common component and σ_w^2 is set to 1 in order to normalize the common component; roots of $(1 - \phi_1 L - \phi_2 L^2) = 0$ lie outside the unit circle; roots of $(1 - \psi_{i1} L - \psi_{i2} L^2) = 0, i = 1, 2, 3, 4$, lie outside the unit circle; and all the shocks are assumed to be independent.

In the above specification, the common component ΔC_t enters each equation in (3.112) with a different weight, $\gamma_i, i = 1, 2, 3, 4$. For each of the four series, $D_i + e_{it}, i = 1, 2, 3, 4$ represents the individual or the idiosyncratic component.

Note that the first population moment for the i-th indicator, ΔY_{it}, consists of two parameters:

$$E(\Delta Y_{it}) = D_i + \gamma_i \delta. \tag{3.115}$$

Given the corresponding sample first moment, $\Delta \bar{Y}_i$, however, the parameters D_i and δ are not separately identified. As a way to avoid the identification problem in the maximum likelihood estimation of the model, Stock and Watson suggest writing the model in deviation from means, thus concentrating the $D_i + \gamma_i \delta$ terms, $i = 1, 2, 3, 4$, out of the likelihood function:

Model in Deviation from Means

$$\Delta y_{it} = \gamma_i \Delta c_t + e_{it}, \quad i = 1, 2, 3, 4, \tag{3.116}$$

$$\Delta c_t = \phi_1 \Delta c_{t-1} + \phi_2 \Delta c_{t-2} + w_t, \quad w_t \sim \text{i.i.d.} N(0, 1), \tag{3.117}$$

$$e_{it} = \psi_{i1} e_{i,t-1} + \psi_{i2} e_{i,t-2} + \epsilon_{it}, \quad \epsilon_{it} \sim \text{i.i.d.} N(0, \sigma_i^2), \quad i = 1, 2, 3, 4, \tag{3.118}$$

where $\Delta y_{it} = \Delta Y_{it} - \Delta \bar{Y}_i$ and $\Delta c_t = \Delta C_t - \delta$.

Once the above model in deviation from means is written in state-space form, the Kalman filter is readily available for maximum likelihood estimation of the model based on the prediction error decomposition, as well as for inferences on Δc_t. A state-space representation of the model is given by

Measurement Equation

$$
\begin{bmatrix} \Delta y_{1t} \\ \Delta y_{2t} \\ \Delta y_{3t} \\ \Delta y_{4t} \end{bmatrix} = \begin{bmatrix} \gamma_1 & 0 & 1 & 0 & 0 & 0 & 0 & 0 & 0 & 0 \\ \gamma_2 & 0 & 0 & 0 & 1 & 0 & 0 & 0 & 0 & 0 \\ \gamma_3 & 0 & 0 & 0 & 0 & 0 & 1 & 0 & 0 & 0 \\ \gamma_4 & 0 & 0 & 0 & 0 & 0 & 0 & 0 & 1 & 0 \end{bmatrix} \begin{bmatrix} \Delta c_t \\ \Delta c_{t-1} \\ e_{1t} \\ e_{1,t-1} \\ e_{2t} \\ e_{2,t-1} \\ e_{3t} \\ e_{3,t-1} \\ e_{4t} \\ e_{4,t-1} \end{bmatrix}, \qquad (3.119)
$$

$(\Delta y_t = H \beta_t)$,

Transition Equation

$$
\begin{bmatrix} \Delta c_t \\ \Delta c_{t-1} \\ e_{1t} \\ e_{1,t-1} \\ e_{2t} \\ e_{2,t-1} \\ e_{3t} \\ e_{3,t-1} \\ e_{4t} \\ e_{4,t-1} \end{bmatrix} = \begin{bmatrix} \phi_1 & \phi_2 & 0 & 0 & \cdots & 0 & 0 \\ 1 & 0 & 0 & 0 & \cdots & 0 & 0 \\ 0 & 0 & \psi_{11} & \psi_{12} & \cdots & 0 & 0 \\ 0 & 0 & 1 & 0 & \cdots & 0 & 0 \\ \vdots & \vdots & \vdots & \vdots & \ddots & 0 & 0 \\ 0 & 0 & 0 & 0 & \cdots & \psi_{41} & \psi_{42} \\ 0 & 0 & 0 & 0 & \cdots & 1 & 0 \end{bmatrix} \begin{bmatrix} \Delta c_{t-1} \\ \Delta c_{t-2} \\ e_{1,t-1} \\ e_{1,t-2} \\ e_{2,t-1} \\ e_{2,t-2} \\ e_{3,t-1} \\ e_{3,t-2} \\ e_{4,t-1} \\ e_{4,t-2} \end{bmatrix} + \begin{bmatrix} w_t \\ 0 \\ \epsilon_{1t} \\ 0 \\ \epsilon_{2t} \\ 0 \\ \epsilon_{3t} \\ 0 \\ \epsilon_{4t} \\ 0 \end{bmatrix},
$$

$$(3.120)$$

$(\beta_t = F \beta_{t-1} + v_t)$

Thus, one can estimate the parameters of the model using the MLE method based on the prediction error decomposition, and given the estimates of the parameters, one can run the Kalman filter to get $\beta_{t|t}$. Then, the $(1, 1)$ element of $\beta_{t|t}$ is $\Delta c_{t|t}$.

3.5.2   Decomposing $\bar{Y}_i$ into D_i and δ, $i = 1, 2, 3, 4$

Given $\Delta c_{t|t}$, $t = 1, 2, \ldots, T$, we need an estimate of δ to construct a new coincident index, $C_{t|t}$, $t = 1, 2, \ldots, T$, since we have

$$C_{t|t} = C_{t|t-1} + \Delta c_{t|t} + \delta. \tag{3.121}$$

Suppose all the parameters of the model are known and the Kalman filter is applied to a model given by (3.112)–(3.114) to obtain $C_{t|t}$, $t = 1, 2, \ldots, T$. The relationship between $C_{t|t}$ and $\Delta Y_t = [\, \Delta Y_{1t} \quad \Delta Y_{2t} \quad \Delta Y_{3t} \quad \Delta Y_{4t} \,]'$ can be given by

$$\Delta C_{t|t} = W(L)\Delta Y_t, \tag{3.122}$$

which states that $\Delta C_{t|t}$ is a function of current and past values of ΔY_1, ΔY_2, ΔY_3, and ΔY_4. Taking expectations on both sides of the above equation, we have:

$$E[\Delta C_{t|t}] = E[W(L)\Delta Y_t], \tag{3.123}$$

$$\Longrightarrow\ \delta = W(1)E(\Delta Y), \tag{3.124}$$

$$\Longrightarrow\ \hat{\delta} = W(1)\Delta \bar{Y}, \tag{3.125}$$

from which we can see that, once $W(L)$ is identified, δ is easily estimated given $\Delta \bar{Y}$. But note that the relation between $\Delta c_{t|t}$ and Δy_t is also given by

$$\Delta c_{t|t} = W(L)\Delta y_t, \tag{3.126}$$

which suggests that $W(L)$, and thus, $W(1)$, may be identified from the model in deviation from means. The following explains Stock and Watson's (1991) approach to identifying $W(1)$.

From the Kalman filter recursion applied to the state-space model written in deviation from means, we have

$$\beta_{t|t} = \beta_{t|t-1} + K_t \eta_{t|t-1}, \tag{3.127}$$

$$\beta_{t|t} = \beta_{t|t-1} + K_t(\Delta y_t - H\beta_{t|t-1}), \tag{3.128}$$

$$\beta_{t|t} = F\beta_{t-1|t-1} + K_t\Delta y_t - K_t H\beta_{t|t-1}, \tag{3.129}$$

$$\beta_{t|t} = F\beta_{t-1|t-1} + K_t\Delta y_t - K_t HF\beta_{t-1|t-1}, \tag{3.130}$$

$$\beta_{t|t} = (I - K_t H)F\beta_{t-1|t-1} + K_t\Delta y_t. \tag{3.131}$$

Harvey (1989) shows that for a stationary transition equation, the Kalman gain, K_t, approaches a steady-state Kalman gain, K, as $t \to \infty$. Given parameter estimates of the model, apply the Kalman filter to the model in deviation from means. The Kalman gain at the last iteration, K_T, is the steady-state Kalman Gain. If one prints K_t for $t = 1, 2, \ldots, T$, one will notice that K_t converges to a steady-state value reasonably fast. Thus at a steady state, we have $\beta_{t|t} = \beta_{t-1|t-1}$ and $K_t = K$, and from equation (3.131), we get

$$\beta_{t|t} = (I - (I - KH)FL)^{-1} K \Delta y_t, \tag{3.132}$$

where L is the lag operator. Because the (1,1) element of $\beta_{t|t}$ is $\Delta c_{t|t}$, $W(L)$ is given by the (1,1) element of $(I - (I - KH)FL)^{-1}K$. Thus, $W(1)$ in (3.125) is given by the (1,1) element of $(I - (I - KH)F)^{-1}K$.

3.5.3 Empirical Results

In this section, we apply Stock and Watson's (1991) model to the four coincident variables for the updated sample period 1960.1–1995.1. In addition, Δy_{4t} in equation (3.116) is replaced by

$$\Delta y_{4t} = \gamma_{40}\Delta c_t + \gamma_{41}\Delta c_{t-1} + \gamma_{42}\Delta c_{t-2} + \gamma_{43}\Delta c_{t-3} + e_{4t}, \tag{3.133}$$

in order to account for the possibility that the employment variable, ΔY_{4t}, might be slightly lagging. The state-space representation of the model then is given by

Measurement Equation

$$
\begin{bmatrix} \Delta y_{1t} \\ \Delta y_{2t} \\ \Delta y_{3t} \\ \Delta y_{4t} \end{bmatrix} = \begin{bmatrix} \gamma_1 & 0 & 0 & 0 & 1 & 0 & 0 & 0 & 0 & 0 & 0 & 0 \\ \gamma_2 & 0 & 0 & 0 & 0 & 0 & 1 & 0 & 0 & 0 & 0 & 0 \\ \gamma_3 & 0 & 0 & 0 & 0 & 0 & 0 & 1 & 0 & 0 & 0 \\ \gamma_{40} & \gamma_{41} & \gamma_{42} & \gamma_{43} & 0 & 0 & 0 & 0 & 0 & 0 & 1 & 0 \end{bmatrix} \begin{bmatrix} \Delta c_t \\ \Delta c_{t-1} \\ \Delta c_{t-2} \\ \Delta c_{t-3} \\ e_{1t} \\ e_{1,t-1} \\ e_{2t} \\ e_{2,t-1} \\ e_{3t} \\ e_{3,t-1} \\ e_{4t} \\ e_{4,t-1} \end{bmatrix},
$$

$$\tag{3.134}$$

Transition Equation

$$
\begin{bmatrix}
\Delta c_t \\
\Delta c_{t-1} \\
\Delta c_{t-2} \\
\Delta c_{t-3} \\
e_{1t} \\
e_{1,t-1} \\
e_{2t} \\
e_{2,t-1} \\
e_{3t} \\
e_{3,t-1} \\
e_{4t} \\
e_{4,t-1}
\end{bmatrix}
=
\begin{bmatrix}
\phi_1 & \phi_2 & 0 & 0 & 0 & 0 & \cdots & 0 & 0 \\
1 & 0 & 0 & 0 & 0 & 0 & \cdots & 0 & 0 \\
0 & 1 & 0 & 0 & 0 & 0 & \cdots & 0 & 0 \\
0 & 0 & 1 & 0 & 0 & 0 & \cdots & 0 & 0 \\
0 & 0 & 0 & 0 & \psi_{11} & \psi_{12} & \cdots & 0 & 0 \\
0 & 0 & 0 & 0 & 1 & 0 & \cdots & 0 & 0 \\
\vdots & \vdots & \vdots & \vdots & \vdots & \vdots & \ddots & 0 & 0 \\
0 & 0 & 0 & 0 & 0 & 0 & \cdots & \psi_{41} & \psi_{42} \\
0 & 0 & 0 & 0 & 0 & 0 & \cdots & 1 & 0
\end{bmatrix}
\begin{bmatrix}
\Delta c_{t-1} \\
\Delta c_{t-2} \\
\Delta c_{t-3} \\
\Delta c_{t-4} \\
e_{1,t-1} \\
e_{1,t-2} \\
e_{2,t-1} \\
e_{2,t-2} \\
e_{3,t-1} \\
e_{3,t-2} \\
e_{4,t-1} \\
e_{4,t-2}
\end{bmatrix}
+
\begin{bmatrix}
w_t \\
0 \\
0 \\
0 \\
\epsilon_{1t} \\
0 \\
\epsilon_{2t} \\
0 \\
\epsilon_{3t} \\
0 \\
\epsilon_{4t} \\
0
\end{bmatrix}.
$$

$$(3.135)$$

Parameter estimates of the model are reported in table 3.3. For various issues related to the specification tests, refer to Stock and Watson 1991. Given these parameter estimates, we get $\Delta c_{t|t}$, $t = 1, 2, \ldots, T$, by running the Kalman filter again. Then, following the steps in section 3.5.2, we get an estimate of δ, the mean of the first differences of C_t. Notice that the new coincident index is identified only up to an arbitrary choice of the initial value. Thus, with an arbitrary starting values for $C_{0|0}$, we calculate $C_{t|t}$, $t = 1, 2, \ldots, T$ using equation (3.121):

$$C_{t|t} = C_{t|t-1} + \Delta c_{t|t} + \hat{\delta}.$$

For direct comparison of the new coincident index to the DOC coincident index, the following adjustments are made to the new coincident index:

$$C_{t|t}^* = C_{t|t} * SD(\Delta C_t^{\text{DOC}})/SD(\Delta c_{t|t}), \qquad (3.136)$$

where $SD(\Delta C_t^{\text{DOC}})$ and $SD(\Delta c_{t|t})$ refer to standard deviations of the first differences of the DOC index and of $\Delta c_{t|t}$, respectively. Finally, $C_{t|t}^*$ is adjusted again so that it is equal to the value of the DOC index in January 1970. The resulting new index of coincident indicators is depicted in figure 3.15 against the DOC coincident index. The new index reveals higher growth in the 1970s and lower growth in the 1980s and 1990s than the DOC index.

Table 3.3
Parameter estimates of stock and Watson's (1991) Dynamic Factor Model of Coincident Indicators

Variables	Parameters	Estimates	
Δc_t	ϕ_1	0.5505	(0.0816)
	ϕ_2	0.0079	(0.0759)
	γ_1	0.6412	(0.0414)
Δy_{1t}	ψ_{11}	−0.0903	(0.0872)
	ψ_{12}	−0.0020	(0.0039)
	σ_1^2	0.2439	(0.0327)
	γ_2	0.2420	(0.0234)
Δy_{2t}	ψ_{21}	−0.3156	(0.0509)
	ψ_{22}	−0.0249	(0.0080)
	σ_2^2	0.3079	(0.0223)
	γ_3	0.5071	(0.0404)
Δy_{3t}	ψ_{31}	−0.3703	(0.0541)
	ψ_{32}	−0.0343	(0.0100)
	σ_3^2	0.6412	(0.0497)
	γ_{40}	0.1402	(0.0110)
	γ_{41}	0.0081	(0.0131)
Δy_{4t}	γ_{42}	0.0105	(0.0129)
	γ_{43}	0.0438	(0.0100)
	ψ_{41}	−0.0261	(0.0671)
	ψ_{42}	0.3435	(0.0751)
	σ_4^2	0.0191	(0.0021)
Log likelihood		305.19	

Note: Standard errors are in parentheses.

Appendix: GAUSS Programs to Accompany Chapter 3

1. TVP.OPT: A time-varying-parameter model of U.S. monetary growth function (based on Kim and Nelson 1989).

2. UC_UNI.OPT: A univariate unobserved components model of U.S. real GDP (based on Clark 1987).

3. UC_BI.OPT: A bivariate unobserved components model of U.S. real GDP and unemployment rate (based on Clark 1989).

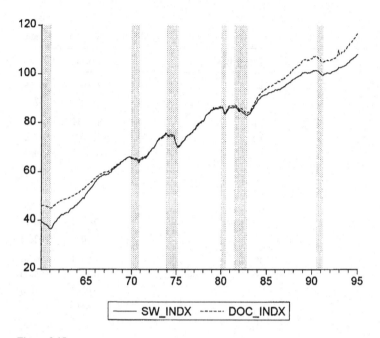

Figure 3.15
The Stock and Watson index from dynamic factor model vs. DOC coincident index

4. S&W.OPT: A dynamic factor model of four coincident economic indicators: an experimental coincident index (based on Stock and Watson 1991).

References

Antoncic, Madelyn. 1986. "High and Volatile Real Interest Rates: Where Does the Fed Fit In?" *Journal of Money, Credit, and Banking,* 18(1), 18–27.

Bera, Anil K., and Sangkyu Lee. 1993. "Information Matrix Test, Parameter Heterogeneity and ARCH: A Synthesis." *Review of Economic Studies,* 60, 229–240.

Burmeister, Edwin, and Kent D. Wall. 1982. "Kalman Filtering Estimation of Unobserved Rational Expectations with an Application to German Hyperinflation." *Journal of Econometrics,* 20, 255–284.

Burmeister, Edwin, Kent D. Wall, and James Hamilton. (1986). "Estimation of Unobserved Expected Monthly Inflation Using Kalman Filtering." *Journal of Business and Economic Statistics,* 4, 147–160.

Burns, A. F., and W. C. Mitchell. 1946. *Measuring Business Cycles.* New York: National Bureau of Economic Research.

Clark, Peter K. 1987. "The Cyclical Component of U.S. Economic Activity." *Quarterly Journal of Economics,* 102, 797–814.

Clark, Peter K. 1989. "Trend Reversion in Real Output and Unemployment." *Journal of Econometrics*, 40, 15–32.

Engle, R. F. 1982. "Autoregressive Conditional Heteroskedasticity with Estimates of the Variance of U.K. Inflation." *Econometrica*, 46 (50) 987–1007.

Engle, Robert F., and Mark Watson. 1981. "A One-Factor Multivariate Time Series Model of Metropolitan Wage Rates." *Journal of the American Statistical Association*, 76(376), Applications Section, 774–781.

Engle, Robert F., and Mark Watson. 1987. "Kalman Filter: Applications to Forecasting and Rational-Expectations Models." In *Advances in Econometrics*, Fifth World Congress, of the Econometric Society, ed. Truman Bewley, vol. 1, 245–281.

Garbade, Kenneth D., and Paul Wachtel. (1978). "Time Variation in the Relationship between Inflation and Interest Rates." *Journal of Monetary Economics*, 4, 775–765.

Hai, Weike, Nelson C. Mark, and Yangru Wu. 1996. "Understanding Spot and Forward Exchange Rate Regressions." Working paper no. 96-03, Ohio State University, Columbus.

Hamilton, James D. 1994a. *Time Series Analysis*. Princeton, NJ: Princeton University Press.

Hamilton, James D. 1994b. "State-Space Models." In *Handbook of Econometrics*, ed. R. F. Engel and D. L. McFadden, vol. 4, chap. 50, 3014–3077.

Harrison, P. J., and C. F. Stevens. 1976. "Bayesian Forecasting." *Journal of the Royal Statistical Society*, Series B, 38, 205–247.

Harvey, A. C. 1987. "Applications of the Kalman Filter in Econometrics." In *Advances in Econometrics*, Fifth World Congress of the Econometric Society, ed. by Truman Bewley, vol. 1., 285–313.

Harvey, Andrew C. 1989. *Forecasting, Structural Time Series Models and the Kalman Filter.* Cambridge: Cambridge University Press.

Harvey, Andrew C. 1990. *The Econometric Analysis of Time Series*. 2d ed. Cambridge: MIT Press.

Kalman, R. E. 1960. "A New Approach to Linear Filtering and Prediction Problems." *Transactions ASME Journal of Basic Engineering*, D82, 35–45.

Kim, Chang-Jin, and Charles R. Nelson. 1989. "The Time-Varying-Parameter Model for Modeling Changing Conditional Variance: The Case of the Lucas Hypothesis." *Journal of Business and Economic Statistics*, 7(4) 433–440.

Kim, Chang-Jin, and Charles R. Nelson. 1997. "Friedman's Plucking Model of Business Fluctuations: Tests and Estimates of Permanent and Transitory Components." Working paper, University of Washington, Seattle.

McNees, S. K. 1986. "Modeling the Fed: A Forward-Looking Monetary Policy Reaction Function." *New England Economic Review*, Nov./Dec., 3–8.

Nelson, Charles R. 1988. "Spurious Trend and Cycle in the State Space Decomposition of a Time Series with a Unit Root." *Journal of Economic Dynamics and Control*, 12, 475–488.

Nelson, C. R., and C. I. Plosser. 1982. "Trends and Random Walks in Macroeconomic Time Series: Some Evidence and Implications." *Journal of Monetary Economics*, 10, 139–162.

Perron, P. 1990. "Testing for a Unit Root in a Time Series with a Changing Mean." *Journal of Business and Economic Statistics*, 8, 153–162.

Stock, James H., and Mark W. Watson. 1991. "A Probability Model of the Coincident Economic Indicators." In *Leading Economic Indicators: New Approaches and Forecasting Records*, ed. K. Lahiri and G. H. Moore. Cambridge: Cambridge University Press 63–89.

Tsay, Ruey S. 1987. "Conditional Heteroscedastic Time Series Models." *Journal of the American Statistical Association*, (82)(398) Theory and Methods, 590–604.

4 Markov-Switching Models

Model instability is sometimes defined as a switch in a regression equation from one subsample period (or regime) to another. An F-test proposed by Chow (1960) may be applied in testing for structural changes in the case where the dates that separate subsamples are known.

In many cases, however, researchers may have little information on the dates at which parameters change, and thus need to make inferences about the turning points as well as the significance of parameter shifts. Quandt (1958, 1960), Farley and Hinich (1970), and H. Kim and Siegmund (1989), for example, consider models in which they permitted at most one switch in the data series with an unknown turning point. Quandt (1972), Goldfeld and Quandt (1973), Brown, Durbin, and Evans (1975), Ploberger Kramer, and Kontrus (1989), and I.-M. Kim and Maddala (1991) considered models that allow for more than one switch. For example, Quandt's model assumes that the probability of a switch does not depend upon what regime is in effect, whereas Goldfeld and Quandt's model explicitly allows for such a dependence by introducing Markov switching. For tests of structural change with unknown change point, see Andrews 1993 and the references therein. See also Wecker 1979, Sclove 1983, and Neftci 1984, for other related models of predicting turning points. An interesting and important aspect of these models is that the time at which a structural change occurs is endogenous to the model.

Recently, Hamilton's (1989) state-dependent Markov-switching model has drawn attention in modeling structural changes in dependent data. His model can be viewed as an extension of Goldfeld and Quandt's (1973) model to the important case of structural changes in the parameters of an autoregressive process. This chapter focuses on Markov-switching models with selected applications. For alternative expositions of the topics, readers are referred to Hamilton 1993.

4.1 Introduction: Serially Uncorrelated Data and Switching

Consider the following regression model without any switching:

$$y_t = x_t \beta + e_t, \quad e_t \sim \text{i.i.d.} N(0, \sigma^2), \tag{4.1}$$

where x_t is a $1 \times k$ vector of exogenous variables. To estimate the parameters of the model in this simple case, the log likelihood function, given by

$$\ln L = \sum_{t=1}^{T} \ln(f(y_t)), \tag{4.2}$$

where

$$f(y_t) = \frac{1}{\sqrt{2\pi\sigma^2}} \exp(-\frac{(y_t - x_t\beta)^2}{2\sigma^2}), \qquad (4.3)$$

can be maximized with respect to β and σ^2.

For a model with structural breaks in the parameters, we have:

$$y_t = x_t\beta_{S_t} + e_t, \quad t = 1, 2, \ldots, T, \qquad (4.4)$$

$$e_t \sim N(0, \sigma_{S_t}^2), \qquad (4.5)$$

$$\beta_{S_t} = \beta_0(1 - S_t) + \beta_1 S_t, \qquad (4.6)$$

$$\sigma_{S_t}^2 = \sigma_0^2(1 - S_t) + \sigma_1^2 S_t, \qquad (4.7)$$

$$S_t = 0 \text{ or } 1, \quad (\text{Regime } 0 \text{ or } 1), \qquad (4.8)$$

where under regime 1, parameters are given by β_1 and σ_1^2, and under regime 0, parameters are given by β_0 and σ_0^2.

If S_t, $t = 1, 2, \ldots, T$, is known a priori, that is, if the dates of regime switching or structural breaks are known a priori, the above is nothing more than a dummy variable model, where the dummy variable, S_t, equals 0 in regime 0 and 1 in regime 1. In this case, the log likelihood function is given by:

$$\ln L = \sum_{t=1}^{T} \ln(f(y_t \mid S_t)), \qquad (4.9)$$

where

$$f(y_t \mid S_t) = \frac{1}{\sqrt{2\pi\sigma_{S_t}^2}} \exp(-\frac{\{y_t - x_t\beta_{S_t}\}^2}{2\sigma_{S_t}^2}), \qquad (4.10)$$

and (4.9) can be maximized with respect to β_0, β_1, σ_0^2, and σ_1^2.

A major problem with the model given by (4.4)–(4.8) arises when S_t, $t = 1, 2, \ldots, T$, is not observed. In this case, as a rule of thumb, we use the following two steps to determine the log likelihood function:

STEP 1 First, consider the joint density of y_t and the unobserved S_t variable, which is the product of the conditional and marginal densities:

$$f(y_t, S_t \mid \psi_{t-1}) = f(y_t \mid S_t, \psi_{t-1}) f(S_t \mid \psi_{t-1}), \tag{4.11}$$

where ψ_{t-1} refers to information up to time $t-1$.

STEP 2   Then, to obtain the marginal density of y_t, integrate the S_t variable out of the above joint density by summing over all possible values of S_t:

$$
\begin{aligned}
f(y_t \mid \psi_{t-1}) &= \sum_{S_t=0}^{1} f(y_t, S_t \mid \psi_{t-1}) \\
&= \sum_{S_t=0}^{1} f(y_t \mid S_t, \psi_{t-1}) f(S_t \mid \psi_{t-1}) \\
&= \frac{1}{\sqrt{2\pi\sigma_0^2}} \exp(-\frac{\{y_t - x_t\beta_0\}^2}{2\sigma_0^2}) \times Pr[S_t = 0 \mid \psi_{t-1}] \\
&+ \frac{1}{\sqrt{2\pi\sigma_1^2}} \exp(-\frac{\{y_t - x_t\beta_1\}^2}{2\sigma_1^2}) \times Pr[S_t = 1 \mid \psi_{t-1}].
\end{aligned}
\tag{4.12}
$$

The log likelihood function then is given by

$$\ln L = \sum_{t=1}^{T} \ln\{ \sum_{S_t=0}^{1} f(y_t \mid S_t, \psi_{t-1}) Pr[S_t \mid \psi_{t-1}]\}.$$

The marginal density given above can be interpreted as a weighted average of the conditional densities given $S_t = 0$ and $S_t = 1$, respectively. To derive the marginal density of y_t in (4.12), and thus, the log likelihood function, we need to calculate appropriately the weighting factors, $Pr[S_t = 0 \mid \psi_{t-1}]$ and $Pr[S_t = 1 \mid \psi_{t-1}]$. Without a priori assumptions about the stochastic behavior of the S_t variable, however, this will not be possible. In sections 4.1.1 and 4.1.2, we deal with different assumptions about the evolution of S_t and discuss ways to calculate appropriately the weighting factors in (4.12), given these assumptions.

4.1.1   The Case of Independent Switching

When the discrete variable S_t evolves independently of its own past values, we can specify probabilities very simply as

$$Pr[S_t = 1] = p = \frac{\exp(p_0)}{1 + \exp(p_0)}, \tag{4.13}$$

$$Pr[S_t = 0] = 1 - p = 1 - \frac{\exp(p_0)}{1 + \exp(p_0)}, \tag{4.14}$$

where p_0 is an unconstrained parameter. Furthermore, if the stochastic behavior of S_t is not dependent upon any other exogenous or predetermined variables, we have $Pr[S_t = j \mid \psi_{t-1}] = Pr[S_t = j]$, and the log likelihood function can be maximized with respect to β_0, β_1, σ_0^2, σ_1^2, and p_0.

In a more complicated case, even when S_t evolves independently of its own past values, it may be dependent upon some exogenous or predetermined variables, Z_{t-1}. Then probability terms in equation (4.12) are given by

$$Pr[S_t = 1 \mid \psi_{t-1}] = p_t = \frac{\exp(p_0 + Z'_{t-1}p_1)}{1 + \exp(p_0 + Z'_{t-1}p_1)}, \tag{4.15}$$

$$Pr[S_t = 0 \mid \psi_{t-1}] = 1 - p_t = 1 - \frac{\exp(p_0 + Z'_{t-1}p_1)}{1 + \exp(p_0 + Z'_{t-1}p_1)}, \tag{4.16}$$

and the log likelihood function can be maximized with respect to β_0, β_1, σ_0^2, σ_1^2, p_0, and p_1.

4.1.2   The Case of Markov Switching

The evolution of the discrete variable S_t may be dependent upon S_{t-1}, S_{t-2}, $\ldots$, S_{t-r}, in which case the process of S_t is named as an r-th order Markov-switching process. In this section, we consider the simplest case of a two-state, first-order Markov-switching process for S_t, with the following transition probabilities:

$$Pr[S_t = 1 \mid S_{t-1} = 1] = p = \frac{\exp(p_0)}{1 + \exp(p_0)}, \tag{4.17}$$

$$Pr[S_t = 0 \mid S_{t-1} = 0] = q = \frac{\exp(q_0)}{1 + \exp(q_0)}. \tag{4.18}$$

An alternative specification of the transition probabilities for a two-state, first-order Markov switching is given as follows:

$$Pr[S_t = 1] = Pr[S_t^* \geq 0], \quad Pr[S_t = 0] = Pr[S_t^* < 0],$$

where S_t^* is a latent variable defined by $S_t^* = \alpha_0 + \alpha_1 S_{t-1} + \xi_t$, with $\xi_t \sim$ i.i.d. $N(0, 1)$. Thus, we have

$$Pr[S_t = 1 \mid S_{t-1} = 1] = p = Pr[\xi_t \geq -\alpha_0 - \alpha_1] = 1 - \Phi(-\alpha_0 - \alpha_1),$$

$$Pr[S_t = 0 \mid S_{t-1} = 0] = q = Pr[\xi_t < -\alpha_0] = \Phi(-\alpha_0),$$

where $\Phi(.)$ is the c.d.f. (cumulative distributive function) of the standard normal distribution.

Dealing with the problem of unobserved S_t in the above model is exactly the same as before. Calculation of the weighting terms in (4.12), $Pr[S_t = j \mid \psi_{t-1}]$, $j = 0, 1$, however, is not as straightforward as in section 4.1.1. We adopt the following filter for the calculation of the weighting terms:

STEP 1   Given $Pr[S_{t-1} = i \mid \psi_{t-1}]$, $i = 0, 1$, at the beginning of time t or the t-th iteration, the weighting terms $Pr[S_t = j \mid \psi_{t-1}]$, $j = 0, 1$, are calculated as

$$Pr[S_t = j \mid \psi_{t-1}] = \sum_{i=0}^{1} Pr[S_t = j, S_{t-1} = i \mid \psi_{t-1}]$$

$$\hspace{4cm} (4.19)$$

$$= \sum_{i=0}^{1} Pr[S_t = j \mid S_{t-1} = i] Pr[S_{t-1} = i \mid \psi_{t-1}],$$

where $Pr[S_t = j \mid S_{t-1} = i]$, $i = 0, 1$, $j = 0, 1$, are the transition probabilities.

STEP 2   Once y_t is observed at the end of time t, or at the end of the t-th iteration, we can update the probability term in the following way:

$$Pr[S_t = j \mid \psi_t] = Pr[S_t = j \mid \psi_{t-1}, y_t] = \frac{f(S_t = j, y_t \mid \psi_{t-1})}{f(y_t \mid \psi_{t-1})}$$

$$= \frac{f(y_t \mid S_t = j, \psi_{t-1}) Pr[S_t = j \mid \psi_{t-1}]}{\sum_{j=0}^{1} f(y_t \mid S_t = j, \psi_{t-1}) Pr[S_t = j \mid \psi_{t-1}]}, \hspace{1cm} (4.20)$$

where $\psi_t = \{\psi_{t-1}, y_t\}$.

The above two steps may be iterated to get $Pr[S_t = j \mid \psi_{t-1}]$, $t = 1, 2, \ldots, T$. To start the above filter at time $t = 1$, however, we need $Pr[S_0 \mid \psi_0]$. We can employ the following steady-state or unconditional probabilities of S_t:

$$\pi_0 = Pr[S_0 = 0 \mid \psi_0] = \frac{1-p}{2-p-q} \tag{4.21}$$

$$\pi_1 = Pr[S_0 = 1 \mid \psi_0] = \frac{1-q}{2-p-q} \tag{4.22}$$

By now, it is clear that the marginal density in (4.12), and thus the log likelihood function, is a function of β_0, β_1, σ_0^2, σ_1^2, p, and q.

4.2   Serially Correlated Data and Markov Switching

In general, an autoregressive model of order k with first-order, M-state Markov-switching mean and variance may be written as

$$\phi(L)(y_t - \mu_{S_t}) = e_t, \quad e_t \sim N(0, \sigma_{S_t}^2), \tag{4.23}$$

$$Pr[S_t = j \mid S_{t-1} = i] = p_{ij}, \quad i, j = 1, 2, \ldots, M, \tag{4.24}$$

$$\sum_{j=1}^{M} p_{ij} = 1, \tag{4.25}$$

$$\mu_{S_t} = \mu_1 S_{1t} + \mu_2 S_{2t} + \ldots + \mu_M S_{Mt}, \tag{4.26}$$

$$\sigma_{S_t}^2 = \sigma_1^2 S_{1t} + \sigma_2^2 S_{2t} + \ldots + \sigma_M^2 S_{Mt}, \tag{4.27}$$

where

$$S_{mt} = 1, \text{ if } S_t = m, \text{ and } S_{mt} = 0, \text{ otherwise.} \tag{4.28}$$

To make the analysis simple, we focus on an AR(1) model. However, an extension of the procedure to the general AR(k) case would be straightforward. For the AR(1) case, we have

$$(y_t - \mu_{S_t}) = \phi_1(y_{t-1} - \mu_{S_{t-1}}) + e_t, \quad e_t \sim \text{i.i.d.} N(0, \sigma_{S_t}^2) \tag{4.29}$$

As before, if S_t, $t = 1, \ldots, T$, were known a priori, the above would be nothing more than a dummy variable model. Calculation of the density of y_t given past information (ψ_{t-1}) and the log likelihood function would be straightforward:

$$f(y_t \mid \psi_{t-1}, S_t, S_{t-1})$$

$$= \frac{1}{\sqrt{2\pi\sigma_{S_t}^2}} \exp\left(-\frac{\{(y_t - \mu_{S_t}) - \phi_1(y_{t-1} - \mu_{S_{t-1}})\}^2}{2\sigma_{S_t}^2}\right), \tag{4.30}$$

$$\ln L = \sum_{t=1}^{T} \ln(f(y_t \mid \psi_{t-1}, S_t, S_{t-1})). \tag{4.31}$$

4.2.1 Dealing with the Problem of Unobserved S_t

In writing the density of y_t given past infomation ψ_{t-1}, we need S_t and S_{t-1}, which are unobserved. To solve the problem, we proceed in exactly the same way as in section 4.1, except instead of considering a joint density of y_t and S_t, we now consider the joint density of y_t, S_t, and S_{t-1}:

STEP 1   Derive the joint density of y_t, S_t, and S_{t-1}, conditional on past information ψ_{t-1}:

$$f(y_t, S_t, S_{t-1} \mid \psi_{t-1}) = f(y_t \mid S_t, S_{t-1}, \psi_{t-1}) Pr[S_t, S_{t-1} \mid \psi_{t-1}], \tag{4.32}$$

where $f(y_t \mid S_t, S_{t-1}, \psi_{t-1})$ is given by (4.30).

STEP 2   To get $f(y_t \mid \psi_{t-1})$, integrate S_t and S_{t-1} out of the joint density by summing the joint density over all possible values of S_t and S_{t-1}:

$$f(y_t \mid \psi_{t-1}) = \sum_{s_t=1}^{M} \sum_{s_{t-1}=1}^{M} f(y_t, S_t, S_{t-1} \mid \psi_{t-1})$$

$$\tag{4.33}$$

$$= \sum_{s_t=1}^{M} \sum_{s_{t-1}=1}^{M} f(y_t \mid S_t, S_{t-1}, \psi_{t-1}) Pr[S_t, S_{t-1} \mid \psi_{t-1}],$$

where the marginal density $f(y_t \mid \psi_{t-1})$ is a weighted average of M^2 conditional densities, weights being $Pr[S_t = j, S_{t-1} = i \mid \psi_{t-1}]$, $i = 1, \ldots, M$, $j = 1, 2, \ldots, M$.

Then the log likelihood function is given by:

$$\ln L = \sum_{t=1}^{T} \ln\{\sum_{s_t=1}^{M} \sum_{s_{t-1}=1}^{M} f(y_t \mid S_t, S_{t-1}, \psi_{t-1}) Pr[S_t, S_{t-1} \mid \psi_{t-1}]\}. \tag{4.34}$$

To complete the above procedure, we still need to deal with the problem of calculating $Pr[S_t = j, S_{t-1} = i \mid \psi_{t-1}]$.

4.2.2 Filtering

The following two steps enable us to calculate $Pr[S_t = j, S_{t-1} = i \mid \psi_{t-1}]$.

STEP 1   Given $Pr[S_{t-1} = i \mid \psi_{t-1}]$, $i = 1, 2, \ldots, M$, at the beginning of time t or the t-th iteration, the weighting terms $Pr[S_t = j, S_{t-1} = i \mid \psi_{t-1}]$, $i = 1, \ldots, M$, $j = 1, \ldots, M$, are calculated as

$$Pr[S_t = j, S_{t-1} = i \mid \psi_{t-1}] = Pr[S_t = j \mid S_{t-1} = i]Pr[S_{t-1} = i \mid \psi_{t-1}],$$

(4.35)

where $Pr[S_t = j \mid S_{t-1} = i]$, $i = 1, \ldots, M$, $j = 1, \ldots, M$, are the transition probabilities.

STEP 2   Once y_t is observed at the end of time t, or at the end of the t-th iteration, we can update the probability terms in the following way:

$$\begin{aligned}
&Pr[S_t = j, S_{t-1} = i \mid \psi_t] \\
&= Pr[S_t = j, S_{t-1} = i \mid \psi_{t-1}, y_t] \\
&= \frac{f(S_t = j, S_{t-1} = i, y_t \mid \psi_{t-1})}{f(y_t \mid \psi_{t-1})} \\
&= \frac{f(y_t \mid S_t = j, S_{t-1} = i, \psi_{t-1})Pr[S_t = j, S_{t-1} = i \mid \psi_{t-1}]}{\sum_{S_t=1}^{M} \sum_{S_{t-1}=1}^{M} f(y_t \mid S_t = j, S_{t-1} = i, \psi_{t-1})Pr[S_t = j, S_{t-1} = i \mid \psi_{t-1}]},
\end{aligned}$$

(4.36)

with

$$Pr[S_t = j \mid \psi_t] = \sum_{S_{t-1}=1}^{M} Pr[S_t = j, S_{t-1} = i \mid \psi_t].$$

(4.37)

Iterating the above two steps for $t = 1, 2, \ldots, T$ provides us with the appropriate weighting terms in (4.33). To start the above filter at time $t = 1$, we can employ the steady-state or unconditional probabilities to be derived in section 4.3. For a summary of the Hamilton filter, refer to a flow chart in figure 4.1. For a two-state, first-order Markov switching, the steady-state probabilities are given by

$$l(\theta) = 0$$

$$\Pr(S_0) = \pi_j \ \ \text{(Steady - State Prob.)}$$

$\Downarrow$

$\Downarrow$

$$\Pr(S_t, S_{t-1} \mid \psi_{t-1}) = \Pr(S_t \mid S_{t-1}) \Pr(S_{t-1} \mid \psi_{t-1})$$

$\Downarrow$

$$f(y_t \mid \psi_{t-1}) = \sum_{S_t} \sum_{S_{t-1}} f(y_t \mid S_t, S_{t-1}, \psi_{t-1}) \Pr(S_t, S_{t-1} \mid \psi_{t-1})$$

$\Downarrow$

$$\{ l(\theta) = l(\theta) + \ln(f(y_t \mid \psi_{t-1})) \}$$

$\Downarrow$

$$\Pr(S_t, S_{t-1} \mid \psi_t) = \frac{f(y_t, S_t, S_{t-1} \mid \psi_{t-1})}{f(y_t \mid \psi_{t-1})} = \frac{f(y_t \mid S_t, S_{t-1}, \psi_{t-1}) \Pr(S_t, S_{t-1} \mid \psi_{t-1})}{f(y_t \mid \psi_{t-1})}$$

$\Downarrow$

$$\Pr(S_t \mid \psi_t) = \sum_{S_{t-1}} \Pr(S_t, S_{t-1} \mid \psi_{t-1})$$

$\Downarrow$ $\qquad\qquad\qquad$ t - 1 = t

$\Downarrow$

$$\left\{ l(\theta) = \sum_{t=1}^{T} \ln(f(y_t \mid \psi_{t-1})) \right\}$$

Figure 4.1
Flowchart for Hamilton's Markov-switching model (an AR(1) model with switching mean)

$$\pi_1 = Pr[S_0 = 1 \mid \psi_0] = \frac{1 - p_{22}}{2 - p_{22} - p_{11}}, \tag{4.38}$$

$$\pi_2 = Pr[S_0 = 2 \mid \psi_0] = \frac{1 - p_{11}}{2 - p_{22} - p_{11}}. \tag{4.39}$$

For a general AR(k) process with switching mean, it is straightforward to extend the above process. In this case, as $S_t, S_{t-1}, \ldots, S_{t-k}$ show up in the model as unobserved variables, we consider the joint density of $y_t, S_t, S_{t-1}, \ldots,$ and S_{t-k}. Thus, the marginal density $f(y_t \mid \psi_{t-1})$ is a weighted average of M^{k+1} conditional densities. For details, refer to Hamilton 1989.

In general, the inference problem in a Markov-switching model consists of (i) estimating the parameters of the model by maximizing the log likelihood function, and (ii) making inferences about $S_t, t = 1, 2, \ldots, T$. In the classical approach, inferences on the state variable S_t are usually made conditional on the parameter estimates of the model. As in the state-space model in chapter 3, depending on the amount of information used in making inferences on S_t, we have filtered probabilities or smoothed probabilities. Filtered probabilities refer to inferences about S_t conditional on information up to t: ψ_t. These are obtained by the filter provided in section 4.2.2. Smoothed probabilities refer to inferences about S_t conditional on all the information in the sample: ψ_T. These are obtained by the smoothing algorithm provided in the next section.

4.3   Issues Related to Markov-Switching Models

4.3.1   Kim's Smoothing Algorithm

Given parameter estimates of the model, we can make inferences on S_t using all the information in the sample. This gives us $Pr[S_t = j \mid \psi_T]$ ($t = 1, 2, \ldots, T$), which is the smoothed probability (as opposed to $Pr[S_t = j \mid \psi_t]$ ($t = 1, 2, \ldots, T$), which is the filtered probability discussed in the previous section). Here, it is assumed that we have an AR(1) model with Markov-switching mean.

Consider the following derivation of the joint probability that $S_t = j$ and $S_{t+1} = k$ based on full information:

$$Pr[S_t = j, S_{t+1} = k \mid \psi_T]$$

$$= Pr[S_{t+1} = k \mid \psi_T] \times Pr[S_t = j \mid S_{t+1} = k, \psi_T]$$

$$= Pr[S_{t+1} = k \mid \psi_T] \times Pr[S_t = j \mid S_{t+1} = k, \psi_t]$$

$$= \frac{Pr[S_{t+1} = k \mid \psi_T] \times Pr[S_t = j, S_{t+1} = k \mid \psi_t]}{Pr[S_{t+1} = k \mid \psi_t]} \tag{4.40}$$

$$= \frac{Pr[S_{t+1} = k \mid \psi_T] \times Pr[S_t = j \mid \psi_t] \times Pr[S_{t+1} = k \mid S_t = j]}{Pr[S_{t+1} = k \mid \psi_t]},$$

and

$$Pr[S_t = j \mid \psi_T] = \sum_{k=1}^{M} Pr[S_t = j, S_{t+1} = k \mid \psi_T]. \tag{4.41}$$

Given $Pr[S_T \mid \psi_T]$ at the last iteration of the basic filter in section 4.2.2, the above can be iterated for $t = T - 1, T - 2, \ldots, 1$ to get the smoothed probabilities, $Pr[S_t \mid \psi_T]$, $t = T - 1, T - 2, \ldots, 1$.

To consider the validity of going from the second line to the third line of equation (4.40), define $\tilde{h}_{t+1,T} = (y_{t+1}, y_{t+2}, \ldots, y_T)'$, for $T > t$. That is, $\tilde{h}_{t+1,T}$ is the vector of observations from date $t + 1$ to T. Then we have

$$Pr[S_t = j \mid S_{t+1} = k, \psi_T]$$

$$= Pr[S_t = j \mid S_{t+1} = k, \tilde{h}_{t+1,T}, \psi_t)$$

$$= \frac{f(S_t = j, \tilde{h}_{t+1,T} \mid S_{t+1} = k, \psi_t)}{f(\tilde{h}_{t+1,T} \mid S_{t+1} = k, \psi_t)} \tag{4.42}$$

$$= \frac{Pr(S_t = j \mid S_{t+1} = k, \psi_t) f(\tilde{h}_{t+1,T} \mid S_{t+1} = k, S_t = j, \psi_t)}{f(\tilde{h}_{t+1,T} \mid S_{t+1} = k, \psi_t)}$$

$$= Pr[S_t = j \mid S_{t+1} = k, \psi_t].$$

The above holds as $f(\tilde{h}_{t+1,T} \mid S_{t+1} = k, S_t = j, \psi_t) = f(\tilde{h}_{t+1,T} \mid S_{t+1} = k, \psi_t)$, which suggests that if S_{t+1} were somehow known, then y_{t+1} would contain no information about S_t beyond that contained in S_{t+1} and ψ_t. Note that in a state-space model with Markov switching considered by Kim (1994) and in chapter 5 of this book, this does not hold exactly, and the smoothed algorithm provided involves an approximation.

The smoothing algorithm derived above can be generalized to a general AR(k) model with Markov switching considered by Hamilton (1989):

$Pr[S_{t-k+1}, \ldots, S_t, S_{t+1} \mid \psi_T]$

$$= \frac{Pr[S_{t-k+2}, \ldots, S_t, S_{t+1} \mid \psi_T] \times Pr[S_{t-k+1}, \ldots, S_t, S_{t+1} \mid \psi_t]}{Pr[S_{t-k+2}, \ldots, S_t, S_{t+1} \mid \psi_t]} \qquad (4.43)$$

$$= \frac{Pr[S_{t-k+2}, \ldots, S_t, S_{t+1} \mid \psi_T] \times Pr[S_{t-k+1}, \ldots, S_t \mid \psi_t] \times Pr[S_{t+1} \mid S_t]}{Pr[S_{t-k+2}, \ldots, S_t, S_{t+1} \mid \psi_t]}.$$

The algorithm for a general AR(k) model with Markov-switching mean looks complicated. However, it is not difficult to show that equation (4.43) collapses to equation (4.40) for $t \le T - k + 1$. Notice that these algorithms are vastly more efficient than those in Hamilton 1989 and Lam 1990 in terms of simplicity and computation time.

4.3.2   Derivation of Steady-State Probabilities Used to Start the Filter

The transition probabilities for a first-order, M-state Markov-switching process S_t in equations (4.24) and (4.25) can be put in the following matrix notation:

$$P^* = \begin{bmatrix} p_{11} & p_{21} & \cdots & p_{M1} \\ p_{12} & p_{22} & \cdots & p_{M2} \\ \vdots & \vdots & \ddots & \vdots \\ p_{1M} & p_{2M} & \cdots & p_{MM} \end{bmatrix}, \qquad (4.44)$$

where $i'_M P^* = i'_M$, with $i_M = [\, 1 \quad 1 \quad \cdots \quad 1 \,]'$. If we let π_t be a vector of $M \times 1$ steady-state probabilites, we have

$$\pi_t = \begin{bmatrix} Pr[S_t = 1] \\ Pr[S_t = 2] \\ \cdots \\ Pr[S_t = M] \end{bmatrix} = \begin{bmatrix} \pi_{1t} \\ \pi_{2t} \\ \vdots \\ \pi_{Mt} \end{bmatrix}, \qquad (4.45)$$

$$i'_M \pi_t = 1. \qquad (4.46)$$

Then according to the definition of steady state probabilities, we have $\pi_{t+1} = P^* \pi_t$ and $\pi_{t+1} = \pi_t$, and thus

$$\pi_t = P^* \pi_t \implies (I_M - P^*) \pi_t = 0_M, \qquad (4.47)$$

where 0_M is an $M \times 1$ matrix of zeros. Combining equations (4.46) and (4.47), we have:

$$\begin{bmatrix} I_M - P^* \\ i'_M \end{bmatrix} \pi_t = \begin{bmatrix} 0_M \\ 1 \end{bmatrix}, \quad \text{or } A\pi_t = \begin{bmatrix} 0_M \\ 1 \end{bmatrix}. \tag{4.48}$$

Multiply both sides of the above equation by $(A'A)^{-1}A'$. Then,

$$\pi_t = (A'A)^{-1}A' \begin{bmatrix} 0_M \\ 1 \end{bmatrix} \tag{4.49}$$

That is, the matrix of steady-state probabilities, π_t, is the last column of the matrix $(A'A)^{-1}A'$.

4.3.3   Expected Duration of a Regime in a Markov-Switching Model

The diagonal elements of the matrix of the transition probabilities (4.44) contain important information on the expected duration of a state or regime. The relevant question is: Given that we are currently in regime j or state j ($S_t = j$), how long, on average, will the regime j last? Note that if we define D as the duration of state j, we have:

$D = 1$, if $S_t = j$ and $S_{t+1} \neq j$; $Pr[D = 1] = (1 - p_{jj})$

$D = 2$, if $S_t = S_{t+1} = j$ and $S_{t+2} \neq j$; $Pr[D = 2] = p_{jj}(1 - p_{jj})$

$D = 3$, if $S_t = S_{t+1} = S_{t+2} = j$ and $S_{t+3} \neq j$; $Pr[D = 3] = p_{jj}^2(1 - p_{jj})$

$D = 4$, if $S_t = S_{t+1} = S_{t+2} = S_{t+3} = j$ and $S_{t+4} \neq j$; $Pr[D = 4] = p_{jj}^3(1 - p_{jj})$

$\vdots$

Then, the expected duration of regime j can be derived as

$$E(D) = \sum_{j=1}^{\infty} j \, Pr[D = j]$$

$$= 1 \times Pr[S_{t+1} \neq j \mid S_t = j]$$

$$+ 2 \times Pr[S_{t+1} = j, S_{t+2} \neq j \mid S_t = j]$$

$$+ 3 \times Pr[S_{t+1} = j, S_{t+2} = j, S_{t+3} \neq j \mid S_t = j]$$

$$+ 4 \times Pr[S_{t+1} = j, S_{t+2} = j, S_{t+3} = j, S_{t+4} \neq j \mid S_t = j]$$

$$+ \ldots$$

$$= 1 \times (1 - p_{jj}) + 2 \times p_{jj}(1 - p_{jj}) + 3 \times p_{jj}^2(1 - p_{jj}) + \dots$$

$$= \frac{1}{1 - p_{jj}}. \tag{4.50}$$

For example, in an AR(4) model of the growth of quarterly real GNP (1952:II–1984:IV) with a two-state Markov-switching mean, Hamilton's (1989) estimates of transition probabilities p_{11} and p_{22} are 0.7550 and 0.9049, where state 1 is a recession and state 2 is a boom. Thus, expected durations of a recession and a boom are

$$\frac{1}{1 - 0.7550} = 4.08$$

and

$$\frac{1}{1 - 0.9040} = 10.42,$$

suggesting that, on average, a recession and a boom last 4.08 quarters and 10.42 quarters, respectively.

4.3.4 Time-Varying Transition Probabilities and Expected Duration of a Regime

The Markov-switching models are useful tools for capturing occasional but recurrent and endogenous regime shifts in time series. Whereas Hamilton (1989) assumes that probability of switching from one regime to another is constant with an implication of a constant expected duration of a regime, Diebold, Lee, and Weinbach (1994) and Filardo (1994) assume that the probability of switching may be dependent on some underlying economic fundamentals. Diebold, Lee, and Weinbach suggest that in a Markov-switching model of exchange rates, it may be reasonable to assume that the likelihood of exchange rate revaluation increases under progressively more severe over- or undervaluation on the basis of economic fundamentals. In a Markov-switching model of the business cycle, Filardo considers time-varying transition probabilities that are functions of leading economic indicators.

Extending Markov-switching models to allow for time-varying transition probabilities is straightforward. Assuming that Z_{t-1} is a vector of economic fundamentals that affect the likelihood of regime switches, the time-varying transition probabilities may have the following logistic form:

$$p_{ij,t} = Pr[S_t = j \mid S_{t-1} = i, Z_{t-1}] = \frac{\exp(\lambda_{ij,0} + Z'_{t-1}\lambda_{ij,1})}{1 + \exp(\lambda_{ij,0} + Z'_{t-1}\lambda_{ij,1})}, \qquad (4.51)$$

$$i = 1, 2, \ldots, M; \; j = 1, 2, \ldots, M - 1,$$

$$p_{iM,t} = Pr[S_t = M \mid S_{t-1} = i, Z_{t-1}] = 1 - \sum_{j=1}^{M-1} p_{ij,t}, \; i = 1, 2, \ldots, M. \quad (4.52)$$

When $M = 2$, the time-varying transition probabilities also have the following probit specifications:

$$Pr[S_t = 1] = Pr[S_t^* < 0] \quad \text{and} \quad Pr[S_t = 2] = Pr[S_t^* \geq 0], \qquad (4.53)$$

where S_t^* is a latent variable defined by

$$S_t^* = g_1 S_{1,t-1} + g_2 S_{2,t-1} + Z'_{t-1}\gamma + \xi_t, \quad \xi_t \sim \text{i.i.d.} N(0, 1), \qquad (4.54)$$

where $S_{i,t-1} = 1$ if $S_{t-1} = i$ and $S_{i,t-1} = 0$, otherwise, as in (4.28). Hence, the transition probabilities are given by

$$p_{11,t} = Pr[S_t = 1 \mid S_{t-1} = 1, Z_{t-1}] = Pr[\xi_t < -(g_1 + Z'_{t-1}\gamma)]$$
$$= \Phi(-(g_1 + Z'_{t-1}\gamma)), \qquad (4.55)$$

$$p_{12,t} = Pr[S_t = 2 \mid S_{t-1} = 1, Z_{t-1}] = Pr[\xi_t \geq -(g_1 + Z'_{t-1}\gamma)]$$
$$= 1 - \Phi(-(g_1 + Z'_{t-1}\gamma)), \qquad (4.56)$$

$$p_{22,t} = Pr[S_t = 2 \mid S_{t-1} = 2, Z_{t-1}] = Pr[\xi_t \geq -(g_2 + Z'_{t-1}\gamma)]$$
$$= 1 - \Phi(-(g_2 + Z'_{t-1}\gamma)), \qquad (4.57)$$

$$p_{21,t} = Pr[S_t = 1 \mid S_{t-1} = 2, Z_{t-1}] = Pr[\xi_t < -(g_2 + Z'_{t-1}\gamma)]$$
$$= \Phi(-(g_2 + Z'_{t-1}\gamma)), \qquad (4.58)$$

where $\Phi(.)$ refers to the c.d.f. of the standard normal distribution.

Time-varying transition probabilities also imply time-varying expected duration of a regime. A closely related issue in the business cycle literature is duration dependence, or whether the probability of a transition between regimes depends on how long the economy has been in a recession or boom. It is a special form of time-varying transition probabilities in a regime-switching model of the business cycle, in which Z_{t-1} is replaced by length to date of the current regime (boom or recession). Durland and McCurdy (1994), for example, examine the nature of business cycle duration dependence within Hamilton's (1989) univariate Markov-switching model of the business cycle. Kim and Nelson (1998) provide a Bayesian analysis of business cycle duration dependence based on a dynamic factor model with Markov-switching.

4.3.5 EM Algorithm

The EM algorithm, originally motivated by Dempster, Laird, and Rubin (1977), is an alternative method for maximizing the likelihood function for models with missing observations or unobserved variables. Assuming that θ is a vector of the model's unknown parameters, the EM algorithm is an iterative procedure that consists of the following "expectation" and "maximization" steps at the k-th iteration:

1. Given the parameter estimates (θ^{k-1}) obtained from the $(k-1)$-th iteration, expectation of the unobserved variables is formed.

2. Conditional on the expectation of the unobserved variables, the likelihood function is maximized with respect to parameters of the model, resulting in θ^k.

Each iteration results in a higher value of the likelihood function, and thus, with arbitrary initial values of the parameters, θ^0, the above two steps are iterated until θ^k converges.

In this section, we sketch the maximization step of the EM algorithm for a Markov-switching model as discussed in Hamilton 1990 and applied in Engel and Hamilton 1990 and Turner, Startz, and Nelson 1989. Note that the expectation step is nothing more than obtaining the smoothed probabilities of the unobserved Markov-switching variable S_t: $Pr[S_t \mid \psi_T]$, $t = 1, 2, \ldots, T$. We consider the following regression model with Markov-switching parameters:

$$y_t = x_t \beta_{s_t} + e_t, \tag{4.59}$$

$$e_t \sim N(0, \sigma_{s_t}^2), \tag{4.60}$$

$$\beta_{s_t} = \beta_0(1 - S_t) + \beta_1 S, t \tag{4.61}$$

$$\sigma_{S_t}^2 = \sigma_0^2(1 - S_t) + \sigma_1^2 S_t, \tag{4.62}$$

$$Pr[S_t = 1 \mid S_{t-1} = 1] = p_{11}, \quad Pr[S_t = 0 \mid S_{t-1} = 0] = p_{00}, \tag{4.63}$$

where x_t is exogenous or predetermined and conditional on S_{t-1}, and S_t is independent of x_t. By grouping the parameters of the above model as $\theta = [\theta_1' \quad \theta_2']'$, where $\theta_1 = [\beta_0' \quad \beta_1' \quad \sigma_0^2 \quad \sigma_1^2]'$ and $\theta_2 = [p_{00} \quad p_{11}]'$, and by denoting $\tilde{y}_T = [y_1 \quad y_2 \quad y_3 \quad \dots \quad y_T]'$, $\tilde{S}_T = [S_1 \quad S_2 \quad S_3 \quad \dots \quad S_T]'$, the joint density of $\tilde{y}_T$ and $\tilde{S}_T$ and the log likelihood function can be written as

$$p(\tilde{y}_T, \tilde{S}_T; \theta) = p(\tilde{y}_T \mid \tilde{S}_T; \theta_1) \times p(\tilde{S}_T; \theta_2)$$

$$= \prod_{t=1}^{T} p(y_t \mid S_t; \theta_1) \times \prod_{t=1}^{T} p(S_t \mid S_{t-1}; \theta_2). \tag{4.64}$$

$$\ln[p(\tilde{y}_T, \tilde{S}_T; \theta)] = \sum_{t=1}^{T} \ln[p(y_t \mid S_t; \theta_1)] + \sum_{t=1}^{T} \ln[p(S_t \mid S_{t-1}; \theta_2)] \tag{4.65}$$

If $\tilde{S}_T$ were observed, the parameter vector θ_2 would be irrelevant and the log likelihood function would be maximized with respect to θ_1 only:

$$\frac{\partial \ln[p(\tilde{y}_T, \tilde{S}_T; \theta)]}{\partial \theta_1} = \sum_{t=1}^{T} \frac{\partial \ln[p(y_t \mid S_t; \theta_1)]}{\partial \theta_1} = 0 \tag{4.66}$$

If $\tilde{S}_t$ is not observed, however, as an alternative to the approach discussed in section 4.2, one may consider maximizing the following expected log likelihood function:

$$Q(\theta; \tilde{y}_T, \theta^{k-1}) = \int_{\tilde{S}_T} \ln[p(\tilde{y}_T, \tilde{S}_T; \theta)] p(\tilde{y}_T, \tilde{S}_T; \theta^{k-1})$$

$$= \int_{\tilde{S}_T} \ln[p(\tilde{y}_T \mid \tilde{S}_T; \theta_1) p(\tilde{S}_T; \theta_2)] p(\tilde{y}_T, \tilde{S}_T; \theta^{k-1}), \tag{4.67}$$

where the expection is formed conditional on θ^{k-1} and $\int_{\tilde{S}_T} = \sum_{s_1} \sum_{s_1} \cdots \sum_{s_T}$.

Focusing on the maximation of the *expected* log likelihood function with respect to θ_1, we have

$$\frac{\partial Q(\theta; \tilde{y}_T, \theta^{k-1})}{\partial \theta_1} = \int_{\tilde{S}_T} \frac{\partial \ln[p(\tilde{y}_T \mid \tilde{S}_T; \theta_1)]}{\partial \theta_1} p(\tilde{y}_T, \tilde{S}_T; \theta^{k-1}) = 0 \qquad (4.68)$$

Divide both sides of equation (4.68) by $p(\tilde{y}_T; \theta^{k-1})$, and we get

$$\int_{\tilde{S}_T} \frac{\partial \ln[p(\tilde{y}_T \mid \tilde{S}_T; \theta_1)]}{\partial \theta_1} \frac{p(\tilde{y}_T, \tilde{S}_T; \theta^{k-1})}{p(\tilde{y}_T; \theta^{k-1})} = 0, \qquad (4.69)$$

$$==> \int_{\tilde{S}_T} \frac{\partial \ln[p(\tilde{y}_T \mid \tilde{S}_T; \theta_1)]}{\partial \theta_1} p(\tilde{S}_T \mid \tilde{y}_T; \theta^{k-1}) = 0, \qquad (4.70)$$

$$==> \int_{\tilde{S}_T} \sum_{t=1}^{T} \frac{\partial \ln[p(y_t \mid S_t)]}{\partial \theta_1} p(\tilde{S}_T \mid \tilde{y}_T; \theta^{k-1}) = 0, \qquad (4.71)$$

$$==> \sum_{t=1}^{T} \sum_{S_t=0}^{1} \frac{\partial \ln[p(y_t \mid S_t)]}{\partial \theta_1} p(S_t \mid \tilde{y}_T; \theta^{k-1}) = 0, \qquad (4.72)$$

where $p(S_t \mid \tilde{y}_T; \theta^{k-1})$ is the smoothed probability. Comparing (4.72) with (4.66), it is straightforward to get the intuition behind the EM algorithm. Equation (4.72) states that θ_1^k, the estimate of θ_1 at the k-th iteration, is obtained by equating the sum of the weighted average of the scores to 0, the weights being the smoothed probabilities of S_t obtained from the expectation step, conditional on θ^{k-1}, the parameter estimates from the previous iteration.

One nice thing about equation (4.72) is that it provides us with closed-form solutions for $\theta^k = [\begin{array}{cccc} \beta_0^{k'} & \beta_1^{k'} & \sigma_0^{2k} & \sigma_1^{2k} \end{array}]'$. Given $S_t = j$, we have

$$\ln[p(y_t \mid S_t = j; \theta_1)] = -\frac{1}{2}\log(2\pi) - \frac{1}{2}\ln(\sigma_j^2) - \frac{1}{2}\frac{(y_t - x_t'\beta_j)^2}{\sigma_j^2}. \qquad (4.73)$$

The first order conditions in equation (4.72) with respect to β_j and σ_j^2, $j = 0, 1$, are given by

$$\sum_{t=1}^{T} \sum_{S_t=0}^{1} \frac{\partial \ln[p(y_t \mid S_t)]}{\partial \beta_j} p(S_t \mid \tilde{y}_T; \theta^{k-1}) =$$

$$\sum_{t=1}^{T} \frac{x_t(y_t - x_t'\beta_j)}{\sigma_j^2} p(S_t = j \mid \tilde{y}_T; \theta^{k-1}) = 0, \qquad (4.74)$$

$$\sum_{t=1}^{T} \sum_{S_t=0}^{1} \frac{\partial \ln[p(y_t \mid S_t)]}{\partial \sigma_j^2} p(S_t \mid \tilde{y}_T; \theta^{k-1})$$

$$(4.75)$$

$$= \sum_{t=1}^{T} \left\{ -\frac{1}{2} \frac{1}{\sigma_j^2} + \frac{1}{2} \frac{(y_t - x_t' \beta_j)^2}{\sigma_j^4} \right\} p(S_t = j \mid \tilde{y}_T; \theta^{k-1}) = 0,$$

which provide us with the following solutions for β_j^k and σ_j^{2k}:

$$\beta_j^k = \left(\sum_t x_t x_t' p(S_t = j \mid \tilde{y}_T; \theta^{k-1}) \right)^{-1} \left(\sum_t x_t y_t p(S_t = j \mid \tilde{y}_T; \theta^{k-1}) \right),$$

$$j = 0, 1, \qquad\qquad\qquad\qquad\qquad\qquad\qquad\qquad (4.76)$$

$$\sigma_j^{2k} = \frac{\sum_t (y_t - x_t' \beta_j^k)^2 p(S_t = j \mid \tilde{y}_T; \theta^{k-1})}{\sum_t p(S_t = j \mid \tilde{y}_T; \theta^{k-1})}, \quad j = 0, 1. \qquad (4.77)$$

Note that β_j^k can alternatively be obtained in a regression of

$$y_t \times \sqrt{p(S_t = j \mid \tilde{y}_T; \theta^{k-1})}$$

on

$$x_t \times \sqrt{p(S_t = j \mid \tilde{y}_T; \theta^{k-1})}.$$

By differentiating the expected log likelihood function in equation (4.77), we can also obtain the following solution for p_{jj}^k:

$$p_{jj}^{k} = \frac{\sum_t p(S_t = j, S_{t-1} = j \mid \tilde{y}_T; \theta^{k-1})}{\sum_t p(S_{t-1} = j \mid \tilde{y}_T; \theta^{k-1})}, \quad j = 0, 1. \qquad (4.78)$$

One potential strength of the EM algorithm is its simplicity in the presence of the closed-form solutions for the parameters at the maximization step. Unlike the approach in section 4.2, this one does not require a numerical optimization procedure. In addition, Hamilton (1990) reports that the EM algorithm is, in general, relatively robust with respect to poorly chosen starting values of the parameters, quickly moving to a reasonable region of the likelihood surface.

For more details of the above derivations and the EM algorithm in general, refer to Hamilton 1990.

4.4   Application 1: Hamilton's Markov-Switching Model of
Business Fluctuations

In Markov-switching models of business fluctuations, the turning point is treated as a structural event that is inherent in the data-generating process. An important feature of such models is that they can capture a particular form of nonlinear dynamics or asymmetry in the business fluctuations. For example, Hamilton (1989) allows the mean of the growth in real GNP to be evolving according to a two-state Markov-switching process, thus allowing the dynamics of recessions to be qualitatively distinct from those of expansions. Growth in real GNP is modeled as an AR(4) process:

$$(\Delta y_t - \mu_{s_t}) = \phi_1(\Delta y_{t-1} - \mu_{s_{t-1}})$$

$$+ \phi_2(\Delta y_{t-2} - \mu_{s_{t-2}}) + \ldots + \phi_4(\Delta y_{t-4} - \mu_{s_{t-4}}) + e_t \qquad (4.79)$$

$$e_t \sim \text{i.i.d.} N(0, \sigma^2), \qquad (4.80)$$

$$\mu_{s_t} = \mu_0(1 - S_t) + \mu_1 S_t \qquad (4.81)$$

$$Pr[S_t = 1 \mid S_{t-1} = 1] = p, \quad Pr[S_t = 0 \mid S_{t-1} = 0] = q, \qquad (4.82)$$

where roots of $\phi(L) = (1 - \phi_1 L - \ldots - \phi_4 L^4) = 0$ lie outside the unit circle and y_t is the log of real GDP or real GNP.

We first apply the above model to real GDP for the sample period employed by Hamilton (1989): 1952:II–1984:IV. Parameter estimates of the model are close to those reported in Hamilton 1989 for the case of real GNP. Our estimates are reported in the second column of table 4.1. Figures 4.2 and 4.3 depict the filtered probabilities of a recession ($Pr[S_t = 0 \mid \tilde{y}_t]$) and the smoothed probabilities of a recession ($Pr[S_t = 0 \mid \tilde{y}_T]$), respectively, where $\tilde{y}_t = [\, y_1 \quad \ldots \quad y_t \,]'$. The shaded areas represent the NBER dating of recessions. The filtered and smoothed probabilities are clearly in close agreement with the NBER reference cycle.

When the sample is extended to include 11 more years of recent data (1952:II–1995:III), however, the model fails to provide reasonable parameter estimates and thus fails to provide reasonable inferences on the probabilities of a recession or a boom. One potential reason is that the model lacks a mechanism to account for a productivity slowdown in the more recent sample. The model assumes that the average growth rate of output during a boom or a recession is the same over the entire sample. Another potential reason is that even

Table 4.1
Maximum likelihood estimates of the Hamilton model (real GDP; 1952:II–1984:IV; 1952:II–1995:III)

	1952:II-1984:IV		1952:II-1995:III			
	(No dummy variable)		(With a dummy variable)			
p	0.9008	(0.0443)	0.9113	(0.0363)	0.9187	(0.0309)
q	0.7606	(0.1206)	0.7658	(0.0857)	0.7668	(0.0863)
ϕ_1	0.0898	(0.1981)	0.0496	(0.1347)	0.0477	(0.1117)
ϕ_2	−0.0186	(0.2082)	−0.0495	(0.1295)	−0.0422	(0.1103)
ϕ_3	−0.1743	(0.1381)	−0.2112	(0.1129)	−0.2095	(0.1008)
ϕ_4	−0.0839	(0.1248)	−0.0953	(0.1140)	−0.0984	(0.0970)
σ	0.7962	(0.0858)	0.6902	(0.0505)	0.6939	(0.0474)
μ_0	−0.2132	(0.2613)	−0.2996	(0.1892)	−0.2328	(0.1895)
μ_1	1.1283	(0.1596)	1.1479	(0.0768)	1.1510	(0.0776)
μ_0^*	—		0.4516	(0.3209)	—	
μ_1^*	—		−0.3346	(0.1340)	−0.3699	(0.1244)
Log likelihood	−175.24		−212.17		−212.99	

Note: Standard errors are in parentheses.

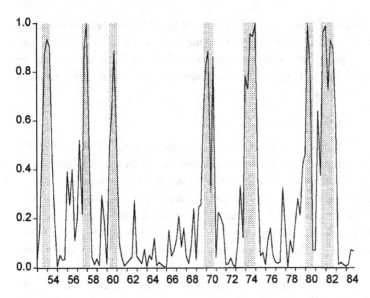

Figure 4.2
Filtered probability of a recession (GDP: 1952:II–1984:IV)

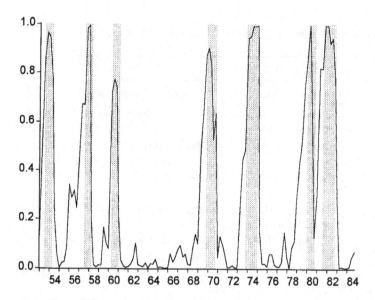

Figure 4.3
Smoothed probability of a recession (GDP: 1952:II–1984:IV)

in the absence of a productivity slowdown in the U.S. economy, if monetary
policy has had a more stabilizing effect on the economy in recent years, the gap
between average growth rates of output during boom and recession would be
smaller than in the earlier sample. To account for these possibilities, equation
(4.81) is replaced by

$$\mu_{s_t} = (\mu_0 + \mu_0^* D_t)(1 - S_t) + (\mu_1 + \mu_1^* D_t)S_t, \tag{4.83}$$

where D_t is a dummy variable set equal to 1 for the subsample 1983:I–1995:III,
and 0 for an earlier sample period. The inclusion of a dummy variable potentially captures a change in the mean growth rates during boom or recession.

The second and third columns of table 4.1 report parameter estimates from
the above model. Although μ_0^* is statistically insignificant, μ_1^* is negative and
statistically significant. Though the choice of 1983:I is ad hoc, the average
growth rate of output during boom seems to have decreased in the more recent
subsample. Figures 4.4 and 4.5 depict filtered and smoothed probabilities of
a recession, obtained from a model that accounts for a recent change in the
average growth rate during boom only. The probabilities are in close agreement
with the NBER reference cycle.

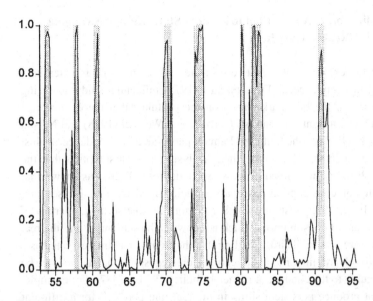

Figure 4.4
Filtered probability of a recession (GDP: 1952:II–1995:III; model with dummy variables)

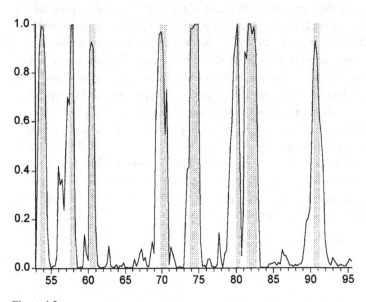

Figure 4.5
Smoothed probability of a recession (GDP: 1952:II–1995:III; model with dummy variables)

4.5   Application 2: A Unit Root in a Three-State Markov-Switching Model of the Real Interest Rate

Assessing the existence of a unit root in the real interest rate is potentially interesting in many aspects. First, Fama's (1975) influential study analyzing the efficiency of the bill market rests on the postulate that the ex ante real interest rate is constant. In contrast, Garbade and Wachtel (1978) and Nelson and Schwert (1977), who criticize Fama's paper and find evidence against a constant real interest rate, base their analysis on the assumption that the real rate follows an integrated process. Second, Rose (1988) has shown that the viability of consumption-based asset-pricing models (e.g., Hansen and Singleton 1982, 1983) rests on whether or not the time series properties of the growth rate of consumption, which is known to be stationary, and the real interest rate are similar. Third, a finding that the ex ante real interest rate has a unit root would have important implications for suggestions that the real rate be used as a guide to the conduct of monetary policy (Walsh 1987). For example, factors that produce persistent shifts in the real rate may call for a different policy response than factors that produce temporary changes in the real rate. For other related issues, readers are referred to Rose 1988.

Literature on the tests of the stationarity of the real interest rate reports mixed results. After testing for the presence of a unit root in the nominal interest rate and the inflation rate, Rose (1988) concludes that the ex ante real interest rate must have a unit root. Walsh (1987) also fails to reject the presence of a unit root in the real interest rate by analyzing the ex post real interest rate. On the contrary, Perron (1990) rejects the unit root hypothesis by incorporating regime shifts in the ex post real interest rate. He argues that unit root tests are biased toward nonrejection of the unit root hypothesis when the series contains a sudden change in the mean.

Garcia and Perron (1996) employ Hamilton's (1989) Markov-switching model to explicitly account for regime shifts in an autoregressive model of the ex post real interest rate. They employ the following AR(2) process with 3-state Markov-switching mean and variance:

$$(y_t - \mu_{s_t}) = \phi_1(y_{t-1} - \mu_{s_{t-1}}) + \phi_2(y_{t-2} - \mu_{s_{t-2}}) + e_t, \tag{4.84}$$

$$e_t \sim N(0, \sigma_{s_t}^2), \tag{4.85}$$

$$\mu_{s_t} = \mu_1 S_{1t} + \mu_2 S_{2t} + \mu_3 S_{3t}, \tag{4.86}$$

$$\sigma_{s_t}^2 = \sigma_1^2 S_{1t} + \sigma_2^2 S_{2t} + \sigma_3^2 S_{3t}, \tag{4.87}$$

$$S_{jt} = 1, \text{ if } S_t = j, \text{ and } S_{jt} = 0, \quad \text{otherwise}, \quad j = 1, 2, 3, \tag{4.88}$$

$$p_{ij} = Pr[S_t = j \mid S_{t-1} = i], \quad \sum_{j=1}^{3} p_{ij} = 1, \tag{4.89}$$

where y_t is the ex post real interest rate calculated by subtracting the (CPI) inflation rate from the nominal interest rate (three-month Treasury bill rate).

Of particular interest is the sum of the AR coefficients ($\phi_1 + \phi_2$). Perron's (1990) conjecture is that if the true data generating process is given by a model like that in (4.84)–(4.89), yet one forces the mean of the series, μ_{s_t}, to be constant in estimation, then the sum of the estimated AR coefficients will be biased toward unity even though the true sum is close to 0.

The model above is estimated for the sample period 1960:I–1990:IV (quarterly data) in table 4.2. The first column of the table reports estimation results for a model without regime shifts. An AR(4) specification is employed in order to make the residuals white noise. The sum of the AR coefficients is estimated to be 0.841. As reported in the second column of the table however, after allowing for regime shifts, the sum of the estimated AR coefficients is very close to 0. Figures 4.6a through 4.6c depict filtered probabilities ($Pr[S_t = j \mid \tilde{y}_t]$) for each regime. In figure 4.7, the estimated ex ante interest rate is depicted against the ex post interest rate.

The ex ante interest rate for an AR(2) process is estimated in the following way:

$$E(y_t \mid \tilde{y}_{t-1}) = E(\mu_{s_t} \mid \tilde{y}_t) + \phi_1 E(y_{t-1} - \mu_{s_{t-1}} \mid \tilde{y}_t) + \phi_2 E(y_{t-2} - \mu_{s_{t-2}} \mid \tilde{y}_t),$$

where $\tilde{y}_t = [\, y_1 \quad \ldots \quad y_t \,]$. This expression can be interpreted as the ex ante interest rate, under the assumption of rational expectations, because the only difference between this expression and the ex post interest rate is a white noise "forecast" error.

Various specification tests employed by Garcia and Perron (1996) suggest that the real interest rate may not have a unit root. Instead, shocks to the real interest rate may be temporary in nature with a tendency to revert to some mean value, which is subject to infrequent shifts.

Table 4.2
Maximum likelihood estimates of a three-state Markov-switching model of the real interest rate (quarterly; 1960:I–1990:IV)

Parameters	Linear model		Markov-switching model	
p_{11}	—		0.9630	(0.0330)
p_{12}	—		0.0000	(0.0000)
p_{21}	—		0.0096	(0.0119)
p_{22}	—		0.9904	(0.0119)
p_{31}	—		0.0000	(0.0000)
p_{32}	—		0.0106	(0.0135)
ϕ_1	0.2459	(0.0878)	0.0187	(0.0940)
ϕ_2	0.0423	(0.0882)	0.0012	(0.0952)
ϕ_3	0.2607	(0.0896)	—	
ϕ_4	0.2920	(0.0895)	—	
σ_1^2	4.4389		4.6303	(1.2674)
σ_2^2	—		1.3976	(0.2905)
σ_3^2	—		6.0466	(1.3418)
μ_1	1.5552	(1.1803)	−1.5760	(0.4081)
μ_2	—		1.3765	(0.1705)
μ_3	—		3.9928	(0.3885)
Log likelihood		−270.13	−254.89	

Note: Standard errors are in parentheses.

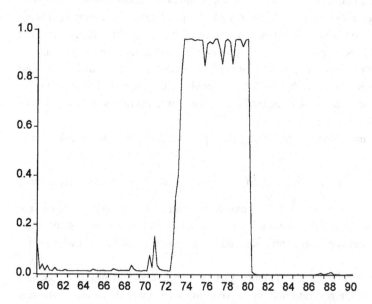

Figure 4.6a
Filtered probability of a regime with low interest rate

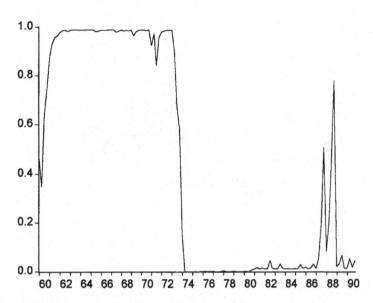

Figure 4.6b
Filtered probability of a regime with medium interest rate

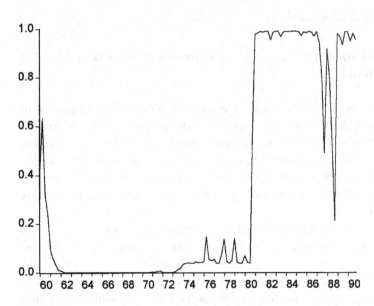

Figure 4.6c
Filtered probability of a regime with high interest rate

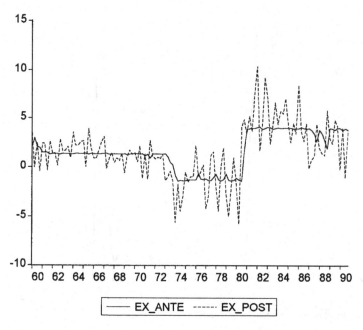

Figure 4.7
Ex ante versus ex post real interest rates

4.6   Application 3: A Three-State Markov-Switching Variance Model of Stock Returns

In this section, we consider Kim, Nelson, and Startz's 1998 application of a three-state Markov-switching variance model to monthly stock returns for the period 1926:1–1986:12. Though they consider the model in order to deal with tests of mean reversion in heteroskedastic data, our focus in this section will be whether a three-state Markov-switching model of heteroskedasticity is a good approximation of the underlying data-generating process for monthly stock returns.

Figures 4.8a and 4.8b show that stock returns tend to exhibit nonnormal unconditional sampling distributions in the form of skewness and excess kurtosis, a fact known at least since Fama (1963) and Mandlebrot (1963). The pronounced peak and heavy tails in the distribution of stock returns, as mentioned in Turner, Startz, and Nelson 1989, are typical of unconditional densities of normal observations subject to heteroskedasticity.

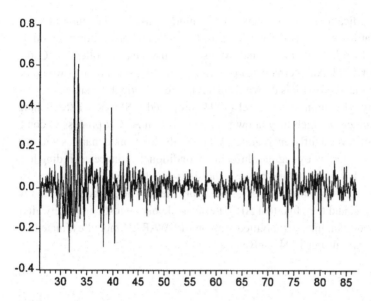

Figure 4.8a
Plot of historical stock returns: EW excess returns, 1926–1986.12

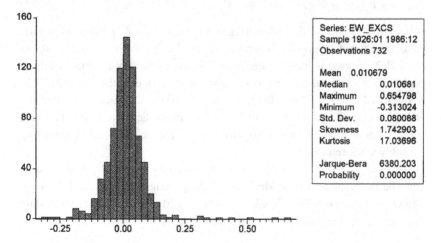

Figure 4.8b
Distribution of historical stock returns: EW excess returns, 1926–1986.12

The specification that has been most commonly used in the study of stock return volatility or heteroskedasticity is the GARCH model developed by Engle (1982) and Bollerslev (1986), and extensively surveyed in Bollerslev, Chou, and Kroner 1992. An alternative approach to modeling stock returns would be to assume that the return is drawn from a mixture of normal densities.

Recently, Hamilton and Susmel (1994) proposed a SWARCH (Switching ARCH) model in which they allow parameters of an ARCH process to come from one of several different regimes. Whereas the long-run dynamics within a regime are governed by regime shifts in unconditional variance according to a first-order Markov-switching process, the short-run dynamics are governed by an ARCH process. Hamilton and Susmel apply the SWARCH model to weekly stock returns, and they find that ARCH effects die out almost completely after a month. For example, a simplified version of SWARCH model estimated by Hamilton and Susmel 1994 is given by

$$y_t = \sigma_{s_t} u_t, \tag{4.90}$$

$$u_t = h_t v_t, \tag{4.91}$$

$$v_t \sim \text{i.i.d. with Student } t \text{ Distribution}, \tag{4.92}$$

$$h_t = \alpha_0 + \alpha_1 u_{t-1}^2 + \alpha_2 u_{t-2}^2 + \beta d_{t-1} u_{t-1}^2, \tag{4.93}$$

where σ_{s_t} captures Markov-switching variances and the d_{t-1} is a dummy variable introduced to capture leverage effects. In the above specification, an ARCH(2) process is incorporated within a given volatility regime. Hamilton and Susmel's estimates of the model using weekly stock returns (1962–1987) show that $\hat{\lambda} = \hat{\alpha}_1 + \hat{\alpha}_2 = 0.48$. Note that $\hat{\lambda}^4 = 0.05$, and this means that the volatility effects captured by u_t or by ARCH effects die out almost completely after a month, suggesting that no ARCH term may be necessary in modeling monthly stock returns.

This suggests that volatility or heteroskedasticity in monthly stock returns may be modeled as a pure Markov-switching variance model, as in Turner, Startz, and Nelson 1989. This leads us to consider the following three state Markov-switching model of monthly stock returns:

$$y_t \sim N(0, \sigma_t^2), \tag{4.94}$$

$$\sigma_t^2 = \sigma_1^2 S_{1t} + \sigma_2^2 S_{2t} + \sigma_3^2 S_{3t}, \tag{4.95}$$

Table 4.3
Maximum likelihood estimates of a three-state Markov-switching model of heteroskedasticity for stock returns (monthly CRSP equal-weighted excess returns, 1926:1–1986:12)

Parameters	Estimates	
p_{11}	0.973620	(0.017667)
p_{12}	0.026380	(0.017667)
p_{21}	0.019715	(0.011953)
p_{22}	0.968596	(0.014220)
p_{31}	0.002752	(0.019303)
p_{32}	0.046039	(0.037638)
σ_1^2	0.001226	(0.000188)
σ_2^2	0.004004	(0.000475)
σ_3^2	0.031022	(0.005684)
Log likelihood	-1001.90	

Note: Standard errors are in parentheses.

$$S_{kt} = 1 \text{ if } S_t = k, \text{ and } S_{kt} = 0, \quad \text{otherwise;} \quad k = 1, 2, 3, \tag{4.96}$$

$$Pr[S_t = j \mid S_{t-1} = i] = p_{ij}, \quad i, j = 1, 2, 3, \tag{4.97}$$

$$\sum_{j=1}^{3} p_{ij} = 1, \tag{4.98}$$

$$\sigma_1^2 < \sigma_2^2 < \sigma_3^2, \tag{4.99}$$

where y_t is the demeaned monthly stock return and S_t is an unobserved state variable that evolves according to a first-order Markov process with transition probabilities given in (4.97).

Table 4.3 reports parameter estimates for such a model along with their standard errors. Figures 4.9a–4.9c depict the smoothed probabilities of low-, medium-, and high-variance states, respectively: $Pr[S_t = j \mid \tilde{y}_T]$, $j = 1, 2, 3$, where $\tilde{y}_T = [\, y_1 \quad y_2 \quad \ldots \quad y_T \,]'$. Given these smoothed probabilities and parameter estimates, we can calculate the variance of the stock returns in the following way:

$$E(\sigma_t^2 \mid \tilde{y}_T) = \hat{\sigma}_1^2 E[S_t = 1 \mid \tilde{y}_T] + \hat{\sigma}_2^2 E[S_t = 2 \mid \tilde{y}_T] + \hat{\sigma}_3^2 E[S_t = 3 \mid \tilde{y}_T].$$

Figure 4.10 shows the estimated variance.

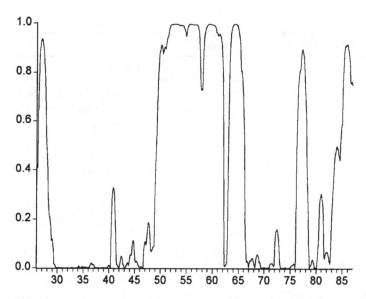

Figure 4.9a
Smoothed probability of a low-variance state for stock returns

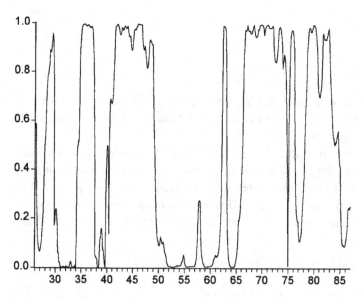

Figure 4.9b
Smoothed probability of a medium-variance state for stock returns

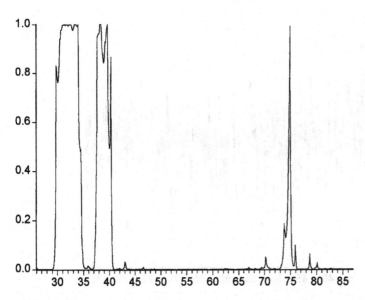

Figure 4.9c
Smoothed probability of a high-variance state for stock returns

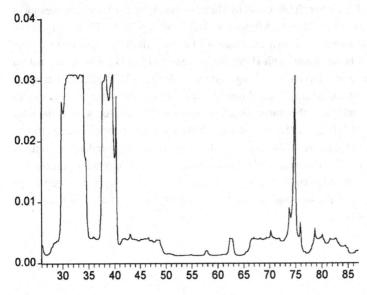

Figure 4.10
Estimated variance of historical stock returns

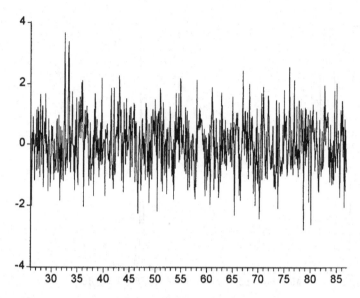

Figure 4.11a
Plot of standardized stock returns

To check whether the three-state Markov-switching variance captures most of the dynamics in the stock return variance, we applied ARCH tests to the standardized returns shown in figure 4.11a. No ARCH effects were found. Again, this is consistent with Hamilton and Susmel (1994), who show that, in the presence of Markov-switching variance, all the ARCH effects that apear in weekly stock returns data almost completely die out after four weeks (a month). In addition, the standardized returns show little excess kurtosis, with a p-value of 0.073 for the Jarque-Bera joint test of normality. (Refer to figure 4.11b.) That is, we cannot reject the hypothesis that the standardized returns are normally distributed at a 5% significance level. These results suggest that the three-state Markov-switching variance model provides a reasonable approximation of the heteroskedasticity in monthly stock returns for the period 1926.1–1986.12.

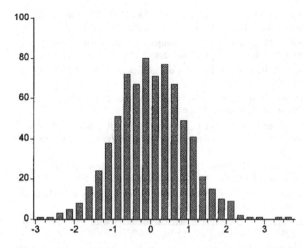

Figure 4.11b
Distribution of standardized stock returns

Appendix: GAUSS Programs to Accompany Chapter 4

1. HMT4_KIM.OPT: An AR(4) model with a two-state Markov-switching mean (based on Hamilton's (1989) filter and Kim's (1994) smoothing).

2. HMT4_DMY.OPT: An AR(4) model with a two-state Markov-switching mean (based on Hamilton's (1989) filter and Kim's (1994) smoothing; dummy variables are incorporated for the mean growth rates).

3. INTR_S3.OPT: A three-state Markov-switching mean-variance model of the real interest rate (based on Garcia and Perron 1996).

4. STCK_V3.OPT: A three-state Markov-switching variance model of stock returns (based on Kim, Nelson, and Startz 1998).

5. HMT_TVP.OPT: An AR(4) model with a Markov-switching mean (two-state) and time-varying transition probabilities (based on Filardo 1994).

References

Andrews, D. W. K. 1993. "Tests for Parameter Instability and Structural Change with Unknown Change Point." *Econometrica*, 62, 1383–1414.

Bollerslev, Tim. 1986. "Generalized Autoregressive Conditional Heteroskedasticity," *Journal of Econometrics,* 31, 307–317.

Bollerslev, Tim, Ray Y. Chou, and Kenneth F. Kroner. 1992. "ARCH Modeling in Finance: A Review of the Theory and Empirical Evidence." *Journal of Econometrics*, 52, 5–59.

Brown, R. L., J. Durbin, and J. M. Evans. 1975. "Techniques for Testing the Constancy of Regression Relationships over Time." *Journal of the Royal Statistical Society*, B37, 149–192.

Chow, G. 1960. "Tests of the Equality between Two Sets of Coefficients in Two Linear Regressions." *Econometrica*, 28, 561–605.

Dempster, A. P., N. M. Laird, and D. B. Rubin. 1977. "Maximum Likelihood from Incomplete Data via the EM Algorithm." *Journal of the Royal Statistical Society*, B39, 1–38.

Diebold, Francis X., Joon-Haeng Lee, and Gretchen C. Weinbach. 1994. "Regime Switching with Time-Varying Transition Probabilities." In *Nonstationary Time Series Analysis and Cointegration*, ed. C. Hargreaves. Oxford: Oxford University Press, 283–302.

Durland, J. Michael, and Thomas H. McCurdy. 1994. "Duration-Dependent Transitions in a Markov Model of U.S. GNP Growth." *Journal of Business and Economic Statistics*, 12, 279–288.

Engel, Charles, and James Hamilton. 1990. "Long Swings in the Dollar: Are They in the Data and Do Markets Know It?" *American Economic Review*, 80(4), 689–713.

Engle, Robert F. 1982. "Autoregressive Conditional Heteroskedasticity with Estimates of the Variance of United Kingdom Inflation." *Econometrica*, 50, 987–1007.

Fama, Eugene F. 1963. "Mandlebrot and the Stable Paretian Hypothesis." *Journal of Business*. 4, 420-429.

Fama, Eugene F. 1975. "Short-Term Interest Rates as Predictors of Inflation." *American Economic Review*, 65, 269–282.

Farley, J. U., and M. J. Hinich. 1970. "A Test for a Shifting Slope Coefficient in a Linear Model." *Journal of the American Statistical Association*, 65, 1320–1329.

Filardo Andrew J. 1994. "Business Cycle Phases and Their Transitional Dynamics." *Journal of Business and Economic Statistics*, 12, 299–308.

Garbade, K., and P. Wachtel. 1978. "Time Variation in the Relationship between Inflation and Interest Rates." *Journal of Monetary Economics*, 4, 755–765.

Garcia, Rene, and Pierre Perron. 1996. "An Analysis of Real Interest under Regime Shift." *Review of Economics and Statistics*, 78, 111–125.

Goldfeld, S. M., and R. E. Quandt. 1973. "A Markov Model for Switching Regression." *Journal of Econometrics*, 1, 3–16.

Hamilton, James D. 1989. "A New Approach to the Economic Analysis of Nonstationary Time Series and the Business Cycle." *Econometrica*, 57(2), 357–384.

Hamilton, James D. 1990. "Analysis of Time Series Subject to Changes in Regime." *Journal of Econometrics*, 45, 39–70.

Hamilton, James D. 1993. "Estimation, Inference, and Forecasting of Time-Series Subject to Changes in Regime." In ed. G. D. Maddala, C. R. Rao, and H. D. Vinod, *Handbook of Statistics*, Vol. 11, 231–259. New York: Elsevie Science Publishers B.V.

Hamilton, James D., and Raul Susmel. 1994. "Autoregressive Conditional Heteroskedasticity and Changes in Regime." *Journal of Econometrics*, 64, 307–333.

Hansen, Lars P., and Kenneth J. Singleton. 1982. "Generalized Instrumental Variables Estimation of Nonlinear Rational Expectations Models." *Econometrica*, 50, 1269–1288.

Hansen, Lars P., and Kenneth J. Singleton. 1983. "Stochastic Consumption, Risk Aversion and the Temporal Behavior of Asset Patterns." *Journal of Political Economy*, 91, 249–265.

Kim, Chang-Jin. 1994. "Dynamic Linear Models with Markov-Switching." *Journal of Econometrics*, 60, 1–22.

Kim, Chang-Jin, and Charles R. Nelson. 1998. "Business Cycle Turning Points, A New Coincident Index, and Tests of Duration Dependence Based on A Dynamic Factor Model with Regime-Switching." *Review of Economics and Economic Statistics*, 80, 188–201.

Kim, Chang-Jin, Charles R. Nelson, and Richard Startz. 1998. " Testing for Mean Reversion in Heteroskedastic Data Based on Gibbs-Sampling-Augmented Randomization." *Journal of Empirical Finance*, 5, 131–154.

Kim, H. J., and D. Siegmund. 1989. "The Likelihood Ratio Test for a Change-Point in Simple Linear Regression." *Biometrika*, 76, 409–423.

Kim, I.-M., and G. S. Maddala. 1991. "Multiple Structural Breaks and Unit Roots in the Nominal and Real Exchange Rates." Unpublished manuscript. Department of Economics, The University of Florida.

Lam, Pok-sang. 1990. "The Hamilton Model with a General Autoregressive Component: Estimation and Comparison with Other Models of Economic Time Series." *Journal of Monetary Economics*, 26, 409–432.

Mandlebrot, Benoit. 1963. "The Variation of Certain Speculative Prices." *Journal of Business*, 4, 394–419.

Neftci, S. N. 1984. "Are Economic Time Series Asymmetric over the Business Cycle?" *Journal of Political Economy*, 92(2), 306–328.

Nelson, Charles R., and G. William Schwert. 1977. "Short-Term Interest Rates as Predictors of Inflation: On Testing the Hypothesis That the Real Interest Rate is Constant." *American Economic Review*, 67, 478–486.

Perron, Pierre. 1990. "Testing for a Unit Root in a Time Series with a Changing Mean." *Journal of Business and Economic Statistics*, 8(2), 153–162.

Ploberger, W., W. Kramer, and K. Kontrus. 1989. "A New Test for Structural Stability in the Linear Regression Model." *Journal of Econometrics*, 40, 307–318.

Quandt, R. E. 1958. "The Estimation of the Parameters of a Linear Regression System Obeying Two Separate Regimes." *Journal of the American Statistical Association*, 53, 873–880.

Quandt, R. E. 1960. "Tests of the Hypothesis that a Linear Regression System Obeys Two Separate Regimes." *Journal of the American Statistical Association*, 55, 324–330.

Quandt, R. E. 1972. "A New Approach to Estimating Switching Regressions." *Journal of the American Statistical Association*, 67, 306–310.

Rose, Andrew K. 1988. "Is the Real Interest Rate Stable?" *Journal of Finance*. 43, 1095–1112.

Sclove, S. L. 1983. "Time-Series Segmentation: A Model and a Method." *Information Sciences*, 29, 7–25.

Turner, Christopher M., Richard Startz, and Charles R. Nelson. 1989. "A Markov Model of Heteroskedasticity, Risk, and Learning in the Stock Market." *Journal of Financial Economics*, 25, 3–22.

Walsh, Carl E. 1987. "Three Questions Concerning Nominal and Real Interest Rates." *Economic Review*, Federal Reserve Bank of San Franscisco, no. 4, 5–20.

Wecker, W. E., 1979. "Predicting the Turning Points of a Time Series." *Journal of Business*, 52(1), 35–50.

5 State-Space Models with Markov Switching

The purpose of this chapter is to extend Hamilton's (1988, 1989) Markov-switching model to the state-space representation of the general dynamic linear model introduced in chapter 3, which includes ARIMA and classical regression models as special cases. The methods in this chapter were first presented in Kim 1994.

The multiregime model of Harrison and Stevens (1976) allows for regime switching according to a Markov chain, but it is assumed that the parameters in different regimes are known and that there are known transition probabilities from one regime to the next (Harvey 1989, p. 348). One of the most recent applications of the switching approach in state-space models includes that by Shumway and Stoffer (1991), who considered a dynamic linear model with measurement matrices that switch endogenously according to an independent random process. Their approach was motivated primarily by the problem of tracking a large number of possible moving targets using a vector of sensors. (For surveys of related issues, see Shumway and Stoffer 1991 and Bar-Shalom 1978.) By restricting the switching to the measurement equations and assuming regimes to be serially independent, they simplified the Kalman filter recursions considerably. In economics, however, the shifts in regimes are unlikely to be serially independent; once the economy is in a regime (recession or expansion), that regime may persist for a while.

Building on ideas introduced in Hamilton 1988, 1989, Cosslett and Lee 1985, and Harrison and Stevens 1976, Kim (1994) presents basic filtering and smoothing algorithms for a Markov-switching state-space model, along with maximum likelihood estimation of the models unknown parameters. The state-space representation is a very flexible form, and the approach allows for estimation of a broad class of models that could not be handled before. For example, consider an MA(1) process with a switching mean. This model is an autoregressive process of infinite order with a switching mean, and from chapter 4 we know that inferences for such a model are infeasible. However, the model can be put into a state-space form, and the algorithm, presented below, may be applied to obtain approximate inferences. In general, Kim's 1994 algorithm can be used, under some regularity conditions, to obtain inferences about any dynamic time series model with Markov switching that can be put in state-space form. In addition, Kim presents an algorithm, also discussed below, for calculating smoothed inferences on the unobserved states that is vastly more efficient than those previously used in the literature.

5.1 Specification of the Model

Consider the following state-space representation of a dynamic linear model with switching in both measurement and transition equations:

$$y_t = H_{S_t}\beta_t + A_{S_t}z_t + e_t, \tag{5.1}$$

$$\beta_t = \tilde{\mu}_{S_t} + F_{S_t}\beta_{t-1} + G_{S_t}v_t, \tag{5.2}$$

$$\begin{pmatrix} e_t \\ v_t \end{pmatrix} \sim N\left(0, \begin{pmatrix} R_{S_t} & 0 \\ 0 & Q^*_{S_t} \end{pmatrix}\right), \tag{5.3}$$

where the measurement equation (5.1) describes the evolution of a vector of an $N \times 1$ observed time series as a function of a $J \times 1$ vector of unobserved β_t and a $K \times 1$ vector of weakly exogenous or lagged dependent variables; the transition equation (5.2) describes the dynamics of the unobserved state vector β_t as a function of an $L \times 1$ vector of shocks v_t; H_{S_t} is of dimension $N \times J$, A_{S_t} is of dimension $N \times K$, F_{S_t} is of dimension $J \times J$, and finally, G_{S_t} is of dimension $J \times L$.

The subscripts in H_{S_t}, A_{S_t}, $\tilde{\mu}_{S_t}$, F_{S_t}, G_{S_t}, R_{S_t}, and $Q^*_{S_t}$ imply that some of the parameters in these matrices are dependent on an unobserved, discrete-valued, M-state Markov-switching variable S_t ($S_t = 1, 2, 3, \ldots, M$) with transition probabilities given by

$$p = \begin{pmatrix} p_{11} & p_{21} & \cdots & p_{M1} \\ p_{12} & p_{22} & \cdots & p_{M2} \\ \vdots & \vdots & \ddots & \vdots \\ p_{1M} & p_{2M} & \cdots & p_{MM} \end{pmatrix}, \tag{5.4}$$

where $p_{ij} = Pr[S_t = j | S_{t-1} = i]$ with $\sum_{j=1}^{M} p_{ij} = 1$ for all i.

When the F_{S_t} matrices, for example, are known under different states, F_m ($m = 1, 2, \ldots, M$) refers to the known parameter matrix when the state or regime m prevails. When a particular element of the F_{S_t} matrix switches from one state to another, and when the values of that element are unknown under different states, it can be modeled in the following way. Assuming that the state variable S_t can take on the values of $1, 2, \ldots, M$, the (a, b)-th element of the F_{S_t} can be specified as

$$f_{a,b,S_t} = f_{a,b,1}S_{1t} + \ldots + f_{a,b,M}S_{Mt}, \tag{5.5}$$

where S_{mt} takes on the value 1 when S_t is equal to m and 0 otherwise. The $f_{i,j,m}$s $(m = 1, 2, \ldots, M)$ are, in principle, part of the parameters to be estimated. As a comparison, Harrison and Stevens (1976) suggested the use of discrete-valued grids, covering a range likely to include plausible values for the variances when the variances of measurement or transition equations are assumed to be heteroskedastic.

5.2 The Basic Filter and Estimation of the Model

5.2.1 Difficulties Associated with Inference and a Solution Based on Approximations

Suppose the parameters of the model specified in the previous section are known. Let ψ_{t-1} denote the vector of observations available as of time $t-1$. In the usual derivation of the Kalman filter for a fixed-coefficient state-space model, the goal is to form a forecast of the unobserved state vector β_t based on ψ_{t-1}, denoted $\beta_{t|t-1}$:

$$\beta_{t|t-1} = E[\beta_t|\psi_{t-1}]. \tag{5.6}$$

Similarly, in the conventional fixed-coefficient case, the matrix $P_{t|t-1}$ denotes the mean squared error of the forecast:

$$P_{t|t-1} = E[(\beta_t - \beta_{t|t-1})(\beta_t - \beta_{t|t-1})'|\psi_{t-1}]. \tag{5.7}$$

Here in the state-space model with Markov switching, the goal is to form a forecast of β_t based not just on ψ_{t-1} but also conditional on the random variable S_t taking on the value j and on S_{t-1} taking on the value i:

$$\beta_{t|t-1}^{(i,j)} = E[\beta_t|\psi_{t-1}, S_t = j, S_{t-1} = i]. \tag{5.8}$$

The proposed algorithm calculates a battery of M^2 such forecasts for each date t, corresponding to every possible value for i and j. Associated with these forecasts are M^2 different mean squared error matrices:

$$P_{t|t-1}^{(i,j)} = E[(\beta_t - \beta_{t|t-1})(\beta_t - \beta_{t|t-1})'|\psi_{t-1}, S_t = j, S_{t-1} = i]. \tag{5.9}$$

Conditional on $S_{t-1} = i$ and $S_t = j$, the Kalman filter algorithm is as follows:

$$\beta_{t|t-1}^{(i,j)} = \tilde{\mu}_j + F_j \beta_{t-1|t-1}^i,$$ (5.10)

$$P_{t|t-1}^{(i,j)} = F_j P_{t-1|t-1}^i F_j' + G_j Q_j^* G_j',$$ (5.11)

$$\eta_{t|t-1}^{(i,j)} = y_t - H_j \beta_{t|t-1}^{(i,j)} - A_j z_t,$$ (5.12)

$$f_{t|t-1}^{(i,j)} = H_j P_{t|t-1}^{(i,j)} H_j' + R_j,$$ (5.13)

$$\beta_{t|t}^{(i,j)} = \beta_{t|t-1}^{(i,j)} + P_{t|t-1}^{(i,j)} H_j' [f_{t|t-1}^{(i,j)}]^{-1} \eta_{t|t-1}^{(i,j)},$$ (5.14)

$$P_{t|t}^{(i,j)} = (I - P_{t|t-1}^{(i,j)} H_j' [f_{t|t-1}^{(i,j)}]^{-1} H_j) P_{t|t-1}^{(i,j)},$$ (5.15)

where $\beta_{t-1|t-1}^i$ is an inference on β_{t-1} based on information up to time $t - 1$, given $S_{t-1} = i$; $\beta_{t|t-1}^{(i,j)}$ is an inference on β_t based on information up to time $t - 1$, given $S_t = j$ and $S_{t-1} = i$; $P_{t|t-1}^{(i,j)}$ is the mean squared error matrix of $\beta_{t|t-1}^{(i,j)}$ conditional on $S_t = j$ and $S_{t-1} = i$; $\eta_{t|t-1}^{(i,j)}$ is the conditional forecast error of y_t based on information up to time $t - 1$, given $S_{t-1} = i$ and $S_t = j$; and $f_{t|t-1}^{(i,j)}$ is the conditional variance of forecast error $\eta_{t|t-1}^{(i,j)}$.

As noted by Gordon and Smith (1988) and Harrison and Stevens (1976), each iteration of the above Kalman filter produces an M-fold increase in the number of cases to consider. (Even when M, the total number of different regimes, is 2, there would be more than 1,000 cases to consider by the time $t = 10$!) It is necessary to introduce some approximations to make the above Kalman filter operable. The key is to collapse terms in the right way at the right time. Therefore, it remains to somehow reduce the $(M \times M)$ posteriors $(\beta_{t|t}^{(i,j)}$ and $P_{t|t}^{(i,j)})$ into M posteriors $(\beta_{t|t}^j$ and $P_{t|t}^j)$ to complete the above Kalman filter. In generalizing the Kalman filter and the dynamic linear model to account for a Markov process of the M processes, Highfield (1990) "collapses" the Kalman filter to a single posterior at each t as in Gordon and Smith 1988. For the quality of various approaches to collapsing, refer to Smith and Markov 1980. We employ approximations similar to those proposed by Harrison and Stevens (1976). Consider the following approximation:

If $\beta_{t|t}^{(i,j)}$ in (5.14) represented $E[\beta_t | S_{t-1} = i, S_t = j, \psi_t]$, it would be straight-forward to show that

$$\beta_{t|t}^j = \frac{\sum_{i=1}^M Pr[S_{t-1} = i, S_t = j | \psi_t] \beta_{t|t}^{(i,j)}}{Pr[S_t = j | \psi_t]},$$ (5.16)

where $\beta_{t|t}^{j}$ would represent $E[\beta_t | S_t = j, \psi_t]$. In this case, by denoting

$$\Delta_t = \frac{Pr[S_{t-1} = i, S_t = j | \psi_t]}{Pr[S_t = j | \psi_t]},$$

the mean squared error matrix of β_t conditional on ψ_t and $S_t = j$ could be derived in the following way:

$$P_{t|t}^{j} = E[(\beta_t - E[\beta_t | S_t = j, \psi_t])(\beta_t - E[\beta_t | S_t = j, \psi_t])' | S_t = j, \psi_t]$$

$$= E[(\beta_t - \beta_{t|t}^{j})(\beta_t - \beta_{t|t}^{j})' | S_t = j, \psi_t]$$

$$= \sum_{i=1}^{M} \Delta_t E[(\beta_t - \beta_{t|t}^{j})(\beta_t - \beta_{t|t}^{j})' | S_{t-1} = i, S_t = j, \psi_t]$$

$$= \sum_{i=1}^{M} \Delta_t E[(\beta_t - \beta_{t|t}^{(i,j)} + \beta_{t|t}^{(i,j)} - \beta_{t|t}^{j})(\beta_t - \beta_{t|t}^{(i,j)} + \beta_{t|t}^{(i,j)} - \beta_{t|t}^{j})'$$

$$| S_{t-1} = i, S_t = j, \psi_t]$$

$$= \sum_{i=1}^{M} \Delta_t \{ E[(\beta_t - \beta_{t|t}^{(i,j)})(\beta_t - \beta_{t|t}^{(i,j)})' | S_{t-1} = i, S_t = j, \psi_t] \tag{5.17}$$

$$+ (\beta_{t|t}^{j} - \beta_{t|t}^{(i,j)})(\beta_{t|t}^{j} - \beta_{t|t}^{(i,j)})' \}$$

$$+ \sum_{i=1}^{M} \Delta_t (E[\beta_t | S_{t-1} = i, S_t = j, \psi_t] - \beta_{t|t}^{(i,j)})(\beta_{t|t}^{(i,j)} - \beta_{t|t}^{j})'$$

$$+ \sum_{i=1}^{M} \Delta_t (\beta_{t|t}^{(i,j)} - \beta_{t|t}^{j})(E[\beta_t | S_{t-1} = i, S_t = j, \psi_t] - \beta_{t|t}^{(i,j)})'$$

$$= \sum_{i=1}^{M} \Delta_t \{ E[(\beta_t - \beta_{t|t}^{(i,j)})(\beta_t - \beta_{t|t}^{(i,j)})' | S_{t-1} = i, S_t = j, \psi_t]$$

$$+ (\beta_{t|t}^{j} - \beta_{t|t}^{(i,j)})(\beta_{t|t}^{j} - \beta_{t|t}^{(i,j)})' \}.$$

Here, if $P_{t|t}^{(i,j)}$ in (5.15) represented $E[(\beta_t - \beta_{t|t}^{(i,j)})(\beta_t - \beta_{t|t}^{(i,j)})' | S_{t-1} = i, S_t = j, \psi_t]$, then (5.17) could be rewritten as:

$$P_{t|t}^j =$$

$$\frac{\sum_{i=1}^{M} Pr[S_{t-1} = i, S_t = j \mid \psi_t]\{P_{t|t}^{(i,j)} + (\beta_{t|t}^j - \beta_{t|t}^{(i,j)})(\beta_{t|t}^j - \beta_{t|t}^{(i,j)})'\}}{Pr[S_t = j \mid \psi_t]}.$$

$$(5.17')$$

At the end of each iteration, we employ equations (5.16) and (5.17') to collapse $M \times M$ posteriors in (5.14) and (5.15) into $M \times 1$ to make the filter operable. Notice, however, that these collapsed posteriors involve approximations, as $\beta_{t|t}^{(i,j)}$ and $P_{t|t}^{(i,j)}$ in (5.14) and (5.15) do not calculate $E[\beta_t \mid S_{t-1} = i, S_t = j, \psi_t]$ and $E[(\beta_t - \beta_{t|t}^{(i,j)})(\beta_t - \beta_{t|t}^{(i,j)})' \mid S_{t-1} = i, S_t = j, \psi_t]$ exactly. This is because β_t conditional on ψ_{t-1}, $S_t = j$, and $S_{t-1} = i$ is a mixture of normals for $t > 2$. One can still motivate (5.14) as the linear projection of β_t on y_t and $\beta_{t-1|t-1}^i$ (taking S_t and S_{t-1} as given). Thus, the algorithm is certainly calculating a sensible inference about β_t. Notice, however, that (5.14) is not calculating the linear projection of β_t on $y_t, y_{t-1}, \ldots$, because $\beta_{t-1|t-1}^i$ is a nonlinear function of $y_{t-1}, y_{t-2}, \ldots$.

5.2.2 How Do We Make Inferences on the Probability Terms to Complete the Filter?

To complete the Kalman filter with the proposed approximation, we need to make inferences on the appropriate probability terms that show up in equations (5.16) and (5.17'). The basic principle is the same as in chapter 4.

STEP 1: At the beginning of the t-th iteration, given the $Pr[S_{t-1} = i \mid \psi_{t-1}]$ term ($i = 1, 2, \ldots, M$), we can calculate

$$Pr[S_t = j, S_{t-1} = i \mid \psi_{t-1}] = Pr[S_t = j \mid S_{t-1} = i]Pr[S_{t-1}$$

$$= i \mid \psi_{t-1}], (i, j = 1, 2, \ldots, M), \quad (5.18)$$

where $Pr[S_t = j \mid S_{t-1} = i]$ is the transition probability.

STEP 2: Consider the joint density of y_t, S_t, and S_{t-1}:

$$f(y_t, S_t = j, S_{t-1} = i \mid \psi_{t-1}) = f(y_t \mid S_t = j, S_{t-1} = i, \psi_{t-1})$$

$$Pr[S_t = j, S_{t-1} = i \mid \psi_{t-1}], (i, j = 1, 2, \ldots, M), \quad (5.19)$$

from which the marginal density of y_t is obtained by

$$f(y_t \mid \psi_{t-1}) = \sum_{j=1}^{M} \sum_{i=1}^{M} f(y_t, S_t = j, S_{t-1} = i \mid \psi_{t-1})$$

$$= \sum_{j=1}^{M} \sum_{i=1}^{M} f(y_t \mid S_t = j, S_{t-1} = i, \psi_{t-1})$$

$$Pr[S_t = j, S_{t-1} = i \mid \psi_{t-1}], \tag{5.20}$$

where the conditional density $f(y_t \mid S_{t-1} = i, S_t = j, \psi_{t-1})$ is obtained based on the prediction error decomposition:

$$f(y_t \mid S_{t-1} = i, S_t = j, \psi_{t-1}) =$$

$$(2\pi)^{-\frac{N}{2}} \mid f_{t|t-1}^{(i,j)} \mid^{-\frac{1}{2}} \exp\{-\frac{1}{2}\eta_{t|t-1}^{(i,j)}{}' f_{t|t-1}^{(i,j)}{}^{-1} \eta_{t|t-1}^{(i,j)}\}, (i, j = 1, 2, \ldots, M)$$

$$\tag{5.21}$$

where $\eta_{t|t-1}^{(i,j)}$ and $f_{t|t-1}^{(i,j)}$ are given in equations (5.12) and (5.13). The only difference from the approach in chapter 4 is that in calculating the conditional density, $f(y_t \mid S_t, S_{t-1}, \psi_{t-1})$, we use the conditional forecast error and variance obtained from the Kalman filter recursion in section 5.2.1.

STEP 3: Once Y_t is observed at the end of time t, we can update the probability term in (5.18) to get

$$Pr[S_{t-1} = i, S_t = j \mid \psi_t]$$

$$= Pr[S_{t-1} = i, S_t = j \mid \psi_{t-1}, y_t]$$

$$= \frac{f(S_{t-1} = i, S_t = j, y_t \mid \psi_{t-1})}{f(y_t \mid \psi_{t-1})} \tag{5.22}$$

$$= \frac{f(y_t \mid S_{t-1} = i, S_t = j, \psi_{t-1}) f(S_{t-1} = i, S_t = j \mid \psi_{t-1})}{f(y_t \mid \psi_{t-1})},$$

$$(i, j = 1, 2, \ldots, M)$$

with

$$Pr[S_t = j \mid \psi_t] = \sum_{i=1}^{M} Pr[S_{t-1} = i, S_t = j \mid \psi_t]. \tag{5.23}$$

5.2.3   Summary of the Filter and the Approximate Maximum Likelihood Estimation of the Model

Figure 5.1 presents a flowchart for Kim's (1994) basic filter, discussed in sections 5.2.1 and 5.2.2. The filter for the state-space model with Markov switching may actually be considered a combination of extended versions of the Kalman filter and the Hamilton filter, along with appropriate approximations. Kim's (1994) filter contains the following steps:

1. Run the Kalman filter given in equations (5.10)–(5.15) for $i, j = 1, 2, \ldots, M$.

2. Calculate $Pr[S_t, S_{t-1} \mid \psi_t]$ and $Pr[S_t \mid \psi_t]$, for $i, j = 1, 2, \ldots, M$.

3. Using these probability terms, collapse $M \times M$ posteriors in (5.14) and (5.15) into $M \times 1$ using equations (5.16) and (5.17').

Note that to start the filter, we need initial values $\beta_{0|0}^j$ and $P_{0|0}^j$ for the Kalman filter portion and $Pr[S_t = j \mid \psi_0]$ for the Hamilton filter portion. These initial values are obtained in exactly the same way as in chapters 3 and 4.

As a by-product of the filter, we get the density of y_t conditional on past information, $f(y_t \mid \psi_{t-1})$, $t = 1, 2, \ldots, T$, from equation (5.20). Then the approximate log likelihood function is given by

$$LL = \ln[f(y_1, y_2, \ldots, y_T)] = \sum_{t=1}^{T} \ln[f(y_t \mid \psi_{t-1})]. \qquad (5.24)$$

To estimate the parameters of the model, we use a nonlinear optimization procedure to maximize the approximate log likelihood function with respect to the underlying unknown parameters.

An important note is in order, concerning the accuracy of the maximum likelihood estimation (MLE) results and the inferences on S_t and β_t, $t = 1, 2, \ldots, T$. In the filter presented in the previous sections, we derived the distribution of β_t conditional on ψ_{t-1}, $S_t = j$, and $S_{t-1} = i$ ($i, j = 1, 2, \ldots, M$). Instead, we could have derived the distribution of β_t conditional on ψ_{t-1}, $S_t = j$, $S_{t-1} = i$, and $S_{t-2} = h$ ($h, i, j = 1, 2, \ldots, M$) to obtain more accurate inferences. In this case, the superscripts (i, j) and i in equations (5.10)–(5.15) would be changed to (h, i, j) and (i, j), respectively. Also, we would need to collapse the M^3 posteriors to M^2 at the end of each iteration. Thus, equations (5.16) and (5.17') would be rewritten as

$$l(\theta) = 0 \; ; \; \beta_{0|0}^{j}, \; P_{0|0}^{j}$$

$$\Pr(S_0) = \pi_i \; (\text{Steady} - \text{State Prob.})$$

$$\Downarrow \qquad \longleftarrow$$

Kalman Filter

$$\beta_{t|t-1}^{(i,j)}, \; P_{t|t-1}^{(i,j)}, \; \eta_{t|t-1}^{(i,j)}, \; f_{t|t-1}^{(i,j)}, \beta_{t|t-1}^{(i,j)}, \; P_{t|t-1}^{(i,j)}$$

Hamilton Filter

$$\Pr(S_t, S_{t-1} \mid \psi_{t-1}) = \Pr(S_t \mid S_{t-1}) \Pr(S_{t-1} \mid \psi_{t-1})$$

$$f(y_t \mid \psi_{t-1}) = \sum_{S_t} \sum_{S_{t-1}} f(y_t \mid S_t, S_{t-1}, \psi_{t-1}) \Pr(S_t, S_{t-1} \mid \psi_{t-1})$$

$$l(\theta) = l(\theta) + \ln(f(y_t \mid \psi_{t-1}))$$

$$\Pr(S_t, S_{t-1} \mid \psi_t) = \frac{f(y_t, S_t, S_{t-1} \mid \psi_{t-1})}{f(y_t \mid \psi_{t-1})} = \frac{f(y_t \mid S_t, S_{t-1}, \psi_{t-1}) \Pr(S_t, S_{t-1} \mid \psi_{t-1})}{f(y_t \mid \psi_{t-1})}$$

$$\Pr(S_t \mid \psi_t) = \sum_{S_{t-1}} \Pr(S_t, S_{t-1} \mid \psi_t)$$

$$\Downarrow$$

Approximations

$$\beta_{t|t}^{j} = \frac{\sum_{i=1}^{M} \Pr(S_{t-1} = i, S_t = j \mid \psi_t) \beta_{t|t}^{(i,j)}}{\Pr(S_t = j \mid \psi_t)}$$

$$P_{t|t}^{j} = \frac{\sum_{i=1}^{M} \Pr(S_{t-1} = i, S_t = j \mid \psi_t) \{P_{t|t}^{(i,j)} + (\beta_{t|t}^{j} - \beta_{t|t}^{(i,j)})(\beta_{t|t}^{j} - \beta_{t|t}^{(i,j)})'\}}{\Pr(S_t = j \mid \psi_t)}$$

t-1 = t

$$\Downarrow$$

$$l(\theta) = \sum_{t=1}^{T} \ln(f(y_t \mid \psi_{t-1}))$$

Figure 5.1
Flowchart for Kim's (1994) filter: state-space models with Markov switching

$$\beta_{t|t}^{i,j} = \sum_{h=1}^{M} \Delta_{ijh,t} \times \beta_{t|t}^{(h,i,j)}, \tag{5.25}$$

and

$$P_{t|t}^{i,j} = \sum_{h=1}^{M} \Delta_{ijh,t} \times \{P_{t|t}^{(h,i,j)} + (\beta_{t|t}^{(i,j)} - \beta_{t|t}^{(h,i,j)})(\beta_{t|t}^{(i,j)} - \beta_{t|t}^{(h,i,j)})'\}, \tag{5.26}$$

where

$$\Delta_{ijh,t} = \frac{Pr[S_{t-2} = h, S_{t-1} = i, S_t = j \mid \psi_t]}{Pr[S_{t-1} = i, S_t = j \mid \psi_t]}.$$

In general, as we carry more states at each iteration, we can get more efficient inferences, but only at the cost of increased computation time and the model's tractability. As a rule of thumb, when only S_t or S_t and S_{t-1} show up in the state-space representation, carrying M^2 states is usually enough. The marginal benefit derived from the increase in efficiency in carrying more states is small and likely does not exceed the marginal cost of increased computation time. When $S_t, S_{t-1}, \ldots, S_{t-r}$ ($r > 1$) show up in the state-space representation of a dynamic system, however, Kim (1994) recommends carrying at least M^{r+1} states at each iteration.

5.3   Smoothing

Once parameters are estimated, we can get inferences on S_t and β_t using all the information in the sample: $Pr[S_t = j \mid \psi_T]$ and $\beta_{t|T}$ ($t = 1, 2, \ldots, T$). Here, it is assumed that only S_t or S_t and S_{t-1} show up in the state-space representation of the model. For the derivation of a similar smoothing algorithm in the context of a general non-Gaussian state-space model, refer to Kitagawa 1987; also refer to Hamilton 1994 for related issues.

As in section 4.3.1, consider the following derivation of the joint probability that $S_t = j$ and $S_{t+1} = k$ based on full information:

$$Pr[S_t = j, S_{t+1} = k \mid \psi_T]$$

$$= Pr[S_{t+1} = k \mid \psi_T] \times Pr[S_t = j \mid S_{t+1} = k, \psi_T]$$

$$\approx Pr[S_{t+1} = k \mid \psi_T] \times Pr[S_t = j \mid S_{t+1} = k, \psi_t]$$

$$= \frac{Pr[S_{t+1} = k \mid \psi_T] \times Pr[S_t = j, S_{t+1} = k \mid \psi_t]}{Pr[S_{t+1} = k \mid \psi_t]}$$

$$= \frac{Pr[S_{t+1} = k \mid \psi_T] \times Pr[S_t = j \mid \psi_t] \times Pr[S_{t+1} = k \mid S_t = j]}{Pr[S_{t+1} = k \mid \psi_t]},$$

(5.27)

and

$$Pr[S_t = j \mid \psi_T] = \sum_{k=1}^{M} Pr[S_t = j, S_{t+1} = k \mid \psi_T]. \tag{5.28}$$

Notice that the algorithm in (5.27) involves an approximation as we go from the first line to the second line. To investigate the nature of the approximation involved, define $h_{t+1,T} = (y'_{t+1}, y'_{t+2}, \ldots, y'_T, z'_{t+1}, z'_{t+2}, \ldots, z'_T)'$, for $T > t$. That is, $h_{t+1,T}$ is the vector of observations from date $t+1$ to T. Then we have

$$Pr[S_t = j \mid S_{t+1} = k, \psi_T]$$

$$= Pr[S_t = j \mid S_{t+1} = k, h_{t+1,T}, \psi_t)$$

$$= \frac{f(S_t = j, h_{t+1,T} \mid S_{t+1} = k, \psi_t)}{f(h_{t+1,T} \mid S_{t+1} = k, \psi_t)}$$

(5.29)

$$= \frac{Pr(S_t = j \mid S_{t+1} = k, \psi_t) f(h_{t+1,T} \mid S_{t+1} = k, S_t = j, \psi_t)}{f(h_{t+1,T} \mid S_{t+1} = k, \psi_t)}.$$

Provided that

$$f(h_{t+1,T} \mid S_{t+1} = k, S_t = j, \psi_t) = f(h_{t+1,T} \mid S_{t+1} = k, \psi_t), \tag{5.30}$$

we have $Pr[S_t = j \mid S_{t+1} = k, \psi_T] = Pr[S_t = j \mid S_{t+1} = k, \psi_t]$, and (5.27) would be exact. However, unlike the smoothing algorithm in section 4.3.1 for the Hamilton model, (5.30) does not hold exactly, and this is why (5.27) involves an approximation.

Keeping equation (5.27) in mind, we now turn to the derivation of the smoothing algorithm for the vector β_t. Like the filter, the smoothing algorithm for the vector β_t can be written as follows, given that $S_t = j$ and $S_{t+1} = k$:

$$\beta_{t|T}^{(j,k)} = \beta_{t|t}^j + \tilde{P}_t^{(j,k)}(\beta_{t+1|T}^k - \beta_{t+1|t}^{(j,k)}), \tag{5.31}$$

$$P_{t|T}^{(j,k)} = P_{t|t}^j + \tilde{P}_t^{(j,k)}(P_{t+1|T}^k - P_{t+1|t}^{(j,k)})\tilde{P}_t^{(j,k)\prime}, \tag{5.32}$$

where $\tilde{P}_t^{(j,k)} = P_{t|t}^j F_k' [P_{t+1|t}^{(j,k)}]^{-1}$; $\beta_{t|T}^{(j,k)}$ is an inference of β_t based on full sample and $P_{t|T}^{(j,k)}$ is the mean squared error matrix of $\beta_{t|T}^{(j,k)}$; and $\beta_{t|t}^j$ and $P_{t|t}^j$ are given by equations (5.16) and (5.17').

Because $Pr[S_t = j \mid \psi_T]$ is not dependent on $\beta_{t|T}$, we can first calculate smoothed probabilities, and these smoothed probabilities can then be used to get smoothed values of β_t, $\beta_{t|T}$. Given the above smoothing algorithms, actual smoothing can be performed by applying approximations similar to those introduced in the basic filtering.

STEP 1   Run through the basic filter in the previous section for $t = 1, \ldots, T$ and store the resulting sequences $\beta_{t|t-1}^{(i,j)}$, $P_{t|t-1}^{(i,j)}$, $\beta_{t|t}^j$, $P_{t|t}^j$, $Pr[S_t = j \mid \psi_{t-1}]$ and $Pr[S_t = j \mid \psi_t]$ from equations (5.14), (5.15), (5.16), (5.17'), (5.18) and (5.23), respectively, for $t = 1, 2, \ldots, T$.

STEP 2   For $t = T - 1, T - 2, \ldots, 1$, get the smoothed joint probability $Pr[S_t = j, S_{t+1} = k \mid \psi_T]$ and $Pr[S_t = j \mid \psi_T]$ according to (5.27) and (5.28), and save them. Here, $Pr[S_T = j \mid \psi_T]$, the starting value for smoothing, is given by the final iteration of the basic filter.

STEP 3   Then we can use the smoothed probabilities from step 2 to collapse the $M \times M$ elements of $\beta_{t|T}^{(j,k)}$ and $P_{t|T}^{(j,k)}$ into M by taking weighted averages. At each iteration of (5.31) and (5.32), for $t = T - 1, T - 2, \ldots, 1$, collapse the $M \times M$ elements into M in the following way by taking weighted averages over state S_{t+1}:

$$\beta_{t|T}^j = \frac{\sum_{k=1}^{M} Pr[S_t = j, S_{t+1} = k \mid \psi_T]\beta_{t|T}^{(j,k)}}{Pr[S_t = j \mid \psi_T]}, \tag{5.33}$$

and

$$P_{t|T}^j =$$

$$\frac{\sum_{k=1}^{M} Pr[S_t = j, S_{t+1} = k \mid \psi_T]\{P_{t|T}^{(j,k)} + (\beta_{t|T}^j - \beta_{t|T}^{(j,k)})(\beta_{t|T}^j - \beta_{t|T}^{(j,k)})'\}}{Pr[S_t = k \mid \psi_T]}.$$

$$\tag{5.34}$$

STEP 4   From step 3, the smoothed value of $\beta_{t|T}^j$ is dependent only upon states at time t. By taking a weighted average over the states at time t, we can get $\beta_{t|T}$ from

$$\beta_{t|T} = \sum_{j=1}^{M} Pr[S_t = j \mid \psi_T]\beta_{t|T}^j. \tag{5.35}$$

5.4   An Evaluation of the Kim Filter and Approximate MLE

One real advantage of the Kim filter is that it allows for inference in a large class of Markov-switching models that previously could not be handled within the classical framework. A Monte Carlo experiment based on generated sets of data could be employed to evaluate the approximation methodology, but in the absence of an alternative methodology, such an evaluation would not be particularly meaningful. Instead of performing a Monte Carlo experiment for a model that could not be handled without the proposed algorithm, Kim (1994) took an example from a class of Markov-switching models for which maximum likelihood estimation and inferences are possible without approximations. Using Lam's (1990) generalized Hamilton model, he evaluated the effects of approximations by comparing inferences based on the proposed algorithm with approximations and those based on Lam's algorithm without approximations.

5.4.1   The Hamilton Model versus Lam's Generalized Hamilton Model

The Hamilton model and Lam's (1990) generalized Hamilton model bear quite different economic implications in terms of the nature of the shocks and business cycle asymmetry. In the Hamilton model with a unit root in the autoregressive component, all the shocks are permanent and the business cycle asymmetry shows up in the growth rate of output. On the contrary, Lam's model allows for the possibility that the economy may be subject to both permanent and transitory shocks. In this case, the business cycle asymmetry shows up in the permanent component of output.

Consider the following decomposition of the log of real GNP into a stochastic trend and an autoregressive component:

$$y_t = n_t + x_t, \tag{5.36}$$

$$n_t = n_{t-1} + \delta_{S_t}, \tag{5.37}$$

$$\phi^*(L)x_t = u_t, \tag{5.38}$$

$$u_t \sim \text{i.i.d.} N(0, \sigma^2), \tag{5.39}$$

$$\delta_{S_t} = \delta_0 + \delta_1 S_t, \qquad \delta_1 > 0, \tag{5.40}$$

$$Pr[S_t = 1 \mid S_{t-1} = 1] = p, \quad Pr[S_t = 0 \mid S_{t-1} = 0] = q, \tag{5.41}$$

where n_t is a stochastic trend and x_t is a deviation of y_t from the trend. The variable n_t may be considered a time trend with a Markov-switching growth rate. Alternatively, it may be considered a random walk component with a discrete shock, given by δ_{S_t}. Lam (1990) assumes either that the roots of $\phi^*(L) = 0$ lie outside the unit circle or that one of the roots is unity.

In case $\phi^*(L) = 0$ has a unit root (i.e., $\phi^*(L) = \phi(L)(1 - L)$, with the roots of $\phi(L) = 0$ being outside the unit circle), the first difference of y_t collapses to Hamilton's (1989) autoregressive model with a Markov-switching mean. In this case, because both n_t and x_t terms have a unit root, the two components are not identified. By multiplying both sides of (5.36) by $\phi(L)(1 - L) = \phi^*(L)$, where L is the lag operator, we have

$$\phi(L)(1 - L)y_t = \phi(L)(1 - L)n_t + \phi^*(L)x_t, \tag{5.42}$$

$$\phi(L)\Delta y_t = \phi(L)\delta_{S_t} + u_t, \tag{5.43}$$

$$\Longrightarrow \quad \phi(L)(\Delta y_t - \delta_{S_t}) = u_t. \tag{5.44}$$

When the roots of $\phi^*(L) = 0$ lie outside the unit circle, x_t represents a transitory deviation of y_t from its trend component n_t and the two components can be identified. By taking first differences on both sides of (5.36), we have

$$\Delta y_t = \delta_0 + \delta_1 S_t + (x_t - x_{t-1}). \tag{5.36'}$$

Unlike in the original Hamilton model with a unit root in (5.38), one difficulty here is that the states of an observation include the whole history of the Markov process. This is clear from the following expression for x_t, which is obtained by solving equation (5.36') backward in time:

$$x_t = \sum_{i=1}^{t} \Delta y_i - \delta_0 t - \delta_1 (\sum_{i=1}^{t-1} S_i + S_t) + x_0. \tag{5.45}$$

Lam (1990) treats the sum of previous states ($\sum_{i=1}^{t-1} S_i$) as an additional state variable and provides inferences of the model based on exact MLE. This is possible because the sum of previous states is also Markovian.

5.4.2 A State-Space Representation of Lam's Generalized Hamilton Model and Approximate MLE: An Evaluation

Even though exact MLE is possible for the model introduced in section 5.4.1, Kim (1994) puts the model in the following state-space form and applies the approximate MLE in section 5.2 for the purpose of evaluating the effects of the approximations:

$$\Delta y_t = \begin{bmatrix} 1 & -1 & 0 & \dots & 0 \end{bmatrix} \begin{bmatrix} x_t \\ x_{t-1} \\ x_{t-2} \\ \vdots \\ x_{t-r+1} \end{bmatrix} + \delta_{S_t}, \tag{5.46}$$

$$(\Delta y_t = H\beta_t + \delta_{S_t})$$

$$\begin{bmatrix} x_t \\ x_{t-1} \\ x_{t-2} \\ \vdots \\ x_{t-r+1} \end{bmatrix} = \begin{bmatrix} \phi_1^* & \phi_2^* & \phi_3^* & \dots & \phi_r^* \\ 1 & 0 & 0 & \dots & 0 \\ 0 & 1 & 0 & \dots & 0 \\ \vdots & \vdots & \vdots & \ddots & \vdots \\ 0 & 0 & 0 & \dots & 0 \end{bmatrix} \begin{bmatrix} x_{t-1} \\ x_{t-2} \\ x_{t-3} \\ \vdots \\ x_{t-r} \end{bmatrix} + \begin{bmatrix} u_t \\ 0 \\ 0 \\ \vdots \\ 0 \end{bmatrix}, \tag{5.47}$$

$$(\beta_t = F\beta_{t-1} + v_t).$$

Table 5.1 reports the estimation results for the real GNP series [1952:2–1984:4] obtained by applying both Lam's (1990) algorithm with no approximations and Kim's (1994) algorithm with approximations. In the usual estimation of the state-space models, the initial values for the state vector and its mean squared error matrix are set to their steady-state values when the transition equation is stationary. Lam treats x_0, the initial value for the autoregressive component, as an additional parameter to be estimated. Following his strategy, we also treat each element of $\beta_{0|0} = [x_0 \ x_{-1}]'$, the initial condition for the state vector (β_t) in our state-space representation, as an additional parameter to be estimated. In this case, because we are assuming that elements in $\beta_{0|0}$ are some unknown constants, each element in $P_{0|0}$, the mean squared error matrix of $\beta_{0|0}$, is fixed at 0 when estimating the model. Estimates of the parameters from the state-space model are close to those from Lam. Except for the initial values of the autoregressive component, all the estimates from the state-space model are within one standard error of Lam's.

Table 5.1
Maximum likelihood estimates of the Hamilton model with general autoregressive component:
comparison of estimates from Lam's (1990) model and the state-space model

Parameters	Estimates			
	Lam's (1990) model		State-space model	
$\hat{p}$	0.957	(0.019)	0.954	(0.022)
$\hat{q}$	0.508	(0.101)	0.465	(0.170)
$\hat{\delta}_0$	−1.483	(0.151)	−1.457	(0.420)
$\hat{\delta}_1$	2.447	(0.160)	2.421	(0.424)
$\hat{\sigma}$	0.771	(0.047)	0.773	(0.052)
$\hat{\phi}_1$	1.244	(0.063)	1.246	(0.087)
$\hat{\phi}_2$	−0.382	(0.064)	−0.367	(0.086)
$\hat{x}_0$	6.376	(0.127)	5.224	(1.684)
$\hat{x}_{-1}$	—	0.535		(2.699)
Log likelihood value	−174.97		−176.33	

Note: Model is estimated using 100 times the log-difference in quarterly real GNP. Standard errors
are in parentheses. Second column is taken from Lam 1990.

Figures 5.2a and 5.2b compare the probability that the economy is in the
high-growth state from Lam's estimation with the probability from the state-
space estimation, based on current and full information. The relative magni-
tudes of these probabilities are almost the same, and inferences about the periods of low growth are almost the same. Figures 5.3 and 5.4 plot the estimated
stochastic trend against actual real GDP and the implied cyclical component,
respectively. The estimates are conditional on information up to time t and are
based on the Kim algorithm.

We would expect Lam's estimation procedure to be more efficient than the
state-space estimation procedure, because the latter is based on an approximation whereas the former is not. Indeed, the standard errors of the estimates are
somewhat larger and the log likelihood value is somewhat smaller for the state-
space procedure. It might appear, then, that the main advantage of employing
the algorithm introduced in this chapter is a significant reduction in the computation costs, when the loss in efficiency is only marginal. However, if an exact
MLE procedure is at all possible for a model, *even at high computation costs*,
the state-space procedure and approximate MLE are not recommended. The
purpose of employing the approximation-based algorithm to the generalized

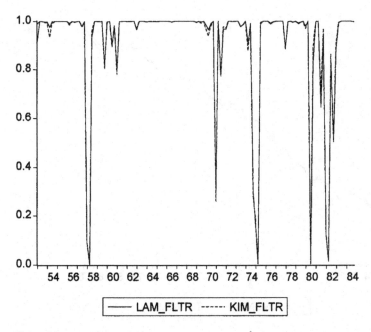

Figure 5.2a
Filtered probabilities of a high-growth state based on Lam's algorithm
without approximations and Kim's algorithm with approximations

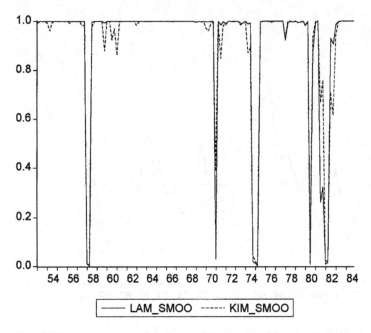

Figure 5.2b
Smoothed probabilities of a high-growth state based on Lam's algorithm without
approximations and Kim's algorithm with approximations

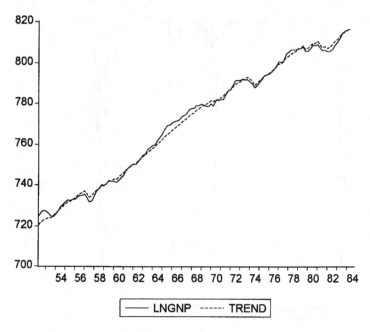

Figure 5.3
Real GNP and Markov-switching trend component from Lam's generalized
Hamilton model: Kim's algorithm

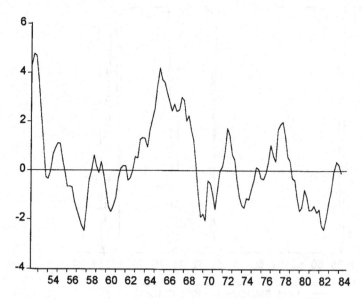

Figure 5.4
Cyclical component from Lam's generalized Hamilton model: Kim's algorithm

Hamilton model in this section is merely to show that the approximations are quite accurate.

Most of the potential applications of Kim's (1994) state-space models with Markov switching are for models in which exact maximum likelihood estimation may not be feasible at all. In these cases, the approximation-based algorithm should be employed, because the marginal benefit of employing the proposed approximation-based algorithm is clearly infinity, whereas the marginal cost is only minimal.

5.5 Application 1: Sources of Monetary Growth Uncertainty and Economic Activity

A large body of research suggests that uncertainty about aggregate demand or monetary growth is an important determinant of the performance of the macroeconomy (see, for example, Barro 1976; Lucas 1973; Friedman 1977; Makin 1982; and Kim and Nelson 1989). However, these studies do not account for the possibility that there may be more than one source of uncertainty. Thus, they do not consider that uncertainty from different sources may have different effects on economic agents' decision making and therefore on economic activity.

Kim (1993b) assumes that there are two types of uncertainty within a regression context: uncertainty that arises due to heteroskedasticity in the disturbance terms and uncertainty that arises as economic agents are obliged to infer the unknown or changing regression coefficients. For example, Harrison and Stevens (1976) have argued that "a person's uncertainty about the future arises not simply because of future random terms but also because of uncertainty about current parameter values and of the model's ability to link the present to the future" (p. 208). This section is based on Kim's analysis of the two sources of U.S. monetary growth uncertainty within a context of the time-varying-parameter model with heteroskedasticity.

5.5.1 A Time-Varying-Parameter Model with Heteroskedastic Disturbances for U.S. Monetary Growth Uncertainty

In section 3.4, we considered Kim and Nelson's (1989) application of the following time-varying-parameter (TVP) model for modeling the changing conditional variance of U.S. monetary growth uncertainty:

$$\Delta M_t = \beta_{0t} + \beta_{1t}\Delta i_{t-1} + \beta_{2t}INF_{t-1} + \beta_{3t}SURP_{t-1} + \beta_{4t}\Delta M_{t-1} + e_t,$$

$$(5.48)$$

$$\beta_{it} = \beta_{it-1} + v_{it}, \qquad\qquad\qquad\qquad\qquad\qquad\qquad\qquad (5.49)$$

$$e_t \sim \text{i.i.d.} N(0, \sigma^2), \qquad\qquad\qquad\qquad\qquad\qquad\qquad\qquad (5.50)$$

$$v_{it} \sim \text{i.i.d.} N(0, \sigma_{vi}^2), \quad i = 0, 1, \ldots, 4, \qquad\qquad\qquad\qquad (5.51)$$

or, in vector notation,

$$\Delta M_t = X_{t-1}\beta_t + e_t, \qquad\qquad\qquad\qquad\qquad\qquad\qquad (5.48)'$$

$$\beta_t = \beta_{t-1} + v_t, \qquad\qquad\qquad\qquad\qquad\qquad\qquad\qquad (5.49)'$$

$$e_t \sim \text{i.i.d.} N(0, \sigma^2), \qquad\qquad\qquad\qquad\qquad\qquad\qquad\qquad (5.50)'$$

$$v_t \sim \text{i.i.d.} N(0, Q), \qquad\qquad\qquad\qquad\qquad\qquad\qquad\qquad (5.51)'$$

where ΔM, Δi, INF, and $SURP$ stand for U.S. figures for the quarterly M1 growth rate, changes in the interest rate as measured by the three-month T-bill rate, the inflation rate as measured by the CPI, and the detrended full employment budget surplus, respectively; v_i, $i = 0, 1, \ldots, 4$, are assumed to be independent. The uncertainty about monetary growth varies as uncertainty about the state vector β_t varies.

Kim and Nelson (1989) applied the above model to a sample that covers 1962.I–1985:IV (quarterly data). The standardized forecast errors and their conditional variances that result from the model do not show significant evidence of serial correlation, which suggests that the model specification is appropriate. Kim and Nelson argue that the very strong ARCH effects present in estimates of a fixed coefficient version of the U.S. monetary growth function could be purely due to the misspecification of changing coefficients in the underlying model.

When the sample is extended to include observations until 1989:II, however, different results are obtained in Kim 1993b. Although no significant serial correlation is found in the standardized forecast errors (Q-statistics are Q(12)=11.5, Q(24)=17.6, Q(36)=26.1), the Q-statistics are significant even at the 1% significance level for the squares of standardized forecast errors (Q(12)=34.6, Q(24)=61.0, Q(36)=74.3). This suggests that the model does not fully explain some of the dynamics in the conditional variance of the forecast error. The TVP model, therefore, cannot be considered an appropriate model for the U.S. monetary growth function for the period 1962:I–1989:II. The remaining serial correlation in the squares of standardized forecast errors may be due to changing conditional variance in the disturbance term, e_t. Ignoring this form of heteroskedasticity results in an inappropriate use of new information when priors are updated in the Kalman filter.

Kim (1993b) also considers a constant regression coefficients model (except for a major structural change) with Markov-switching heteroskedasticity in the disturbance term. After regime shifts are accounted for in the variance of the disturbance term, no statistically significant ARCH effects remain. Standardized forecast errors and squares of standardized forecast errors reveal no statistically significant serial correlations, suggesting little model misspecification. However, whereas the TVP model fails to incorporate changing uncertainty due to future random shocks, the Markov-switching variance model with constant regression coefficients fails to incorporate the learning process of economic agents. These considerations suggest a general model that encompasses changing conditional variance due to time-varying coefficients and Markov-switching heteroskedasticity in the disturbance term:

$$\Delta M_t = X_{t-1}\beta_t + e_t, \quad t = 1, 2, \ldots, T, \tag{5.52}$$

$$\beta_t = \beta_{t-1} + v_t, \tag{5.53}$$

$$v_t \sim N(0, Q), \tag{5.54}$$

$$e_t \sim N(0, \sigma^2_{e,s_t}), \tag{5.55}$$

$$\sigma^2_{s_t} = \sigma^2_0 + (\sigma^2_1 - \sigma^2_0)S_t, \quad \sigma^2_1 > \sigma^2_0, \tag{5.56}$$

$$Pr[S_t = 1 \mid S_{t-1} = 1] = p_{11}, \quad Pr[S_t = 0 \mid S_{t-1} = 0] = p_{00}. \tag{5.57}$$

This model may be viewed as an alternative to that in Evans 1991, which considers a time-varying-parameter model with ARCH disturbance terms. A major difference between ARCH and Markov-switching heteroskedasticity is that whereas the unconditional variance is constant for the former, the unconditional variance itself is subject to shifts (structural changes) for the latter. By considering the Markov-switching heteroskedasticity in the disturbance term of the above model, we actually regard part of the changes in conditional variance of the forecast error as resulting from endogenous regime changes in the variance structure.

Table 5.2
Estimates of the time-varying-parameter model of U.S. monetary growth uncertainty (1962:I–1989:II)

Parameters	Model 1		Model 2	
σ_{v1}	0.0708	(0.0479)	0.0000	—
σ_{v2}	0.0429	(0.0351)	0.0000	—
σ_{v3}	0.0239	(0.0419)	0.0000	—
σ_{v4}	0.0001	(0.0075)	0.0000	—
σ_{v5}	0.0000	(0.0014)	0.0000	—
σ_{e0}	0.3607	(0.0502)	0.4128	(0.0485)
σ_{e1}	0.8944	(0.1314)	0.9772	(0.1331)
p_{00}	0.9327	(0.0757)	0.9378	(0.0718)
p_{11}	0.9599	(0.0401)	0.9563	(0.0416)
Log likelihood	−106.017		−110.947	

Note: Standard errors are in parentheses.

5.5.2 Specification Tests and a Decomposition of Monetary Growth Uncertainty into Two Sources: (1964:I–1989:II)

Table 5.2 reports the maximum likelihood estimation of the model. Using these results, we test the validity of the random walk specification for the regression coefficients and the validity of the heteroskedasticity in the disturbance terms assumptions. When we perform a likelihood ratio test for the null hypothesis of stable regression coefficients, $\sigma_{vi}^2 = 0$, $i = 1, 2, \ldots, 5$, we reject the null at the 10% significance level (p-value = 0.0793). Kendall and Stuart (1973) and Garbade (1977) have argued that under the null hypothesis of a stable regression coefficient, the likelihood statistic will be more concentrated toward the origin than a χ^2 distribution. Thus using a χ^2 distribution to determine critical values of the likelihood ratio leads to a conservative test. For more rigorous tests for parameter constancy against nonstationary alternatives such as a random walk or a martingale, readers are referred to Leybourne and McCabe 1989, Nabeya and Tanaka 1990, and Nyblom 1989.

Under the assumption of no heteroskedasticity ($\sigma_0^2 = \sigma_1^2$), the general model of this section reduces to the TVP model. But the parameters p_{11} and p_{00} are not identified under the null. Therefore, we follow Engel and Hamilton (1990) by testing a slightly more general null hypothesis ($p_{00} + p_{11} = 1$) against the alternative ($p_{00} + p_{11} > 1$). This in effect tests whether some persistent heteroskedasticity is left after the effects of time-varying or unknown regression coefficients on uncertainty are taken into account. The likelihood ratio test statistic is 6.8452, rejecting the null hypothesis at the 1% significance level.

Finally, further tests reveal no significant serial correlation in the general model for either the standardized forecast errors or the squares of the standardized forecast errors (Q-statistics for the squared standardized forecast errors, for example, are Q(12)=4.8, Q(24)=15.5, and Q(36)=24.6.) This suggest that the serial correlation in the squares of the standardized forecast errors from the pure TVP model in the previous section was due to heteroskedasticity. Overall, the test results suggest that the model of this section provides a more appropriate characterization of monetary growth uncertainty.

For the time-varying-parameter model with heteroskedastic disturbances, given $S_{t-1} = i$ and $S_t = j$, the conditional variance of the monetary forecast error can be represented as a modified version of equation (5.13):

$$f_{t|t-1}^{(i,j)} = X_{t-1} P_{t|t-1}^i X_{t-1}' + \sigma_j^2, \tag{5.13'}$$

where H is replaced by a vector of explanatory variables X_{t-1} and R_j is replaced by σ_j^2. The above equation states that the conditional variance of the forecast errors consists of two distinct terms: the conditional variance due to changing (or unknown) regression coefficients $[f_{1t} = X_{t-1} P_{t|t-1}^i X_{t-1}', \ i = 0, 1]$ and the conditional variance due to the heteroskedasticity of the disturbance terms $[f_{2t} = \sigma_0^2 + (\sigma_1^2 - \sigma_0^2)j, \ j = 0, 1]$. The former is dependent on S_{t-1}, the state at time $t - 1$, and the latter is dependent upon S_t, the state at time t. Thus, in reducing the 2×1 elements in each of f_{1t} and f_{2t} into one, the appropriate weights would be $Pr[S_{t-1} = i \mid \psi_{t-1}]$, $(i = 0, 1)$, and $Pr[S_t = j \mid \psi_{t-1}]$, $(j = 0, 1)$, respectively. Using these weights, the uncertainty terms can be calculated as

$$\tilde{f}_t = \tilde{f}_{1t} + \tilde{f}_{2t}, \tag{5.58}$$

$$\tilde{f}_{1t} = X_{t-1} \tilde{P}_{t|t-1} X_{t-1}', \quad \text{and} \tag{5.59}$$

$$\tilde{f}_{2t} = \sum_{j=0}^{1} Pr[S_t = j \mid \psi_{t-1}] \sigma_j^2 = \sigma_0^2 + (\sigma_1^2 - \sigma_0^2) Pr[S_t = 1 \mid \psi_{t-1}], \tag{5.60}$$

where

$$\tilde{P}_{t|t-1} = \sum_{i=0}^{1} Pr[S_{t-1} = i \mid \psi_{t-1}] \{ P_{t|t-1}^i + (\tilde{\beta}_{t|t-1} - \beta_{t|t-1}^i)(\tilde{\beta}_{t|t-1} - \beta_{t|t-1}^i)' \},$$

$$\tag{5.61}$$

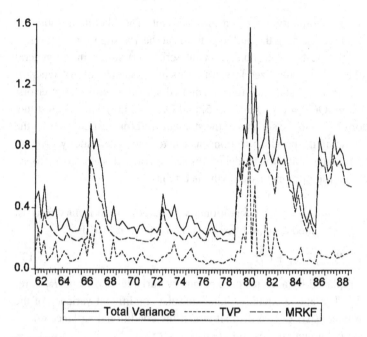

Figure 5.5
Decomposition of monetary growth uncertainty based on a TVP model with Markov-switching
heteroskedasticity

and where $\tilde{\beta}_{t|t-1} = \sum_{i=0}^{1} Pr[S_{t-1} = i \mid \psi_{t-1}]\beta_{t|t-1}^{i}$, and $P_{t|t-1}^{i}$ is the mean
squared error matrix of $\beta_{t|t-1}^{i}$. Figure 5.5 gives the plots of the overall uncer-
tainty $(\tilde{f}_t)$ and the decomposed uncertainty $(\tilde{f}_{1t}$ and $\tilde{f}_{2t})$ from Kim's (1993b)
general model.

We can observe from figure 5.5 that the overall monetary growth uncertainty
is in general higher in the 1980s than in the earlier period. During the sample
period 1962:1–1979:3, the average level of monetary growth uncertainty (as
measured by the conditional variance of monetary forecast errors) is 0.3483,
approximately 72% of which is due to the heteroskedasticity in the disturbance
terms. In contrast, during the sample period 1979:4–1989:2, the average level
of monetary growth uncertainty rose to 0.7235, with heteroskedasticity in
the disturbance terms explaining approximately 80% of the total variation
in the forecast errors. The portion of uncertainty due to heteroskedasticity
in the disturbance terms during the 1979.4–1989.2 period was 2.31 times as
high as that during the earlier period. The financial deregulation that started

in late 1979 may be one of the factors that explain the sizable increase in the uncertainty due to heteroskedasticity in the disturbance terms, and the switches in the Fed's monetary targeting procedure in 1979:4 and 1982:4 may be reflected in the increase in the TVP portion of uncertainty around those two periods.

5.5.3 Sources of Monetary Growth Uncertainty and Economic Activity

Of special interest in this section is the examination of the effects of different sources of monetary growth uncertainty on economic activity. Here, two econometric issues are involved. The first is the appropriate decomposition of the real GNP series into secular (or trend) and cyclical components. We follow Lam (1990) by assuming that real GNP consists of the sum of two independent unobserved components: one following a random walk with drift, which evolves according to a two-state Markov process, and the other following an autoregressive process either with or without a unit root. The specification for real GNP is

$$\tilde{y}_t = T_t + C_t, \tag{5.62}$$

$$T_t = T_{t-1} + \gamma_{S_t} + \alpha_1 \tilde{f}_{1t} + \alpha_2 \tilde{f}_{2t}, \tag{5.63}$$

$$C_t = \phi_1 C_{t-1} + \phi_2 C_{t-2} + \delta \tilde{\eta}_{t|t-1} + u_t, \quad u_t \sim \text{i.i.d.} N(0, \sigma^2), \tag{5.64}$$

$$\gamma_{S_t} = \gamma_0 + \gamma_1 S_t, \quad S_t = 0, 1, \tag{5.65}$$

$$Pr[S_t = 0 \mid S_{t-1} = 0] = q_{00} \quad \text{and} \quad Pr[S_t = 1 \mid S_{t-1} = 1] = q_{11}, \tag{5.66}$$

where $\tilde{y}_t$ is the log of real GNP; T_t and C_t are the trend and cyclical components of real GNP, respectively; γ_{S_t} is the drift term, which evolves according to a two-state Markov process given by (5.65); $\tilde{\eta}_{t|t-1} = \sum_{i=0}^{1} Pr[S_{t-1} = i \mid \psi_{t-1}] \eta_{t|t-1}^i$ is the conditional forecast error of monetary growth; $\tilde{f}_{1t}$ and $\tilde{f}_{2t}$ are decomposed conditional variances defined in (5.59) and (5.60). It is assumed that innovations in the real GNP are independent of innovations in the monetary growth. The inclusion of the conditional variances of monetary forecast errors in the trend component follows Froyen and Waud (1984) and Friedman (1977).

The second econometric issue involved is the two-step versus joint estimation of the monetary growth and output equations, discussed in Mishkin 1982 and Pagan 1984. Because the output equations (5.63)–(5.64) include generated

Table 5.3
Different sources of monetary growth uncertainty and economic activity: joint estimation results (output equation)

Parameters	Model 1		Model 2		Model 3	
ϕ_1	1.029	(0.170)	0.914	(0.202)	0.960	(0.133)
ϕ_2	−0.062	(0.186)	−0.079	(0.129)	−0.064	(0.115)
δ	0.255	(0.140)	0.161	(0.149)	0.223	(0.143)
σ	0.683	(0.092)	0.694	(0.068)	0.726	(0.067)
γ_0	−0.259	(0.424)	0.026	(0.392)	−0.160	(0.293)
γ_1	1.632	(0.384)	1.532	(0.380)	1.345	(0.228)
q_{11}	0.924	(0.057)	0.944	(0.054)	0.924	(0.043)
q_{00}	0.567	(0.289)	0.655	(0.244)	0.785	(0.124)
α_1	−4.035	(1.680)	−3.193	(1.053)	—	
α_2	0.715	(0.744)	—		−0.121	(0.530)
Log likelihood	−245.21		−245.62		−248.54	

Note: The output equation is estimated using 100 times the log difference in quarterly real GNP. Standard errors are in parentheses.

regressors, we may get biased standard errors in the second-step regression of the two-step estimation procedure. Following Pagan, we employ a maximum likelihood estimation procedure to estimate jointly the monetary growth and output equations.

Table 5.3 reports the estimates of the output equation from the joint estimation procedure. There is strong support for the hypothesis that uncertainty due to changing coefficients discourages economic activity. Uncertainty due to heteroskedasticity in the disturbance terms has a positive effect on economic activity, but the effect is not statistically significant.

These empirical results can be reconciled with the existing literature on the relationship between irreversible investment and uncertainty (see Bernanke 1983; Pindyck 1988; Cukierman 1980; and Henry 1974, for examples). The literature positively associates uncertainty and the value of new information. However, within our framework, different sources of uncertainty have different effects on the value of new information. Consider a forecast of monetary growth y_{t+1}. (Assume that y_t is yet to be realized. At the end of time t, y_t is a piece of new information.) From the modified Kalman filter recursion, we have (superscripts are omitted):

$$\Delta M_{t+1|t} = X_t \beta_{t+1|t} = X_t \beta_{t|t}$$

$$= X_t \beta_{t|t-1} + X_t K_t \eta_{t|t-1}$$

$$= X_t \beta_{t|t-1} + (X_{t-1} + \Delta X_t (X'_{t-1} X_{t-1})^{-1} X'_{t-1} X_{t-1}) K_t \eta_{t|t-1} \quad (5.67)$$

$$= X_t \beta_{t|t-1} + Z_t \eta_{t|t-1},$$

where $K_t = P_{t|t-1} X'_{t-1} f_{t|t-1}^{-1}$ is the Kalman gain; $\eta_{t|t-1}$ is the conditional forecast error which contains new information at time t; $\tilde{f}_{2t}$ is the uncertainty associated with heteroskedasticity;

$$Z_t = \{1 + \Delta X_t (X'_{t-1} X_{t-1})^{-1} X'_{t-1}\} \left\{ \frac{\tilde{f}_{1t}}{\tilde{f}_{1t} + \tilde{f}_{2t}} \right\}$$

and

$$\tilde{f}_{1t} = X_{t-1} \tilde{P}_{t|t-1} X'_{t-1}$$

is the uncertainty associated with regression coefficients. It is evident that, for a given change in the vector X_t (ΔX_t),

$$\frac{\partial Z_t}{\partial \tilde{f}_{1t}} > 0$$

and

$$\frac{\partial Z_t}{\partial \tilde{f}_{2t}} < 0.$$

In forming a new forecast, when uncertainty associated with changing regression coefficients ($\tilde{f}_{1t}$) increases, the value of new information ($\eta_{t|t-1}$) increases. This gives economic agents more incentive to delay an irreversible decision. But when uncertainty from the other source ($\tilde{f}_{2t}$) increases, there is little gain in delaying a decision because new information is less valuable. Therefore, if we assume economic agents are Bayesian in principle, and if we believe that monetary growth is one variable that economic agents consider in making their irreversible decisions, the empirical evidence in this section is consistent with the basic ideas in the existing literature on irreversible investment and uncertainty.

5.6   Application 2: Friedman's Plucking Model of Business Fluctuations and Implied Business Cycle Asymmetry

More than 30 years ago, Milton Friedman proposed a "plucking" model of business fluctuations in which output cannot exceed a ceiling level, but is from time to time, plucked downward by recession. The model implies that business fluctuations are asymmetric and that recessions have only a temporary effect on output. Subsequent literature (see Goodwin and Sweeney 1993; Beaudry and Koop 1993; and Sichel 1994 for examples) has provided copious empirical support for these propositions, especially for the asymmetric behavior of real output in its transitory or cyclical component. But econometric models of business fluctuations have not incorporated these features.

Recently, Kim and Nelson 1998a have proposed a general econometric time series model that incorporates asymmetric movements of business fluctuations off the trend and asymmetric persistence of shocks during recessionary and normal times. A version of the proposed model is

$$y_t = n_t + x_t \tag{5.68}$$

Transitory Component

$$x_t = \phi_1 x_{t-1} + \phi_2 x_{t-2} + \tau S_t + u_t, \quad \tau \neq 0, \tag{5.69}$$

$$u_t \sim N(0, \sigma_u^2), \tag{5.70}$$

$$Pr[S_t = 1 \mid S_{t-1} = 1] = p, \tag{5.71}$$

$$Pr[S_t = 0 \mid S_{t-1} = 0] = q. \tag{5.72}$$

Trend Component

$$n_t = g_{t-1} + n_{t-1} + v_t, \tag{5.73}$$

$$g_t = g_{t-1} + w_t, \tag{5.74}$$

$$w_t \sim N(0, \sigma_w^2), \tag{5.75}$$

$$v_t \sim N(0, \sigma_v^2), \tag{5.76}$$

where S_t is a first-order Markov-switching variable that determines the state of the economy.

Most of the existing literature on the decomposition of real GDP based on linear unobserved-components models (see Clark 1987; Kuttner 1994; and

Watson 1986 for examples) views economic fluctuations as symmetric movements around a stochastic trend. These models may be viewed as restricted versions of the model presented in this section, the restriction being $\tau = 0$.

The term τS_t in the transitory component is incorporated to account for its potential asymmetric behavior. In addition, if $\sigma_u^2 = 0$ with $\tau < 0$, this implies an existence of the trend ceiling component or the maximum feasible output as suggested in Friedman's plucking model. Thus the period of $S_t = 1$ with $\tau < 0$ would be interpreted as a period during which the economy is plucked down below its trend ceiling component.

Note that recent attempts to incorporate asymmetry in the time series models of economic fluctuations have been limited to the growth rate of real output itself or to the trend component. Hamilton's (1989) Markov-switching model of the growth of real GNP and Lam's (1990) generalized Hamilton model with a Markov-switching trend growth component and a symmetric transitory component are two examples. The above model may also be extended to include asymmetry in the trend component as well, in the following way:

$$n_t = g_{t-1} + n_{t-1} + \gamma S_t + v_t. \tag{5.73'}$$

Estimation of the model given in (5.68)–(5.76) based on Kim 1994 is straightforward once we put the above model in state-space form:

$$y_t = [\,1 \quad 1 \quad 0 \quad 0\,] \begin{bmatrix} n_t \\ x_t \\ x_{t-1} \\ g_t \end{bmatrix}, \tag{5.77}$$

$(y_t = H\beta_t),$

$$\begin{bmatrix} n_t \\ x_t \\ x_{t-1} \\ g_t \end{bmatrix} = \begin{bmatrix} 0 \\ \tau S_t \\ 0 \\ 0 \end{bmatrix} + \begin{bmatrix} 1 & 0 & 0 & 1 \\ 0 & \phi_1 & \phi_2 & 0 \\ 0 & 1 & 0 & 0 \\ 0 & 0 & 0 & 1 \end{bmatrix} \begin{bmatrix} n_{t-1} \\ x_{t-1} \\ x_{t-2} \\ g_{t-1} \end{bmatrix} + \begin{bmatrix} v_t \\ u_t \\ 0 \\ w_t \end{bmatrix}, \tag{5.78}$$

$(\beta_t = \tilde{\mu}_{S_t} + F\beta_{t-1} + V_t),$

$$E(V_t V_t') = \begin{bmatrix} \sigma_v^2 & 0 & 0 & 0 \\ 0 & \sigma_u^2 & 0 & 0 \\ 0 & 0 & 0 & 0 \\ 0 & 0 & 0 & \sigma_w^2 \end{bmatrix}. \tag{5.79}$$

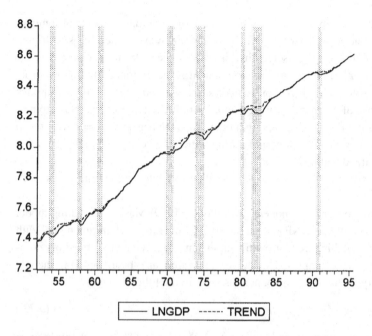

Figure 5.6
Real GDP and its trend component based on a plucking model

By estimating various versions of the proposed model, Kim and Nelson (1997) have shown that the stochastic behavior of quarterly real GDP [1951:I– 1995:III] is well characterized by Friedman's plucking model of business fluctuations. Figures 5.6 and 5.7 depict the trend and the cyclical components of real GDP as implied by Friedman's plucking model. For further discussion and an analysis of the unemployment rate series, refer to Kim and Nelson 1997.

5.7 Application 3: A Dynamic Factor Model with Markov Switching: Business Cycle Turning Points and a New Coincident Index

In their pioneering study, Burns and Mitchell (1946) established two defining characteristics of the business cycle: comovement among economic variables through the cycle and nonlinearity in the evolution of the business cycle, that is, regime switching at the turning points of the business cycle. As noted by Diebold and Rudebusch (1996), these two aspects of the business cycle have generally been considered in isolation from one another in the lit-

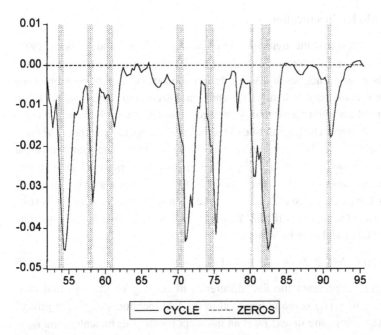

Figure 5.7
Asymmetric transitory component based on a plucking model

erature. Two of the most recent and influential examples include Stock and
Watson's (1989, 1991, 1993) linear dynamic factor model and Hamilton's
(1989) regime-switching model. In Stock and Watson's dynamic factor model,
introduced in chapter 3, comovement among economic variables is captured
by a composite index, and Hamilton's regime-switching model introduced in
chapter 4, features nonlinearity in an individual economic variable. After an
extensive survey of related literature, and based on both theoretical and empirical foundations, Diebold and Rudebusch proposed a multivariate dynamic
factor model with regime switching that encompasses the two key features
of the business cycle. In this section, we deal with inferences on the dynamic factor model with Markov switching based on Kim's (1994) approximate MLE, as successfully implemented by M. Kim and Yoo (1995) and
Chauvet (1997). Kim and Nelson's (1998b) approach via Bayesian Gibbs-
sampling to approximation-free inferences of the same model is discussed
in chapter 10. The following section is taken from section 2 of Kim and
Nelson 1998b.

5.7.1 Model Specification

In the synthesis of the dynamic factor model of Stock and Watson (1989, 1991, 1993) and the regime-switching model of Hamilton (1989) proposed by Diebold and Rudebusch (1996), the growth rate of each of four observed individual coincident indicators depends on current and lagged values of an unobserved common factor that is interpreted as the composite index of coincident indicators. The growth rate of the index is in turn dependent on whether the economy is in the recession state or the boom state. The four coincident indicators involved are industrial production (IP), total personal income less transfer payments in 1987 dollars (GMYXPQ), total manufacturing and trade sales in 1987 dollars (MTQ), and employees on nonagricultural payrolls (LP-NAG). The abbreviations IP, GMYXPQ, MTQ, and LPNAG are DRI variable names. The model may be written as

$$\Delta Y_{it} = \gamma_i(L)\Delta C_t + D_i + e_{it}, \quad i = 1, 2, 3, 4, \tag{5.80}$$

where ΔY_{it} represents the first difference of the log of the i-th indicator, $i = 1, \ldots, 4$; $\gamma_i(L)$ is the polynomial in the lag operator; ΔC_t is the growth rate of the composite index; D_i is an intercept for the i-th indicator; and e_{it} is a process with AR representation:

$$\psi_i(L)e_{it} = \epsilon_{it}, \quad \epsilon_{it} \sim \text{i.i.d.} N(0, \sigma_i^2). \tag{5.81}$$

Thus, each indicator ΔY_{it}, $i = 1, 2, 3, 4$, consists of an individual component $(D_i + e_{it})$ and a linear combination of current and lagged values of the common factor or index (ΔC_t). In Kim and Nelson 1998, the common factor is assumed to be generated by an AR process with a long-run growth and Markov-switching deviations from the long-run growth,

$$\phi(L)(\Delta C_t - \mu_{s_t} - \delta) = v_t, \quad v_t \sim \text{i.i.d.} N(0, 1), \tag{5.82}$$

v_t and ϵ_{it} are independent of one another for all t and i, and the variance of v_t is taken to be unity for identification of the model. Whereas δ is constant over time, μ_{s_t} depends on whether the economy is in a recession ($S_t = 0$) or a boom ($S_t = 1$), as follows:

$$\mu_{s_t} = \mu_0 + \mu_1 S_t, \quad \mu_1 > 0, \ S_t = \{0, 1\}. \tag{5.83}$$

Transitions between regimes or states of the economy are then governed by the following Markov process:

$$Pr[S_t = 1 \mid S_{t-1} = 1] = p, \quad Pr[S_t = 0 \mid S_{t-1} = 0] = q. \tag{5.84}$$

This model differs from Stock and Watson's (1991) linear dynamic factor model of the business cycle, discussed in chapter 3, by allowing the mean growth rate of the coincident index, given by $(\mu_{s_t} + \delta)$, to switch between the two regimes of the business cycle. We note that the means of the variables are overdetermined in this parameterization. Imposing a mean of 0 on the μ_{s_t} process, δ determines the long-run growth rate of the index and μ_{s_t} produces deviations from that long-run growth rate according to whether the economy is in a recession or a boom.

Because the parameters D_i, $i = 1, 2, 3, 4$, and δ overdetermine the means of the processes, as alluded to above, the model is not identified. However, when the data are expressed as deviations from means ($\Delta y_{it} = \Delta Y_{it} - \Delta \bar{Y}_i$), equations (5.80)–(5.82) can be replaced by

$$\Delta y_{it} = \gamma_i(L)\Delta c_t + e_{it}, \quad i = 1, 2, 3, 4, \tag{5.85}$$

$$\phi(L)(\Delta c_t - \mu_{s_t}) = v_t, \tag{5.86}$$

where $\Delta c_t = \Delta C_t - \delta$. Notice that we have

$$\Delta \bar{Y}_i = D_i + \gamma_i(1)\delta. \tag{5.87}$$

By putting (5.85) and (5.86) into state-space form, one can readily apply Kim's (1994) approximate MLE, introduced earlier in this chapter, to estimate the model's parameters. We adopt second-order autoregressive specifications for the error processes of both the common component and the four idiosyncratic components in (5.86) and (5.81): $\phi(L) = (1 - \phi_1 L - \phi_2 L^2)$ and $\psi_i(L) = (1 - \psi_{i1}L - \psi_{i2}L^2)$, $i = 1, 2, 3, 4$. Stock and Watson (1989, 1991) point out that the payroll variable, Δy_{4t}, may not be exactly coincident, but slightly lagging the unobserved common component. Following them, we adopt $\gamma_i(L) = \gamma_i$, for $i = 1, 2, 3$, and $\gamma_4(L) = \gamma_{40} + \gamma_{41}L + \gamma_{42}L^2 + \gamma_{43}L^3$. Then the state-space representation of the model is given by

$$y_t = H\beta_t, \tag{5.88}$$

$$\beta_t = M_{\phi(L)S_t} + F\beta_{t-1} + v_t, \tag{5.89}$$

or

Measurement Equation

$$
\begin{bmatrix} \Delta y_{1t} \\ \Delta y_{2t} \\ \Delta y_{3t} \\ \Delta y_{4t} \end{bmatrix} = \begin{bmatrix} \gamma_1 & 0 & 0 & 0 & 1 & 0 & 0 & 0 & 0 & 0 & 0 & 0 \\ \gamma_2 & 0 & 0 & 0 & 0 & 0 & 1 & 0 & 0 & 0 & 0 & 0 \\ \gamma_3 & 0 & 0 & 0 & 0 & 0 & 0 & 0 & 1 & 0 & 0 & 0 \\ \gamma_{40} & \gamma_{41} & \gamma_{42} & \gamma_{43} & 0 & 0 & 0 & 0 & 0 & 0 & 1 & 0 \end{bmatrix} \begin{bmatrix} \Delta c_t \\ \Delta c_{t-1} \\ \Delta c_{t-2} \\ \Delta c_{t-3} \\ e_{1t} \\ e_{1,t-1} \\ e_{2t} \\ e_{2,t-1} \\ e_{3t} \\ e_{3,t-1} \\ e_{4t} \\ e_{4,t-1} \end{bmatrix}
$$

$$(5.90)$$

Transition Equation

$$
\begin{bmatrix} \Delta c_t \\ \Delta c_{t-1} \\ \Delta c_{t-2} \\ \Delta c_{t-3} \\ e_{1t} \\ e_{1,t-1} \\ \vdots \\ e_{4t} \\ e_{4,t-1} \end{bmatrix} = \begin{bmatrix} \phi(L)\mu_{s_t} \\ 0 \\ 0 \\ 0 \\ 0 \\ 0 \\ \vdots \\ 0 \\ 0 \end{bmatrix}
$$

$$
+ \begin{bmatrix} \phi_1 & \phi_2 & 0 & 0 & 0 & 0 & \cdots & 0 & 0 \\ 1 & 0 & 0 & 0 & 0 & 0 & \cdots & 0 & 0 \\ 0 & 1 & 0 & 0 & 0 & 0 & \cdots & 0 & 0 \\ 0 & 0 & 1 & 0 & 0 & 0 & \cdots & 0 & 0 \\ 0 & 0 & 0 & 0 & \psi_{11} & \psi_{12} & \cdots & 0 & 0 \\ 0 & 0 & 0 & 0 & 1 & 0 & \cdots & 0 & 0 \\ \vdots & \vdots & \vdots & \vdots & \vdots & \vdots & \ddots & \vdots & \vdots \\ 0 & 0 & 0 & 0 & 0 & 0 & \cdots & \psi_{41} & \psi_{42} \\ 0 & 0 & 0 & 0 & 0 & 0 & \cdots & 1 & 0 \end{bmatrix} \begin{bmatrix} \Delta c_{t-1} \\ \Delta c_{t-2} \\ \Delta c_{t-3} \\ \Delta c_{t-4} \\ e_{1,t-1} \\ e_{1,t-2} \\ \vdots \\ e_{4,t-1} \\ e_{4,t-2} \end{bmatrix} + \begin{bmatrix} v_t \\ 0 \\ 0 \\ 0 \\ \epsilon_{1t} \\ 0 \\ \vdots \\ \epsilon_{4t} \\ 0 \end{bmatrix}, \quad (5.91)
$$

where $\phi(L)\mu_{s_t} = \mu_{s_t} - \phi_1 \mu_{s_{t-1}} - \phi_2 \mu_{s_{t-2}}$.

5.7.2   An Empirical Model and Approximate MLE

When current and r-lagged Markov-switching variables show up in a state-space model with M-state Markov-switching variables, Kim (1994) recommends carrying at least M^{r+1} states at each interation of the Kalman filter. In the state-space representation of the model presented in section 5.7.1, the current and two lagged state variables, S_t, S_{t-1}, and S_{t-2}, show up. Because S_t is a two-state Markov-switching variable in our present application, we may have to carry at least 2^3 states at each iteration of the Kalman filter. Instead M.-J. Kim and Yoo (1995) and Chauvet (1995) assume that the intercept term of the common component, not the mean of the common component, is Markov switching. Equation (5.86) is modified as follows:

$$\phi(L)\Delta c_t = \mu_{S_t} + v_t, \tag{5.86'}$$

which results in a state-space representation of the model that depends only on S_t, allowing one to carry only 2^2 states at each iteration of the Kalman filter. The transition equation in (5.89) is replaced by

$$\beta_t = M_{S_t} + F\beta_{t-1} + v_t, \tag{5.89'}$$

where $M_{\phi(L)S_t}$ is replaced by $M_{S_t} = [\ \mu_{S_t} \quad 0 \quad 0 \quad \dots \quad 0\ ]'$ in (5.91).

   Table 5.4 presents parameter estimates of the model that results from an application of Kim's (1994) approximate MLE carrying 2^2 states. Of particular interest in this section would be an inference on C_t, $t = 1, 2, \dots, T$, the new coincident index. However, one potential difficulty in applying Kim's filter is that the effects of approximations employed on the steady state Kalman gain are unknown, and this complicates the task of decomposing $\Delta \bar{Y}_i$ into D_i and δ, which is necessary to extract the new composite coincident index, $C_t = C_{t-1} + \Delta c_t + \delta$.

   Thus, based on $\Delta c_{t|t}$, estimates of Δc_t conditional on information up to t, from the filter, the new coincident index is calculated so that its first difference has the same mean and standard deviation as the first difference of the DOC coincident index:

$$C_t = C_{t-1} + \Delta c_{t|t} * SD(\Delta C_t^{DOC})/SD(\Delta c_{t|t}) + \text{Mean}(\Delta C_t^{DOC}), \tag{5.92}$$

where $SD(\Delta C_t^{DOC})$ and $\text{Mean}(\Delta C_t^{DOC})$ refer to standard deviation and mean of the first differences of the DOC coincident index, respectively, and $SD(\Delta c_{t|t})$ refers to standard deviation of $\Delta c_{t|t}$. The new index is then adjusted so that it is equal to the value of the DOC index in January 1970.

Table 5.4
Parameter estimates of the dynamic factor model of coincident indicators with Markov switching

Variables	Parameters	Estimates	
ΔC_t	q	0.8409	(0.0664)
	p	0.9728	(0.0107)
	ϕ_1	0.3459	(0.0776)
	ϕ_2	−0.0299	(0.0134)
	μ_0	−1.4986	(0.1758)
	μ_1	0.2619	(0.0712)
Δ_{1t}	ψ_{11}	−0.0169	(0.0585)
	ψ_{12}	−0.0001	(0.0005)
	γ_1	0.5584	(0.0375)
Δ_{2t}	σ_1^2	0.5082	(0.0317)
	ψ_{21}	−0.3199	(0.0507)
	ψ_{22}	−0.0256	(0.0081)
	γ_2	0.2151	(0.0205)
	σ_2^2	0.5535	(0.0193)
Δ_{3t}	ψ_{31}	−0.3612	(0.0548)
	ψ_{32}	−0.0326	(0.0099)
	γ_3	0.4468	(0.0310)
	σ_3^2	0.8029	(0.0314)
Δ_{4t}	ψ_{41}	−0.1044	(0.0841)
	ψ_{42}	0.2640	(0.0891)
	γ_4	0.1223	(0.0095)
	γ_{41}	0.0114	(0.0111)
	γ_{42}	0.0110	(0.0110)
	γ_{43}	0.0406	(0.0085)
	σ_4^2	0.1360	(0.0076)
Log likelihood	315.19		

Note: Standard errors are in parentheses.

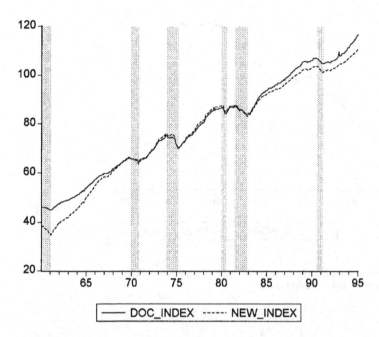

Figure 5.8
New coincident index from dynamic factor model with Markov switching versus
DOC coincident index

Figures 5.8 and 5.9 depict the new coincident index from this section against
the DOC coincident index and the Stock and Watson coincident index from
section 3.5, respectively. The new index is remarkably close to the Stock and
Watson index. Figures 5.10 and 5.11 depict filtered and smoothed probabilities
respectively, of recessions that result from the model. These probabilities are in
close agreement with the NBER reference cycle, as represented by the shaded
area.

Appendix: GAUSS Programs to Accompany Chapter 5

1. KIM_JE0.OPT: A state-space representation of Lam's (1990) generalized
Hamilton model and Kim's (1994) filter (original version: treats the elements
of initial state vector as unknown parameters to be estimated).

2. KIM_JE1.OPT: A state-space representation of Lam's (1990) generalized
Hamilton model and Kim's (1994) filter (easier version).

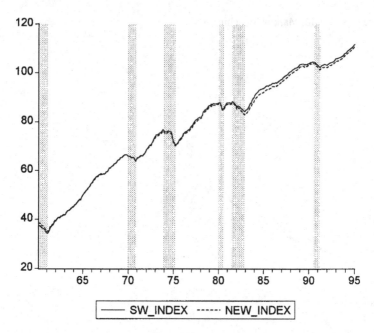

Figure 5.9
New coincident index from dynamic factor model with Markov switching versus
the Stock and Watson coincident index

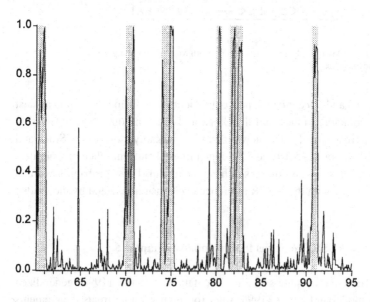

Figure 5.10
Filtered probability of a recession based on information up to t:
dynamic factor model with Markov switching

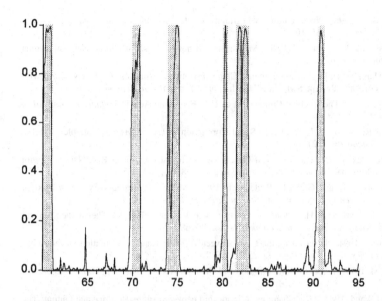

Figure 5.11
Smoothed probability of a recession based on information up to T:
dynamic factor model with Markov switching

3. TVPMRKF.OPT: Time-varying-parameter model with Markov-switching heteroskedasticity (based on Kim 1993b).

4. TVPM_JNT.OPT: Time-varying-parameter model with Markov-switching heteroskedasticity (based on Kim 1993; a joint estimation of the output equation and the monetary growth equation).

5. SW_MS.OPT: Dynamic factor model with Markov switching (a new coincident index); an application of Kim's (1994) algorithm by Chauvet (1997) and M.-J. Kim and Yoo (1995).

References

Barro, R. J. 1976. "Rational Expectations and the Role of Monetary Policy." *Journal of Monetary Economics,* 2, 1–32.

Bar-Shalom, Y. 1978. "Tracking Methods in a Multi-Target Environment." *IEEE Trans. Automatic Control,* AC-23, 618–626.

Beaudry, P., and G. Koop. 1993. "Do Recessions Permanently Change Output?" *Journal of Monetary Economics.* 31, 149–163.

Bernanke, Ben S. 1983. "Irreversibility, Uncertainty, and Cyclical Investment." *Quarterly Journal of Economics,* February, 85–106.

Burns, A. F., and W. C. Mitchell. 1946. "Measuring Business Cycles." New York: National Bureau of Economic Research.

Chauvet, Marcelle. 1997. "An Econometric Characterization of Business Cycle Dynamics with Factor Structure and Regime Switching." Forthcoming, *International Economic Review*

Clark, P. K. 1987. "The Cyclical Component of U.S. Economic Activity." *Quarterly Journal of Economics,* 102, 797–814.

Cosslett, S. R., and L.-F. Lee. 1985. " Serial Correlation in Latent Discrete Variable Models." *Journal of Econometrics,* 27, 79–97.

Cukierman, Alex. 1980. "The Effects of Uncertainty on Investment Under Risk Neutrality with Endogenous Information." *Journal of Political Economy,* 88(3), 462–475

Diebold, Francis X., and Glenn D. Rudebusch. 1996. "Measuring Business Cycles: A Modern Perspective." *Review of Economics and Statistics,* 78, 67–77.

Engel, Charles, and James Hamilton. 1990. "Long Swings in the Dollar: Are They in the Data and Do Markets Know It?" *American Economic Review,* 80, 689–713.

Evans, Martin. 1991. "Discovering the Link between Inflation Rates and Inflation Uncertainty." *Journal of Money, Credit, and Banking,* 23(2), 169–184.

Friedman, M. 1977. "Nobel Lecture: Inflation and Unemployment." *Journal of Political Economy,* 85, 451–472.

Froyen and Waud. 1984. "The Changing Relationship between Aggregate Price and Output: The British Experience." *Economica,* 51, 53–67.

Garbade, K. 1977. "Two Methods for Examining the Stability of Regression Coefficients." *Journal of the American Statistical Association,* 72(357), Applications Section, 54–63.

Goodwin, T. H., and R. J. Sweeney. 1993. "International Evidence on Friedman's Theory of the Business Cycle." *Economic Inquiry,* April, 178–193.

Gordon, K., and A. F. M. Smith. 1988. "Modeling and Monitoring Discontinuous Changes in Time Series." In *Bayesian Analysis of Time Series and Dynamic Linear Models,* ed. J. C. Spall, pp. 359–392, New York: Marcel Dekker.

Hamilton, James. 1988. "Rational Expectations Econometric Analysis of Changes in Regimes: An Investigation of the Term Structure of Interest Rates." *Journal of Economic Dynamics and Control,* 12, 385–432.

Hamilton, James. 1989. "A New Approach to the Economic Analysis of Nonstationary Time Series and the Business Cycle." *Econometrica,* 57(2), 357–384.

Hamilton, James. 1984. "State-Spare Models." In *Handbook of Econometrics,* Vol. 4, ed. Robert F. Engle and Daniel McFadden. Amsterdam: Elsevier Science Publishing Co. 3041–3081.

Harrison, P. J., and C. F. Stevens. 1976. "Bayesian Forecasting." *Journal of the Royal Statistical Society,* Series B, 38, 205–247.

Harvey, Andrew C. 1989. *Forecasting, Structural Time Series Models and the Kalman Filter.* Cambridge: Cambridge University Press.

Henry, Claude. 1974. "Investment Decisions under Uncertainty: The Irreversibility Effect." *American Economic Review,* (64(6), 1006–1012.

Highfield, R. A. 1990. "Bayesian Approaches to Turning Point Prediction." In *Proceedings of the Business and Economics Section,* pp. 89–98 Washington: American Statistical Association.

Kendall, Maurice G. and Alan Stuart. 1973. *The Advanced Theory of Statistics.* Vol. 2. 3d ed. New York: Hafner Publishing Co.

Kim, Chang-Jin. 1993a. "Unobserved-Component Time Series Models with Markov-Switching Heteroskedasticity: Changes in Regime and the Link between Inflation Rates and Inflation Uncertainty." *Journal of Business and Economic Statistics.* 11, 341–349.

Kim, Chang-Jin. 1993b. "Sources of Monetary Growth Uncertainty and Economic Activity: The Time-Varying-Parameter Model with Heteroskedastic Disturbances." *Review of Economics and Statistics,* 75, 483–492.

Kim, Chang-Jin. 1994. "Dynamic Linear Models with Markov-Switching." *Journal of Econometrics,* 60, 1–22.

Kim, Chang-Jin, and Charles R. Nelson. 1989. "The Time-Varying-Parameter Model for Modeling Changing Conditional Variance: The Case of the Lucas Hypothesis." *Journal of Business and Economic Statistics,* 7(4), 433–440.

Kim, Chang-Jin, and Charles R. Nelson. 1998a. "Friedman's Plucking Model of Business Fluctuations: Tests and Estimates of Permanent and Transitory Components." Forthcoming, *Journal of Money, Credit, and Banking.*

Kim, Chang-Jin and Charles R. Nelson. 1998b. "Business Cycle Turning Points, A New Coincident Index, and Tests of Duration Dependence Based on A Dynamic Factor Model with Regime-Switching." *Review of Economics and Economic Statistics,* 80, 188–201.

Kim, Myung-Jig, and Ji-Sung Yoo. 1995. "New Index of Coincident Indicators: A Multivariate Markov Switching Factor Model Approach." *Journal of Monetary Economics,* 36, 607–630.

Kitagawa, Genshiro. 1987. "Non-Gaussian State-Space Modeling of Nonstationary Time Series." *Journal of American Statistical Association,* 82(400), Theory and Method, 1032–1063.

Kuttner, Kenneth N. 1994. "Estimating Potential Output as a Latent Variable." *Journal of Business and Economic Statistics,* 12(3), 361–368.

Lam, Pok-sang. 1990. "The Hamilton Model with a General Autoregressive Component: Estimation and Comparison with Other Models of Economic Time Series." *Journal of Monetary Economics,* 26, 409–432.

Leybourne, S. J., and B. P. M. McCabe. 1989. "On the Distribution of Some Test Statistics for Coefficient Constancy." *Biometrika,* 76, 169–177.

Lucas, R. E., Jr. 1973. "Some International Evidence on Output-Inflation Tradeoffs." *American Economic Review,* 63, 326–334.

Makin, John H. 1982. "Anticipated Money, Inflation Uncertainty and Real Economic Activity." *Review of Economics and Statistics,* 64, 126–134.

Mishkin, F. 1982. "Does Anticipated Monetary Policy Matter? An Econometric Investigation." *Journal of Political Economy,* 90, 22–51.

Nabeya, S., and K. Tanaka. 1990. "Asymptotic Theory of a Test for Constancy of Regression Coefficients against the Random Walk Alternative." *The Annals of Statistics,* 16, 218–235.

Nyblom, J. 1989. "Testing for the Constancy of Parameters of Time." *Journal of American Statistical Association,* 84, 223–230.

Pagan, Adrian. 1984. "Econometric Issues in the Analysis of Regressions with Generated Regressors." *International Economic Review,* 25(1), 221–247.

Pindyck, Robert. 1988. "Irreversible Investment, Capacity Choice, and the Value of the Firm." *The American Economic Review,* 78(5), 969–985.

Shumway, R. H., and D. S. Stoffer. 1991. "Dynamic Linear Models with Switching." *Journal of American Statistical Association,* 86, 763–769.

Sichel, D. E. 1994. "Inventories and the Three Phases of the Business Cycle." *Journal of Business and Economic Statistics,* 12(3), 269–277.

Smith, A. F. M., and U. E. Makov. 1980. "Bayesian Detection and Estimation of Jumps in Linear Systems." In *Analysis and Optimization of Stochastic Systems,* ed. O. L. R. Jacobs, M. H. A. Davis, M. A. H. Dempster, C. J. Harris, and P. C. Parks. New York: Academic Press. pp. 333–345.

Stock, James H., and Mark W. Watson. 1989. "New Indexes of Coincident and Leading Economic Indicators." In *NBER Macroeconomics Annual,* eds. O. Blanchard and S. Fischer. Cambridge: MIT Press, 351–394.

Stock, James H., and Mark W. Watson. 1991. "A Probability Model of the Coincident Economic Indicators." In *Leading Economic Indicators: New Approaches and Forecasting Records,* K. Lahiri and G. H. Moore. Cambridge: Cambridge University Press, 63–89.

Stock, James H., and Mark W. Watson. 1993. "A Procedure for Predicting Recessions with Leading Indicators: Econometric Issues and Recent Experience." In *Business Cycles, Indicators and Forecasting,* J. H. Stock and M. W. Watson, Chicago: University of Chicago Press for NBER, 255–284.

Watson, M. W. 1986. "Univariate Detrending Methods with Stochastic Trends." *Journal of Monetary Economics,* 18, 29–75.

6 State-Space Models with Heteroskedastic Disturbances

Consider the following state-space model for an $n \times 1$ vector of observations y_t:

$$y_t = H_t \beta_t + A_t z_t + e_t, \tag{6.1}$$

$$\beta_t = \tilde{\mu}_t + F_t \beta_{t-1} + v_t, \tag{6.2}$$

$$\begin{pmatrix} e_t \\ v_t \end{pmatrix} \sim N \left(0, \begin{pmatrix} R_t & 0 \\ 0 & Q_t \end{pmatrix} \right), \tag{6.3}$$

where β_t is a $k \times 1$ vector of unobserved state variables; H_t is an $n \times k$ matrix that links the observed y_t vector and the unobserved β_t; z_t is an $r \times 1$ vector of exogenous or predetermined variables; $\tilde{\mu}_t$ is $k \times 1$; and v_t is $k \times 1$.

The preceding model is called *time invariant* or *time homogeneous* if the subscripts on H_t, A_t, $\tilde{\mu}_t$, F_t, R_t, and Q_t can be dropped. This time-invariant model has been employed in many applications of the state space-model and the Kalman filter, as in chapter 3. Kim (1994) considers cases in which some of the parameters in these matrices may be Markov switching, and these are dealt with in chapter 5.

In this chapter, we focus on models in which the disturbance terms of the measurement and/or transition equations are heteroskedastic. We consider two different types of heteroskedasticity: ARCH-type conditional heteroskedasticity and Markov-switching heteroskedasticity. These two types of heteroskedasticity are fundamentally different. First, the unconditional variance is constant under ARCH but subject to abrupt shifts under Markov-switching heteroskedasticity. Second, as suggested by Hamilton and Susmel (1994), whereas long-run variance dynamics may be governed by regime shifts (or Markov switching) in unconditional variance, short-run variance dynamics within a regime may be governed by an ARCH-type process. Thus, Markov-switching heteroskedasticity may be more appropriate for low-frequency data over a long period of time, whereas ARCH-type heteroskedasticity may be more appropriate for high-frequency data over a short period of time. However, for a given time series, it may be difficult to distinguish statistically between the two types of heteroskedasticity, because the two models are non-nested. Besides, even though the unconditional variance is not defined for an integrated ARCH or an integrated GARCH, Diebold (1986), Lastrapes (1989), Lamoureux and Lastrapes (1990), and others suggest that a failure to allow for regime shifts leads to an overstatement of the persistence of the variance of a series, possibly leading to an integrated ARCH or GARCH.

In section 6.1, we discuss state-space models with ARCH-type conditional heteroskedasticity as developed by Harvey, Ruiz, and Sentana (1992). An example is provided in the context of a time-varying-parameter model with GARCH disturbances. In section 6.2, we discuss Kim's (1993a) state-space models with Markov-switching heteroskedasticity, which may be considered a straightforward generalization of Kim 1994. We then deal with specific applications of Markov-switching heteroskedasticity to issues related to the inflation series and stock prices in sections 6.3 and 6.4.

6.1   State-Space Models with ARCH Disturbances

6.1.1   Model Specification

We consider the following state-space model with ARCH disturbances proposed by Harvey, Ruiz, and Sentana (1992):

$$y_t = H\beta_t + Az_t + \epsilon_t + \Lambda\epsilon_t^*, \tag{6.4}$$

$$\beta_t = \tilde{\mu} + F\beta_{t-1} + \omega_t + \lambda\omega_t^*, \tag{6.5}$$

$$\epsilon_t \sim N(0, R), \qquad \omega_t \sim N(0, Q), \tag{6.6}$$

where Λ is $n \times 1$ and λ is $k \times 1$, and ϵ_t^* and ω_t^* are 1×1. Dimensions of all the other matrices are the same as before.

This model differs from the usual time-invariant model in chapter 3 by an addition of the $\Lambda\epsilon_t^*$ and $\lambda\omega_t^*$ terms. The ARCH effects are introduced via the following scalar disturbances:

$$\epsilon_t^*|\psi_{t-1} \sim N(0, h_{1t}), \tag{6.7}$$

$$\omega_t^*|\psi_{t-1} \sim N(0, h_{2t}), \tag{6.8}$$

where, for simplicity, an ARCH(1) is assumed for h_{1t} and h_{2t}, and ψ_{t-1} refers to information up to $t - 1$:

$$h_{1t} = \alpha_0 + \alpha_1\epsilon_{t-1}^{*}{}^2, \tag{6.9}$$

$$h_{2t} = \gamma_0 + \gamma_1\omega_{t-1}^{*}{}^2. \tag{6.10}$$

Λ and λ are the loading matrices that determine which individual shocks in the system are subject to ARCH effects. Note that Λ and α_0 (λ and γ_0) cannot both be identidied. Thus, for example, α_0 (γ_0) needs to be normalized.

If, for example, $\Lambda = 0_n$ and $\lambda = 0_k$, then there is no ARCH effect and the model reduces to the usual time-invariant model. If the first element of Λ is nonzero with the others being zero, only the first shock in the measurement equation is subject to an ARCH effect. If all the elements of Λ are nonzero, then all the shocks in the measurement equation are subject to a common ARCH effect. The same argument applies for the transition equation.

In addition, if we define

$$e_t = \epsilon_t + \Lambda \epsilon_t^*, \tag{6.11}$$

$$v_t = \omega_t + \lambda \omega_t^*, \tag{6.12}$$

then we have

$$e_t | \psi_{t-1} \sim N(0, R_t), \tag{6.13}$$

$$v_t | \psi_{t-1} \sim N(0, Q_t), \tag{6.14}$$

where

$$R_t = R + \Lambda h_{1t} \Lambda' \quad \text{and} \quad Q_t = Q + \lambda h_{2t} \lambda' \tag{6.15}$$

6.1.2   Difficulties Associated with Inference and a Solution Based on Approximations

Given the model's parameters, let us consider the linear Kalman filter introduced in chapter 3. The linear Kalman filter for the model introduced in the previous section consists of the following six equations:

$$\beta_{t|t-1} = \tilde{\mu} + F\beta_{t-1|t-1} \tag{6.16}$$

$$P_{t|t-1} = FP_{t-1|t-1}F' + Q + \lambda h_{2t}\lambda', \tag{6.17}$$

$$\eta_{t|t-1} = y_t - H\beta_{t|t-1} - Az_t, \tag{6.18}$$

$$f_{t|t-1} = HP_{t|t-1}H' + R + \Lambda h_{1t}\Lambda', \tag{6.19}$$

$$\beta_{t|t} = \beta_{t|t-1} + P_{t|t-1}H'f_{t|t-1}^{-1}\eta_{t|t-1}, \tag{6.20}$$

$$P_{t|t} = P_{t|t-1} - P_{t|t-1}H'f_{t|t-1}^{-1}HP_{t|t-1}. \tag{6.21}$$

To process equations (6.17) and (6.19), however, we need to calculate $h_{1t} = \alpha_0 + \alpha_1\epsilon_{t-1}^{*2}$ and $h_{2t} = \gamma_0 + \gamma_1\omega_{t-1}^{*2}$, which are functions of the squares of past unobserved shocks ϵ_{t-1}^{*2} and ω_{t-1}^{*2}. Thus, the above Kalman filter is not operable.

Harvey, Ruiz, and Sentana (1992) solve the problem of the unobserved ${\epsilon_{t-1}^*}^2$ and ${\omega_{t-1}^*}^2$ by replacing them with their conditional expectations:

$$h_{1t} = \alpha_0 + \alpha_1 E[{\epsilon_{t-1}^*}^2|\psi_{t-1}], \tag{6.22}$$

$$h_{2t} = \gamma_0 + \gamma_1 E[{\omega_{t-1}^*}^2|\psi_{t-1}]. \tag{6.23}$$

Thus, their algorithm involves approximations. To get the conditional expectations of the squares of the unobserved shocks of interest, Harvey, Ruiz, and Sentana augment the heteroskedastic shocks into the original state vector in the transition equation in the following way:

$$\begin{bmatrix} \beta_t \\ \epsilon_t^* \\ \omega_t^* \end{bmatrix} = \begin{bmatrix} \tilde{\mu} \\ 0 \\ 0 \end{bmatrix} + \begin{bmatrix} F & 0_k & 0_k \\ 0_k' & 0 & 0 \\ 0_k' & 0 & 0 \end{bmatrix} \begin{bmatrix} \beta_{t-1} \\ \epsilon_{t-1}^* \\ \omega_{t-1}^* \end{bmatrix} + \begin{bmatrix} I_k & 0_k & \lambda \\ 0_k' & 1 & 0 \\ 0_k' & 0 & 1 \end{bmatrix} \begin{bmatrix} \omega_t \\ \epsilon_t^* \\ \omega_t^* \end{bmatrix}, \tag{6.24}$$

$$(\beta_t^* = \tilde{\mu}^* + F^*\beta_{t-1}^* + G^*v_t^*), \tag{6.24'}$$

where

$$E[v_t^* v_t^{*\prime}|\psi_{t-1}] = \begin{bmatrix} Q & 0_k & 0_k \\ 0_k' & h_{1t} & 0 \\ 0_k' & 0 & h_{2t} \end{bmatrix} = Q_t^*, \tag{6.25}$$

where 0_k is a $k \times 1$ vector of zeros. Then, the measurement equation should be replaced by

$$y_t = [\, H \quad \Lambda \quad 0_n \,] \begin{bmatrix} \beta_t \\ \epsilon_t^* \\ \omega_t^* \end{bmatrix} + Az_t + \epsilon_t, \tag{6.26}$$

$$(y_t = H^*\beta_t^* + Az_t + \epsilon_t), \tag{6.26'}$$

where 0_n is an $n \times 1$ vector of 0s and

$$E(\epsilon_t \epsilon_t') = R. \tag{6.27}$$

Applying the Kalman filter recursions to the model given by (6.24'), (6.25), (6.26'), and (6.27), we have

$$\beta^*_{t|t-1} = \tilde{\mu}^* + F^*\beta^*_{t-1|t-1}, \tag{6.28}$$

$$P^*_{t|t-1} = F^*P^*_{t-1|t-1}F^{*'} + G^*Q^*_tG^{*'}, \tag{6.29}$$

$$\eta^*_{t|t-1} = y_t - H^*\beta^*_{t|t-1} - Az_t, \tag{6.30}$$

$$f^*_{t|t-1} = H^*P^*_{t|t-1}H^{*'} + R, \tag{6.31}$$

$$\beta^*_{t|t} = \beta^*_{t|t-1} + P^*_{t|t-1}H^{*'}f^{*-1}_{t|t-1}\eta^*_{t|t-1}, \tag{6.32}$$

$$P^*_{t|t} = P^*_{t|t-1} - P^*_{t|t-1}H^{*'}f^{*-1}_{t|t-1}H^*P^*_{t|t-1}. \tag{6.33}$$

To process the above Kalman filter, we need

$$h_{1t} = \alpha_0 + \alpha_1 E[\epsilon^{*2}_{t-1}|\psi_{t-1}]$$

and

$$h_{2t} = \gamma_0 + \gamma_1 E[\omega^{*2}_{t-1}|\psi_{t-1}]$$

in the Q^*_t matrix of equation (6.29).

Under this specification, calculation of the terms,

$$E[\epsilon^{*2}_{t-1}|\psi_{t-1}]$$

and

$$E[\omega^{*2}_{t-1}|\psi_{t-1}]$$

is straightforward. Because we know

$$\epsilon^*_{t-1} = E[\epsilon^*_{t-1}|\psi_{t-1}] + (\epsilon_{t-1} - E[\epsilon^*_{t-1}|\psi_{t-1}]) \tag{6.34}$$

and

$$\omega^*_{t-1} = E[\omega^*_{t-1}|\psi_{t-1}] + (\omega_{t-1} - E[\omega^*_{t-1}|\psi_{t-1}]), \tag{6.35}$$

it is easy to show that

$$E[\epsilon^{*2}_{t-1}|\psi_{t-1}] = E[\epsilon^*_{t-1}|\psi_{t-1}]^2 + E[(\epsilon^*_{t-1} - E(\epsilon^*_{t-1}|\psi_{t-1}))^2], \tag{6.36}$$

$$E[\omega^{*2}_{t-1}|\psi_{t-1}] = E[\omega^*_{t-1}|\psi_{t-1}]^2 + E[(\omega^*_{t-1} - E(\omega^*_{t-1}|\psi_{t-1}))^2], \tag{6.37}$$

where $E[\epsilon^*_{t-1}|\psi_{t-1}]$ and $E[\omega^*_{t-1}|\psi_{t-1}]$ are obtained from the last two elements of $\beta^*_{t-1|t-1}$ and their mean squared errors, $E[(\epsilon_{t-1} - E(\epsilon_{t-1}|\psi_{t-1}))^2]$ and

$E[(\omega_{t-1} - E(\omega_{t-1}|\psi_{t-1}))^2]$, are obtained from the last two diagonal elements of $P^*_{t-1|t-1}$.

As by-products of the above Kalman filter, we obtain the prediction error $(\eta^*_{t|t-1})$ and its variance $(f^*_{t|t-1})$ from equations (6.30) and (6.31). Based on this prediction error decomposition, the approximate log likelihood can easily be calculated as

$$\ln L = -\frac{1}{2}\sum_{t=1}^{T}\ln((2\pi)^n|f^*_{t|t-1}|) - \frac{1}{2}\sum_{t=1}^{T}\eta^{*\prime}_{t|t-1}f^{*\ -1}_{t|t-1}\eta^*_{t|t-1}, \qquad (6.38)$$

which can be maximized with respect to the unknown parameters of the model for an approximate MLE.

6.1.3   An Example: A Time-Varying-Parameter Model with GARCH Disturbances

In modeling the U.S. monetary growth function [1962:I–1989:II] in section 5.5, we considered a time-varying-parameter model with Markov-switching heteroskedasticity. A natural alternative would be a time-varying-parameter model with GARCH disturbances of the following form:

$$\Delta M_t = X_{t-1}\beta_t + \epsilon^*_t, \qquad (6.39)$$

$$\beta_t = \beta_{t-1} + v_t, \qquad (6.40)$$

$$\epsilon^*_t|\psi_{t-1} \sim N(0, h_t), \qquad (6.41)$$

$$h_t = \alpha_0 + \alpha_1 \epsilon^{*\ 2}_{t-1} + \alpha_2 h_{t-1}, \qquad (6.42)$$

$$v_t \sim N(0, Q), \qquad (6.43)$$

where X_{t-1} is a 1×5 vector of explanatory variables and the scalar shock ϵ^*_t in the measurement equation is subject to GARCH(1,1).

A straightforward application of section 6.1.2 leads us to consider the following modified model in which the ϵ^*_t term is augmented into the state vector of the measurement equation:

$$\Delta M_t = \begin{bmatrix} X_{t-1} & 1 \end{bmatrix} \begin{bmatrix} \beta_t \\ \epsilon^*_t \end{bmatrix}, \qquad (6.44)$$

$$(\Delta M_t = X^*_{t-1}\beta^*_t), \qquad (6.44')$$

Table 6.1
Estimates of a time-varying-parameter model with GARCH disturbances: U.S. monetary growth model (1962:I–1989:II)

Parameters	Model 1	
σ_{v1}	0.1170	(0.0898)
σ_{v2}	0.0430	(0.0437)
σ_{v3}	0.0000	(0.0513)
σ_{v4}	0.1765	(0.1486)
σ_{v5}	0.0119	(0.0375)
α_0	0.0427	(0.0324)
α_1	0.3206	(0.2185)
α_2	0.5573	(0.2314)
Log likelihood	-109.979	

Note: Standard errors are in parentheses.

$$\begin{bmatrix} \beta_t \\ \epsilon_t^* \end{bmatrix} = \begin{bmatrix} I_5 & 0 \\ 0 & 0 \end{bmatrix}\begin{bmatrix} \beta_{t-1} \\ \epsilon_{t-1}^* \end{bmatrix} + \begin{bmatrix} v_t \\ \epsilon_t^* \end{bmatrix},$$ (6.45)

$$(\beta_t^* = F^*\beta_{t-1}^* + v_t^*),$$ (6.45')

where

$$E(v_t^* v_t^{*\prime}) = \begin{bmatrix} Q & 0 \\ 0 & h_t \end{bmatrix} = Q_t^*.$$ (6.46)

Table 6.1 presents parameter estimates of the model based on the modified state-space form above and the approximations suggested by Harvey, Ruiz, and Sentana (1992) are reported in table 6.1. As in the case of the Markov-switching disturbance terms in section 5.5, the standardized forecast errors and their squares exhibit no significant serial correlation. (Q-statistics for the standardized forecast errors are Q(12)=10.3, Q(24)=20.6, and Q(36)=32.4, and Q-statistics for the squares of the standardized forecast errors are Q(12)=5.2, Q(24)=12.4, and Q(36)=21.0.)

In figure 6.1a, the time-varying monetary growth uncertainty that results from the model is decomposed into two components: uncertainty due to time-varying regression coefficients and uncertainty due to GARCH disturbance terms. It is interesting to compare the results in figure 6.1a with those in figure 6.1b, which are based on the time-varying-parameter model with Markov-switching heteroskedasticity in section 5.5. The two figures are remarkably close to identical except that the GARCH portion of uncertainty in figure 6.1a is in general higher than the Markov-switching portion of uncertainty in figure 6.1b. Apparently, distinguishing between the two alternative types of heteroskedasticity in the disturbance terms is difficult for the present application.

6.2 State-Space Models with Markov-Switching Heteroskedasticity

In this section, as an alternative to the state-space model with ARCH-type conditional heteroskedasticity, we assume that R_t and Q_t in equation (6.3) are dependent on Markov-switching variables that which are outcomes of unobserved discrete-time, discrete-state, first-order Markov processes. As mentioned earlier, in addition to the fundamental differences between the ARCH-type and Markov-switching heteroskedasticity an important motivation for considering a state-space model with Markov-switching heteroskedasticity is due to Lastrapes (1989) and Lamoureux and Lastrapes (1990), who show that failure to allow for regime shifts may lead to an overstatement of the persistence of the variance of a series. For example, Raymond and Rich (1992) argue that regime changes are a major source of conditional heteroskedasticity in the U.S. inflation series.

6.2.1 Model Specification

Consider the following state-space model with Markov-switching heteroskedasticity in the disturbance terms, as in Kim 1993a:

$$y_t = H\beta_t + Az_t + e_t, \tag{6.47}$$

$$\beta_t = \tilde{\mu} + F\beta_{t-1} + v_t, \tag{6.48}$$

$$E(v_t v_t') = Q_{S_{1t}}, \tag{6.49}$$

$$E(e_t e_t') = R_{S_{2t}}, \tag{6.50}$$

$$E(e_t v_s') = 0, \tag{6.51}$$

$$Q_{S_{1t}} = Q_1 \Theta_{1,1t} + Q_2 \Theta_{1,2t} + \cdots + Q_\omega \Theta_{1,\omega t}, \tag{6.52}$$

$$R_{S_{2t}} = R_1 \Theta_{2,1t} + R_2 \Theta_{2,2t} + \cdots + R_\omega \Theta_{2,\omega t}, \tag{6.53}$$

where $\Theta_{r,jt} = 1$ if $S_{rt} = j$, and $\Theta_{r,jt} = 0$ if $S_{rt} \neq j$, $r = 1, 2$, $j = 1, 2, \ldots, \omega$. The two independent unobserved state variables, S_{1t} and S_{2t}, evolve according to first-order Markov processes with transition probabilities:

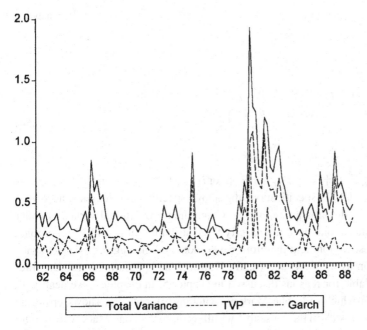

Figure 6.1a
Decomposition of monetary growth uncertainty based on a TVP model with
GARCH(1,1) heteroskedasticity

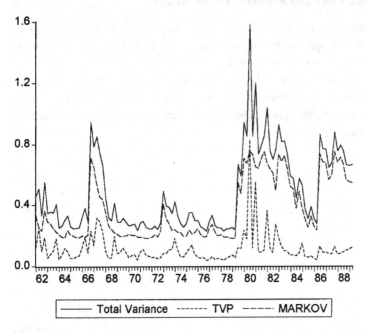

Figure 6.1b
Decomposition of monetary growth uncertainty based on a TVP model with
Markov-switching heteroskedasticity

$$
p_r = \begin{pmatrix} p_{r,11} & p_{r,12} & \cdots & p_{r,1\omega} \\ p_{r,21} & p_{r,22} & \cdots & p_{r,2\omega} \\ \vdots & \vdots & \ddots & \vdots \\ p_{r,\omega 1} & p_{r,\omega 2} & \cdots & p_{r,\omega\omega} \end{pmatrix}, \quad r = 1, 2, \tag{6.54}
$$

where $p_{r,ji} = Pr[S_{rt} = j | S_{r,t-1} = i]$, for $i, j = 1, 2, \ldots, \omega$, and $\sum_{j=1}^{\omega} p_{ji} = 1$. Unlike the ARCH specification, the above specification does not need past values of the disturbances e_t and v_t. Given the unconditional variances under different states, one need not specify the distribution of e_t and v_t conditional on past observation, and therefore we do not need the augmented state-space formulation as in (6.24) and (6.26). However, an approximation to the filter is unavoidable for reasons discussed in chapter 5. In chapter 5, we dealt with the case in which only one Markov-switching variable, S_t, shows up in the state-space model. In the sense that we allow more than one Markov-switching variable in a state-space model, this section may be considered a generalization of chapter 5.

6.2.2 Basic Filter and Estimation of the Model

Making inferences on β_t, $t = 1, 2, \ldots, T$, and estimating the parameters of the model are straightforward applications of chapter 5. For given realizations of the state variables at times t and $t - 1$ ($S_{1,t-1} = m$, $S_{1t} = m'$, $S_{2,t-1} = n$, and $S_{2t} = n'$, where $m, m' = 1, 2, \ldots$, or ω, and $n, n' = 1, 2, \ldots$, or ω), the Kalman filter can be represented as follows. The notation $\gamma_t^{m,n'}$, for example, means that the variable γ_t is dependent on the realizations of the state variables $S_{1,t-1} = m$ and $S_{2t} = n'$.

Prediction

$$
\beta_{t|t-1}^{m,n} = \tilde{\mu} + F\beta_{t-1|t-1}^{m,n}, \tag{6.55}
$$

$$
P_{t|t-1}^{m,n,m'} = F P_{t-1|t-1}^{m,n} F' + Q^{m'}, \tag{6.56}
$$

$$
\eta_{t|t-1}^{m,n} = y_t - H\beta_{t|t-1}^{m,n} - Az_t, \tag{6.57}
$$

$$
f_{t|t-1}^{m,n,m',n'} = H P_{t|t-1}^{m,n,m'} H' + R^{n'}. \tag{6.58}
$$

Updating

$$
\beta_{t|t}^{m,n,m',n'} = \beta_{t|t-1}^{m,n} + K_t^{m,n,m',n'} \eta_{t|t-1}^{m,n}, \tag{6.59}
$$

$$P_{t|t}^{m,n,m',n'} = (I - K_t^{m,n,m',n'} H) P_{t|t-1}^{m,n,m'},$$ (6.60)

where

$$K_t^{m,n,m',n'} = P_{t|t-1}^{m,n,m'} H' (f_{t|t-1}^{m,n,m',n'})^{-1}$$ (6.61)

is the Kalman gain and other notations are the same as in chapters 3 and 5.

Each iteration of the above Kalman filter produces an ω^2-fold increase in the number of cases to consider. Thus to make the above Kalman filter operable, we need to reduce the $(\omega^2 \times \omega^2)$ posteriors ($\beta_{t|t}^{m,n,m',n'}$ and $P_{t|t}^{m,n,m',n'}$) into $(\omega \times \omega)$ by taking appropriate weighted averages over states at $t-1$ at the end of each iteration. The following, which is an extension of chapter 5, explains how this can be done:

Approximations

$$\beta_{t|t}^{m',n'} = \sum_{m=1}^{\omega} \sum_{n=1}^{\omega} [\beta_{t|t}^{m,n,m',n'}$$

$$\times \frac{Pr[S_{1,t-1} = m, S_{2,t-1} = n, S_{1t} = m', S_{2t} = n'|\psi_t]}{Pr[S_{1t} = m', S_{2t} = n'|\psi_t]}]$$ (6.62)

$$P_{t|t}^{m',n'} = \sum_{m=1}^{\omega} \sum_{n=1}^{\omega} [\{P_{t|t}^{m,n,m',n'} + (\beta_{t|t}^{m',n'} - \beta_{t|t}^{m,n,m',n'})(\beta_{t|t}^{m',n'} - \beta_{t|t}^{m,n,m',n'})'\}$$
(6.63)

$$\times \frac{Pr[S_{1,t-1} = m, S_{2,t-1} = n, S_{1t} = m', S_{2t} = n'|\psi_t]}{Pr[S_{1t} = m', S_{2t} = n'|\psi_t]}],$$

where ψ_t refers to information available at time t.

The appropriate probability terms necessary for the above collapsing can be obtained as follows:

$$Pr[S_{1,t-1} = m, S_{2,t-1} = n, S_{1t} = m', S_{2t} = n'|\psi_t]$$

$$= \frac{Pr[y_t, S_{1,t-1} = m, S_{2,t-1} = n, S_{1t} = m', S_{2t} = n'|\psi_{t-1}]}{Pr[y_t|\psi_{t-1}]}$$

$$= \left(\frac{Pr[y_t|S_{1,t-1} = m, S_{2,t-1} = n, S_{1t} = m', S_{2t} = n', \psi_{t-1}]}{Pr[y_t|\psi_{t-1}]} \right)$$
(6.64)

$$\times Pr[S_{1,t-1} = m, S_{2,t-1} = n, S_{1t} = m', S_{2t} = n'|\psi_{t-1}],$$

where

$$Pr[y_t|S_{1,t-1} = m, S_{2,t-1} = n, S_{1t} = m', S_{2t} = n', \psi_{t-1}]$$

$$= (2\pi)^{-\frac{N}{2}}|f_{t|t-1}^{m,n,m',n'}|^{-\frac{1}{2}} \exp\{-\frac{1}{2}\eta_{t|t-1}^{m,n}{}' f_{t|t-1}^{m,n,m',n'}{}^{-1}\eta_{t|t-1}^{m,n}\}, \tag{6.65}$$

$$Pr[y_t|\psi_{t-1}]$$

$$= \sum_{m=1}^{\omega}\sum_{n=1}^{\omega}\sum_{m'=1}^{\omega}\sum_{n'=1}^{\omega} Pr[y_t, S_{1,t-1} = m, S_{2,t-1} = n, S_{1t} = m', S_{2t} = n'|\psi_{t-1}], \tag{6.66}$$

and

$$Pr[S_{1,t-1} = m, S_{2,t-1} = n, S_{1t} = m', S_{2t} = n'|\psi_{t-1}]$$

$$= Pr[S_{1t} = m'|S_{1,t-1} = m] \times Pr[S_{2t} = n'|S_{2,t-1} = n] \tag{6.67}$$

$$\times Pr[S_{1,t-1} = m, S_{2,t-1} = n|\psi_{t-1}],$$

with

$$Pr[S_{1,t-1} = m, S_{2,t-1} = n|\psi_{t-1}]$$

$$= \sum_{i=1}^{\omega}\sum_{j=1}^{\omega} Pr[S_{1,t-2} = i, S_{1,t-1} = m, S_{2,t-2} = j, S_{2,t-1} = n|\psi_{t-1}]. \tag{6.68}$$

Notice that equation (6.67) results from the assumption that the two state variables, S_{1t} and S_{2t}, are independent.

As by-products of the filter, we get the density of y_t conditional on past information, $f(y_t|\psi_{t-1})$, $t = 1, 2, \ldots, T$, from equation (6.66). Then the approximate log likelihood function is given by

$$LL = \ln[f(y_1, y_2, \ldots, y_T)] = \sum_{t=1}^{T} \ln[f(y_t|\psi_{t-1})], \tag{6.69}$$

which may be numerically maximized with respect to the unknown parameters of the model for approximate MLE.

Finally, a useful comment is in order. An alternative way of dealing with more than one Markov-switching variable within a state-space model is to represent the dynamics of the multivariate Markov-switching variables using a single Markov-switching process. For example, assume each of the two Markov-switching variables S_{1t} and S_{2t} in the model given by (6.47)–(6.54) is subject to two states ($\omega = 2$). Then their dynamics can be represented using a single Markov-switching variable, S_t, in the following way:

$S_t = 1$, if $S_{1t} = 0$ and $S_{2t} = 0$,

$S_t = 2$, if $S_{1t} = 0$ and $S_{2t} = 1$,

$S_t = 3$, if $S_{1t} = 1$ and $S_{2t} = 0$,

$S_t = 4$, if $S_{1t} = 1$ and $S_{2t} = 1$,

with

$$Pr[S_t = j | S_{t-1} = i] = p_{ij}, \qquad i, j = 1, 2, 3, 4,$$

$$\sum_{j=1}^{4} p_{ij} = 1, \qquad i = 1, 2, 3, 4,$$

where p_{ij}, $i, j = 1, 2, 3, 4$, is appropriately defined.

Independence between S_{1t} and S_{2t} amounts to restrictions in the matrix of transition probabilities that describes the dynamics of the newly defined S_t variable. In the absence of these restrictions, the whole analysis in this section collapses to that of chapter 5.

6.3 Application 1: The Link between the Inflation Rate and Inflation Uncertainty

This section deals with Kim's (1993a) application of the unobserved-components model with Markov-switching heteroskedasticity to the investigation of the link between inflation and its uncertainty. Following Ball and Cecchetti (1990), we assume that inflation is subject to permanent shocks and temporary shocks, the variances of which shift according to discrete-valued, first-order Markov processes. By incorporating regime shifts in both mean and variance structures within a four-state, Markov-switching, unobserved-components model of U.S. inflation, we analyze the interaction of mean and variance over long and short horizons. In particular, we are interested in the relation between inflation and its uncertainty over short and long horizons. Notice that whereas Ball and Cecchetti addressed the same issue using cross-country analysis, Kim's analysis, introduced in this section is based on a time series analysis within a country, as in Evans 1991. Empirical results show that inflation is costly, because higher inflation is associated with higher long-run uncertainty.

6.3.1 Motivation and Practical Issues Involved

Although most economists agree that inflation is costly, there is no consensus about why. One view (Okun 1971 and Friedman 1977) implies that understanding the costs of inflation requires that we understand the connection between the level of inflation and its uncertainty. But earlier empirical studies of the inflation-uncertainty relation report conflicting results, and the issue appears unsettled, as documented in Ball and Cecchetti 1990. For example, Engle (1983) and Cosimano and Jansen (1988) find little evidence of a link between the relatively high rates of inflation in the 1970s in the United States and uncertainty measured by the conditional variance of inflation. By contrast, evidence from cross-sectional survey studies of inflationary expectations appear to support a link. (See Wachtel 1977.)

In trying to resolve the empirical standoff, Ball and Cecchetti (1990) focused on the distinction between short-term and long-term uncertainty. By assuming that there are both temporary (white noise) and permanent (random walk) components in the inflation series, they investigated the inflation-uncertainty relation. [They cannot reject the null hypothesis that the inflation series has a unit root. Barsky (1987) also finds that changes in quarterly U.S. inflation are largely permanent since 1960.] This unobserved-components specification is consistent with an MA(1) process for the difference of the inflation series, and based on the Schwartz criterion, they actually chose an MA(1) for the differences of inflation series for most of the countries considered. Under the assumption that the permanent and transitory shocks are independent, we can indirectly estimate the variances of shocks to the random walk component and the white noise component by estimating the parameters of the MA(1) model. Ball and Cecchetti first assumed that the two variances are constant for a given country and estimated the cross-country relationship between the variances and the average inflation rates. From this analysis, they concluded that both short-term and long-term uncertainty are positively related to the average inflation rate across the countries considered. Then they divided each country's data into five-year periods and estimated the relationship between the variances and the average inflation rates across periods. From this analysis, they concluded that inflation has a major impact on the long-term uncertainty.

One of the shortcomings of Ball and Cecchetti's (1990) time series analysis within each country is that they have at most six nonoverlapping measures of variances and average inflation rates across periods. Based on a time series analysis of the U.S. monthly CPI inflation rate, Evans (1991) found evidence of a positive link between the level of inflation and uncertainty about inflation in the long run. His analysis is based on a time-varying-parameter AR(1) model with an ARCH disturbance term, in which the intercept and slope coefficients are assumed to follow random walks. This analysis involves indirect tests of the link between inflation and its short and steady-state uncertainty.

In the next section, we apply a modified version of the state-space model with Markov-switching heteroskedasticity introduced in section 6.2 to modeling the behavior of the U.S. inflation rate (measured by GNP deflator, quarterly, 1958.I–1990.IV). Our model shares its basic idea with that of Ball and Cecchetti (1990), and the approach used is similar to that of Evans (1991). Based on the analysis of Cosimano and Jansen (1988) and Raymond and Rich (1992), it is assumed that regime changes may be an important source of persistence in the conditional variance of U.S. inflation. By incorporating regime shifts in both mean and variance structures, we can perform a direct test of the link between inflation and its uncertainty over different time horizons.

6.3.2   A Time Series Model of U.S. Inflation and Its Uncertainty over Short and Long Horizons (1958.I–1990.IV, GNP Deflator)

Following Ball and Cecchetti (1990), we assume that inflation consists of a stochastic trend (random walk) component and a stationary autoregressive component. Trend inflation, for example, is determined by trend money growth, and the deviation of inflation from its trend is determined by monetary and other demand and supply shocks. Consider the following specification for the U.S. inflation rate:

$$\pi_t = T_t + C_t + \mu_2 S_{1t} + \mu_3 S_{2t} + \mu_4 S_{1t} S_{2t}, \tag{6.70}$$

$$T_t = T_{t-1} + (Q_0 + Q_1 S_{1t})v_t, \qquad v_t \sim N(0, 1), \tag{6.71}$$

$$\phi(L)C_t = (h_0 + h_1 S_{2t})e_t, \qquad e_t \sim N(0, 1), \tag{6.72}$$

where S_{1t} and S_{2t} are unobserved state variables that determine the regime. S_{1t} and S_{2t} are assumed to evolve independently of each other according to first-order, discrete, two-state Markov processes with the following transition probabilities:

$$Pr[S_{1t} = 0 | S_{1,t-1} = 0] = p_{00}, \quad Pr[S_{1t} = 1 | S_{1,t-1} = 1] = p_{11}, \tag{6.73}$$

$$Pr[S_{2t} = 0 | S_{2,t-1} = 0] = q_{00}, \qquad Pr[S_{2t} = 1 | S_{2,t-1} = 1] = q_{11}. \tag{6.74}$$

In the above specification, we have four different regimes. They may be defined, for convenience, as regime 1: a low Q_t and low h_t ($S_{1t} = 0$, $S_{2t} = 0$) regime, regime 2: a low Q_t and high h_t ($S_{1t} = 0$, $S_{2t} = 1$) regime, regime 3: a high Q_t and low h_t ($S_{1t} = 1$, $S_{2t} = 0$) regime, and regime 4: a high Q_t and high h_t ($S_{1t} = 1$, $S_{2t} = 1$) regime. This four-regime specification is consistent with Raymond and Rich's (1992) four-state Markov model of the U.S. inflation rate. The parameters μ_2, μ_3, and μ_4 are incorporated to capture the possible interactions between mean and variance shifts. (The state variables S_{1t} and S_{2t} work like dummy variables. For instance, μ_2 captures a shift in the mean of inflation during regime 2 relative to that during regime 1; μ_3 captures a shift in the mean during regime 3 relative to that during regime 1; and $\mu_2 + \mu_3 + \mu_4$ captures a shift in the mean during regime 4 relative to that during regime 1.)

When the above model is applied to the sample period 1950.I–1990.IV (observations between 1948.II and 1949.IV are used to obtain initial values for the filter), an important structural change in the variance of transitory shocks is observed in 1954.I. The probability of high variance for the transitory shocks is close to 1 before 1954.I and it is close to 0 starting from 1954.I, with $h_0 = 0.307$ and $h_1 = 0.582$. The timing of the structural break in the variance of transitory shocks is the same as that found in Cosimano and Jansen 1988. When the same model is applied to the sample period 1958.I–1990.IV (observations between 1954.I and 1957.IV are used to obtain initial values for the filter), h_0 is 0.150 and h_1 is significant at 0.183. This clearly indicates the possibility of a model with a three-state variance structure for the transitory shocks for the period 1950.I–1990.IV. Whereas Barro (1989) views the exceptionally high variance of inflation in the early 1950s as resulting from the price controls during World War II and the Korean War, Cosimano and Jansen (1988) view it as resulting from substantial revisions to the GNP deflator during that period. Therefore, instead of applying a model with a three-state variance structure for the transitory shocks to the entire sample, the model specified above (with two-state variance structures for both transitory and permanent shocks) is applied to the subsample that excludes observations prior to 1954.I. [An AR(1) specification is employed for the transitory component of inflation (i.e., $\phi(L) = 1 - \phi L$). But the AR coefficients are close to 0 and insignificant for both sample periods, which validates Ball and Cecchetti's (1990) white noise specification of the transitory component.]

Table 6.2 presents estimates of the model for the sample period 1958.I–1990.IV with $\phi(L) = 1$. The estimate of μ_4 is close to 0 and insignificant. This allows for straightforward interpretation of the parameters μ_2 and μ_3. For

Table 6.2
Estimation of the inflation model (U.S. GNP deflator, 1958.I–1990.IV)

Model

$$\pi_t = T_t + \mu_2 S_{1t} + \mu_3 S_{2t} + \mu_4 S_{1t} S_{2t} + (h_0 + h_1 S_{2t})e_t,$$

$$T_t = T_{t-1} + (Q_0 + Q_1 S_{1t})v_t,$$

$$v_t \sim N(0, 1), \quad e_t \sim N(0, 1),$$

$$Pr[S_{1t} = 0 | S_{1,t-1} = 0] = p_{00} \quad Pr[S_{1t} = 1 | S_{1,t-1} = 1] = p_{11},$$

$$Pr[S_{2t} = 0 | S_{2,t-1} = 0] = q_{00}, \quad Pr[S_{2t} = 1 | S_{2,t-1} = 1] = q_{11}.$$

Parameters	Estimates	
$\hat{Q}_0$	0.0419	(0.0378)
$\hat{Q}_1$	0.3546	(0.1175)
$\hat{h}_0$	0.1505	(0.0435)
$\hat{h}_1$	0.1808	(0.0487)
$\hat{\mu}_2$	0.5192	(0.2018)
$\hat{\mu}_3$	−0.2856	(0.1355)
$\hat{\mu}_4$	−0.0861	(0.4876)
$\hat{p}_{00}$	0.8373	(0.1044)
$\hat{p}_{11}$	0.9641	(0.0247)
$\hat{q}_{00}$	0.9704	(0.0247)
$\hat{q}_{11}$	0.9463	(0.0570)
Log likelihood value	−65.2415	

Note: Standard errors are in parentheses. S_{1t} and S_{2t} evolve independently of one another. Observations between 1954.I and 1957.IV were used to obtain initial values for the filter.

example, μ_2 can be interpreted as a shift in mean during a high permanent-shock variance state relative to a low permanent-shock variance state; and μ_3 as a shift in mean during a high transitory-shock variance state relative to a low transitory-shock variance state.

Estimates of μ_2, μ_3, Q_1, and h_1 suggest that high uncertainty about long-run inflation is associated with a positive shift in inflation, and high uncertainty about short-run inflation with a negative shift in inflation. Figures 6.2 and 6.3 show the association of the inflation rate with the short-run and long-run uncertainty. The positive association of long-run uncertainty and level of inflation is consistent with Ball and Cecchetti 1990 and Evans 1991. If

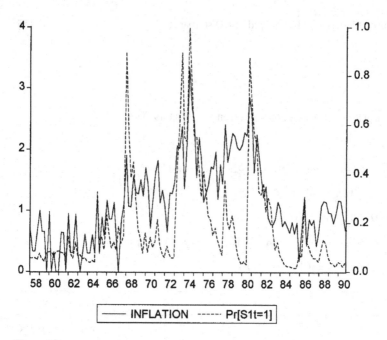

Figure 6.2
Inflation rate and probability of high variance state for permanent shocks

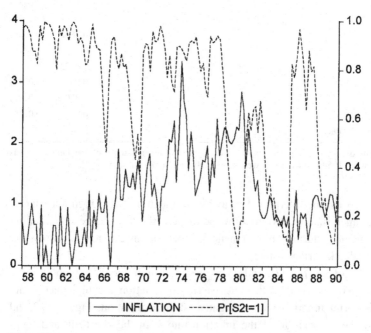

Figure 6.3
Inflation rate and probability of high variance state for transitory shocks

inflation increases above normal (the low Q_t and low h_t state, or regime 1, may be considered as a normal state), it increases long-run uncertainty by making monetary policy less stable. For example, the Federal Reserve may face a dilemma between disinflation policy and accommodation policy. This interpretation results from Ball and Cecchetti, who assume that trend inflation is determined by trend money growth. One possible interpretation for the negative association between short-run uncertainty and inflation is that when inflation falls below normal, the Federal Reserve may have more room to maneuver monetary aggregates for stabilization purposes, which may result in less-stable short-run monetary policy. But this interpretation is less clear. It seems from figure 6.3 that the negative association of inflation and its short-run uncertainty is mostly due to the 1960s and late 1980s, during which periods inflation was low and the variance of transitory shocks was high.

The ratio of high to low variances of permanent shocks is much larger than that of transitory shocks. Furthermore, Q_0 (the variance of permanent shocks when low) is close to 0, and periods of high permanent-shock variance are short-lived. This suggests that infrequent permanent shocks to the GNP deflator account for most of the persistence in the GNP deflator, as in Balke and Fomby 1991. Figure 6.2 shows three major positive shifts in the variance of permanent shocks, around years 1968, 1974–5, and 1982–3, which is consistent with earlier findings by Balke and Fomby and Evans (1991). Based on an outlier search, Balke and Fomby found substantial evidence of large, infrequent shocks to the GNP deflator in 1968 and 1983. Evans found a dramatic increase in the persistence of the CPI inflation series during the oil shock period of 1970s.

6.4 Application 2: Transient Fads and the Crash of '87 in the U.S. Stock Market

Another application of the unobserved-components model or the state-space model with Markov-switching heteroskedasticity is Kim and M. Kim's (1996) analysis of the U.S. stock market with a focus on the 1987 crash. Using a fad model with Markov-switching heteroskedasticity in both the fundamental and fad components (UC-MS model), Kim and Kim examined the possibility that the 1987 stock market crash was an example of a short-lived fad. Although we usually think of fads as speculative bubbles, the UC-MS model seems to be picking up is unwarranted pessimism that the market exhibited with the OPEC oil shock and with the '87 crash.

The model can capture some short-run dynamics that might otherwise not be captured by variance ratio tests (see Poterba and Summers 1988; Lo and MacKinlay 1988; and Kim, Nelson, and Startz 1991), by autoregression test (see Fama and French 1988), or by conventional unobserved-components models (see Clark 1987 and Watson 1986). These models, which do not explicitly address the importance of heteroskedasticity, may miss some important short-run dynamics of interest, especially during unusual periods such as the '87 crash.

Furthermore, the conditional variance implied by the UC-MS model captures most of the dynamics in the GARCH specification of stock return volatility. Yet unlike the GARCH measure of volatility's the UC-MS measure of volatility is consistent with volatility reverting to its normal level very quickly after the crash.

6.4.1 Motivation for a Model of Stock Returns with a Fad Component

Consider the following model by Summers (1986) and Poterba and Summers (1988), which is often referred to as a "fad" model:

$$P_t = P_t^* + z_t, \tag{6.75}$$

$$P_t^* = \mu + P_{t-1}^* + e_t, \quad e_t \sim N(0, \sigma_{et}^2), \tag{6.76}$$

$$z_t = \psi(L)u_t, \quad u_t \sim N(0, \sigma_{ut}^2), \tag{6.77}$$

where P_t is the natural log of stock price; P^* is the "fundamental," which is assumed to evolve slowly over time; and z_t is a persistent but stationary component. In this case the return, defined as a log-differenced price, is given by

$$y_t = P_t - P_{t-1} = \mu_t + e_t + (z_t - z_{t-1}). \tag{6.78}$$

When the transitory component z_t has a root close to, but not equal to, unity, a given change in price tends to be reversed over a long period of time by a predictable change in the opposite direction. (See Fama and French 1988 for the detailed discussion of the behavior of long autocorrelations implied by such models.) De Long, et al. (1990), for example, developed a theory in which shocks to the z_t component may be caused by the noisy traders' misperceptions. In the noisy-trader model, an important proportion of the market consists of noisy traders, that is, investors who bid prices away from fundamentals, and changes in noisy traders' price misperception can result in very large and persistent changes in prices. The significance of mean reversion in stock prices, or the significance of the fad component could be tested, at least in principle, by decomposing the stock price into the two components.

Several authors have proposed methods of decomposing a univariate series into permanent and transitory components. For example, Nelson and Plosser (1982) matched a model consisting of permanent and temporary components to an autocorrelation function to get the relative size of each component. Watson (1986) and Clark (1987) used unobserved-components models to decompose GNP series into two components. Campbell and Mankiw (1987), using parameters of the low-order autoregressive ARMA representation of a series, estimated the effect of a shock on long-run forecasts to assess the importance of the permanent or transitory component. Recently, alternative methods have been employed to detect mean reversion and/or fads in stock prices. For example, Poterba and Summers (1988), Lo and MacKinlay (1988), and M. Kim, Nelson, and Startz (1991) employed the variance ratio methodology of Cochrane (1988) and Fama and French (1988) employed an autoregression test in analyzing mean reversion in stock prices. These studies reported mixed evidence on the existence of mean reversion in stock prices.

In assessing the importance of the transitory component, none of the studies of mean reversion in stock prices, however, consider the possibility of extremely unusual, temporal deviations of stock prices from a random walk component that last only a very brief period of time. Or the mean reversion in stock price may be seasonal. Jegadeesh (1991), for example, argues that mean reversion in stock prices is entirely concentrated in the month of January. The October 1987 market crash could be one such case. Variance ratio tests or other methods of decomposition surveyed above are likely to miss some important short-run dynamics in the presence of transitory shocks of this kind. The goal of this section is to assess the possibility of such transitory shocks and to introduce an empirical model that can capture the important short-run dynamics in stock prices that other models are likely to miss.

6.4.2 An Empirical Model of Stock Returns with a Possibility of Transient Fads

To set the stage, consider the following empirical model for excess returns with Markov-switching (MS) heteroskedasticity by Turner, Startz, and Nelson (1989):

$$y_t^* = \mu_t + e_t, \qquad e_t \sim N(0, \sigma_{et}^2), \tag{6.79}$$

$$\sigma_{et}^2 = (1 - S_t)\sigma_0^2 + S_t\sigma_1^2, \tag{6.80}$$

where y_t^* is the excess return measured by log differences of stock prices adjusted for dividends less risk-free interest, and μ_t is the time-varying risk premium. S_t is given by the two-state, first-order Markov process with the following transition probabilities:

$$Pr[S_t = 1|S_{t-1} = 1] = p_{11}, \qquad Pr[S_t = 0|S_{t-1} = 0] = p_{00}. \tag{6.81}$$

This model can be regarded as an alternative to a popular specification of changing volatility, namely, the ARCH-class models. For example, the GARCH(1,1) model specifies the conditional variance as

$$e_t|\psi_{t-1} \sim N(0, h_t), \tag{6.82}$$

$$h_t = \alpha_0 + \alpha_1 e_{t-1}^2 + \alpha_2 h_{t-1}, \tag{6.83}$$

where ψ_{t-1} refers to the available information up to time $t - 1$. As Kim and M. Kim (1996) have shown, the two-state Markov-switching model of Turner, Startz, and Nelson (1989) does not seem to capture enough variation in volatility when compared to the GARCH model, but it allows faster decay of volatility. (Figure 6.4 depicts volatilities implied by these two models of stock returns.) Moreover, neither allows for the possibility of transitory shocks.

Kim and M. Kim (1996) propose a model that allows for the possibility of a transitory component in the Turner, Startz, and Nelson model. For an AR(2) specification of the transitory component z_t and a constant mean μ, the expression for stock returns from the model in (6.75)–(6.78) can be rewritten in the following state-space form:

$$y_t = \mu + [\,1 \quad -1\,] \begin{bmatrix} z_t \\ z_{t-1} \end{bmatrix} + e_t, \tag{6.84}$$

$$(y_t = \mu + H\beta_t + e_t), \tag{6.84'}$$

$$\begin{bmatrix} z_t \\ z_{t-1} \end{bmatrix} = \begin{bmatrix} \phi_1 & \phi_2 \\ 1 & 0 \end{bmatrix} \begin{bmatrix} z_{t-1} \\ z_{t-2} \end{bmatrix} + \begin{bmatrix} u_t \\ 0 \end{bmatrix}, \tag{6.85}$$

$$(\beta_t = F\beta_{t-1} + v_t) \tag{6.85'}$$

where Markov-switching variances are assumed for the two shocks,

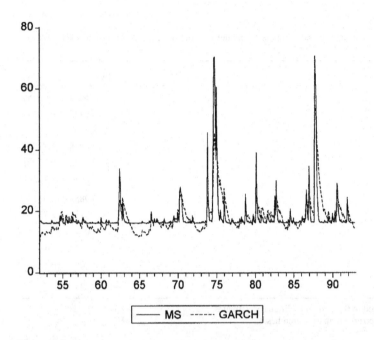

Figure 6.4
Stock returns volatility from a two-state Markov-switching variance model and GARCH(1,1)
model

$$\sigma_{et}^2 = (1 - S_{et})\sigma_{e0}^2 + S_{et}\sigma_{e1}^2, \quad \sigma_{e1}^2 > \sigma_{e0}^2, \tag{6.86}$$

$$\sigma_{ut}^2 = (1 - S_{ut})\sigma_{u0}^2 + S_{ut}\sigma_{u1}^2, \quad \sigma_{u1}^2 > \sigma_{u0}^2, \tag{6.87}$$

and S_{et} and S_{ut} are discrete-valued, unobserved first-order Markov-switching
variables that evolve independently of each other according to the following
transition probabilities:

$$Pr[S_{et} = 0|S_{e,t-1} = 0] = p_{e0}, \quad Pr[S_{et} = 1|S_{e,t-1} = 1] = p_{e1}, \tag{6.88}$$

$$Pr[S_{ut} = 0|S_{u,t-1} = 0] = p_{u0}, \quad Pr[S_{ut} = 1|S_{u,t-1} = 1] = p_{u1}. \tag{6.89}$$

6.4.3 Empirical Results: The October 1987 Market Crash

The data series examined in this section is the monthly S&P 500 index covering the 1952.1 to 1992.12 period. (The series is constructed from the monthly
closing prices, taken from Ibbotson Associates, 1993, *SBBI Yearbook*, Chicago.) The beginning of the sample period roughly matches the year of the

Table 6.3
Estimates of the unobserved components model of stock returns with transient fads (1952:1–1992:12)

Parameters	Estimates[2]	
$\hat{p}_{e1}$	0.9944	(0.0077)
$\hat{p}_{e0}$	0.9338	(0.0622)
$\hat{\sigma}_{e1}$	3.8903	(0.1791)
$\hat{\sigma}_{e0}$	2.0965	(0.4874)
$\hat{\mu}$	0.3132	(0.1706)
$\hat{p}_{u1}$	0.6470	(0.1897)
$\hat{p}_{u0}$	0.9853	(0.0113)
$\hat{\sigma}_{u1}$	8.8134	(2.7363)
$\hat{\sigma}_{u0}$	0.0^1	—
$\hat{\phi}_1$	1.1682	(0.1463)
$\hat{\phi}_2$	−0.2937	(0.1399)
Log likelihood	−1383.29	

1. Constrained to 0 based on preliminary estimates.
2. Standard errors are in the parentheses.

structural change in the dividend process identified by the previous studies, for example, Campbell 1991 and Hodrick 1992. The S&P 500 index is deflated by the CPI, and the continuously compounded return is calculated as 100 times the log differences of the real S&P 500 index.

Table 6.3 reports ML estimates of the UC-MS model given in (6.84)–(6.89). Of special interest are the parameter estimates of the transitory components of stock prices. The standard error of the transitory shocks (σ_u) is not significantly different from 0 for the low-volatility state ($S_{ut} = 0$), but it is significant and very large for the high-volatility state ($S_{ut} = 1$), so the fad is either on or off. Estimates of transition probabilities (p_{u0} and p_{u1}) indicate that the low- (zero-) volatility state dominates the high-volatility state. The duration of the high-volatility state for the transitory shocks, as implied by the estimate of the transition probability (p_{u1}), is only 2.84 months. (Refer to figures 6.5 and 6.6 for probabilities of high-variance states for transitory and permanent components, respectively.)

Estimates of the transitory components of stock prices from the Kalman filter are drawn in figure 6.7, as well as two standard-error confidence bands.

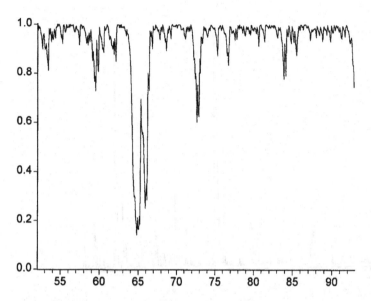

Figure 6.5
Probability of a high-variance state for permanent component

During the sample period, only two episodes of statistically significant transitory components are identified; one during the OPEC oil shock and the other during the 1987 stock market crash. Kim and M. Kim (1996) showed that this result continues to hold even after parameter uncertainty underlying the model has been taken into account. These results confirm that, if there exist transitory components in stock prices, they are only transient. In fact, this possibility was conjectured by Fama and French (1988).

The existence of transitory components, even though they might be short-lived, should be interpreted with care. Nelson (1988) demonstrated that the unobserved-components model tends to incorrectly detect cyclical variations around a smooth trend, when data are generated by a random walk. Thus, a persistent transitory component may merely be a statistical artifact. Though it is not clear to what extent Nelson's argument applies to our model, we cannot rule out the possibility that we have found two different types of permanent shocks in the stock prices, one of which is transient. Therefore, the evidence is only suggestive.

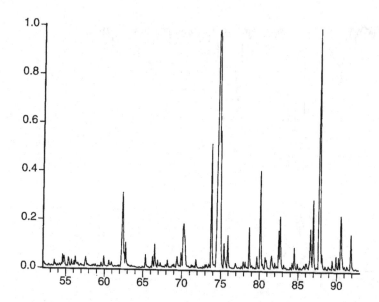

Figure 6.6
Probability of a high-variance state for transitory component

6.4.4 Volatility Implied by the Model

The UC-MS model provides a convenient tool for modeling volatility of stock returns and its persistence. Volatility of returns from this model can be computed as the sum of a highly persistent component and a less persistent component. From the Kalman filter algorithm provided in section 6.2, the conditional forecast error variance is given by

$$f_{t|t-1}^{m,m',n,n'} = H P_{t|t-1}^{m,n,m'} H' + \sigma_{et}^{2\,n'}, \tag{6.90}$$

which is dependent upon states at time t and $t-1$ (i.e., $S_{ut} = m'$, $S_{u,t-1} = m$, $S_{et} = n'$, $S_{e,t-1} = n$, with m, m', n, $n' = 0$, or 1). The first element in the right-hand side of (6.90) is the portion of return volatility that is less persistent and is a function of σ_{ut}^2 (degree of persistence: $\hat{p}_{u0} + \hat{p}_{u1} - 1 = 0.6326$). The second element of (6.90) is the portion of volatility that is highly persistent ($\hat{p}_{e0} + \hat{p}_{e1} - 1 = 0.9343$). These two components of volatility with different levels of persistence could be interpreted as transitory and trend volatility, respectively, as in the case of Engle and Lee 1992.

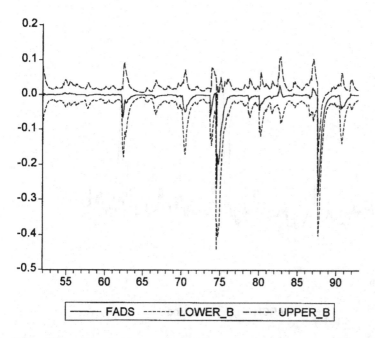

Figure 6.7
Fads component and two standard-error confidence bands

Using (6.90) and filtered probabilities of states, the conditional variance of returns based on available information can be calculated as

$$\sum_{n=0}^{1}\sum_{n'=0}^{1}\sum_{m=0}^{1}\sum_{m'=0}^{1} Pr[S_{u,t-1}=n, S_{u,t}=n', S_{e,t-1}=m,$$

$$S_{e,t}=m'|\psi_{t-1}]f_{t|t-1}^{n,n',m,m'}, \tag{6.91}$$

where ψ_{t-1} is information available at time $t-1$. Figure 6.8 depicts conditional variance of returns calculated in this way and compares it to that of a GARCH specification. The conditional variance from the UC-MS model captures most of the dynamics in the GARCH measure of volatility, and yet the implication is very different. That is, because of the transient nature of the shocks for the 1987 crash period, figures 6.5 and 6.6 suggest that unusually high stock return volatility right after the 1987 crash was mainly driven by the

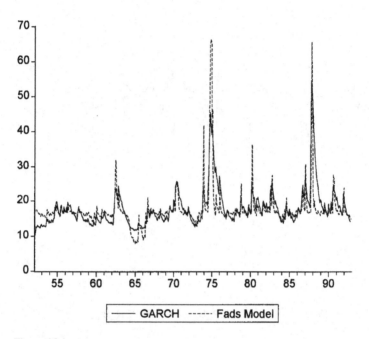

Figure 6.8
Volatility implied by the fads model and the GARCH(1,1) model

jump in volatility of the fad component rather than the fundamental. Furthermore, volatility reverted to normal levels very quickly after the crash. Volatility
dropped to precrash levels by early 1988 and remained low, which confirms
Schwert's (1990) finding. The market responded "correctly" to the temporary
shock by recovering stock return volatility quickly after the crash, as documented in Schwert 1990 and Engle and Lee 1992.

Appendix: GAUSS Programs to Accompany Chapter 6

1. TVPGRCH.OPT: A time-varying-parameter model with GARCH(1,1) disturbances (based on Harvey, Ruiz, and Sentana 1992).

2. INF_FNL.OPT: A state-space model with Markov-switching heteroskedasticity: a model of inflation rate (large and infrequent permanent shocks to inflation), based on Kim 1993.

3. STCK.OPT: A fad model of stock returns (transient fads), based on Kim and M. Kim 1996.

4. GARCH.OPT: GARCH(1,1) model of stock returns.

5. STCK_V2.OPT: A two-state Markov-switching model of stock returns.

References

Ball, Laurence, and Stephen G. Cecchetti. (1990). "Inflation and Uncertainty at Short and Long Horizons." *Brookings Papers on Economic Activity*, 1, 215–254.

Balke, N. S., and T. B. Fomby. 1991. "Shifting Trends, Segmented Trends, and Infrequent Permanent Shocks." *Journal of Monetary Economics*, 28, 61–85.

Barro, R. J. 1989. "Interest Rate Targeting." *Journal of Monetary Economics*, 23, 3–30.

Barsky, Robert B. 1987. "The Fisher Hypothesis and Forecastability and Persistence of Inflation." *Journal of Monetary Economics*, 19, 3–24.

Campbell, John Y. 1991. "A Variance Decomposition for Stock Returns." *Economic Journal*, 101, 157–179.

Campbell, John Y., and N. Gregory Mankiw. 1987. "Are Output Fluctuation Transitory?" *Quarterly Journal of Economics*, 102, 857–880.

Clark, Peter K. 1987. "The Cyclical Component of U.S. Economic Activity." *Quarterly Journal of Economics*, 102, 797–814.

Cochrane, John H. 1988. "How Big Is the Random Walk in GNP?" *Journal of Political Economy*, 96, 893–920.

Cosimano, Thomas F., and Dennis W. Jansen. 1988. "Estimates of the Variance of U.S. Inflation Based upon the ARCH Model: Comment." *Journal of Money, Credit, and Banking*, 20(3), 409–421.

De Long, J. Bradford, Andrei Shleifer, Lawrence H. Summers, and Robert J. Waldmann. 1990. "Noise Trader Risk in Financial Markets." *Journal of Political Economy*, 98, 703–738.

Diebold, F. X. 1986. "Modeling the Persistence of Conditional Variances: A Comment." *Econometric Reviews*, 5, 51–56.

Engle, Robert F. 1983. "Estimates of the Variance of U.S. Inflation Based upon the ARCH Model." *Journal of Money, Credit, and Banking*, 15, 286–301.

Engle, Robert F., and Chowdhury Mustafa. 1992. "Implied ARCH Models from Options Prices." *Journal of Econometrics*, 52, 289–311.

Engle, Robert F., and Gary G. J. Lee. 1992. "A Permanent and Transitory Component Model of Stock Return Volatility." Discussion paper no. 92-44, University of California, San Diego.

Evans, Martin. 1991. "Discovering the Link between Inflation Rates and Inflation Uncertainty." *Journal of Money, Credit, and Banking*, 23(2), 169–184.

Fama, Eugine F., and Kenneth R. French. 1988. "Permanent and Temporary Components of Stock Prices.' *Journal of Political Economy*, 96, 246–273.

Friedman, Milton. 1977. "Nobel Lecture: Inflation and Unemployment." *Journal of Political Economy*, 85, 451–472.

Hamilton, James D., and Raul Susmel. 1994. "Autoregressive Conditional Heteroskedasticity and Changes in Regime." *Journal of Econometrics*, 64, 307–333.

Harvey, Andres C., Esther Ruiz, and Enrique Sentana. 1992. "Unobserved Component Time Series Models with ARCH Disturbances." *Journal of Econometrics*, 52, 129–157.

Hodrick, Robert J. 1992. "Dividend Yields and Expected Stock Returns: Alternative Procedures for Inference and Measurement." *Review of Financial Studies*, 5, 357–386.

Jegadeesh, Narasimhan. 1991. "Seasonality in Stock Price mean Reversion: Evidence from the U.S. and the U.K." *Journal of Finance*, 46, 1427–1444.

Kim, Chang-Jin. 1993a. "Unobserved-Component Time Series Models with Markov-Switching Heteroskedasticity: Changes in Regime and the Link between Inflation Rates and Inflation Uncertainty." *Journal of Business and Economic Statistics*, 11, 341–349.

Kim, Chang-Jin. 1993b. "Sources of Monetary Growth Uncertainty and Economic Activity: The Time-Varying-Parameter Model with Heteroskedastic Disturbances." *Review of Economics and Statistics*, 75, 483–492.

Kim, Chang-Jin. 1994. "Dynamic Linear Models with Markov-Switching." *Journal of Econometrics*, 60, 1–22.

Kim, Chang-Jin, and Myung-Jig Kim. 1996. "Transient Fads and the Crash of '87." *Journal of Applied Econometrics*, 11, 41–58.

Kim, Myung-Jig, Charles R. Nelson, and Richard Startz. 1991. "Mean Reversion in Stock Prices? A Reappraisal of the Empirical Evidence." *Review of Economic Studies*, 58, 515–528.

Lamoureux, Christopher G., and William Lastrapes. 1990. "Persistence in Variance, Structural Change, and the GARCH Model." *Journal of Business and Economic Statistics*, 8(2), 225–234.

Lastrapes, William D. 1989. "Exchange Rate Volatility and U.S. Monetary Policy: An ARCH application." *Journal of Money, Credit, and Banking*, 21(1), 66–77.

Lo, A. W., and A. C. MacKinlay. 1988. "Stock Market Prices Do Not Follow Random Walks: Evidence from a Simple Specification Test." *Review of Financial Studies*, 1, 41–66.

Nelson, Charles R. 1988. "Spurious Trend and Cycle in the State Space Decomposition of a Time Series with a Unit Root." *Journal of Economic Dynamics and Control*, 12, 475–488.

Nelson, Charles R., and Charles I. Plosser. 1982. "Trends and Random Walks in Macroeconomic Time Series: Some Evidence and Implications." *Journal of Monetary Economics*, 10, 139–162.

Okun, Arthur M. 1971. "The Mirage of Steady Inflation." *Brookings Papers on Economic Activity*, 2, 486–498.

Poterba, James M., and Lawrence H. Summers. 1988. "Mean Reversion in Stock Prices: Evidence and Implications." *Journal of Financial Economics*, 22, 27–59.

Raymond, Jennie, and Robert W. Rich. 1992. "Changes in Regime and the Behavior of Inflation." Working paper, Department of Economics, Vanderbilt University, Nashville, TN.

Schwert, G. William. 1990. "Stock Volatility and the Crash of '87." *Review of Financial Studies*, 3, 77–102.

Summers, Lawrence. 1986. "Does the Stock Market Rationality Reflect Fundamental Values?" *Journal of Finance*, 41, 591–601.

Turner, Christopher M., Richard Startz, and Charles R. Nelson. 1989. "A Markov Model of Heteroscedasticity, Risk, and Learning in the Stock Market." *Journal of Financial Economics*, 25, 3–22.

Wachtel, P. A. 1977. "Survey Measures of Expected Inflation and Their Potential Usefulness." in *Analysis of Inflation 1964–1974*, ed. J. Popkin, Cambridge, MA: Ballinger.

Watson, Mark W. 1986. "Univariate Detrending Methods with Stochastic Trends." *Journal of Monetary Economics*, 18, 49–75.

II THE GIBBS-SAMPLING APPROACH

7 An Introduction to Bayesian Inference and Gibbs-Sampling

7.1 Classical versus Bayesian Analysis: Fundamental Differences

To illustrate the differences between classical and Bayesian inference, we begin by considering the familiar linear regression model:

$$Y = X\beta + e, \quad e \sim N(0, \sigma^2 I_T), \tag{7.1}$$

where Y and e are $T \times 1$ vectors, and X is a $T \times K$ matrix of rank K containing the fixed regressors, $X_1, \ldots, X_K$. Within the classical framework, β and σ^2 are treated as unknown constants to be estimated, and the ordinary least squares method provides us with the best linear unbiased estimator of β,

$$\hat{\beta} = (X'X)^{-1}X'Y, \tag{7.2}$$

whereas an unbiased estimator of σ^2 is given by

$$\hat{\sigma}^2 = \frac{\hat{e}'\hat{e}}{T - K}, \tag{7.3}$$

where $\hat{e} = Y - X\hat{\beta}$. These estimators are random variables with the following distributions:

$$\hat{\beta} \sim N(\beta, \sigma^2(X'X)^{-1}), \tag{7.4}$$

$$(T - K)\frac{\hat{\sigma}^2}{\sigma^2} \sim \chi^2(T - K). \tag{7.5}$$

These estimators are evaluated within a repeated sampling context for qualities such as unbiasedness and consistency. Suppose that we have J sets of sample data on X and Y taken from a population with given β and σ^2. We thus have J different estimates of β and σ^2, for J different samples: $\{(\hat{\beta})^1, (\hat{\beta})^2, \ldots, (\hat{\beta})^J\}$ and $\{(\hat{\sigma}^2)^1, (\hat{\sigma}^2)^2, \ldots, (\hat{\sigma}^2)^J\}$. An unbiased estimator of β, for example, is the one that has the following property:

$$p \lim_{J \to \infty} \frac{1}{J} \sum_{j=1}^{J} \hat{\beta}^j = \beta, \tag{7.6}$$

which states that in infinitely repeated sampling, the estimator

$$\hat{\beta} = (X'X)^{-1}X'Y$$

on average gives us the correct answer. Unfortunately, however, we have only one set of sample data in usual applications. Even in this case, the estimator $\hat{\beta}$ is the "best" one in the sense of being closest to the correct β, in an expected value sense. Thus, in making inferences in a classical framework, we are interested in a high probability of being close to the correct result. Evaluation takes place within a repeated-sampling context. Furthermore, probability is defined in terms of the limit of relative frequency and is objective.

Within a Bayesian framework, the parameters of the model, $\theta = [\beta \ \sigma^2]'$, are treated as random variables having probability distributions. These distributions are used to summarize the status of knowledge about the model's parameters. A probability distribution, $g(\theta)$, employed by a researcher to summarize his or her knowledge of θ before observing sample observations on X and Y is called a *prior* distribution. Different researchers may have different knowledge about the parameters, and that knowledge may be subjective, reflecting prior beliefs. Thus, Bayesian inference is subjective in the sense that it incorporates an individual's belief about how likely are different values of the parameters.

Once Y is observed, a Bayesian researcher revises the distribution of the parameters by combining the prior distribution with the information contained in the sample, using Bayes' theorem. To see the steps in this process, denote the distribution of the sample observations Y given the parameters by $f(Y \mid \theta)$, the joint distribution of the data and parameters by $h(\theta, Y)$, and the marginal distribution of the data by $f(Y)$. The posterior distribution of the parameters given the data is denoted by $p(\theta \mid Y)$. Now the joint density $h(\theta, Y)$ is alternatively factored as

$$h(\theta, Y) = f(Y \mid \theta)g(\theta) = p(\theta \mid Y)f(Y), \tag{7.7}$$

from which we obtain Bayes' theorem:

$$p(\theta \mid Y) = \frac{f(Y \mid \theta)g(\theta)}{f(Y)}, \tag{7.8}$$

or because $f(Y)$ has no operational significance,

$$p(\theta \mid Y) \propto f(Y \mid \theta)g(\theta). \tag{7.9}$$

It is customary, noting the functional equivalence of $f(Y \mid \theta)$ and the likelihood function $L(\theta \mid Y)$, to express the posterior distribution as

$$p(\theta \mid Y) \propto L(\theta \mid Y)g(\theta). \tag{7.10}$$

This shows how the posterior distribution combines the likelihood function with the prior distribution.

Notice that whereas classical inferences are based only on sample information and thus are is purely objective, one can take advantage of subjective and/or nonsample prior information in Bayesian inference. When the prior information is not available, a "flat" prior is adopted in Bayesian analysis. Such a prior distribution is called a *diffuse* or *noninformative* prior and reflects the researcher's ignorance about the parameters.

7.2 Bayesian Analysis: An Introduction

Bayesian methods have a long history in econometrics; the classical reference work is Zellner 1971. In Bayesian analysis, choice of the prior distribution may be problematic. In principle, a prior distribution of any functional form can be combined with the likelihood function to form a posterior density. (This does not mean that any density will do; a normal density may not be used as a prior density for σ^2, because variances cannot take on negative values.) Among the group of densities that may reasonably represent prior information, certain densities may be more easily combined with the likelihood function than others. A *natural conjugate prior* is an example. When a natural conjugate prior is combined with the likelihood function, the posterior density has the same form as the prior density. Throughout this section, we employ such natural conjugate priors.

7.2.1 Example 1: A Bayesian Inference of β When σ^2 Is Known

Assuming that the prior distribution of β in (7.1) is given by a multivariate normal distribution of the following form:

Prior Distribution of β

$$\beta \mid \sigma^2 \sim N(\beta_0, \Sigma_0), \tag{7.11}$$

where β_0 and Σ_0 are known, the prior density can be written as

$$==> g(\beta \mid \sigma^2) = (2\pi)^{-\frac{K}{2}} \mid \Sigma_0 \mid \exp\{-\frac{1}{2}(\beta - \beta_0)'\Sigma_0^{-1}(\beta - \beta_0)\}$$

$$\propto \exp\{-\frac{1}{2}(\beta - \beta_0)'\Sigma_0^{-1}(\beta - \beta_0)\}, \tag{7.12}$$

where $(2\pi)^{-\frac{K}{2}} \mid \Sigma_0 \mid$ is a known constant.

Because of the assumption of normality in (7.1), the likelihood function is given by

$$L(\beta \mid \sigma^2, Y) = (2\pi\sigma^2)^{-\frac{T}{2}} \exp(-\frac{1}{2\sigma^2}(Y - X\beta)'(Y - X\beta))$$

$$\propto \exp\{-\frac{1}{2\sigma^2}(Y - X\beta)'(Y - X\beta)\}, \tag{7.13}$$

where $(2\pi\sigma^2)^{-\frac{T}{2}}$ is a known constant.

Combining the prior density, which summarizes the nonsample information, and the likelihood function, which summarizes the sample information, according to equation (7.10), we get the following posterior density of β:

$$p(\beta \mid \sigma^2, Y) \propto g(\beta \mid \sigma^2)L(\beta \mid \sigma^2, Y)$$

$$\propto \exp\{-\frac{1}{2}(\beta - \beta_0)'\Sigma_0^{-1}(\beta - \beta_0) - \frac{1}{2\sigma^2}(Y - X\beta)'(Y - X\beta)\}. \tag{7.14}$$

Notice that given a normal density for the prior of β, the posterior density in (7.14) is also of normal form. Thus, the normal density is the natural conjugate prior for β. Rearranging terms, it can be shown (see Judge et al. 1982) that the posterior distribution of β is given by the following normal distribution:

Posterior Distribution of β

$$\beta \mid \sigma^2, Y \sim N(\beta_1, \Sigma_1), \tag{7.15}$$

where

$$\beta_1 = (\Sigma_0^{-1} + \sigma^{-2}X'X)^{-1}(\Sigma_0^{-1}\beta_0 + \sigma^{-2}X'Y), \tag{7.16}$$

$$\Sigma_1 = (\Sigma_0^{-1} + \sigma^{-2}X'X)^{-1}. \tag{7.17}$$

From (7.16), an alternative representation for the posterior mean β_1 would be

$$\beta_1 = (\Sigma_0^{-1} + \sigma^{-2}X'X)^{-1}(\Sigma_0^{-1}\beta_0 + \sigma^{-2}X'Xb), \tag{7.18}$$

where $b = (X'X)^{-1}X'Y$ summarizes the sample estimate of β and β_0 is the prior mean of β. Thus the posterior mean, β_1, of β is a matrix average of β_0 and b. In the simplest case in which X is a vector of 1s, b refers to the sample mean of Y, and the posterior mean of β is the weighted average of the sample mean and the prior mean, the weights being the precision (inverse of the variance) of the two measures.

7.2.2   Example 2: Bayesian Inference for σ^2 When β Is Known

The natural conjugate prior for σ^2 is the inverted Gamma distribution. Or alternatively, the natural conjugate prior for $\frac{1}{\sigma^2}$ is the Gamma distribution. So we begin this section with a review of the Gamma distribution.

NOTE   Let z_t be i.i.d. normal with mean 0 and variance $\frac{1}{\delta}$:

$$z_t \sim \text{i.i.d.} N(0, \frac{1}{\delta}), \quad t = 1, 2, \ldots, \nu \tag{7.19}$$

Then, we have

$$W = \sum_{t=1}^{\nu} z_t^2 \sim \Gamma(\frac{\nu}{2}, \frac{\delta}{2}), \tag{7.20}$$

where the density function for the Gamma distribution is given by

$$g(W) \propto W^{\frac{\nu}{2}-1} \exp(-\frac{W\delta}{2}), \tag{7.21}$$

with

$$E(W) = \frac{\nu}{\delta}, \tag{7.22}$$

$$\text{Var}(W) = 2\frac{\nu}{\delta^2}. \tag{7.23}$$

Note also that, when $\delta = 1$, $W \sim \chi^2(\nu)$ with $E(W) = \nu$ and $\text{Var}(W) = 2\nu$.

Assuming that the prior distribution of $1/\sigma^2$ is given by a Gamma distribution of the form

Prior Distribution of $1/\sigma^2$

$$\frac{1}{\sigma^2} \mid \beta \sim \Gamma(\frac{\nu_0}{2}, \frac{\delta_0}{2}), \tag{7.24}$$

where ν_0 and δ_0 are known. By letting $W = 1/\sigma^2$ in (7.21), the prior density of $1/\sigma^2$ can be written as

$$g(\frac{1}{\sigma^2} \mid \beta) \propto (\frac{1}{\sigma^2})^{\frac{\nu_0}{2}-1} \exp(-\frac{\delta_0}{2\sigma^2}). \tag{7.25}$$

As in section 7.1, because of the assumption of normality in the model given by (7.1), the likelihood function is given by

$$L(\frac{1}{\sigma^2} \mid \beta, Y) = (2\pi\sigma^2)^{-\frac{T}{2}} \exp(-\frac{1}{2\sigma^2}(Y - X\beta)'(Y - X\beta))$$

$$\propto (\sigma^2)^{-\frac{T}{2}} \exp(-\frac{1}{2\sigma^2}(Y - X\beta)'(Y - X\beta)).$$

(7.26)

We then multiply the prior density (7.25) and the likelihood function (7.26) to get the following posterior density for $1/\sigma^2$:

$$p(\frac{1}{\sigma^2} \mid \beta, Y) \propto g(\frac{1}{\sigma^2} \mid \beta)L(\frac{1}{\sigma^2} \mid \beta, Y)$$

$$\propto (\frac{1}{\sigma^2})^{\frac{\nu_0}{2}-1} \exp(-\frac{\delta_0}{2\sigma^2}) \times (\sigma^2)^{-\frac{T}{2}} \exp(-\frac{1}{2\sigma^2}(Y - X\beta)'(Y - X\beta))$$

$$= (\frac{1}{\sigma^2})^{\frac{\nu_0}{2}-\frac{T}{2}-1} \exp(-\frac{1}{2\sigma^2}(\delta_0 + (Y - X\beta)'(Y - X\beta))$$

$$= (\frac{1}{\sigma^2})^{\frac{\nu_1}{2}-1} \exp(-\frac{\delta_1}{2\sigma^2}),$$

(7.27)

Notice that given a Gamma density for the prior of $1/\sigma^2$, the posterior density is also a Gamma density. Thus the Gamma density is the natural conjugate prior for $1/\sigma^2$. The density function in (7.27) suggests that the posterior distribution of $1/\sigma^2$ is given by:

Posterior Distribution of $1/\sigma^2$

$$\frac{1}{\sigma^2} \mid \beta, Y \sim \Gamma(\frac{\nu_1}{2}, \frac{\delta_1}{2}),$$

(7.28)

where

$$\nu_1 = \nu_0 + T,$$

(7.29)

$$\delta_1 = \delta_0 + (Y - X\beta)'(Y - X\beta).$$

(7.30)

Alternatively, the prior and posterior distributions of σ^2 may be represented as

Prior Distribution of σ^2

$$\sigma^2 \mid \beta \sim IG(\frac{\nu_0}{2}, \frac{\delta_0}{2}),$$

(7.31)

Posterior Distribution of σ^2

$$\sigma^2 \mid \beta, Y \sim IG(\frac{\nu_1}{2}, \frac{\delta_1}{2}), \tag{7.32}$$

where IG refers to inverted Gamma distribution and ν_1 and δ_1 are defined in (7.29) and (7.30).

7.2.3 Example 3: Bayesian Inference When Both β and σ^2 Are Unknown

When both β and σ^2 are unknown, we first specify the joint prior distribution for these parameters. Assuming a Gamma distribution for the marginal prior p.d.f. for $1/\sigma^2$ and a normal distribution for the conditional prior p.d.f. for $\beta \mid 1/\sigma^2$, we have the following joint prior density:

Joint Prior Density

$$g(\beta, \frac{1}{\sigma^2}) = g(\beta \mid \frac{1}{\sigma^2})g(\frac{1}{\sigma^2}), \tag{7.33}$$

where

$$\beta \mid \frac{1}{\sigma^2} \sim N(\beta_2, \Sigma_2), \tag{7.34}$$

$$\frac{1}{\sigma^2} \sim \Gamma(\frac{\nu_2}{2}, \frac{\delta_2}{2}), \tag{7.35}$$

where β_2, Σ_2, ν_2, and δ_2 are known.

Combining the above joint prior density and the likelihood function, it can be shown that the joint posterior density of β and $1/\sigma^2$ is given by

Joint Posterior Density

$$p(\beta, \frac{1}{\sigma^2} \mid Y) = g(\beta, \frac{1}{\sigma^2})L(\beta, \frac{1}{\sigma^2} \mid Y)$$

$$= p(\beta \mid \frac{1}{\sigma^2}, Y)p(\frac{1}{\sigma^2} \mid Y), \tag{7.36}$$

where the posterior distribution of β conditional on $1/\sigma^2$ is a normal distribution and the marginal posterior distribution of $1/\sigma^2$ is a Gamma distribution:

$$\beta \mid \frac{1}{\sigma^2}, Y \sim N(\beta_3, \Sigma_3), \tag{7.37}$$

$$\frac{1}{\sigma^2} \mid Y \sim \Gamma(\frac{\nu_3}{2}, \frac{\delta_3}{2}),\tag{7.38}$$

where β_3, Σ_3, ν_3, and δ_3 can be shown to be appropriately defined. For detailed derivation and results, refer to chapter 7 of Judge et al. 1982.

Given the above joint posterior density, to make an inference on β, we need to obtain the marginal posterior distribution of β by integration:

Marginal Posterior Distribution of β

$$g(\beta \mid Y) = \int_0^\infty g(\beta, \frac{1}{\sigma^2} \mid Y)d\sigma^2,\tag{7.39}$$

which can be shown to have a multivariate t-distribution.

As this example suggests, Bayesian analysis usually requires integration to get the marginal posterior distributions of individual parameters from a joint posterior distribution of all unknown parameters of the model. These integrals, however, may be difficult to solve, and sometimes, the joint posterior density itself, from which the marginal densities are to be derived, is difficult to derive. The Gibbs-sampling methodology introduced in the next section offers an easy way to solve these problems, given that conditional posterior distributions such as those in of sections 7.2.1 and 7.2.2 are readily available. Although the integral involved in (7.39) or the derivation of the joint posterior density in (7.36) are feasible, the Gibbs-sampling approach may be employed to obtain easily the marginal distribution of β without integration and without having to know the joint density.

7.3   Gibbs-Sampling: Motivation and Basic Idea

Gibbs-sampling is a Markov chain Monte Carlo simulation method for approximating joint and marginal distributions by sampling from conditional distributions. (Useful references are Casella and George 1993; Geman and Geman 1984; Gelfand and Smith 1990; and Gelfand et al. 1990.)

Suppose we are given a joint density of k random variables, $f(z_1, z_2, \ldots, z_k)$, and that we are interested in obtaining characteristics of the marginal density

$$f(z_t) = \int \ldots \int f(z_1, z_2, \ldots, z_k)dz_1 \ldots dz_{t-1}dz_{t+1} \ldots dz_k,\tag{7.40}$$

such as the mean or variance. However, the joint density may not be given, or even if the joint density is known, the integrations in (7.40) may be difficult to perform. If we are given the complete set of conditional densities, denoted $f(z_t \mid z_{j \neq t})$, $t = 1, 2, \ldots, k$, with $z_{j \neq t} = \{z_1, \ldots, z_{t-1}, z_{t+1}, \ldots, z_k\}$, then the Gibbs-sampling technique allows us to generate a sample $z_1^j, z_2^j, z_3^j, \ldots, z_k^j$, from the joint density $f(z_1, \ldots, z_k)$ without requiring that we know either the joint density or the marginal densities $f(z_t)$, $t = 1, 2, \ldots, k$. The following explains the basic idea of the Gibbs-sampling methodology: Given an arbitrary starting set of values $(z_2^0, \ldots, z_k^0)$,

1. Draw z_1^1 from $f(z_1 \mid z_2^0, \ldots, z_k^0)$.
2. Then draw z_2^1 from $f(z_2 \mid z_1^1, z_3^0, \ldots, z_k^0)$.
3. Then draw z_3^1 from $f(z_3 \mid z_1^1, z_2^1, z_4^0 \ldots, z_k^0)$.

$\vdots$

k. Finally draw z_k^1 from $f(z_k \mid z_1^1, \ldots, z_{k-1}^1)$ to complete one iteration.

Steps 1 through k can be iterated J times to get $(z_1^j, z_2^j, \ldots, z_k^j)$, $j = 1, 2, \ldots, J$. Geman and Geman (1984) have shown that the joint and marginal distributions of generated $(z_1^j, z_2^j, \ldots, z_k^j)$ converge at an exponential rate to the joint and marginal distributions of $z_1, z_2, \ldots, z_k$, as $J \to \infty$. Thus the joint and marginal distributions of $z_1, z_2, \ldots, z_k$ can be approximated by the empirical distributions of M simulated values $(z_1^j, z_2^j, \ldots, z_k^j)$ $(j = L + 1, L + M)$, where L is large enough that the Gibbs-sampler has converged. M can be chosen to give sufficient precision to the empirical distribution of interest. For example, the mean of the marginal distribution of z_i may be approximated by

$$\frac{\sum_{j=1}^M z_i^{L+j}}{M},$$

and the marginal distribution of z_i may be approximated by the empirical distribution of $(z_i^{L+1}, z_i^{L+2}, \ldots, z_i^{L+M})$.

Convergence of the Gibbs-sampling is also an important issue. McCulloch and Rocci (1994) suggest plotting the estimates of the posterior densities over Gibbs iterations. If these estimated densities show little variation with additional Gibbs iterations, one may conclude that the Gibbs-sampling has converged. Gelman and Rubin (1992) suggest that a single sequence of samples may give a false impression of convergence, no matter how many draws are chosen. Thus they suggest trying various different sets of starting values for Gibbs-sampling.

7.4   Examples of Gibbs-Sampling in Econometrics

7.4.1   A Univariate Autoregression

This section demonstrates the application of Gibbs-sampling to Bayesian estimation of a univariate autoregression. The data set we employ is the real GDP series for the period 1952:II–1995:III.

Consider the following linear AR(4) model for the first differences of the log real GDP:

$$y_t = \mu + \phi_1 y_{t-1} + \phi_2 y_{t-2} + \phi_3 y_{t-3} + \phi_4 y_{t-4} + e_t, \tag{7.41}$$

$$e_t \sim \text{i.i.d.} N(0, \sigma^2), \tag{7.42}$$

where roots of $(1 - \phi_1 L - \phi_2 L^2 - \phi_3 L^3 - \phi_4 L^4) = 0$ lie outside the complex unit circle. In matrix notation, we have

$$Y = X\beta + e, \quad e \sim N(0, \sigma^2 I_T), \tag{7.43}$$

where $\beta = [\, \mu \quad \phi_1 \quad \phi_2 \quad \phi_3 \quad \phi_4 \,]'$ and X is the matrix of 1 and lagged observation on Y.

To apply the Gibbs-sampling approach to the above model, we need conditional posterior distributions of β and σ^2, given appropriate conditional prior distributions. In section 7.2.1, we derived a posterior distribution of β assuming that σ^2 is known. In section 7.2.2, we also derived a posterior distribution of σ^2 assuming that β is known. Although those were for the case of fixed regressors, the results are the same for the case of an autoregression.

We need the following two conditional distributions for Gibbs-sampling:

Conditional Distributions of β, Given σ^2

Prior

$$\beta \mid \sigma^2 \sim N(\beta_0, \Sigma_0)_{I[s(\phi)]}, \tag{7.44}$$

where β_0 and Σ_0 are known and $I[s(\phi)]$ is an indicator function used to denote roots of $\phi(L) = 0$ that lie outside the unit circle.

Posterior

$$\beta \mid \sigma^2, Y \sim N(\beta_1, \Sigma_1)_{I[s(\phi)]}, \tag{7.45}$$

where

$$\beta_1 = (\Sigma_0^{-1} + \sigma^{-2} X'X)^{-1}(\Sigma_0^{-1}\beta_0 + \sigma^{-2}X'Y), \tag{7.46}$$

$$\Sigma_1 = (\Sigma_0^{-1} + \sigma^{-2} X'X)^{-1}. \tag{7.47}$$

Conditional Distributions of σ^2, Given β

Prior

$$\sigma^2 \mid \beta \sim IG(\frac{\nu_0}{2}, \frac{\delta_0}{2}), \tag{7.48}$$

where IG refers to an inverted Gamma distribution and δ_0 and nu_0 are known.

Posterior

$$\sigma^2 \mid \beta, Y \sim IG(\frac{\nu_1}{2}, \frac{\delta_1}{2}), \tag{7.49}$$

$$\nu_1 = \nu_0 + T, \tag{7.50}$$

$$\delta_1 = \delta_0 + (Y - X\beta)'(Y - X\beta). \tag{7.51}$$

Given the conditional posterior distributions in (7.45) and (7.49), it is straightforward to implement Gibbs-sampling. One can start the iteration of Gibbs-sampling with an arbitrary starting value for $\sigma^2 = \{\sigma^2\}^0$. Then the following is iterated for $j = 1, 2, \ldots, L + M$:

1. Conditional on $\sigma^2 = \{\sigma^2\}^{j-1}$, a generated value of σ^2 at the previous iteration, generate β^j from the conditional posterior distribution in (7.45),

2. Conditional on $\beta = \beta^j$, a generated value of β from (1), generate $\{\sigma^2\}^j$ from the conditional posterior distribution in (7.49).

3. Set $j = j - 1$, and go to (1).

In generating $\beta = [\mu \quad \phi_1 \quad \phi_2 \quad \phi_3 \quad \phi_4]'$ from (7.45) we employ "rejection sampling" to ensure that roots of $(1 - \phi_1 L - \phi_2 L^2 - \phi_3 L^3 - \phi_4 L^4) = 0$ lie outside the complex unit circle. For example, if the generated values for ϕ_1, ϕ_2, ϕ_2, and ϕ_4 do not satisfy the stationarity condition, we discard them and they are simulated again until the condition is satisfied.

As a result, we have the following sets of generated values for β and σ^2:

Table 7.1
Bayesian versus classical inferences on parameter estimates: a linear AR(4) model of real GDP
(1952:I–1995:IV)

	Prior		Posterior			MLE results	
	Mean	SD	Mean	SD	MD		
μ	0	1,000	0.506	0.103	0.507	0.505	(0.104)
ϕ_1	0	1,000	0.306	0.076	0.305	0.307	(0.076)
ϕ_2	0	1,000	0.097	0.079	0.100	0.097	(0.079)
ϕ_3	0	1,000	−0.092	0.082	−0.092	−0.091	(0.079)
ϕ_4	0	1,000	−0.031	0.075	−0.031	−0.032	(0.076)
σ^2	−	−	0.781	0.090	0.775	0.749	(0.081)

Note: Standard errors of the ML estimates are reported in parentheses. Prior distribution of σ^2 is improper. SD and MD refer to standard deviation and median, respectively.

$$\beta^1, \beta^2, \beta^3, \ldots, \beta^{L+M},$$

$$\{\sigma^2\}^1, \{\sigma^2\}^2, \{\sigma^2\}^3, \ldots, \{\sigma^2\}^{L+M}.$$

We discard the first L generated values to ensure the convergence of the Gibbs-sampler, then we make inferences (mean, median, standard deviation, posterior probability bands, etc.) of β and σ^2, based on the remaining M generated values. These remaining M values of β and σ^2 provide us with the marginal and joint distributions.

The first 1,000 draws in the Gibbs simulation process are discarded, and then the next 4,000 draws are saved and used to calculate the moments of the marginal posterior distributions. These are reported in table 7.1.

It is interesting the compare the results from the Bayesian Gibbs-sampling with those from the classical MLE approach. As we are employing almost non-informative priors for the parameters, little non-sample information is incorporated in the Bayesian approach. Therefore, we expect the Bayesian inferences to be very close to the classical inferences. Results in table 7.1 confirm this.

7.4.2   A Regression Model with Autocorrelated Disturbances

Consider the following regression model with AR(p) disturbances:

$$y_t = \beta_1 + \beta_2 x_{2t} + \ldots + \beta_k x_{kt} + e_t, \tag{7.52}$$

$$(Y = X\beta + e), \tag{7.52'}$$

$$e_t = \phi_1 e_{t-1} + \ldots + \phi_p e_{t-p} + v_t, \quad v_t \sim \text{i.i.d.} N(0, \sigma^2), \tag{7.53}$$

$$(e = E\phi + v), \tag{7.53'}$$

where X is exogenous, the roots of $(1 - \phi_1 L - \ldots - \phi_p L^p) = 0$ lie outside the complex unit circle, and E is the matrix of lagged values of e.

One nice conditioning feature of this model is that

1. Conditional on β, the problem reduces to making inferences on ϕ and σ^2 from the following AR(p) model:

$$e_t^* = \phi_1 e_{t-1}^* + \ldots + \phi_p e_{t-p}^* + v_t, \quad v_t \sim \text{i.i.d.} N(0, \sigma^2), \tag{7.54}$$

$$(e^* = E^*\phi + v, \quad v \sim N(0, \sigma^2 I_{T-p})), \tag{7.54'}$$

where $e_t^* = y_t - \beta_1 - \beta_2 x_{2t} - \ldots - \beta_k x_{kt}$.

2. Conditional on ϕ and σ^2, the problem reduces to making inferences on β from the following regression model with known variance:

$$y_t^* = \beta_1^* + \beta_2 x_{2t}^* + \ldots + \beta_k x_{kt}^* + v_t, \quad v_t \sim \text{i.i.d.} N(0, \sigma^2), \tag{7.55}$$

$$(Y^* = X^*\beta + v, \quad v \sim N(0, \sigma^2 I_{T-1})), \tag{7.55'}$$

where $y_t^* = y_t - \phi_1 y_{t-1} - \ldots - \phi_p y_{t-p}$, $x_{it}^* = x_t - \phi_1 x_{t-1} - \ldots - \phi_p x_{i,t-p}$, $i = 1, 2, \ldots, k$, and $\beta_1^* = \beta_1 (1 - \phi_1 - \phi_2 - \ldots - \phi_p)$.

The Gibbs-sampling approach to a regression model with autocorrelated disturbances was first considered by Chib (1993). An understanding of the examples in sections 7.2.1 and 7.2.2 is enough to derive the full conditional posterior distributions of the model's parameters. Given the following full conditional posterior distributions of β, ϕ, and σ^2, Gibbs-sampling can easily be implemented:

Conditional Distributions of β, Given ϕ and σ^2

Prior

$$\beta \mid \phi, \sigma^2 \sim N(b_0, A_0), \tag{7.56}$$

where β_0 and A_0 are known.

Posterior

$$\beta \mid \phi, \sigma^2, Y \sim N(b_1, A_1), \tag{7.57}$$

where

$$b_1 = (A_0^{-1} + \sigma^{-2}X^{*\prime}X^*)^{-1}(A_0^{-1}b_0 + \sigma^{-2}X^{*\prime}Y^*), \tag{7.58}$$

$$A_1 = (A_0^{-1} + \sigma^{-2}X^{*\prime}X^*)^{-1}, \tag{7.59}$$

and where X^* and Y^* are given in (7.53′).

Conditional Distributions of ϕ, Given β and σ^2

Prior

$$\phi \mid \beta, \sigma^2 \sim N(c_0, B_0)_{I[s(\phi)]}, \tag{7.60}$$

where $I[s(\phi)]$ is an indicator function used to denote that roots of $\phi(L) = 0$ lie outside the unit circle.

Posterior

$$\phi \mid \beta, \sigma^2, Y \sim N(c_1, B_1)_{I[s(\phi)]}, \tag{7.61}$$

where

$$c_1 = (B_0^{-1} + \sigma^{-2}E^{*\prime}E^*)^{-1}(B_0^{-1}c_0 + \sigma^{-2}E^{*\prime}e^*), \tag{7.62}$$

$$c_1 = (B_0^{-1} + \sigma^{-2}E^{*\prime}E^*)^{-1}, \tag{7.63}$$

and where E^* and e^* are given in (7.54)′.

Conditional Distributions of σ^2, Given β and ϕ

Prior

$$\sigma^2 \mid \beta \sim IG(\frac{\nu_0}{2}, \frac{\delta_0}{2}), \tag{7.64}$$

where IG refers to inverted Gamma distribution and δ_0 and ν_0 are known.

Posterior

$$\sigma^2 \mid \beta, Y \sim IG(\frac{\nu_1}{2}, \frac{\delta_1}{2}), \tag{7.65}$$

$$\nu_1 = \nu_0 + T, \tag{7.66}$$

$$\delta_1 = \delta_0 + (Y^* - X^*\beta)'(Y^* - X^*\beta), \tag{7.67}$$

where X^* and Y^* are given in (7.55)′.

Table 7.2
Bayesian versus classical inferences on parameter estimates: a regression model with autocorrelated disturbances (Generated data set)

	Prior		Posterior			MLE results	
	Mean	SD	Mean	SD	MD		
β_0	0	1,000	−0.011	0.225	−0.012	−0.027	(0.189)
β_1	0	1,000	0.946	0.079	0.947	0.944	(0.078)
ϕ	0	1,000	0.615	0.067	0.617	0.604	(0.066)
σ^2	—	—	0.995	0.122	0.986	0.961	(0.109)

Note: True values of β_0, β_1, ϕ, and σ^2 are 0, 1, 0.5, and 1, respectively. Standard errors of the ML estimates are reported in parentheses. Prior distribution of σ^2 is improper. SD and MD refer to standard deviation and median, respectively.

As in Section 7.3.1, one can start the iteration of Gibbs-sampling with arbitrary starting values, $\phi = \phi^0$ and $\sigma^2 = \{\sigma^2\}^0$. Then the following is iterated for Gibbs simulations:

1. Conditional on $\phi = \phi^{j-1}$ and $\sigma^2 = \{\sigma^2\}^{j-1}$, generate β^j from the conditional posterior distribution in (7.57).

2. Conditional on $\sigma^2 = \{\sigma^2\}^{j-1}$ and $\beta = \beta^j$, generate ϕ^j from the conditional posterior distribution in (7.61).

3. Conditional on $\beta = \beta^j$ and $\phi = \phi^j$, generate $\{\sigma^2\}^j$ from the conditional posterior distribution in (7.65).

4. Set $j = j - 1$, and go to (1).

Following Chib (1993), we apply the above Gibbs-sampling algorithm to a generated data set and compare the results to those from MLE. The data-generating process is given by

$$y_t = \beta_0 + \beta_1 x_t + e_t, \tag{7.68}$$

$$e_t = \phi e_{t-1} + v_t, \quad v_t \sim \text{i.i.d.}N(0, \sigma^2), \tag{7.69}$$

$$x_t = 0.5x_{t-1} + w_t, \quad w_t \sim \text{i.i.d.}N(0, 1), \tag{7.70}$$

where the values assigned for the parameters in the data generation are $\beta_0 = 0$, $\beta_1 = 1$, $\phi = 0.5$, and $\sigma^2 = 1$.

Inferences on β_0, β_1, ϕ, and σ^2 are based on 4,000 draws from the posterior, after 1,000 draws have been discarded. Figures 7.1–7.4 show the marginal posterior distributions (histograms) of these four parameters. Table 7.2 reports

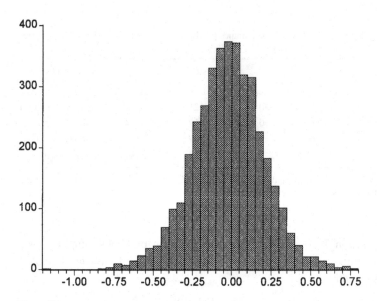

Figure 7.1
Marginal posterior distribution of β_0

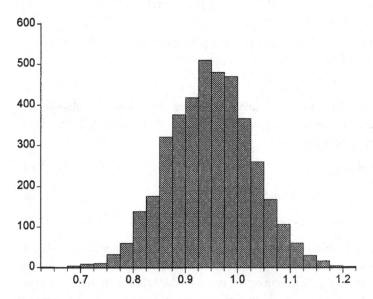

Figure 7.2
Marginal posterior distribution of β_1

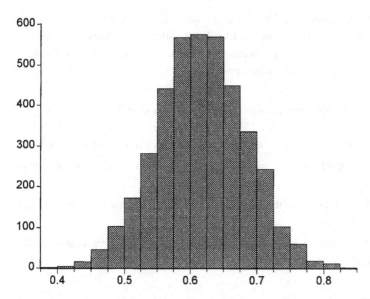

Figure 7.3
Marginal posterior distribution of ϕ

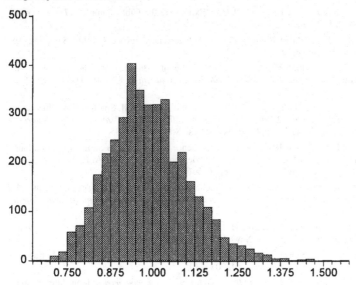

Figure 7.4
Marginal posterior distribution of σ^2

posterior mean, median, and standard deviation of these posterior distibutions. When compared to the maximum likelihood estimation results, with almost noninformative priors for the Bayesian approach, the posterior means are close to the ML estimates of the parameters.

Appendix: GAUSS Programs to Accompany Chapter 7

1. GBS_AR4.PRG: A Gibbs-sampling approach to a linear AR(4) model.

2. MLE_AR4.OPT: A maximum likelihood estimation of a linear AR(4) model.

3. GBS_ATO.PRG: A Gibbs-sampling approach to a regression model with AR(1) disturbances.

4. MLE_ATO.PRG: A maximum likelihood estimation of a regression model with AR(1) disturbances.

References

Casella, George, and Edward I. George. 1993. "Explaining the Gibbs Sampler." *The American Statistician,* 46(3), 167–174.

Chib, Siddhartha. 1993. "Bayes Regression with Autocorrelated Errors: A Gibbs Sampling Approach." *Journal of Econometrics,* 58, 275–294.

Gelfand, Alan E., and Adrian F. M. Smith. 1990. "Sampling-Based Approaches to Calculating Marginal Densities." *Journal of the American Statistical Association,* 85(410), Theory and Methods, 398–409.

Gelfand, Alan E., Susan E. Hills, Amy Racine-Poon, and Adrian F. M. Smith. 1990. "Illustration of Bayesian Inference in normal Data Models Using Gibbs Sampling." *Journal of the American Statistical Association,* 85(412), Applications and Case Studies, 972–985.

Gelman, A., and D. B. Rubin. 1992. "A Single Sequence from the Gibbs Sampler Gives a False Sense of Security." In *Bayesian Statistics,* ed. J. M. Bernardo, J. O. Berger, A. P. Dawid, and A. F. M. Smith, Oxford: Oxford Press University, pp. 625–631.

Geman, Stuart, and Donald Geman. 1984. "Stochastic Relaxation, Gibbs Distributions and the Bayesian Restoration of Images." *IEEE Transactions on Pattern Analysis and Machine Intelligence,* 6, 721–741.

Judge, G. G., R. C. Hill, W. E. Griffiths, H. Lutkepohl, and T.-C. Lee. 1982. *Introduction to the Theory and Practice of Econometrics.* New York: John Wiley & Sons.

McCulloch, Robert, and Peter E. Rossi. 1994. "An Exact Likelihood analysis of Multinomial Probit Model." *Journal of Econometrics,* 64, 207–240.

Zellner, Arnold. 1971. *An Introduction to Bayesian Inference in Econometrics.* John Wiley & Sons.

8 State-Space Models and Gibbs-Sampling

Consider the following state-space model introduced in chapter 3:

$$y_t = H\beta_t + Az_t + e_t, \tag{8.1}$$

$$\beta_t = \tilde{\mu} + F\beta_{t-1} + v_t, \tag{8.2}$$

$$e_t \sim \text{i.i.d.} N(0, R), \tag{8.3}$$

$$v_t \sim \text{i.i.d.} N(0, Q), \tag{8.4}$$

$$E(e_t v_s') = 0, \tag{8.5}$$

where y_t is an $n \times 1$ vector of variables observed at time t; β_t is a $k \times 1$ vector of unobserved state variables; H is an $n \times k$ matrix that links the observed y_t vector and the unobserved state variable β_t; z_t is an $r \times 1$ vector of exogenous or predetermined variables; $\tilde{\mu}$ is $k \times 1$; and v_t is $k \times 1$.

Within the classical framework of chapter 3, the Kalman filter and maximum likelihood estimation based on prediction error decomposition open the way to inference for this model. Defining $\tilde{\beta}_T = [\,\beta_1 \quad \beta_2 \quad \ldots \quad \beta_T\,]'$, one potential disadvantage of the classical approach is that inferences about the state variable $\tilde{\beta}_T$ are conditional on the estimated values of the hyper-parameters (elements of H, A, $\tilde{\mu}$, F, Q, and R) of the model. That is, we first obtain the maximum likelihood estimates of the model's unknown hyperparameters. Then, to get estimates of $\tilde{\beta}_T$, we treat the ML estimates as if they were the true values for the model's nonrandom hyperparameters.

Within the Bayesian approach, however, both the model's hyperparameters and the state variable $\tilde{\beta}_T$ are treated as random variables. In contrast to the classical approach, inference on $\tilde{\beta}_T$ is based on the joint distribution of $\tilde{\beta}_T$ and hyperparameters, not a conditional distribution. In addition, the conditioning feature of the Gibbs-sampling and recent advances in the literature (see Carlin, Polson, and Stoffer 1992; Carter and Kohn 1994; and Shephard 1994 for examples) make Bayesian inference in the state-space model easy to implement.

This chapter deals with fundamental issues that arise in the analysis of state-space models via Bayesian Gibbs-sampling. The basic idea is that the unobserved state vector, $\tilde{\beta}\_T$, along with the model's unknown hyperparameters can be treated as missing data, and they can be generated using the simulation tool of Gibbs-sampling and then analyzed. For Gibbs simulations, the following two steps are iterated until convergence is achieved, with arbitrary starting values for the hyperparameters:

STEP 1   Conditional on the model's hyperparameters and the observed data, generate $\tilde{\beta}_T$.

STEP 2   Conditional on $\tilde{\beta}_T$ and the observed data, generate the model's hyperparameters.

The second step of the above procedure is straightforward to implement. Notice that conditional on $\tilde{\beta}_T$, the measurement and transition equations in (8.1) and (8.2) are two independent sets of linear regression equations, because v_t and e_t are independent. By treating $\tilde{\beta}_T$ generated in step 1 as a set of data, the problem of generating the unknown hyperparameters in each of the two sets of equations collapses to the examples provided in chapter 7.

Methods of generating $\tilde{\beta}_T$ conditional on the model's hyperparameters and the observed data set is what is new in this chapter. Sections 8.1 and 8.2 deal with these issues, as discussed in Carter and Kohn 1994, although the results presented are more general than in Carter and Kohn. In those two sections, it is assumed that the model's hyperparameters are known. In section 8.3, we apply the Bayesian Gibbs-sampling approach to Stock and Watson's (1991) dynamic factor model of the coincident economic indicators considered in chapter 3. Inference for the state vector (or equivalently, the new experimental coincident index) and the unknown parameters of the model are made based on a joint distribution that results from Gibbs-simulations. This analysis allows us to compare the results from the two alternative approaches: the classical approach in chapter 3 and the Bayesian Gibbs-sampling approach in this chapter.

8.1   Generating the State Vector When Q Is Positive-Definite

The literature suggests at least two alternative ways of generating $\tilde{\beta}_T$, given the hyperparameters of the model and the observed data: singlemove Gibbs-sampling and multimove Gibbs-sampling. Single-move Gibbs-sampling, originally suggested by Carlin, Polson, and Stoffer (1992), generates the state vector $\tilde{\beta}_T$ one element at a time, utilizing the Markov properties of the state-space model to condition neighboring states. In this approach, the state vector is generated from the following conditional distribution:

$$p(\beta_t \mid \tilde{\beta}_{\neq t}, \tilde{y}_T), \qquad t = 1, 2, \ldots, T, \tag{8.6}$$

where $\tilde{\beta}_{\neq t}$ is a vector of state variables that excludes β_t and $\tilde{y}_T = [y_1 \ldots y_T]'$ is a vector of observed data in the sample. Multimove Gibbs-sampling, on the contrary, as suggested by Carter and Kohn (1994), generates the whole vector of $\tilde{\beta}_T$ from the following joint distribution:

$$p(\tilde{\beta}_T \mid \tilde{y}_T). \tag{8.7}$$

In this chapter, we employ Carter and Kohn's multimove Gibbs-sampling approach for its computational efficiency and faster convergence. Thus, our purpose is to generate $\tilde{\beta}_T$ from the joint distribution given by

$$p(\tilde{\beta}_T \mid \tilde{y}_T)$$

$$= p(\beta_T \mid \tilde{y}_T) p(\tilde{\beta}_{T-1} \mid \beta_T, \tilde{y}_T)$$

$$= p(\beta_T \mid \tilde{y}_T) p(\beta_{T-1} \mid \beta_T, \tilde{y}_T) p(\tilde{\beta}_{T-2} \mid \beta_{T-1}, \beta_T, \tilde{y}_T)$$

$$= p(\beta_T \mid \tilde{y}_T) p(\beta_{T-1} \mid \beta_T, \tilde{y}_T) p(\beta_{T-2} \mid \beta_{T-1}, \beta_T, \tilde{y}_T)$$

$$\quad p(\beta_{T-3} \mid \beta_{T-2}, \beta_{T-1}, \beta_T, \tilde{y}_T)$$

$$= \ldots$$

$$= p(\beta_T \mid \tilde{y}_T) p(\beta_{T-1} \mid \beta_T, \tilde{y}_T) p(\beta_{T-2} \mid \beta_{T-1}, \tilde{y}_T) \ldots p(\beta_1 \mid \beta_2, \tilde{y}_T)$$

$$= p(\beta_T \mid \tilde{y}_T) p(\beta_{T-1} \mid \beta_T, \tilde{y}_{T-1}) p(\beta_{T-2} \mid \beta_{T-1}, \tilde{y}_{T-2}) \ldots p(\beta_1 \mid \beta_2, \tilde{y}_1)$$

$$= p(\beta_T \mid \tilde{y}_T) \prod_{t=1}^{T-1} p(\beta_t \mid \beta_{t+1}, \tilde{y}_t), \tag{8.8}$$

where $\tilde{y}_t = [\, y_1 \quad y_2 \quad y_3 \quad \ldots \quad y_t \,]'$ and $\tilde{\beta}_t = [\, \beta_1 \quad \beta_2 \quad \beta_3 \quad \ldots \quad \beta_t \,]'$. The validity of going from the third to the fifth line is established by the Markov property of β_t. Conditional on β_{t-1} and $\tilde{y}_T$, for example, β_t contains no information about β_{t-2} beyond that contained in β_{t-1} and $\tilde{y}_T$. A similar argument applies as we go from the fifth to the sixth line in equation (8.8). Conditional on β_{t-1} and $\tilde{y}_{t-2}$, for example, $\{y_{t-1}, y_t, \ldots, y_T\}$ carries no information about β_{t-2} beyond that contained in β_{t-1} and $\tilde{y}_{t-2}$.

Equation (8.8) suggests that the whole vector of $\tilde{\beta}_T = [\beta_1 \, \beta_2 \, \beta_3 \ldots \beta_T]'$ can be generated by first generating β_T from $p(\beta_T \mid \tilde{y}_T)$, and then, for $t = T - 1, T - 2, \ldots, 2, 1$, generating β_t from $p(\beta_t \mid \beta_{t+1}, \tilde{y}_t)$, given the generated values for β_{t+1}.

Because the state-space model in (8.1)–(8.5) is linear and Gaussian, the distribution of β_T given $\tilde{y}_T$ and that of β_t given β_{t+1} and $\tilde{y}_t$ for $t = T - 1, \ldots, 1$ are also Gaussian:

$$\beta_T \mid \tilde{y}_T \sim N(\beta_{T\mid T}, P_{T\mid T}), \tag{8.9}$$

$$\beta_t \mid \tilde{y}_t, \beta_{t+1} \sim N(\beta_{t|t,\beta_{t+1}}, P_{t|t,\beta_{t+1}}), \qquad t = T - 1, T - 2, \ldots, 1, \qquad (8.10)$$

where

$$\beta_{T|T} = E(\beta_T \mid \tilde{y}_T), \qquad (8.11)$$

$$P_{T|T} = \text{Cov}(\beta_T \mid \tilde{y}_T), \qquad (8.12)$$

$$\beta_{t|t,\beta_{t+1}} = E(\beta_t \mid \tilde{y}_t, \beta_{t+1}) = E(\beta_t \mid \beta_{t|t}, \beta_{t+1}), \qquad (8.13)$$

$$P_{t|t,\beta_{t+1}} = \text{Cov}(\beta_t \mid \tilde{y}_t, \beta_{t+1}) = \text{Cov}(\beta_t \mid \beta_{t|t}, \beta_{t+1}). \qquad (8.14)$$

We can take advantage of the Gaussian Kalman filter in chapter 3 to obtain $\beta_{T|T}$ and $P_{T|T}$ as well as $\beta_{t|t,\beta_{t+1}}$ and $P_{t|t,\beta_{t+1}}$, $t = T - 1, T - 2, \ldots, 1$. For example, the last iteration of the usual updating procedure of the Kalman filter provides us with $\beta_{T|T}$ and $P_{T|T}$, and it is straightforward to generate β_T from (8.9). Once β_T is generated in this way, we need to generate β_t, $t = T - 1, T - 2, \ldots, 1$, from (8.10). Thus, our job is to derive $\beta_{t|t,\beta_{t+1}}$ and $P_{t|t,\beta_{t+1}}$.

For this purpose, let us review the Kalman filter derivation of an updated estimate of β_t and its covariance, given $\beta_{t|t-1}$ and new information y_t:

$$\beta_{t|t} = E(\beta_t \mid \tilde{y}_{t-1}, y_t) = E(\beta_t \mid \beta_{t|t-1}, y_t) = \beta_{t|t-1} + P_{t|t-1} H' f_{t|t-1}^{-1} \eta_{t|t-1},$$

$$(3.79)$$

$$P_{t|t} = \text{Cov}(\beta_t \mid \tilde{y}_t) = \text{Cov}(\beta_t \mid \beta_{t|t-1}, y_t) = P_{t|t-1} - P_{t|t-1} H' f_{t|t-1}^{-1} H P_{t|t-1},$$

$$(3.80)$$

where $\beta_{t|t-1} = E(\beta_t \mid \tilde{y}_{t-1})$; $P_{t|t-1} = \text{Cov}(\beta_t \mid \tilde{y}_{t-1})$; $\eta_{t|t-1} = y_t - y_{t|t-1}$ is the conditional forecast error for y_t; $f_{t|t-1} = H P_{t|t-1} H' + R$ is the variance of the conditional forecast error for y_t; and H is the matrix that relates observed y_t and unobserved β_t in the measurement equation, $y_t = H\beta_t + e_t$. Equation (3.79), for example, explains a way to update an estimate of β_t by combining $\beta_{t|t-1}$ and new information contained in y_t.

In our present case, the derivation of $\beta_{t|t,\beta_{t+1}} = E(\beta_t \mid \beta_{t|t}, \beta_{t+1})$, for example, is equivalent to updating an estimate of β_t by combining $\beta_{t|t}$ and information contained in the generated β_{t+1}. Notice that this generated β_{t+1} can be considered an additional vector of observed data that contains information beyond that in $\beta_{t|t}$. Then, proceeding with the problem as if the measurement equation were given by

$$\beta_{t+1} = \tilde{\mu} + F\beta_t + v_{t+1}, \qquad (8.15)$$

the forecast error for β_{t+1} conditional on $\tilde{y}_t$ is given by $\eta^*_{t+1|t} = \beta_{t+1} - \tilde{\mu} - F\beta_{t|t}$, and this amounts to new information in β_{t+1} not contained in $\beta_{t|t}$; its variance is given by $f^*_{t+1|t} = FP_{t|t}F' + Q$. In addition, the matrix that relates observed (realized) β_{t+1} and the unobserved state vector β_t is given by $H^* = F$. Thus the following updating equations can be derived:

$$
\begin{aligned}
\beta_{t|t,\beta_{t+1}} &= E(\beta_t \mid \tilde{y}_t, \beta_{t+1}) \\
&= E(\beta_t \mid \beta_{t|t}, \beta_{t+1}) \\
&= \beta_{t|t} + P_{t|t}H^{*'}f^*_{t+1|t}{}^{-1}\eta^*_{t+1|t} \\
&= \beta_{t|t} + P_{t|t}F'(FP_{t|t}F' + Q)^{-1}(\beta_{t+1} - \tilde{\mu} - F\beta_{t|t}),
\end{aligned}
\tag{8.16}
$$

$$
\begin{aligned}
P_{t|t,\beta_{t+1}} &= \operatorname{Cov}(\beta_t \mid \tilde{y}_t, \beta_{t+1}) \\
&= \operatorname{Cov}(\beta_t \mid \beta_{t|t}, \beta_{t+1}) \\
&= P_{t|t} - P_{t|t}H^{*'}f^*_{t+1|t}{}^{-1}H^*P_{t|t} \\
&= P_{t|t} - P_{t|t}F'(FP_{t|t}F' + Q)^{-1}FP_{t|t}.
\end{aligned}
\tag{8.17}
$$

For a rigorous derivation, the argument in chapter 3 can be used (equations (3.16) and (3.17)). Once $\beta_{t|t,\beta_{t+1}}$ and $P_{t|t,\beta_{t+1}}$ are derived in this way, it is straightforward to gentrate β_t, $t = T - 1, T - 2, \ldots, 1$ from (8.10).

The following dynamic factor model with AR(1) common and individual components provides an example of the type of the model for which the methods presented in this section apply:

$$
y_{1t} = \gamma_1 C_t + e_{1t},
\tag{8.18}
$$

$$
y_{2t} = \gamma_2 C_t + e_{2t},
\tag{8.19}
$$

$$
C_t = \phi C_{t-1} + w_t, \qquad w_t \sim \text{i.i.d.} N(0, 1)
\tag{8.20}
$$

$$
e_{it} = \psi_i e_{i,t-1} + \epsilon_{it}, \qquad \epsilon_{it} \sim \text{i.i.d.} N(0, \sigma_i^2), \qquad i = 1, 2,
\tag{8.21}
$$

where the shocks are independent and the mean of y_{it}, $i = 1, 2$, is assumed to be zero. A state-space representation of the model is given by

$$
\begin{bmatrix} y_{1t} \\ y_{2t} \end{bmatrix} = \begin{bmatrix} \gamma_1 & 1 & 0 \\ \gamma_2 & 0 & 1 \end{bmatrix} \begin{bmatrix} C_t \\ e_{1t} \\ e_{2t} \end{bmatrix},
\tag{8.22}
$$

$$
(y_t = H\beta_t),
$$

$$
\begin{bmatrix} C_t \\ e_{1t} \\ e_{2t} \end{bmatrix} = \begin{bmatrix} \phi & 0 & 0 \\ 0 & \psi_1 & 0 \\ 0 & 0 & \psi_2 \end{bmatrix} \begin{bmatrix} C_{t-1} \\ e_{1,t-1} \\ e_{2,t-1} \end{bmatrix} + \begin{bmatrix} w_t \\ \epsilon_{1t} \\ \epsilon_{2t} \end{bmatrix},
\tag{8.23}
$$

$(\beta_t = F\beta_{t-1} + v_t),$

$$
E(v_t v_t') = Q = \begin{bmatrix} 1 & 0 & 0 \\ 0 & \sigma_1^2 & 0 \\ 0 & 0 & \sigma_2^2 \end{bmatrix},
\tag{8.24}
$$

where Q is positive definite.

8.2   Generating the State Vector When Q Is Singular: A Generalization

This section generalizes the results in section 8.1 to include the case of a singular Q matrix. In many state-space models, the covariance matrix of the shocks to the transition equation, Q, may not be positive-definite. Then the algorithm in section 8.1 needs to be modified. Consider an extension of the example in section 8.1 to include an AR(2) common component:

$$
C_t = \phi_1 C_{t-1} + \phi_2 C_{t-2} + w_t, \qquad w_t \sim \text{i.i.d.} N(0,1),
\tag{8.20$'$}
$$

where roots of $(1 - \phi_1 L - \phi_2 L^2) = 0$ lie outside the complex unit circle.

A state-space representation of the model in (8.18), (8.19), (8.20$'$) and, (8.21), may be given by

$$
\begin{bmatrix} y_{1t} \\ y_{2t} \end{bmatrix} = \begin{bmatrix} \gamma_1 & 1 & 0 & 0 \\ \gamma_2 & 0 & 1 & 0 \end{bmatrix} \begin{bmatrix} C_t \\ e_{1t} \\ e_{2t} \\ C_{t-1} \end{bmatrix},
\tag{8.25}
$$

$(y_t = H\beta_t),$

$$
\begin{bmatrix} C_t \\ e_{1t} \\ e_{2t} \\ C_{t-1} \end{bmatrix} = \begin{bmatrix} \phi_1 & 0 & 0 & \phi_2 \\ 0 & \psi_1 & 0 & 0 \\ 0 & 0 & \psi_2 & 0 \\ 1 & 0 & 0 & 0 \end{bmatrix} \begin{bmatrix} C_{t-1} \\ e_{1,t-1} \\ e_{2,t-1} \\ C_{t-2} \end{bmatrix} + \begin{bmatrix} w_t \\ \epsilon_{1t} \\ \epsilon_{2t} \\ 0 \end{bmatrix},
\tag{8.26}
$$

$(\beta_t = F\beta_{t-1} + v_t),$

State-Space Models and Gibbs-Sampling

195

$$E(v_t v_t') = Q = \begin{bmatrix} 1 & 0 & 0 & 0 \\ 0 & \sigma_1^2 & 0 & 0 \\ 0 & 0 & \sigma_2^2 & 0 \\ 0 & 0 & 0 & 0 \end{bmatrix}. \tag{8.27}$$

Here, the fourth row of the transition equation describes an identity and Q is singular. Note that we want to generate β_t using the distribution of β_t conditional $\tilde{y}_t$ and β_{t+1} in (8.10). However, the fourth row of β_{t+1} and the first row of β_t are an identity, and the fourth row of β_{t+1} cannot be a conditioning factor in the distribution of β_t. If we conditioned the whole vector β_{t+1} to derive the distribution of β_t as in (8.16) and (8.17), $P_{t|t,\beta_{t+1}}$ in (8.17) would be singular, making the generation of β_t using (8.10) impossible. Thus, in generating β_t, only the first three rows of β_{t+1} should be the conditioning factors.

In general, suppose that the first $J \times J$ block of the Q matrix, denoted by Q^*, is positive-definite and that all the other elements of the Q matrix are 0s. (We can always write the state-space model to achieve this form of Q matrix. When $J = k$, where k is the dimension of Q, the analysis in this section collapses to that in section 8.1.) Then in generating β_t, only the first J rows of β_{t+1}, denoted by β_{t+1}^*, can be conditioning factors in the distribution of β_t in (8.10). Equations (8.8), (8.10), (8.13), (8.14), (8.16), and (8.17) should be modified.

In the present case, our purpose is to generate β_t from the following joint distribution:

$$p(\tilde{\beta}_T \mid \tilde{y}_T) = p(\beta_t \mid \tilde{y}_T) \prod_{t=1}^{T-1} p(\beta_t \mid \beta_{t+1}^*, \tilde{y}_t), \tag{8.8'}$$

which is equivalent to generating β_t, $t = T, T-1, \ldots, 1$, from the following distributions:

$$\beta_T \mid \tilde{y}_T \sim N(\beta_{T|T}, P_{T|T}), \tag{8.9}$$

$$\beta_t \mid \tilde{y}_t, \beta_{t+1}^* \sim N(\beta_{t|t,\beta_{t+1}^*}, P_{t|t,\beta_{t+1}^*}), \qquad t = T-1, T-2, \ldots, 1. \tag{8.10'}$$

The following describes a general procedure for generating the state vector via Gibbs-sampling:

STEP 1   Run the Kalman filter algorithm to calculate $\beta_{t|t} = E(\beta_t \mid \tilde{y}_t)$ and $P_{t|t} = \text{Cov}(\beta_t \mid \tilde{y}_t)$ for $t = 1, 2, \ldots, T$ and save them. The last iteration of the

Kalman filter provides us with $\beta_{T|T}$ and $P_{T|T}$, and these can be used to generate β_T based on (8.9).

STEP 2:   For $t = T - 1, T - 2, \ldots, 1$, given $\beta_{t|t}$ and $P_{t|t}$, if we treat the first J elements of the generated β_{t+1}, i.e., β_{t+1}^*, as an additional vector of observations to the system, the distribution $p(\beta_t \mid \tilde{y}_t, \beta_{t+1}^*)$ is easily derived by applying the updating equations of the Kalman filter. β_{t+1}^* is given by

$$\beta_{t+1}^* = F^*\beta_t + v_{t+1}^*, \tag{8.15'}$$

where F^* is the first J rows of F and v_{t+1}^* is the first J rows of v_{t+1}. Defining Q^* the first $J \times J$ block of Q, the updating equations are derived as

$$\beta_{t|t,\beta_{t+1}^*} = E(\beta_t \mid \tilde{y}_t, \beta_{t+1}^*)$$

$$= \beta_{t|t} + P_{t|t}F^{*\prime}(F^*P_{t|t}F^{*\prime} + Q^*)^{-1}(\beta_{t+1}^* - \tilde{\mu} - F^*\beta_{t|t}), \tag{8.16'}$$

$$P_{t|t,\beta_{t+1}^*} = \text{Cov}(\beta_t \mid \tilde{y}_t, \beta_{t+1}^*)$$

$$= P_{t|t} - P_{t|t}F^{*\prime}(F^*P_{t|t}F^{*\prime} + Q^*)^{-1}F^*P_{t|t}. \tag{8.17'}$$

Given (8.16') and (8.17'), we generate β_t, $t = T - 1, \ldots, 1$ based on (8.10'). We keep only the first J elements of the generated β_t, $t = T, T - 1, \ldots, 1$, for inference.

8.3   Application 1: A Gibbs-Sampling Approach to a Linear Dynamic Factor Model and a New Coincident Index

In chapter 3, we discussed Stock and Watson's (1991) application of the state-space model and the Kalman filter to a linear dynamic factor model, for the purpose of extracting an experimental coincident index, the unobserved common component, from four coincident economic indicators: industrial production (Y_1), real personal income less transfer payments (Y_2), real manufacturing and trade sales (Y_3), and employees on nonagricultural payrolls (Y_4). Inference on the unobserved common index component was conditional on the maximum likelihood estimation of the model's parameters. In this section, we present the Bayesian Gibbs-sampling approach to estimating the unobserved common index component and the model's parameters from their joint distribution, as implemented by Kim and Nelson (1998).

The following rewrites the dynamic factor model for the four coincident indicators in deviation from means, as in section 3.5:

$$\Delta y_{it} = \gamma_i \Delta c_t + e_{it}, \qquad i = 1, 2, 3, 4, \tag{8.28}$$

$$\Delta c_t = \phi_1 \Delta c_{t-1} + \phi_2 \Delta c_{t-2} + w_t, \qquad w_t \sim \text{i.i.d.} N(0, 1), \tag{8.29}$$

$$e_{it} = \psi_{i1} e_{i,t-1} + \psi_{i2} e_{i,t-2} + \epsilon_{it}, \qquad \epsilon_{it} \sim \text{i.i.d.} N(0, \sigma_i^2), \quad i = 1, 2, 3, 4, \tag{8.30}$$

where ϵ_{1t}, ϵ_{2t}, ϵ_{3t}, ϵ_{4t}, and w_t are independent of one another; $\Delta y_{it} = \Delta Y_{it} - \Delta \bar{Y}_i$; $\Delta c_t = \Delta C_t - \delta$; $\Delta \bar{Y}_i$ is the mean of the first difference of the i-th indicator; C_t is the new experimental coincident index; and δ is the mean of the first difference of C_t.

Throughout this section, the following notation is employed:

$$\Delta \tilde{c}_T = [\, \Delta c_1 \quad \Delta c_2 \quad \dots \quad \Delta c_T \,]',$$

$$\tilde{\phi} = [\, \phi_1 \quad \phi_2 \,]',$$

$$\tilde{\psi} = [\, \tilde{\psi}_1 \quad \tilde{\psi}_2 \quad \tilde{\psi}_3 \quad \tilde{\psi}_4 \,]', \quad \text{with} \quad \tilde{\psi}_i = [\, \psi_{i1} \quad \psi_{i2} \,],$$

$$\tilde{\sigma}^2 = [\, \sigma_1^2 \quad \sigma_2^2 \quad \sigma_3^2 \quad \sigma_4^2 \,]',$$

$$\tilde{\gamma} = [\, \gamma_1 \quad \gamma_2 \quad \gamma_3 \quad \gamma_4 \,]'.$$

Our job is to draw Bayesian inferences for the above $T + 18$ variates from the following joint posterior distribution:

$$p(\Delta \tilde{c}_T, \tilde{\phi}, \tilde{\gamma}, \tilde{\psi}, \tilde{\sigma}^2 \mid \Delta \tilde{y}_T) = p(\tilde{\phi}, \tilde{\gamma}, \tilde{\psi}, \tilde{\sigma}^2 \mid \Delta \tilde{c}_T, \Delta \tilde{y}_T) p(\Delta \tilde{c}_T \mid \Delta \tilde{y}_T)$$

$$= p(\tilde{\gamma}, \tilde{\psi}, \tilde{\sigma}^2 \mid \Delta \tilde{c}_T, \Delta \tilde{y}_T) p(\tilde{\phi} \mid \Delta \tilde{c}_T) p(\Delta \tilde{c}_T \mid \Delta \tilde{y}_T)$$

$$= \prod_{i=1}^{4} p(\tilde{\gamma}_i, \tilde{\psi}_i, \sigma_i^2 \mid \tilde{c}_T, \Delta \tilde{y}_T) p(\tilde{\phi} \mid \Delta \tilde{c}_T) p(\Delta \tilde{c}_T \mid \Delta \tilde{y}_T), \tag{8.31}$$

where $\tilde{y}_T = [\, \tilde{y}'_{1T} \quad \tilde{y}'_{2T} \quad \tilde{y}'_{3T} \quad \tilde{y}'_{4T} \,]'$ and $\tilde{y}_{iT} = [\, y_{i1} \quad y_{i2} \quad \dots \quad y_{iT} \,]'$, $i = 1, 2, 3, 4$. However, this joint distribution is not readily obtainable directly. Even if it were readily obtainable, the derivation of the marginal distributions would be extremely difficult. But the conditioning features of the model allows us to implement the Gibbs-sampling methodology for Bayesian inference.

Gibbs-sampling can be implemented by successive iteration of the following three steps, given appropriate prior distributions and arbitrary starting values for the model's parameters:

STEP 1   Conditional on data $(\Delta \tilde{y}_T)$ and all the parameters of the model, generate $\Delta \tilde{c}_T$.

STEP 2   Conditional on $\Delta \tilde{c}_T$, generate $\tilde{\phi}$ based on equation (8.29).

STEP 3   Conditional on $\Delta \tilde{c}_T$ and data for the i-th coincident indicator $(\Delta \tilde{y}_{iT})$, generate $\tilde{\psi}_i$, γ_i, σ_i^2 $(i = 1, 2, 3, 4)$ based on the i-th equation in (8.28) and (8.30).

Each iteration of the above three steps provides us with a generated set of $\Delta \tilde{c}_T$ and the model's parameters. However, the calculation of C_t, $t = 1, 2, \ldots, T$, a new coincident index, based on information in $\Delta \tilde{c}_T$ and the mean of ΔY, may be of interest. Thus, a fourth step may be implemented for this purpose.

STEP 4   Conditional on data and the model's generated parameters, calculate δ, the mean of ΔC_t, and calculate C_t, $t = 1, 2, \ldots, T$, given C_0.

The following sections describe each of the above four steps.

8.3.1   Generating $\Delta \tilde{c}_T$, Conditional on the Parameters of the Model and $\Delta \tilde{y}_T$

To employ the procedure introduced in section 8.2, we need to put the model in a state-space form; yet we know that there exists more than one way of representing a model in state-space form. For the purpose of this section, we adopt a different state-space representation of the model than the one employed in section 3.5. By multiplying both sides of each of the four equations in (8.28) by $\psi_i(L) = (1 - \psi_{i1}L - \psi_{i2}L^2)$, $i = 1, 2, 3, 4$, and using (8.30), we get

$$\psi_i(L)\Delta y_{it} = \gamma_i \psi_i(L)\Delta c_t + \epsilon_{it}, \quad i = 1, 2, 3, 4. \tag{8.32}$$

Then, the state-space representation is given by

Measurement Equation

$$\begin{bmatrix} \Delta y_{1t}^* \\ \Delta y_{2t}^* \\ \Delta y_{3t}^* \\ \Delta y_{4t}^* \end{bmatrix} = \begin{bmatrix} \gamma_1 & -\gamma_1\psi_{11} & -\gamma_1\psi_{12} \\ \gamma_2 & -\gamma_2\psi_{21} & -\gamma_2\psi_{22} \\ \gamma_3 & -\gamma_3\psi_{31} & -\gamma_3\psi_{32} \\ \gamma_4 & -\gamma_4\psi_{41} & -\gamma_4\psi_{42} \end{bmatrix} \begin{bmatrix} \Delta c_t \\ \Delta c_{t-1} \\ \Delta c_{t-2} \end{bmatrix} + \begin{bmatrix} \epsilon_{1t} \\ \epsilon_{2t} \\ \epsilon_{3t} \\ \epsilon_{4t} \end{bmatrix}, \tag{8.33}$$

$(\Delta y_t^* = H\beta_t + e_t),$

$$E(e_t e_t') = R = \begin{bmatrix} \sigma_1^2 & 0 & 0 & 0 \\ 0 & \sigma_2^2 & 0 & 0 \\ 0 & 0 & \sigma_3^2 & 0 \\ 0 & 0 & 0 & \sigma_4^2 \end{bmatrix}, \tag{8.34}$$

where $\Delta y_{it}^* = \Delta y_{it} - \psi_{i1} \Delta y_{i,t-1} - \psi_{i2} \Delta y_{i,t-2}$, $i = 1, 2, 3, 4$.

Transition Equation

$$\begin{bmatrix} \Delta c_t \\ \Delta c_{t-1} \\ \Delta c_{t-2} \end{bmatrix} = \begin{bmatrix} \phi_1 & \phi_2 & 0 \\ 1 & 0 & 0 \\ 0 & 1 & 0 \end{bmatrix} \begin{bmatrix} \Delta c_{t-1} \\ \Delta c_{t-2} \\ \Delta c_{t-3} \end{bmatrix} + \begin{bmatrix} w_t \\ 0 \\ 0 \end{bmatrix}, \tag{8.35}$$

$(\beta_t = F\beta_{t-1} + v_t)$,

$$E(v_t v_t') = Q = \begin{bmatrix} 1 & 0 & 0 \\ 0 & 0 & 0 \\ 0 & 0 & 0 \end{bmatrix}. \tag{8.36}$$

In the above state-space representation, the second and third rows of the transition equation describe identities, and all the elements of the Q matrix are 0 except for the (1,1) element. Thus we have a case where $J = 1$ in terms of section 8.2.

8.3.2 Generating $\tilde{\phi}$, Conditional on $\Delta \tilde{c}_T$

Conditional on $\Delta \tilde{c}_T$, equation (8.29) is independent of the rest of the model and the distribution of $\tilde{\phi}$ is independent of the rest of the parameters in the model, as well as data, $\Delta \tilde{y}_T$. Thus, we can focus on equation (8.29) and ignore the rest of the model in generating $\tilde{\phi}$ conditional on $\Delta \tilde{c}_T$. As a result, the problem reduces to that of section 7.4.1.

By writing equation (8.29) in matrix form, we have:

$$\Delta \tilde{c}_T = X\tilde{\phi} + w, \quad w \sim N(0, I). \tag{8.37}$$

We employ a multivariate normal prior for $\tilde{\phi}$ given by

$$\tilde{\phi} \sim N(\underline{\alpha}, \underline{A})_{I[s(\phi)]}, \tag{8.38}$$

where $\underline{\alpha}$ and $\underline{A}$ are known and $I[s(\phi)]$ is an indicator function used to denote that roots of $\phi(L) = 0$ lie outside the unit circle. Combining the likelihood with the above prior distribution, we can derive the following posterior distribution, from which we generate $\tilde{\phi}$:

Posterior

$$\tilde{\phi} \mid \Delta\tilde{c}_T \sim N(\bar{\alpha}, \bar{A})_{I[s(\phi)]},\tag{8.39}$$

where

$$\bar{\alpha} = (\underline{A}^{-1} + X'X)^{-1}(\underline{A}^{-1}\underline{\alpha} + X'\Delta\tilde{c}_T)$$

$$\bar{A} = (\underline{A}^{-1} + X'X)^{-1}.$$

We draw $\tilde{\phi}$ from the untruncated normal posterior and retain the draw if the roots of $\phi(L) = 0$ lie outside the unit circle.

8.3.3 Generating $\tilde{\gamma}_i$, $\tilde{\psi}_i$, and σ_i^2, Conditional on $\Delta\tilde{c}_T$ and $\Delta\tilde{y}_{iT}$, $i = 1, 2, 3, 4$

Conditional on $\Delta\tilde{c}_T$, equations (8.28) and (8.30) result in four independent regression models, each with autocorrelated disturbances. Then the problem is exactly the same as that in section 7.4.2. The following actually summarizes the results in section 7.4.2 within our present context.

We employ normal priors for γ_i and $\tilde{\psi}_i$ and an inverted Gamma distribution for σ_i^2 in the following way:

Priors

$$\gamma_i \mid \tilde{\psi}_i, \sigma_i^2 \sim N(\underline{\alpha}_i, \underline{A}_i), \quad i = 1, 2, 3, 4,\tag{8.40}$$

$$\tilde{\psi}_i \mid \gamma_i, \sigma_i^2 \sim N(\underline{\alpha}_i^*, \underline{A}_i^*)_{I[s(\psi)]}, \quad i = 1, 2, 3, 4,\tag{8.41}$$

$$\sigma_i^2 \mid \gamma_i, \tilde{\psi}_i \sim IG(\frac{\nu_i}{2}, \frac{f_i}{2}), \quad i = 1, 2, 3, 4,\tag{8.42}$$

where $\underline{\alpha}_i$, $\underline{A}_i$, $\underline{\alpha}_i^*$, $\underline{A}_i^*$, ν_i, and f_i, $i = 1, 2, 3, 4$, are known.

Generating γ_i, Conditional on $\tilde{\psi}_i$, σ_i^2, $\Delta\tilde{y}_{iT}$, and $\Delta\tilde{c}_T$, $i = 1, 2, 3, 4$ By multiplying both sides of each of the four equations in (8.28) by $(1 - \psi_{i1}L - \psi_{i2}L^2)$ and using (8.30), we get

$$\Delta y_{it}^* = \gamma_i \Delta c_t^* + \epsilon_{it}, \quad \epsilon_{it} \sim i.i.d. N(0, \sigma_i^2) \ i = 1, 2, 3, 4,\tag{8.43}$$

where $y_{it}^* = y_{it} - \psi_{i1}y_{i,t-1} - \psi_{i2}y_{i,t-2}$ and $c_t^* = c_t - \psi_{i1}c_{t-1} - \psi_{i2}c_{t-2}$. Writing (8.43) in matrix notation, we have

$$\Delta\tilde{y}_{iT}^* = \gamma_i \Delta\tilde{c}_T^* + \epsilon_i, \quad E_i \sim N(0, \sigma_i^2 I_{T-2}), i = 1, 2, 3, 4.\tag{8.44}$$

Combining the likelihood with the prior distribution in (8.40), we can derive
the following posterior distribution, from which we generate γ_i, $i = 1, 2, 3, 4$:

Posterior

$$\gamma_i \mid \psi_i, \sigma_i^2, \Delta \tilde{c}_T, \Delta \tilde{y}_{iT}, \sim N(\bar{\alpha}_i, \bar{A}_i), \tag{8.45}$$

where

$$\bar{\alpha}_i = (\underline{A}_i^{-1} + \sigma_i^{-2} \Delta \tilde{c}_T^{*\prime} \Delta \tilde{c}_T^*)^{-1} (\underline{A}_i^{-1} \underline{\alpha}_i + \sigma_i^{-2} \Delta \tilde{c}_T^{*\prime} \Delta \tilde{y}_{iT}^*),$$

$$\bar{A}_i = (\underline{A}_i^{-1} + \sigma_i^{-2} \Delta \tilde{c}_T^{*\prime} \Delta \tilde{c}_T^*)^{-1}.$$

Generating ψ_i Conditional on γ_i, σ_i^2, $\Delta \tilde{y}_{iT}$, and $\Delta \tilde{c}_T$, $i = 1, 2, 3, 4$ To
derive a posterior distribution of $\tilde{\psi}_i$, we focus on equation (8.30):

$$e_{it} = \psi_{i1} e_{i,t-1} + \psi_{i2} e_{i,t-2} + \epsilon_{it}, \quad i = 1, 2, 3, 4. \tag{8.30}$$

where, from equation (8.28), $e_{it} = \Delta y_{it} - \gamma_i \Delta c_t$ for $i = 1, 2, 3, 4$. In matrix
notation, we have:

$$\tilde{e}_{iT} = E_i \tilde{\psi}_i + \epsilon_i, \quad \epsilon_i \sim N(0, \sigma_i^2 I_{T-2}), \quad i = 1, 2, 3, 4. \tag{8.46}$$

Then, combining the likelihood with the prior distribution in (8.41), we can
derive the following posterior distribution, from which we generate $\tilde{\psi}_i$:

Posterior

$$\tilde{\psi}_i \mid \gamma_i, \sigma_i^2, \Delta \tilde{c}_T, \Delta \tilde{y}_{iT}, \sim N(\bar{\alpha}_i^*, \bar{A}_i^*)_{I[s(\psi)]}, \tag{8.47}$$

where

$$\bar{\alpha}_i^* = (\underline{A}_i^{*-1} + \sigma_i^{-2} E_i^{*\prime} E_i^*)^{-1} (\underline{A}_i^{*-1} \underline{\alpha}_i^* + \sigma_i^{-2} E_i^{*\prime} \tilde{e}_{iT}^\prime),$$

$$\bar{A}_i^* = (\underline{A}_i^{*-1} + \sigma_i^{-2} E_i^{*\prime} E_i^*)^{-1}.$$

As in the case of generating $\tilde{\phi}$, we draw $\tilde{\psi}$ from the untruncated normal
posterior and retain the draw if the roots of $\psi(L) = 0$ lie outside the unit circle.

Generating σ_i^2 Conditional on $\tilde{\psi}_i$, $\tilde{\phi}$, $\Delta \tilde{y}_{iT}$, and $\Delta \tilde{c}_T$, $i = 1, 2, 3, 4$ Lastly,
given $\tilde{\gamma}_i$ and $\tilde{\psi}_i$, we focus on (8.44) to get the likelihood of σ_i^2. Combining the
likelihood with the prior distribution in (8.42), the posterior distribution from
which σ_i^2 is to be drawn is given by

Posterior

$$\sigma_i^2 \mid \tilde{\psi}_i, \tilde{\gamma}_i, \Delta \tilde{c}_T, \Delta \tilde{y}_{iT}$$

$$\sim IG\left(\frac{v_i + (T-2)}{2}, \frac{f_i + (\tilde{e}_{iT} - E_i^* \tilde{\psi}_i)'(\tilde{e}_{iT} - E_i^* \tilde{\psi}_i)}{2}\right), \tag{8.48}$$

$i = 1, 2, 3, 4.$

8.3.4　Generating C_t, an Experimental Coincident Indicator

The mean of each coincident variable $(\Delta \bar{Y}_i)$ consists of the portion due to the idiosyncratic component (D_i) and the portion due to the common component $(\gamma_i \delta$, where δ is the mean of $\Delta C_t)$. Section 3.5.2 discusses a way to calculate δ using the steady-state Kalman gain and the mean of each coincident variable, conditional on parameter estimates of the model in deviation from means. The procedure here is exactly the same, except that we run the Kalman filter conditional on the generated parameters of the model at the end of each run of the Gibbs-sampling. In doing so, we cannot use the state-space representation given in section 8.3.1. (Refer to section 3.5.2 for reasons.) Instead, we use the state-space representation of the model given in section 3.5:

Measurement Equation

$$\begin{bmatrix} \Delta y_{1t} \\ \Delta y_{2t} \\ \Delta y_{3t} \\ \Delta y_{4t} \end{bmatrix} = \begin{bmatrix} \gamma_1 & 0 & 1 & 0 & 0 & 0 & 0 & 0 & 0 & 0 \\ \gamma_2 & 0 & 0 & 0 & 1 & 0 & 0 & 0 & 0 & 0 \\ \gamma_3 & 0 & 0 & 0 & 0 & 0 & 1 & 0 & 0 & 0 \\ \gamma_4 & 0 & 0 & 0 & 0 & 0 & 0 & 0 & 1 & 0 \end{bmatrix} \begin{bmatrix} \Delta c_t \\ \Delta c_{t-1} \\ e_{1t} \\ e_{1,t-1} \\ e_{2t} \\ e_{2,t-1} \\ e_{3t} \\ e_{3,t-1} \\ e_{4t} \\ e_{4,t-1} \end{bmatrix}, \tag{8.49}$$

$(\Delta y_t = H\beta_t)$

Transition Equation

$$
\begin{bmatrix}
\Delta c_t \\
\Delta c_{t-1} \\
e_{1t} \\
e_{1,t-1} \\
e_{2t} \\
e_{2,t-1} \\
e_{3t} \\
e_{3,t-1} \\
e_{4t} \\
e_{4,t-1}
\end{bmatrix}
=
\begin{bmatrix}
\phi_1 & \phi_2 & 0 & 0 & \dots & 0 & 0 \\
1 & 0 & 0 & 0 & \dots & 0 & 0 \\
0 & 0 & \psi_{11} & \psi_{12} & \dots & 0 & 0 \\
0 & 0 & 1 & 0 & \dots & 0 & 0 \\
\vdots & \vdots & \vdots & \vdots & \ddots & 0 & 0 \\
0 & 0 & 0 & 0 & \dots & \psi_{41} & \psi_{42} \\
0 & 0 & 0 & 0 & \dots & 1 & 0
\end{bmatrix}
\begin{bmatrix}
\Delta c_{t,t-1} \\
\Delta c_{t-2} \\
e_{1,t-1} \\
e_{1,t-2} \\
e_{2,t-1} \\
e_{2,t-2} \\
e_{3,t-1} \\
e_{3,t-2} \\
e_{4,t-1} \\
e_{4,t-2}
\end{bmatrix}
+
\begin{bmatrix}
w_t \\
0 \\
\epsilon_{1t} \\
0 \\
\epsilon_{2t} \\
0 \\
\epsilon_{3t} \\
0 \\
\epsilon_{4t} \\
0
\end{bmatrix},
$$

$$(8.50)$$

$$(\beta_t = F\beta_{t-1} + v_t)$$

Then, as in section 3.5.2, δ, the mean of ΔC_t, is given by

$$\delta = E_1'(I_k - (I_k - K^*H)F)^{-1}K^*\Delta\bar{Y}, \tag{8.51}$$

where $E_1' = [\,1 \quad 0 \quad 0 \quad \dots \quad 0\,]$, $\Delta\bar{Y} = [\,\Delta\bar{Y}_1 \quad \dots \quad \Delta\bar{Y}_4\,]$, k is the dimension of the state vector in the above state-space model, and K^* is the steady-state Kalman gain that results from applying the Kalman filter to the above state-space model. K^* is obtained from the last iteration of the Kalman filter.

Once δ is identified, for given generated $\Delta\tilde{c}_T$, and an initial value C_0, we are able to generate our new composite coincident index using

$$C_t = \Delta c_t + C_{t-1} + \delta, \qquad t = 1, 2, \dots, T. \tag{8.52}$$

8.3.5 Empirical Results

We now apply the procedures in the previous sections the four coincident indicators for the sample period 1960.01–1995.01. The fourth equation in (8.28) is replaced by

$$\Delta y_{4t} = \gamma_{40}\Delta c_t + \gamma_{41}\Delta c_{t-1} + \gamma_{42}\Delta c_{t-2} + \gamma_{43}\Delta c_{t-3} + e_{4t}, \tag{8.53}$$

to account for the possibility that the employment variable, Δy_{4t}, might be slightly lagging. The two state-space representations of the modified model are presented below. State-space representation 1 is used to generate Δc_t in section 8.3.1, and representation 2 is used to generate C_t in section 8.3.4.

State-Space Representation 1

$$
\begin{bmatrix} \Delta y_{1t}^* \\ \Delta y_{2t}^* \\ \Delta y_{3t}^* \\ \Delta y_{4t}^* \end{bmatrix} = \begin{bmatrix} \gamma_1 & -\gamma_1\psi_{11} & -\gamma_1\psi_{12} & 0 & 0 & 0 \\ \gamma_2 & -\gamma_2\psi_{21} & -\gamma_2\psi_{22} & 0 & 0 & 0 \\ \gamma_3 & -\gamma_3\psi_{31} & -\gamma_3\psi_{32} & 0 & 0 & 0 \\ \gamma_{40} & \gamma_{41}^* & \gamma_{42}^* & \gamma_{43}^* & \gamma_{44}^* & \gamma_{45}^* \end{bmatrix} \begin{bmatrix} \Delta c_t \\ \Delta c_{t-1} \\ \Delta c_{t-2} \\ \Delta c_{t-3} \\ \Delta c_{t-4} \\ \Delta c_{t-5} \end{bmatrix} + \begin{bmatrix} \epsilon_{1t} \\ \epsilon_{2t} \\ \epsilon_{3t} \\ \epsilon_{4t} \end{bmatrix},
$$

$$(8.33')$$

where $y_{it}^* = y_{it} - \psi_{i1}y_{i,t-1} - \psi_{i2}y_{i,t-2}$, $i = 1, 2, 3, 4$; $\gamma_{41}^* = -\gamma_{40}\psi_{41} + \gamma_{41}$; $\gamma_{42}^* = -\gamma_{40}\psi_{42} - \gamma_{41}\psi_{41} + \gamma_{42}$; $\gamma_{43}^* = -\gamma_{41}\psi_{42} - \gamma_{42}\psi_{41} + \gamma_{43}$; $\gamma_{44}^* = -\gamma_{42}\psi_{42} - \gamma_{43}\psi_{41}$, and $\gamma_{45}^* = -\gamma_{43}\psi_{42}$.

$$
\begin{bmatrix} \Delta c_t \\ \Delta c_{t-1} \\ \Delta c_{t-2} \\ \Delta c_{t-3} \\ \Delta c_{t-4} \\ \Delta c_{t-5} \end{bmatrix} = \begin{bmatrix} \phi_1 & \phi_2 & 0 & 0 & 0 & 0 \\ 1 & 0 & 0 & 0 & 0 & 0 \\ 0 & 1 & 0 & 0 & 0 & 0 \\ 0 & 0 & 1 & 0 & 0 & 0 \\ 0 & 0 & 0 & 1 & 0 & 0 \\ 0 & 0 & 0 & 0 & 1 & 0 \end{bmatrix} \begin{bmatrix} \Delta c_{t-1} \\ \Delta c_{t-2} \\ \Delta c_{t-3} \\ \Delta c_{t-4} \\ \Delta c_{t-5} \\ \Delta c_{t-6} \end{bmatrix} + \begin{bmatrix} w_t \\ 0 \\ 0 \\ 0 \\ 0 \\ 0 \end{bmatrix}.
$$

$$(8.35')$$

State-Space Representation 2

$$
\begin{bmatrix} \Delta y_{1t} \\ \Delta y_{2t} \\ \Delta y_{3t} \\ \Delta y_{4t} \end{bmatrix} = \begin{bmatrix} \gamma_1 & 0 & 0 & 0 & 1 & 0 & 0 & 0 & 0 & 0 & 0 & 0 \\ \gamma_2 & 0 & 0 & 0 & 0 & 0 & 1 & 0 & 0 & 0 & 0 & 0 \\ \gamma_3 & 0 & 0 & 0 & 0 & 0 & 0 & 0 & 1 & 0 & 0 & 0 \\ \gamma_{40} & \gamma_{41} & \gamma_{42} & \gamma_{43} & 0 & 0 & 0 & 0 & 0 & 0 & 1 & 0 \end{bmatrix} \begin{bmatrix} \Delta c_t \\ \Delta c_{t-1} \\ \Delta c_{t-2} \\ \Delta c_{t-3} \\ e_{1t} \\ e_{1,t-1} \\ e_{2t} \\ e_{2,t-1} \\ e_{3t} \\ e_{3,t-1} \\ e_{4t} \\ e_{4,t-1} \end{bmatrix},
$$

$$(8.49')$$

$$
\begin{bmatrix}
\Delta c_t \\
\Delta c_{t-1} \\
\Delta c_{t-2} \\
\Delta c_{t-3} \\
e_{1t} \\
e_{1,t-1} \\
\vdots \\
e_{4t} \\
e_{4,t-1}
\end{bmatrix}
=
\begin{bmatrix}
\phi_1 & \phi_2 & 0 & 0 & 0 & 0 & \ldots & 0 & 0 \\
1 & 0 & 0 & 0 & 0 & 0 & \ldots & 0 & 0 \\
0 & 1 & 0 & 0 & 0 & 0 & \ldots & 0 & 0 \\
0 & 0 & 1 & 0 & 0 & 0 & \ldots & 0 & 0 \\
0 & 0 & 0 & 0 & \psi_{11} & \psi_{12} & \ldots & 0 & 0 \\
0 & 0 & 0 & 0 & 1 & 0 & \ldots & 0 & 0 \\
\vdots & \vdots & \vdots & \vdots & \vdots & \vdots & \ddots & \vdots & \vdots \\
0 & 0 & 0 & 0 & 0 & 0 & \ldots & \psi_{41} & \psi_{42} \\
0 & 0 & 0 & 0 & 0 & 0 & \ldots & 1 & 0
\end{bmatrix}
\begin{bmatrix}
\Delta c_{t-1} \\
\Delta c_{t-2} \\
\Delta c_{t-3} \\
\Delta c_{t-4} \\
e_{1,t-1} \\
e_{1,t-2} \\
\vdots \\
e_{4,t-1} \\
e_{4,t-2}
\end{bmatrix}
+
\begin{bmatrix}
w_t \\
0 \\
0 \\
0 \\
\epsilon_{1t} \\
0 \\
\vdots \\
\epsilon_{4t} \\
0
\end{bmatrix}.
$$

$$(8.50')$$

The first 2,000 draws in the Gibbs-simulation are discarded, and then the next 8,000 draws are used to estimate marginal posterior distributions of the parameters and to make inferences on Δc_t and C_t, $t = 1, 2, \ldots, T$, the new coincident index. Table 8.1 describes the prior and posterior distributions of the model's parameters. The posterior means of the model's parameters are in close agreement with the maximum likelihood estimates of section 3.5. In addition, all the maximum likelihood estimates lie within the 95% posterior bands from the Bayesian analysis. Figure 8.1 depicts the new experimental coincident index from Bayesian Gibbs-sampling against the DOC coincident index. This new coincident index is based on averages of 8,000 draws of C_t, $t = 1, 2, \ldots, T$. Additional adjustments made for comparison with the DOC index are the same as in section 3.5. In figure 8.2, the new coincident index from Gibbs sampling is compared with that from the classical approach in section 3.5. The new indices obtained from the alternative methodologies are very similar.

Appendix: GAUSS Program to Accompany Chapter 8

1. SW_GIBS.PRG: A Gibbs-sampling approach to Stock and Watson's dynamic factor model of four coincident economic indicators: a new experimental coincident index

Table 8.1
Bayesian prior and posterior distributions: the Stock and Watson model

	Prior		Posterior				
	Mean	SD	Mean	SD	MD	95% bands	
ϕ_1	0.0	1	0.533	0.069	0.534	(0.395,	0.669)
ϕ_2	0.0	1	0.029	0.062	0.029	(−0.091,	0.153)
δ	−	−	0.567	0.046	0.566	(0.483,	0.662)
γ_1	0.0	1	0.621	0.041	0.619	(0.544,	0.705)
ψ_{11}	0.0	1	−0.032	0.065	−0.036	(−0.163,	0.095)
ψ_{12}	0.0	1	−0.054	0.065	−0.055	(−0.176,	0.074)
σ_1^2	−	−	0.236	0.034	0.235	(0.173,	0.303)
γ_2	0.0	1	0.231	0.023	0.231	(0.188,	0.278)
ψ_{21}	0.0	1	−0.302	0.052	−0.303	(−0.402,	−0.202)
ψ_{22}	0.0	1	−0.065	0.051	−0.066	(−0.163,	0.033)
σ_2^2	−	−	0.316	0.023	0.315	(0.274,	0.363)
γ_3	0.0	1	0.479	0.038	0.477	(0.406,	0.556)
ψ_{31}	0.0	1	−0.358	0.053	−0.356	(−0.460,	−0.253)
ψ_{32}	0.0	1	−0.153	0.053	−0.153	(−0.256,	−0.051)
σ_3^2	−	−	0.668	0.052	0.666	(0.571,	0.775)
γ_{40}	0.0	1	0.133	0.010	0.133	(0.113,	0.153)
γ_{41}	0.0	1	0.003	0.011	0.003	(−0.018,	0.024)
γ_{42}	0.0	1	0.024	0.010	0.024	(0.004,	0.043)
γ_{43}	0.0	1	0.028	0.008	0.028	(0.011,	0.045)
ψ_{41}	0.0	1	−0.003	0.060	−0.002	(−0.120,	0.110)
ψ_{42}	0.0	1	0.293	0.060	0.294	(0.170,	0.410)
σ_4^2	−	−	0.021	0.002	0.021	(0.017,	0.026)

Note: $y_{1t}, y_{2t}, y_{3t}, y_{4t}$ represent IP, GMYXPQ, MTQ, and LPNAG, respectively. Prior distribution of σ_i^2 is improper. SD and MD refer to standard deviation and median, respectively. 95% bands refers to 95% posterior probability bands.

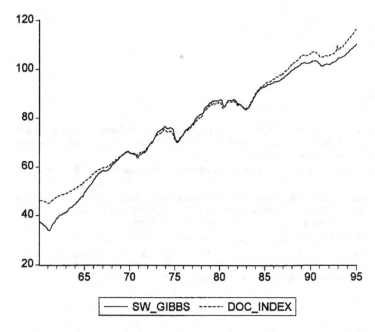

Figure 8.1
DOC index versus Stock and Watson index (from Gibbs-sampling)

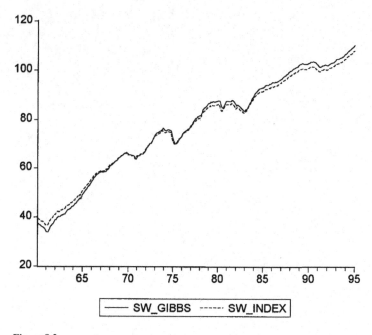

Figure 8.2
Classical versus Bayesian inference for the Stock and Watson index

References

Carlin, Bradley P., Nicholas G. Polson, and David S. Stoffer. 1992. "A Monte Carlo Approach to Nonnormal and Nonlinear State-Space Modeling." *Journal of the American Statistical Association,* 87(418), Theory and Methods, 493–500.

Carter, C. K., and P. Kohn. 1994. "On Gibbs Sampling for State Space Models." *Biometrica,* 81, 541–553.

Kim, Chang-Jin, and Charles R. Nelson. 1998. "Business Cycle Turning Points, a New Coincident Index, and Tests of Duration Dependence Based on a Dynamic Factor Model with Regime-Switching." Forthcoming, *Review of Economics and Economic Statistics.*

Shephard, Neil. 1994. "Partial Non-Gaussian State Space." *Biometrica,* 81, 115–131.

Stock, James H., and Mark W. Watson. 1991. "A Probability Model of the Coincident Economic Indicators." In *Leading Economic Indicators: New Approaches and Forecasting Records,* ed. K. Lahiri and G. H. Moore. Cambridge: Cambridge University Press, 63–89.

9 Markov-Switching Models and Gibbs-Sampling

As discussed in chapter 4, a major difficulty in drawing inferences from Markov-switching models is that some parameters of the model are dependent on an unobserved state variable (S_t) that is an outcome of an unobserved, discrete-time, discrete-state Markov process. In the classical framework, inference on Markov-switching models consists of first estimating the model's unknown parameters, then making inferences on the unobserved Markov-switching variable, $\tilde{S}_T = [\, S_1 \quad S_2 \quad \dots \quad S_T \,]'$, conditional on the parameter estimates. The procedure is quite similar to that for the state-space models of chapter 3. A state-space model also involves an unobserved state vector (β_t), and inferences on $\tilde{\beta}_T = [\, \beta_1 \quad \beta_2 \quad \dots \quad \beta_T \,]'$ are conditional on the parameter estimates.

Whereas chapter 4 deals with the classical approach to inference on Markov-switching models, this chapter provides a Bayesian counterpart. In the Bayesian analysis, both the parameters of the model and the Markov-switching variable, $S_t, t = 1, 2, \dots, T$, are treated as random variables. Thus, in contrast to the classical approach, inference on $\tilde{S}_T$ is based on a joint distribution, not a conditional distribution. In addition, by employing the simulation tool of Gibbs-sampling, Albert and Chib (1993) have made the Bayesian analysis of Markov-switching models easy to implement. As in the case of the Bayesian approach to state-space models in chapter 8, both the parameters of the model and the unobserved Markov-switching variables are treated as missing data, and they are generated from appropriate conditional distributions using Gibbs-sampling and then analyzed.

Section 9.1 reviews the main ideas of Albert and Chib (1993) within the context of a simple Markov-switching model. Sections 9.2 and 9.3 deal with extensions and applications.

9.1 A Basic Model and the Bayesian Gibbs-Sampling Approach

Consider the following simple model with Markov-switching mean and variance:

$$y_t = \mu_{S_t} + e_t, \tag{9.1}$$

$$e_t \sim N(0, \sigma_{S_t}^2), \tag{9.2}$$

$$\mu_{S_t} = \mu_0 + \mu_1 S_t, \tag{9.3}$$

$$\sigma_{S_t}^2 = \sigma_0^2(1 - S_t) + \sigma_1^2 S_t = \sigma_0^2(1 + h_1 S_t), \tag{9.4}$$

$$\mu_1 > 0, \quad h_1 > -1, \tag{9.5}$$

where S_t evolves according to a two-state, first-order Markov-switching process with the following transition probabilities:

$$Pr[S_t = 0 \mid S_{t-1} = 0] = q, \quad Pr[S_t = 1 \mid S_{t-1} = 1] = p. \tag{9.6}$$

A key to the Bayesian approach is that along with S_t, $t = 1, 2, \ldots, T$, the model's unknown parameters, μ_0, μ_1, σ_0^2, σ_1^2, p, and q, are treated as random variables. For Bayesian inference about these $T + 6$ variates, we need to derive the joint posterior density:

$$g(\tilde{S}_T, \mu_0, \mu_1, \sigma_0^2, \sigma_1^2, p, q \mid \tilde{y}_T) = g(\mu_0, \mu_1, \sigma_0^2, \sigma_1^2, p, q \mid \tilde{y}_T, \tilde{S}_T)g(\tilde{S}_T \mid \tilde{y}_T)$$

$$= g(\mu_0, \mu_1, \sigma_0^2, \sigma_1^2 \mid \tilde{y}_T, \tilde{S}_T)g(p, q \mid \tilde{y}_T, \tilde{S}_T)g(\tilde{S}_T \mid \tilde{y}_T)$$

$$= g(\mu_0, \mu_1, \sigma_0^2, \sigma_1^2 \mid \tilde{y}_T, \tilde{S}_T)g(p, q \mid \tilde{S}_T)g(\tilde{S}_T \mid \tilde{y}_T), \tag{9.7}$$

where $\tilde{y}_T = [\, y_1 \quad y_2 \quad \ldots \quad y_T \,]'$ and $\tilde{S}_T = [\, S_1 \quad S_2 \quad \ldots \quad S_T \,]'$.

Equation (9.7) assumes that, conditional on $\tilde{S}_T$, the transition probabilities, p and q, are independent of both the other parameters of the model and the data, $\tilde{y}_T$. Conditional on $\tilde{S}_T$, equations (9.1) and (9.2) are simply a regression model with a known dummy variable, S_t. These conditioning features of the model allow us to employ the simulation tool of Gibbs-sampling for Bayesian inference. To implement Gibbs-sampling, we need to derive the distributions of the blocks of each of the above $T + 6$ variates conditional on all the other blocks of variates. Thus using arbitrary starting values for the parameters of the model, the following three steps can be repeated until convergence occurs:

STEP 1   Generate each S_t from $g(S_t \mid \tilde{S}_{\neq t}, \mu_0, \mu_1, \sigma_0^2, \sigma_1^2, p, q, \tilde{y}_T)$, $t = 1, 2, \ldots, T$, where $\tilde{S}_{\neq t} = [S_1 \ldots S_{t-1} \, S_{t+1} \ldots S_T]'$ refers to a vector of S variables that excludes S_t; or generate the whole block of $\tilde{S}_T$ from $g(\tilde{S}_T \mid \mu_0, \mu_1, \sigma_0^2, \sigma_1^2, p, q, \tilde{y}_T)$.

STEP 2   Generate the transition probabilities, p and q, from $g(p, q \mid \tilde{S}_T)$.

STEP 3   Generate μ_0, μ_1, σ_0^2, σ_1^2, from $g(\mu_0, \mu_1, \sigma_0^2, \sigma_1^2 \mid \tilde{y}_T, \tilde{S}_T)$.

The following sections describe each of the above three steps.

9.1.1 Generating $\tilde{S}_T$ Conditional on $\mu_0, \mu_1, \sigma_0^2, \sigma_1^2, p, q$, and $\tilde{y}_T$

Single-Move Gibbs-Sampling   Single-move Gibbs-sampling, originally motivated by Albert and Chib (1993), refers to simulating $S_t, t = 1, 2, \ldots, T$, one by one from each of the following T conditional distributions:

$$g(S_t \mid \tilde{S}_{\neq t}, \tilde{\phi}, \tilde{\mu}, \sigma_1^2, \sigma_2^2, p, q, \tilde{y}_T), \quad t = 1, 2, \ldots, T. \tag{9.8}$$

Suppressing the conditioning on the parameters, consider the following derivation of the conditional distribution, from which $S_t, t = 1, 2, \ldots, T$, is to be generated:

$$
\begin{aligned}
g(S_t \mid \tilde{y}_T; \tilde{S}_{\neq t}) &= g(S_t \mid \tilde{y}_t, y_{t+1}, \ldots y_T; \tilde{S}_{\neq t}) \\[2mm]
&= \frac{g(S_t, y_{t+1}, \ldots, y_T \mid \tilde{y}_t, \tilde{S}_{\neq t})}{g(y_{t+1}, \ldots, y_T \mid \tilde{y}_t, \tilde{S}_{\neq t})} \\[2mm]
&= \frac{g(S_t \mid \tilde{y}_t, \tilde{S}_{\neq t}) g(y_{t+1}, \ldots, y_T \mid \tilde{y}_t, \tilde{S}_{\neq t}, S_t)}{g(y_{t+1}, \ldots, y_T \mid \tilde{y}_t, \tilde{S}_{\neq t})} \\[2mm]
&= g(S_t \mid \tilde{y}_t, \tilde{S}_{\neq t}) \\[2mm]
&= g(S_t \mid \tilde{y}_{t-1}, y_t, \tilde{S}_{t-1}, S_{t+1}, \ldots, S_T) \\[2mm]
&= \frac{g(S_t, y_t, S_{t+1} \ldots, S_T \mid \tilde{y}_{t-1}, \tilde{S}_{t-1})}{g(y_t, S_{t+1}, \ldots, S_T \mid \tilde{y}_{t-1}, \tilde{S}_{t-1})} \\[2mm]
&\propto g(S_t, y_t, S_{t+1} \ldots, S_T \mid \tilde{y}_{t-1}, \tilde{S}_{t-1}) \\[2mm]
&= g(S_t \mid \tilde{S}_{t-1}, \tilde{y}_{t-1}) g(y_t, S_{t+1}, \ldots, S_T \mid S_t, \tilde{S}_{t-1}, \tilde{y}_{t-1}) \\[2mm]
&= g(S_t \mid S_{t-1}) g(y_t, S_{t+1}, \ldots, S_T \mid S_t, \tilde{S}_{t-1}, \tilde{y}_{t-1}).
\end{aligned}
\tag{9.9}
$$

Note that conditional on $S_t, t = 1, 2, \ldots, T$, the y_t's, $t = 1, 2, \ldots, T$, are independent of one another. In the second term of the numerator from the third line of equation (9.9), $y_{t+1}, \ldots, y_T$ are independent of S_t, given $S_{t+1}, \ldots, S_T$. This guarantees the validity of going from the third line to the fourth line. (For given $S_t, t = 1, 2, \ldots, T$, if the y_t's, $t = 1, 2, \ldots, T$, are not independent, this would not hold.) The validity of going from the eighth line to the ninth line is ensured by the Markov property of S_t. Given S_{t-1}, all other information is irrelevant in predicting S_t.

The second term in the last line of equation (9.9) reduces to

$g(y_t, S_{t+1}, \ldots, S_T \mid S_t, \tilde{S}_{t-1}, \tilde{y}_{t-1})$

$= g(y_t \mid S_t, \tilde{S}_{t-1}, S_{t+1}, \ldots, S_T, \tilde{y}_{t-1}) g(S_{t+1}, \ldots, S_T \mid S_t, \tilde{S}_{t-1}, \tilde{y}_{t-1}, y_t)$

$= g(y_t \mid S_t) g(S_{t+1} \mid S_t, \tilde{S}_{t-1}, \tilde{y}_{t-1}) g(S_{t+2}, \ldots, S_T \mid S_{t+1}, S_t, \tilde{S}_{t-1}, \tilde{y}_{t-1}, y_t)$

$= g(y_t \mid S_t) g(S_{t+1} \mid S_t) g(S_{t+2}, \ldots, S_T \mid S_{t+1})$

$\propto g(y_t \mid S_t) g(S_{t+1} \mid S_t). \tag{9.10}$

From equation (9.9) and (9.10), we have the final result:

$g(S_t \mid \tilde{y}_T; \tilde{S}_{\neq t}) \propto g(S_t \mid S_{t-1}) g(y_t \mid S_t) g(S_{t+1} \mid S_t), \tag{9.11}$

where $g(S_t \mid S_{t-1})$ and $g(S_{t+1} \mid S_t)$ are given by the transition probabilities and

$$g(y_t \mid S_t) = \frac{1}{\sqrt{2\pi\sigma_{S_t}^2}} \exp\{-\frac{1}{2\sigma_{S_t}^2}(y_t - \mu_{S_t})^2\}.$$

Using the above conditional distribution, $Pr[S_t = j \mid \tilde{y}_T, \tilde{S}_{\neq t}]$ can be calculated as

$$Pr[S_t = j \mid \tilde{y}_T, \tilde{S}_{\neq t}] = \frac{g(S_t = j \mid \tilde{y}_T, \tilde{S}_{\neq t})}{\sum_{j=0}^{1} g(S_t = j \mid \tilde{y}_T, \tilde{S}_{\neq t})}. \tag{9.12}$$

Once $Pr[S_t = 1 \mid \tilde{y}_T, \tilde{S}_{\neq t}]$ is calculated, it is straightforward to generate S_t using a uniform distribution. For example, we generate a random number from a uniform distribution between 0 and 1. If the generated number is less than or equal to the calculated value of $Pr[S_t = 1 \mid \tilde{y}_T, \tilde{S}_{\neq t}]$, we set $S_t = 1$. Otherwise, S_t is set equal to 0.

Multimove Gibbs-Sampling   Multi-move Gibbs-sampling, originally motivated by Carter and Kohn (1994) in the context of a state-space model and implemented by Kim and Nelson (1998) in a Markov-switching model, refers to simulating S_t, $t = 1, 2, \ldots, T$, as a block from the following joint conditional distribution:

$$g(\tilde{S}_T \mid \tilde{\phi}, \tilde{\mu}, \sigma_1^2, \sigma_2^2, p, q, \tilde{y}_T). \tag{9.13}$$

Suppressing the conditioning on the model's parameters, consider the following derivation of the joint conditional density:

$$g(\tilde{S}_T \mid \tilde{y}_T)$$

$$= g(S_1, S_2, \ldots, S_T \mid \tilde{y}_T)$$

$$= g(S_T \mid \tilde{y}_T) g(S_{T-1}, S_{T-2}, \ldots, S_1, \mid S_T \tilde{y}_T)$$

$$= g(S_T \mid \tilde{y}_T) g(S_{T-1} \mid S_T, \tilde{y}_T) g(S_{T-2}, \ldots, S_1 \mid S_T, S_{T-1}, \tilde{y}_T)$$

$$= g(S_T \mid \tilde{y}_T) g(S_{T-1} \mid S_T, \tilde{y}_T) g(S_{T-2} \mid S_T, S_{T-1}, \tilde{y}_T) \ldots g(S_1 \mid S_T, S_{T-1},$$

$$\ldots, S_2, \tilde{y}_T)$$

$$= g(S_T \mid \tilde{y}_T) g(S_{T-1} \mid S_T, \tilde{y}_{T-1}) g(S_{T-2} \mid S_{T-1}, \tilde{y}_{T-2}) \ldots g(S_1 \mid S_2, y_1)$$

$$= g(S_T \mid \tilde{y}_T) \prod_{t=1}^{T-1} g(S_t \mid S_{t+1}, \tilde{y}_t). \tag{9.14}$$

The above derivation again depends on the Markov property of S_t: Conditional on S_{t+1}, for example, $S_{t+2}, \ldots, S_T$ and $y_{t+1}, \ldots, y_T$ contain no information beyond that in S_{t+1}. Equation (9.14) suggests that we first generate S_T conditional on $\tilde{y}_T$ and then, for $t = T - 1, T - 2, \ldots, 1$, generate S_t conditional on $\tilde{y}_t$ and the generated S_{t+1}. For this purpose, the following steps can be employed, as in Kim and Nelson 1998:

STEP 1 Run Hamilton's (1989) basic filter to get $g(S_t \mid \tilde{y}_t)$, $t = 1, 2, \ldots, T$, and save them. The last iteration of the filter provides us with $g(S_T \mid \tilde{y}_T)$, from which S_T is generated.

STEP 2 To generate S_t conditional on $\tilde{y}_t$ and S_{t+1}, $t = T - 1, T - 2, \ldots, 1$, we employ the following result:

$$g(S_t \mid \tilde{y}_t, S_{t+1}) = \frac{g(S_t, S_{t+1} \mid \tilde{y}_t)}{g(S_{t+1} \mid \tilde{y}_t)}$$

$$= \frac{g(S_{t+1} \mid S_t, \tilde{y}_t) g(S_t \mid \tilde{y}_t)}{g(S_{t+1} \mid \tilde{y}_t)} \tag{9.15}$$

$$= \frac{g(S_{t+1} \mid S_t) g(S_t \mid \tilde{y}_t)}{g(S_{t+1} \mid \tilde{y}_t)}$$

$$\propto g(S_{t+1} \mid S_t) g(S_t \mid \tilde{y}_t),$$

where $g(S_{t+1} \mid S_t)$ is the transition probability, and $g(S_t \mid \tilde{y}_t)$ has been saved from step 1. Using equation (9.15), generating S_t is the same as in the case of single-move Gibbs-sampling. We first calculate $Pr[S_t = 1 \mid S_{t+1}, \tilde{y}_t]$ in the following way:

$$Pr[S_t = 1 \mid S_{t+1}, \tilde{y}_t] = \frac{g(S_{t+1} \mid S_t = 1)g(S_t = 1 \mid \tilde{y}_t)}{\sum_{j=0}^{1} g(S_{t+1} \mid S_t = j)g(S_t = j \mid \tilde{y}_t)}, \qquad (9.16)$$

and then, as in the case of the single-move Gibbs-sampling, we use a random number drawn from a uniform distribution to generate S_t.

9.1.2 Generating Transition Probabilities, p and q, Conditional on $\tilde{S}_T$

Conditional on $\tilde{S}_T$, notice that p and q are independent of the data set, $\tilde{y}_T$, and the model's other parameters. As we will be using beta distributions as conjugate priors for the transition probabilities, we start this section with a brief review of the beta distribution.

Review of the Beta Distribution A beta distribution, denoted by $z \sim \text{beta}(\alpha_0, \alpha_1)$, is dependent on two hyperparameters, $\alpha_0 > 0$ and $\alpha_1 > 0$, and the density function is given by

$$g(z \mid \alpha_0, \alpha_1) \propto z^{\alpha_0-1}(1-z)^{\alpha_1-1}, \quad \text{for } 0 < z < 1,$$

$$g(z \mid \alpha_0, \alpha_1) = 0, \quad \text{for } z \geq 1 \text{ or } z \leq 0.$$

The expected value and the variance of a beta random variable is given by

$$E(z) = \frac{\alpha_0}{\alpha_0 + \alpha_1},$$

$$\text{Var}(z) = \frac{\alpha_0 \alpha_1}{(\alpha_0 + \alpha_1)^2(\alpha_0 + \alpha_1 + 1)}.$$

Assuming independent beta distributions for the priors of p and q, we have:

Prior

$$p \sim \text{beta}(u_{11}, u_{10}), \qquad (9.17)$$

$$q \sim \text{beta}(u_{00}, u_{01}), \qquad (9.18)$$

with

$$g(p, q) \propto p^{u_{11}-1}(1-p)^{u_{10}-1}q^{u_{00}-1}(1-q)^{u_{01}-1}, \qquad (9.19)$$

where u_{ij}, $i, j = 0, 1$, are known hyperparameters of the priors.

The likelihood function for p and q is given by:

Likelihood Function

$$L(p, q \mid \tilde{S}_T) = p^{n_{11}}(1 - p)^{n_{10}}q^{n_{00}}(1 - q)^{n_{01}}, \tag{9.20}$$

where n_{ij} refers to the transitions from state i to j, which can be easily counted for given $\tilde{S}_T = [\, S_1 \quad S_2 \quad \ldots \quad S_T \,]$.

Combining the prior distribution and the likelihood function, we get the following posterior distribution:

Posterior

$$p(p, q \mid \tilde{S}_T) = g(p, q)L(p, q \mid \tilde{S}_T)$$

$$\propto p^{u_{11}-1}(1 - p)^{u_{10}-1}q^{u_{00}-1}(1 - q)^{u_{01}-1}p^{n_{11}}(1 - p)^{n_{10}}q^{n_{00}}(1 - q)^{n_{01}}$$

$$= p^{u_{11}+n_{11}-1}(1 - p)^{u_{10}+n_{10}-1}q^{u_{00}+n_{00}-1}(1 - q)^{u_{01}+n_{01}-1}, \tag{9.21}$$

which suggests that the posterior distribution is given by the two independent beta distributions:

$$p \mid \tilde{S}_T \sim \text{beta}(u_{11} + n_{11}, u_{10} + n_{10}), \tag{9.22}$$

$$q \mid \tilde{S}_T \sim \text{beta}(u_{00} + n_{00}, u_{01} + n_{01}), \tag{9.23}$$

from which p and q are drawn.

9.1.3 Generating μ_0 and μ_1, Conditional on σ_0^2, σ_1^2, $\tilde{S}_T$, and $\tilde{y}_T$

Equations (9.1), (9.2), and (9.3) can be rewritten as

$$y_t = \mu_0 + \mu_1 S_t + e_t, \quad e_t \sim N(0, \sigma_{S_t}^2). \tag{9.24}$$

Dividing both sides of equation (9.24) by σ_{S_t}, we get

$$y_t^\dagger = \mu_0 x_{0t} + \mu_1 x_{1t} + v_t, \quad v_t \sim \text{i.i.d.}N(0, 1), \tag{9.25}$$

where

$$y_t^\dagger = \frac{y_t}{\sigma_{S_t}},$$

$$x_{0t} = \frac{1}{\sigma_{S_t}},$$

and

$$x_{1t} = \frac{S_t}{\sigma_{S_t}}.$$

Writing equation (9.25) in matrix notation, we have

$$Y^\dagger = X\tilde{\mu} + V, \quad V \sim N(0, I_T), \tag{9.26}$$

where $\tilde{\mu} = [\; \mu_0 \quad \mu_1 \;]'$. We assume a normal prior for μ:

Prior

$$\tilde{\mu} \mid \sigma_0^2, \sigma_1^2 \sim N(b_0, B_0), \tag{9.27}$$

where b and B are known.

Then, the posterior distribution is given by

Posterior

$$\tilde{\mu} \mid \sigma_0^2, \sigma_1^2, \tilde{S}_T, \tilde{y}_T \sim N(b_1, B_1), \tag{9.28}$$

where

$$b_1 = (B_0^{-1} + X'X)^{-1}(B_0^{-1}b_0 + X'Y^\dagger),$$

$$B_1 = (B_0^{-1} + X'X)^{-1}.$$

We first draw $\tilde{\mu} = [\; \mu_0 \quad \mu_1 \;]$ from the above multivariate posterior distribution. To constrain $\mu_1 > 0$, if the generated value of μ_1 is less than or equal to 0, we discard the draws. Otherwise, we save them.

9.1.4 Generating σ_0^2 and σ_1^2, Conditional on μ_0, μ_1, $\tilde{S}_T$, and $\tilde{y}_T$

From equation (9.4), we have

$$\sigma_{S_t}^2 = \sigma_0^2(1 + h_1 S_t), \tag{9.29}$$

where $\sigma_1^2 = \sigma_0^2(1 + h_1)$.

We can first generate σ_0^2, conditional on h_1, and then we can generate $\bar{h}_1 = 1 + h_1$ conditional on σ_0^2. To generate σ_0^2 conditional on h_1, we divide both sides of equation (9.24) by $\sqrt{1 + h_1 S_t}$:

$$y_t^* = \mu_0 x_{0t}^* + \mu_1 x_{1t}^* + v_t^*, \quad v_t^* \sim \text{i.i.d.} N(0, \sigma_0^2), \tag{9.30}$$

where

$$y_t^* = \frac{y_t}{\sqrt{1 + h_1 S_t}},$$

$$x_{0t}^* = \frac{1}{\sqrt{1 + h_1 S_t}},$$

$$x_{1t}^* = \frac{S_t}{\sqrt{1 + h_1 S_t}},$$

and

$$v_t^* = \frac{e_t}{\sqrt{1 + h_1 S_t}}.$$

Then, as in section 7.4, given an inverted Gamma distribution as a conjugate prior for σ_0^2, the posterior distribution for σ_0^2 is easily obtained as follows:

Prior

$$\sigma_0^2 \mid h_1, \mu_0, \mu_1 \sim IG(\frac{v_0}{2}, \frac{\delta_0}{2}), \tag{9.31}$$

where IG refers to an inverted Gamma distribution, and v_0 and δ_0 are known.

Posterior

$$\sigma_0^2 \mid h_1, \mu_0, \mu_1, \tilde{S}_T, \tilde{y}_T \sim IG(\frac{v_1}{2}, \frac{\delta_1}{2}), \tag{9.32}$$

where

$$v_1 = v_0 + T,$$

$$\delta_1 = \delta_0 + \sum_{t=1}^{T} (y_t^* - \mu_0 x_{0t}^* - \mu_1 x_{1t}^*)^2,$$

and T is the sample size.

To generate $\bar{h}_1 = 1 + h_1$ conditional on σ_0^2, we divide both sides of equation (9.24) by σ_0:

$$y_t^{**} = \mu_0 x_{0t}^{**} + \mu_1 x_{1t}^{**} + v_t^{**}, \quad v_t^{**} \sim \text{i.i.d.} N(0, 1 + h_1 S_t), \tag{9.33}$$

where

$$y_t^{**} = \frac{y_t}{\sigma_0},$$

$$x_{0t}^{**} = \frac{1}{\sigma_0},$$

$$x_{1t}^{**} = \frac{S_t}{\sigma_0},$$

and

$$v_t^{**} = \frac{e_t}{\sigma_0}.$$

Note that the likelihood function of h_1 depends only on the values of y_t for which $S_t = 1$. Keeping this in mind, an appropriate prior distribution for $\bar{h}_1$ and the posterior distribution are given below:

Prior

$$\bar{h}_1 \mid \sigma_0^2, \mu_0, \mu_1 \sim IG(\frac{v_3}{2}, \frac{\delta_3}{2}), \qquad\qquad\qquad (9.34)$$

Posterior

$$\bar{h}_1 \mid \sigma_0^2, \mu_0, \mu_1, \tilde{S}_T, \tilde{y}_T \sim IG(\frac{v_4}{2}, \frac{\delta_4}{2}), \qquad\qquad\qquad (9.35)$$

where

$$v_4 = v_3 + T_1,$$

$$\delta_4 = \delta_3 + \sum_{}^{N_1} (y_t^{**} - \mu_0 x_{0t}^{**} - \mu_1 x_{1t}^{**})^2,$$

where IG refers to an inverted Gamma distribution; v_3 and δ_3 are known; $N_1 = \{t : S_t = 1\}$; T_1 is the cardinalities of N_1; and the sum is over the elements N_1.

Once $\bar{h}_1 = 1 + h_1$ is generated from the above posterior distribution, σ_1^2 is calculated by $\sigma_1^2 = \sigma_0^2(1 + h_1)$.

9.1.5   Example: A Markov-Switching Model of Real GDP with No AR Dynamics

Albert and Chib (1993) analyzed an autoregressive model with a first-order, two-state Markov-switching mean (with constant variance) for the first dif-

Table 9.1
Bayesian Gibbs-sampling approach to a Markov-switching AR(0) model of real GDP (1952:II–1984:IV)

	Prior		Posterior		
	Mean	SD	Mean	SD	MD
μ_0	0	1	-0.23331	0.29214	-0.22381
μ_1	0.5	1	1.33857	0.26021	1.33691
σ^2	—	—	0.70430	0.11367	0.69268
p	0.8	0.16	0.88859	0.05456	0.89899
q	0.8	0.16	0.74006	0.10385	0.75066

Note: Prior distribution of σ^2 is improper. SD and MD refer to standard deviation and median, respectively.

ferences of the log of real GNP (1952:II–1984:IV), via the Bayesian Gibbs-sampling approach. By analyzing the marginal distributions of each of the four autoregressive coefficients for an AR(4) Markov-switching model, they suggest that the autoregressive coefficients are not significantly different from 0. They also show that an AR(0) Markov-switching model provides a useful model of the U.S. quarterly output series.

Following Albert and Chib, we apply an AR(0) Markov-switching model to the first differences of the log of real GDP (1952:II–1984:IV). The model we employ is the same as equations (9.1)–(9.6), except that we have homoskedasticity in place of (9.4). Whereas Albert and Chib applied the single-move Gibbs-sampling in generating $\tilde{S}_T$, we apply the multimove Gibbs-sampling in this section. Table 9.1 reports the marginal posterior distributions of the parameters. Figure 9.1 depicts the posterior probabilities of a recession ($Pr[S_t = 0 \mid \tilde{y}_T]$) against the NBER reference cycle. (The shaded areas represent the NBER recessions.) The model seems to predict the NBER recessions reasonably well. Notice that figure 9.1 is directly comparable to the smoothed probabilities of a recession given in figure 4.2. There seems to be no significant difference between the two figures.

9.2   Application 1: A Three-State Markov-Switching Variance Model of Stock Returns

In section 4.6, we considered a classical analysis of the following three-state Markov-switching variance model of U.S. monthly stock returns (CRSP data set, equal-weighted excess returns, 1926.1–1986.12):

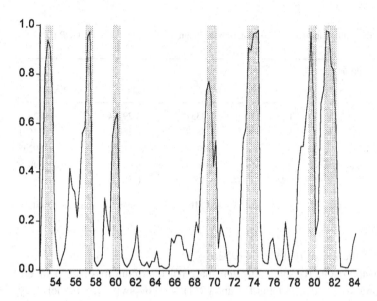

Figure 9.1
Probability of a recession from Gibbs-sampling (GDP, 1953:I–1984IV)

$$y_t \sim N(0, \sigma_t^2), \tag{9.36}$$

$$\sigma_t^2 = \sigma_1^2 S_{1t} + \sigma_2^2 S_{2t} + \sigma_3^2 S_{3t}, \tag{9.37}$$

$$S_{kt} = 1 \text{ if } S_t = k \text{ and } S_{kt} = 0, \text{ otherwise } k = 1, 2, 3, \tag{9.38}$$

$$Pr[S_t = j \mid S_{t-1} = i] = p_{ij}, \quad i, j = 1, 2, 3, \tag{9.39}$$

$$\sum_{j=1}^{3} p_{ij} = 1, \tag{9.40}$$

$$\sigma_1^2 < \sigma_2^2 < \sigma_3^2, \tag{9.41}$$

where y_t is the demeaned stock return, S_t is an unobserved state variable which evolves according to a first-order Markov process with transition probabilities in (9.39).

In this section, we extend the analysis in section 9.1 to deal with a three-state Markov-switching model, and we provide a Bayesian counterpart to section 4.6. The discussion in this section is originally from Kim, Nelson, and Startz 1998. The random variables to be drawn via the Gibbs-sampling in the present case are $\tilde{S}_T = [\, S_1 \quad S_2 \quad \ldots \quad S_T \,]'$, $\tilde{\sigma}^2 = [\, \sigma_1^2 \quad \sigma_2^2 \quad \sigma_3^2 \,]'$, and $\tilde{p} = [\, p_{11} \quad p_{12} \quad p_{21} \quad p_{22} \quad p_{31} \quad p_{32} \,]'$. By successive iteration of the following steps, the procedure simulates a drawing from the joint distribution of all the state variables and the model's parameters, given the data:

STEP 1   Generate $\tilde{S}_T$, conditional on $\tilde{\sigma}^2$, $\tilde{p}$, and $\tilde{y}_T$.

STEP 2   Generate $\tilde{p}$, conditional on $\tilde{S}_T$.

STEP 3   Generate $\tilde{\sigma}^2$, conditional on $\tilde{S}_T$ and the data, $\tilde{y}_T$.

9.2.1   Generating $\tilde{S}_T$, Conditional on $\tilde{\sigma}^2$, $\tilde{p}$, and $\tilde{y}_T$

The derivation of the posterior distribution from which we draw the state variables is exactly the same as that in section 9.1.1. For the case of multimove Gibbs-sampling, and suppressing the conditioning on the parameters of the model, we have

$$g(\tilde{S}_T \mid \tilde{y}_T) = g(S_T \mid \tilde{y}_T) \prod_{t=1}^{T-1} g(S_t \mid S_{t+1}, \tilde{y}_t), \tag{9.42}$$

where $\tilde{y}_t = [\, y_1 \quad \ldots \quad y_t \,]'$.

As in section 9.1.1, to simulate $\tilde{S}_T$ from the above distribution, we first run Hamilton's (1989) basic filter for the model to get $g(S_t \mid \tilde{y}_t)$ and $g(S_t \mid \tilde{y}_{t-1})$, for $t = 1, 2, \ldots, T$. The last iteration of the filter provides us with $g(S_T \mid \tilde{y}_T, \tilde{p}, \tilde{\sigma}^2)$, from which S_T is generated. Then, we can successively generate S_t from $g(S_t \mid S_{t+1}, \tilde{y}_t)$, for $t = T-1, T-2, \ldots, 1$, using the following results:

$$g(S_t \mid S_{t+1}, \tilde{y}_t) \propto g(S_{t+1} \mid S_t) g(S_t \mid \tilde{y}_t). \tag{9.43}$$

Because S_t is a three-state Markov-switching variable, however, we need to pay special attention to its generation based on the uniform distribution. First, we calculate $Pr[S_t = 1 \mid S_{t+1}, \tilde{y}_t]$ in the following way:

$$Pr[S_t = 1 \mid S_{t+1}, \tilde{y}_t] = \frac{g(S_{t+1} \mid S_t = 1) g(S_t = 1 \mid \tilde{y}_t)}{\sum_{j=1}^3 g(S_{t+1} \mid S_t = j) g(S_t = j \mid \tilde{y}_t)}. \tag{9.44}$$

Then, we generate a random number from the uniform distribution. If the generated number is less than or equal to $Pr[S_t = 1 \mid S_{t+1}, \tilde{y}_t]$, we set $S_t = 1$; if it is greater than $Pr[S_t = 1 \mid S_{t+1}, \tilde{y}_t]$, we generate another random number from the uniform distribution. Then, if that generated number is less than or equal to $Pr[S_t = 2 \mid S_{t+1}, \tilde{y}_t, S_t \neq 1]$, we set $S_t = 2$; if it is greater than $Pr[S_t = 2 \mid S_{t+1}, \tilde{y}_t, S_t \neq 1]$, we set $S_t = 3$. We calculate $Pr[S_t = 2 \mid S_{t+1}, \tilde{y}_t, S_t \neq 1]$ in the following way:

$$Pr[S_t = 2 \mid S_{t+1}, \tilde{y}_t, S_t \neq 1] = \frac{g(S_{t+1} \mid S_t = 2) g(S_t = 2 \mid \tilde{y}_t)}{\sum_{j=2}^{3} g(S_{t+1} \mid S_t = j) g(S_t = j \mid \tilde{y}_t)}. \tag{9.45}$$

9.2.2 Generating $\tilde{p} = [\, p_{11} \quad p_{12} \quad p_{21} \quad p_{22} \quad p_{31} \quad p_{32} \,]'$, Conditional on $\tilde{S}_T$

Conditional on $\tilde{S}_T$, the transition probabilities are independent of $\tilde{y}_T$ and the other parameters of the model, as in section 9.1.2. For the three-state Markov-switching model in this section, however, we need to modify the procedures in section 9.1.2.

Given $\tilde{S}_T$, let n_{ij}, $i, j = 1, 2, 3$, be the total number of transitions from state $S_{t-1} = i$ to $S_t = j$, $t = 2, 3, \dots, T$. Define $\bar{p}_{ii} = Pr[S_t \neq i \mid S_{t-1} = i]$, $i = 1, 2, 3$, and $\bar{p}_{ij} = Pr[S_t = j \mid S_{t-1} = i, S_t \neq i]$, for $i \neq j$. We then have $p_{ij} = Pr[S_t = j \mid S_{t-1} = i] = \bar{p}_{ij} \times (1 - p_{ii})$ for $j \neq i$. Similarly, define $\bar{n}_{ii}$ to be the number of transitions from state $S_{t-1} = i$ to $S_t \neq i$.

By taking the beta family of distributions as conjugate priors, it can be shown that the posterior distributions of p_{ii} are given by

$$p_{ii} \mid \tilde{S}_T \sim \text{beta}(u_{ii} + n_{ii}, \bar{u}_{ii} + \bar{n}_{ii}), \quad i = 1, 2, 3, \tag{9.46}$$

where u_{ii} and $\bar{u}_{ii}$ are the known hyperparameters of the priors. Once p_{ii}, $i = 1, 2, 3$, are generated from the above distribution, generation of the other parameters is straightforward. For example, given that p_{11} is generated, p_{12} can be calculated by $p_{12} = \bar{p}_{12} \times (1 - p_{11})$, where $\bar{p}_{12}$ can be generated from the following beta distribution:

$$\bar{p}_{12} \mid \tilde{S}_T \sim \text{beta}(u_{12} + n_{12}, u_{13} + n_{13}), \tag{9.47}$$

where u_{12} and u_{13} are the known hyperparameters of the prior. Given p_{11} and p_{12} generated in this way, we have $p_{13} = 1 - p_{11} - p_{12}$.

For our application of this approach to CRSP excess returns, we employ the following hyperparameters: $u_{ii} = 0.5$ and $\bar{u}_{ii} = 0.5$, and $u_{ij} = 0.5$ and $u_{ik} = 0.5$ for $i \neq j \neq k$. These hyperparameters imply almost noninformative priors for the transition probabilities in the sense that they imply that the expected duration of a state is two months with very high standard deviation.

9.2.3 Generating σ_j^2, $j = 1, 2, 3$, Conditional on $\tilde{S}_T$ and $\tilde{y}_T$

To efficiently impose a constraint that $\sigma_1^2 < \sigma_2^2 < \sigma_3^2$, we can redefine σ_t^2 in equation (9.37) as follows:

$$\sigma_t^2 = \sigma_1^2(1 + S_{2t}h_2)(1 + S_{3t}h_2)(1 + S_{3t}h_3), \tag{9.48}$$

so that σ_2^2 and σ_3^2 are given by

$$\sigma_2^2 = \sigma_1^2(1 + h_2) \text{ and } \sigma_3^2 = \sigma_1^2(1 + h_2)(1 + h_3), \tag{9.49}$$

where $h_2 > 0$ and $h_3 > 0$. In this specification, we first generate σ_1^2, then generate $\bar{h}_2 = 1 + h_2$ and $\bar{h}_3 = 1 + h_3$ to generate σ_2^2 and σ_3^2 indirectly.

Generating σ_1^2, Conditional on h_2 and h_3 To generate σ_1^2, conditional on $1 + h_1$ and $1 + h_2$, we transform equation (9.36) as follows:

$$Y_{1t} = \frac{y_t}{\sqrt{(1 + S_{2t}h_2)(1 + S_{3t}h_2)(1 + S_{3t}h_3)}}, \quad Y_{1t} \sim \text{i.i.d.} N(0, \sigma_1^2). \tag{9.50}$$

By choosing an inverse Gamma distribution as the prior ($IG(\frac{\nu_1}{2}, \frac{\delta_1}{2})$), one can show that the conditional distribution from which we generate σ_1^2 is given by

$$\sigma_1^2 \mid \tilde{y}_T, \tilde{S}_T, h_2, h_3 \sim IG(\frac{\nu_1 + T}{2}, \frac{\delta_1 + \sum_{t=1}^{T} Y_{1t}^2}{2}), \tag{9.51}$$

where ν_1 and δ_1 are the known hyperparameters of the prior distribution.

Generating $\bar{h}_2 = 1 + h_2$, Conditional on σ_1^2 and h_3 To generate $\bar{h}_2 = 1 + h_2$, and thus σ_2^2, we transform equation (9.36) as follows:

$$Y_{2t} = \frac{y_t}{\sqrt{\sigma_1^2(1 + S_{3t}h_3)}}. \tag{9.52}$$

Here, we note that the likelihood function of h_2 depends only on the values of y_t for which $S_t = 2$ or 3 (or, equivalently, $S_{2t} = 1$ or $S_{3t} = 1$). For the observations in which $S_t = 2$ or 3, we have $Y_{2t} \sim \text{i.i.d.} N(0, (1 + h_2))$.

Thus, defining $N_2 = \{t : S_t = 2 \text{ or } 3\}$ and choosing an inverse Gamma distribution for the prior ($IG(\frac{\nu_2}{2}, \frac{\delta_2}{2})I_{[\bar{h}_2 > 1]}$), one can show that the conditional posterior distribution of $\bar{h}_2 = 1 + h_2$ is given by

$$\bar{h}_2 \mid \tilde{y}_T, \tilde{S}_T, \sigma_1^2, h_3 \sim IG(\frac{\nu_2 + T_2}{2}, \frac{\delta_2 + \sum^{N_2} Y_{2t}^2}{2})I_{[\bar{h}_2 > 1]}, \tag{9.53}$$

where I is the indicator function on $[\bar{h}_2 > 1]$; T_2 is the cardinalities of N_2; and the sum is over the elements N_2. A rejection sampling is used to achieve the constraint that $\bar{h}_2 > 1$.

Generating $\bar{h}_3 = 1 + h_3$, Conditional on σ_1^2 and h_2   Finally, to generate $\bar{h}_3 = 1 + h_3$, and thus σ_3^2, we transform equation (9.36) as follows:

$$Y_{3t} = \frac{y_t}{\sqrt{\sigma_1^2(1 + S_{3t}h_2)}} \tag{9.54}$$

Here, we note that the likelihood function of h_3 depends only on the values of y_t for which $S_t = 3$ (or, equivalently, $S_{3t} = 1$). For the values of y_t for which $S_t = 3$, we have $Y_{3t} \sim$ i.i.d.$N(0, (1 + h_3))$.

By defining $N_3 = \{t : S_t = 3\}$ and choosing an inverse Gamma distribution for the priors $(IG(\frac{v_3}{2}, \frac{\delta_3}{2})I_{[\bar{h}_3 > 1]})$, one can show that the conditional posterior distribution of $\bar{h}_3 = 1 + h_3$ is given by

$$\bar{h}_3 \mid \sigma_1^2, h_2, \tilde{y}_T, \tilde{S}_T, \sim IG(\frac{v_3 + T_3}{2}, \frac{\delta_3 + \sum^{N_3} Y_{3t}^2}{2})I_{[\bar{h}_3 > 1]}, \tag{9.55}$$

where I is the indicator function on $[\bar{h}_3 > 1]$; T_3 is the cardinalities of N_3; and the sum is over the elements N_3. Again, a rejection sampling is used to achieve the constraint that $\bar{h}_3 > 1$.

Notice that the quantity v_i, $i = 1, 2, 3$, represents the strength of the priors of σ_1^2, $\bar{h}_2$, and $\bar{h}_3$. For our application of the approach to the U.S. CRSP excess returns, we employ $v_i = 0$ and $\delta_i = 0$ for $i = 1, 2, 3$.

9.2.4 Empirical Results

The procedures for Gibbs-sampling described in the previous sections are applied here to equal-weighted excess returns, 1926.1–1986.12, from the CRSP data file. Gibbs-sampling is run such that the first 2,000 draws are discarded and the next 10,000 are recorded. We employ almost noninformative priors for all the model's parameters. Details of the priors employed are given in the previous sections. Table 9.2 presents the marginal posterior distributions of the parameters that result from Gibbs-sampling. Comparing the results with those from the MLE in section 4.6, the posterior means of the parameters are in close agreement with the ML estimates, and all the ML estimates (in table 4.3) fall within the 95% posterior bands reported in table 9.2.

Table 9.2
Bayesian Gibbs-sampling approach to a three-state Markov-switching model of heteroskedasticity
for CRSP excess returns, equal-weighted portfolio (1926.1–1986.12)

Parameter	Posterior Mean	SD	MD	98% posterior bands
p_{11}	0.9700	0.0204	0.9746	(0.9164, 0.9954)
p_{12}	0.0271	0.0199	0.0225	(0.0020, 0.0791)
p_{21}	0.0302	0.0233	0.0250	(0.0035, 0.0878)
p_{22}	0.9598	0.0248	0.9649	(0.8995, 0.9907)
p_{31}	0.0116	0.0139	0.0066	(0.0001, 0.0510)
p_{32}	0.0250	0.0242	0.0183	(0.0005, 0.0879)
σ_1^2	0.0013	0.0002	0.0013	(0.0009, 0.0017)
σ_2^2	0.0039	0.0007	0.0038	(0.0028, 0.0054)
σ_3^2	0.0258	0.0044	0.0253	(0.0187, 0.0351)

Note: Almost noninformative priors were given for all the parameters of the model; SD and MD
refer to standard deviation and median, respectively.

At the end of each run of Gibbs-sampling, we have a simulated set of $\{S_t, t = 1, 2, \ldots, T\}$, and thus, of $\{S_{jt}, t = 1, 2, \ldots, T, j = 1, 2, 3\}$, $\sigma_j^2, j = 1, 2, 3$, and $\tilde{p}$. (Figures 9.2a, 9.2b, and 9.2c depict probabilities of low-, medium-, and high-variance states for the stock returns that result from the Gibbs-simulations.) Using the particular realizations of the states and the parameters for each run of Gibbs-sampling, we can calculate σ_t^2 for $t = 1, 2, \ldots, T$ using equation (9.37). We can also standardize returns by $y_t^* = \frac{y_t}{\sigma_t}$. Thus when all the iterations are over, we have 10,000 sets of realized return variances $\tilde{\sigma}_T^2 = \{\sigma_t^2, t = 1, 2, \ldots, T\}$ and 10,000 sets of realized standardized returns $\tilde{y}_T^* = \{y_t^*\ t = 1, 2, \ldots, T\}$, each of which is associated with different realizations of the parameters and the state variable. Figure 9.3 plots the average of 10,000 sets of $\tilde{\sigma}_T^2$, which are our estimates of the stock return variance. Figures 9.4a and 9.4b show the plot and the sampling distribution of the standardized returns. These are calculated as the average of 10,000 realized sets of $\tilde{y}^*$ from Gibbs-sampling.

To check whether the three-state Markov-switching model of heteroskedasticity captures most of the dynamics in the stock return variance, we applied ARCH tests to the above standardized returns. No ARCH effects were found. For example, when ARCH tests were performed on the average of 10,000 sets of standardized returns from Gibbs-sampling, the LM test statistics at lags 1

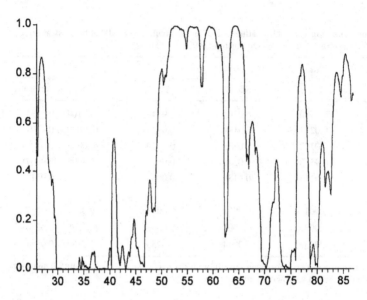

Figure 9.2a
Probability of a low-variance state for stock returns (Gibbs-sampling)

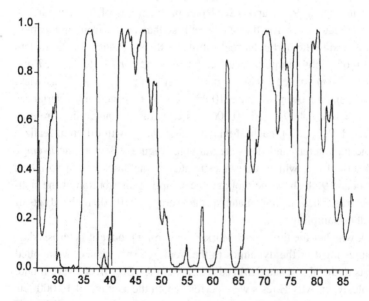

Figure 9.2b
Probability of a medium-variance state for stock returns (Gibbs-sampling)

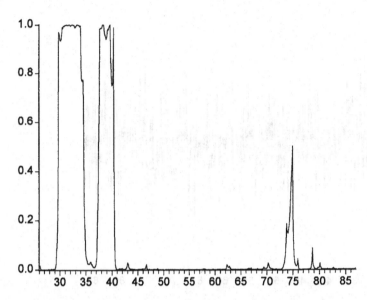

Figure 9.2c
Probability of a high-variance state for stock returns (Gibbs-sampling)

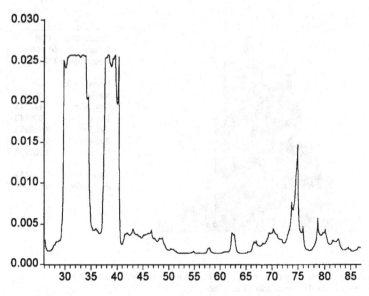

Figure 9.3
Estimated variance of historical returns (three-state Markov-switching variance; Gibbs-sampling): monthly excess returns, EW portfolio, 1926–1986

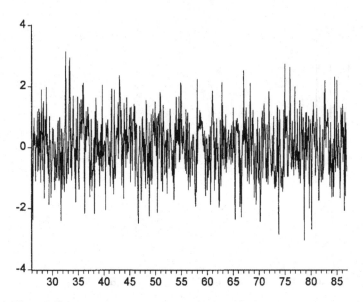

Figure 9.4a
Plot of standardized returns (average of 10,000 realizations from Gibbs-sampling):
monthly excess returns, EW portfolio 1926–1986

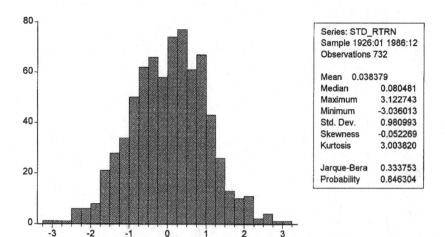

| Series: STD_RTRN |
| Sample 1926:01 1986:12 |
| Observations 732 |

Mean	0.038379
Median	0.080481
Maximum	3.122743
Minimum	-3.036013
Std. Dev.	0.980993
Skewness	-0.052269
Kurtosis	3.003820
Jarque-Bera	0.333753
Probability	0.846304

Figure 9.4b
Plot of standardized returns (average of 10,000 realizations from Gibbs-sampling):
monthly excess returns, EW portfolio 1926–1986

through 5 were 0.001, 0.824, 0.657, 0.754, and 0.678 respectively. This is consistent with the findings of Hamilton and Susmel (1994), who show that all the ARCH effects that show up in weekly stock returns data die out almost completely after four weeks (a month), after allowing for Markov-switching variance. In addition, the standardized returns show little excess kurtosis, with a p-value of 0.846 for the Jarque-Bera joint test of normality. These results suggest that the three-state Markov-switching variance model is a reasonable approximation to the heteroskedasticity in stock returns for the period 1926.1–1986.12.

Comparing the smoothed probabilities of a high-variance state from the classical analysis (figure 4.8c) in section 4.6 with those from the Bayesian analysis (figure 9.2c), an advantage of the Bayesian Gibbs-sampling approach is clear. The stock returns during the mid-1970s of the first oil shock period are not very likely to have come from the same state (i.e., high variance state) as those during the Great Depression period. Whereas the probabilities of a high-variance state during the first oil shock are close to 1 in the classical analysis, they are less than 0.5 in the Bayesian Gibbs-sampling analysis.

9.3   Application 2: A Three-State Markov Switching Mean-Variance Model of the Real Interest Rate

This section provides a Bayesian alternative to the analysis of the three-state Markov-switching mean-variance model of the U.S. real interest rate from section 4.5:

$$(y_t - \mu_{s_t}) = \phi_1(y_{t-1} - \mu_{s_{t-1}}) + \phi_2(y_{t-2} - \mu_{s_{t-2}}) + e_t, \tag{9.56}$$

$$e_t \sim N(0, \sigma_{s_t}^2), \tag{9.57}$$

$$\mu_{s_t} = \mu_1 S_{1t} + \mu_2 S_{2t} + \mu_3 S_{3t}, \quad \mu_1 < \mu_2 < \mu_3, \tag{9.58}$$

$$\sigma_{s_t}^2 = \sigma_1^2 S_{1t} + \sigma_2^2 S_{2t} + \sigma_3^2 S_{3t}, \tag{9.59}$$

$$S_{jt} = 1, \text{ if } S_t = j \text{ and } S_{jt} = 0, \text{ otherwise } j = 1, 2, 3, \tag{9.60}$$

$$p_{ij} = Pr[S_t = j \mid S_{t-1} = i], \quad \sum_{j=1}^{3} p_{ij} = 1, \tag{9.61}$$

where y_t is the ex post real interest rate calculated by subtracting the (CPI) inflation rate from the nominal interest rate (three-month Treasury bill rate).

To guarantee the identification of the model within the Gibbs-sampling framework, the constraint $\mu_1 < \mu_2 < \mu_3$ is included in equation (9.58). Notice that
given the constraint on μ_1, μ_2, and μ_3 above, we should not constrain σ_1^2, σ_2^2,
and σ_3^2, except to stipulate that they are positive.

The above is a straightforward application of the three-state Markov-
switching model in section 9.2 extended to include autoregressive coefficients
and a switching mean. Thus, the Gibbs-sampling procedure includes two more
redundant steps than in section 9.2. Defining $\tilde{S}_T = [\; S_1 \quad S_2 \quad \ldots \quad S_T \;]'$, $\tilde{\sigma}^2 =$
$[\; \sigma_1^2 \quad \sigma_2^2 \quad \sigma_3^2 \;]'$, $\tilde{p} = [\; p_{11} \quad p_{12} \quad p_{21} \quad p_{22} \quad p_{31} \quad p_{32} \;]'$, $\tilde{\mu} = [\mu_1 \mu_2 \mu_3]'$,
and $\tilde{\phi} = [\; \phi_1 \quad \phi_2 \;]$, the Gibbs-sampling procedure is given by successive iter-
ation of the following five steps:

STEP 1   Generate $\tilde{S}_T$, conditional on $\tilde{\sigma}^2$, $\tilde{p}$, $\tilde{\mu}$, $\tilde{\phi}$, and $\tilde{y}_T$.

STEP 2   Generate $\tilde{p}$, conditional on $\tilde{S}_T$.

STEP 3   Generate $\tilde{\sigma}^2$, conditional on $\tilde{\mu}$, $\tilde{\phi}$, $\tilde{S}_T$, and $\tilde{y}_T$.

STEP 4   Generate $\tilde{\mu}$, conditional on $\tilde{\sigma}^2$, $\tilde{\phi}$, $\tilde{S}_T$, and $\tilde{y}_T$.

STEP 5   Generate $\tilde{\phi}$, conditional on $\tilde{\sigma}^2$, $\tilde{\mu}$, $\tilde{S}_T$, and $\tilde{y}_T$.

9.3.1   Generating $\tilde{S}_T$, Conditional on $\tilde{\sigma}^2$, $\tilde{p}$, $\tilde{\mu}$, $\tilde{\phi}$, and $\tilde{y}_T$

The procedure for generating $\tilde{S}_T$ using the multi-move Gibbs-sampling is the
same as in section 9.2.1, except that Hamilton's (1989) basic filter is somewhat
more complicated due to the autoregresive structure in the present case.

9.3.2   Generating $\tilde{p}$, Conditional on $\tilde{S}_T$

The procedure for generating the transition probabilities, $\tilde{p}$, is exactly the same
as that in section 9.2.2.

9.3.3   Generating $\tilde{\sigma}^2$, Conditional on $\tilde{\mu}$, $\tilde{\phi}$, $\tilde{S}_T$, and $\tilde{y}_T$

Again, the procedure is almost the same as that in section 9.2.3, except that y_t
in equations (9.50), (9.52), and (9.54) is replaced by

$$e_t = (y_t - \mu_{s_t}) - \phi_1(y_{t-1} - \mu_{s_{t-1}}) - \phi_2(y_{t-2} - \mu_{s_{t-2}}). \tag{9.62}$$

Also, in generating $\bar{h}_2 = 1 + h_2$ and $\bar{h}_3 = 1 + h_3$ from the inverted Gamma distributions, no constraints are imposed. Thus, no rejection sampling is necessary.

9.3.4 Generating $\tilde{\mu}$, Conditional on $\tilde{\sigma}^2$, $\tilde{\phi}$, $\tilde{S}_T$, and $\tilde{y}_T$

Rearranging equation (9.56), we have

$$y_t^* = \mu_1 S_{1t}^* + \mu_2 S_{2t}^* + \mu_3 S_{3t}^* + e_t, \quad e_t \sim N(0, \sigma_{S_t}^2), \tag{9.63}$$

where $y_t^* = y_t - \phi_1 y_{t-1} - \phi_2 y_{t-2}$ and $S_{it} = S_{it} - \phi_1 S_{i,t-1} - \phi_2 S_{i,t-2}$, $i = 1, 2, 3$. To make the above homoskedastic, we divide both sides by σ_{S_t}:

$$\frac{y_t^*}{\sigma_{S_t}} = \mu_1 \frac{S_{1t}^*}{\sigma_{S_t}} + \mu_2 \frac{S_{2t}^*}{\sigma_{S_t}} + \mu_3 \frac{S_{3t}^*}{\sigma_{S_t}} + v_t, \quad v_t \sim \text{i.i.d.} N(0, 1), \tag{9.64}$$

which, in matrix notation, is given by

$$\tilde{y}_T^* = \tilde{S}_T^* \tilde{\mu} + v, \quad v \sim N(0, I_{T-2}). \tag{9.65}$$

Then it is straightforward to derive the posterior distribution of $\mu = [\ \mu_1 \quad \mu_2 \quad \mu_3\ ]'$, given an appropriate prior distribution:

Prior

$$\tilde{\mu} \mid \tilde{\sigma}^2, \tilde{\phi} \sim N(a_0, A_0)_{I[\mu_1 < \mu_2 < \mu_3]}, \tag{9.66}$$

where a_0 and A_0 are known hyperparameters of the prior distribution and $I[.]$ refers to an indicator function.

Posterior

$$\mu \mid \tilde{\sigma}^2, \tilde{\phi}, \tilde{S}_T, \tilde{y}_T \sim N(a_1, A_1)_{I[\mu_1 < \mu_2 < \mu_3]}, \tag{9.67}$$

where

$$a_1 = (A_0^{-1} + \tilde{S}_T^{*\prime} \tilde{S}_T^*)^{-1} (A_0^{-1} a_0 + \tilde{S}_T^{*\prime} \tilde{y}_T^*),$$

$$A_1 = (A_0^{-1} + \tilde{S}_T^{*\prime} \tilde{S}_T^*)^{-1}.$$

To meet the constraint $\mu_1 < \mu_2 < \mu_3$, we employ rejection sampling.

9.3.5 Generating $\tilde{\phi}$, Conditional on $\tilde{\sigma}^2$, $\tilde{\mu}$, $\tilde{S}_T$, and $\tilde{y}_T$

If we let $y_t^{**} = y_t - \mu_{S_t}$, equation (9.56) is given by

$$y_t^{**} = \phi_1 y_{t-1}^{**} + \phi_2 y_{t-2}^{**} + e_t, \quad e_t \sim N(0, \sigma_{S_t}^2). \tag{9.68}$$

To make the above homoskedastic, we divide both sides by σ_{S_t}:

$$\frac{y_t^{**}}{\sigma_{S_t}} = \phi_1 \frac{y_{t-1}^{**}}{\sigma_{S_t}} + \phi_2 \frac{y_{t-2}^{**}}{\sigma_{S_t}} + v_t, \quad v_t \sim N(0, 1). \tag{9.69}$$

In matrix notation, we have

$$\tilde{y}_T^{**} = X\tilde{\phi} + v, \quad v \sim N(0, I_{T-2}). \tag{9.70}$$

Then, given an appropriate prior distribution, the posterior distribution of $\tilde{\phi} = [\,\phi_1 \quad \phi_2\,]'$ is easily derived:

Prior

$$\tilde{\phi} \mid \tilde{\sigma}^2, \tilde{\mu} \sim N(b_0, B_0)_{I[\phi(L)\in s]}, \tag{9.71}$$

where b_0 and B_0 are known hyperparameters of the prior distribution and $I[.]$ refers to an indicator function used to denote that the roots of $(1 - \phi_1 L - \phi_2 L^2) = 0$ lie outside the unit circle.

Posterior

$$\tilde{\phi} \mid \tilde{\sigma}^2, \tilde{\mu}, \tilde{S}_T, \tilde{y}_T \sim N(b_1, B_1)_{I[\phi(L)\in s]}, \tag{9.72}$$

where

$$b_1 = (B_0^{-1} + X'X)^{-1}(B_0^{-1}b_0 + X'\tilde{y}_T^{**}),$$

$$B_1 = (B_0^{-1} + X'X)^{-1}.$$

To achieve the constraint that the roots of $(1 - \phi_1 L - \phi_2 L^2) = 0$ lie outside the unit circle for the simulated ϕ_1 and ϕ_2, we adopt rejection sampling.

9.3.6   Empirical Results

The procedure described in the previous sections is applied here to the quarterly ex post real interest rate for the sample period 1960:I–1991:IV. The first 2,000 draws of Gibbs-sampling are discarded, and the analysis is based on the next 10,000 draws. Table 9.3 reports the marginal posterior distributions of each of the model's parameters. Comparing the results in this section with those from the maximum likelihood estimation in section 4.5, we can see that

Table 9.3
Bayesian Gibbs-sampling approach to a three-state Markov-switching mean-variance model of the real interest rate (quarterly, 1960.I–1991.IV)

| Parameter | Posterior | | | |
	Mean	SD	MD	98% posterior bands
p_{11}	0.9598	0.0373	0.9715	(0.8646, 0.9987)
p_{12}	0.0150	0.0211	0.0071	(0.0001, 0.0751)
p_{21}	0.0146	0.0158	0.0094	(0.0002, 0.0613)
p_{22}	0.9768	0.0208	0.9829	(0.9202, 0.9992)
p_{31}	0.0083	0.0130	0.0034	(0.0000, 0.0460)
p_{32}	0.0092	0.0156	0.0034	(0.0000, 0.0514)
ϕ_1	0.0503	0.1048	0.0496	(−0.1572, 0.2576)
ϕ_2	0.0617	0.1073	0.0584	(−0.1479, 0.2808)
σ_1^2	5.6335	1.8251	5.3155	(3.0804, 9.9789)
σ_2^2	1.4558	0.3538	1.4039	(0.9195, 2.3096)
σ_3^2	6.6678	1.6415	6.4165	(4.1432, 10.6480)
μ_1	−1.4634	0.5247	−1.4695	(−2.4883, −0.3808)
μ_2	1.3535	0.2092	1.3588	(0.9276, 1.7794)
μ_3	3.9894	0.5071	3.9633	(2.9832, 5.0494)

Note: Almost noninformative priors were given for all the parameters of the model. SD and MD refer to standard deviation and median, respectively.

the posterior means from the Bayesian Gibbs-sampling analysis are in close agreement with the maximum likelihood estimates.

The posterior means for ϕ_1 and ϕ_2 are close to 0 and their 95% posterior bands include 0. Thus, regime switching in the mean seems to account for most of the persistence in the real interest rate. The nonoverlapping posterior bands for μ_1, μ_2, and μ_3 seem to suggest that the mean of the real interest rate is characterized by three distinctive phases. The variance term, however, does not seem to have three phases.

Figures 9.5a, 9.5b, and 9.5c depict the probabilities of low-, medium-, and high-mean states for the real interest rate. These may be considered as smoothed probabilities, because inferences of these probabilities are based on the full sample. At the end of j-th iteration, we have a set of generated parameters, $\tilde{p}^j$, $\tilde{\mu}^j$, $\tilde{\phi}^j$, and the states $\tilde{S}_T^j$, which allow us to calculate $E[y_t \mid \tilde{y}_T, \tilde{p}^j, \tilde{\mu}^j, \tilde{\phi}^j, \tilde{S}_T^j]$, $t = 1, 2, \ldots, T$, $j = 1, 2, \ldots, 10,000$. Averages of these 10,000 values provide us with a measure of the expected real interest. Figure 9.6 depicts this measure, based on the full sample.

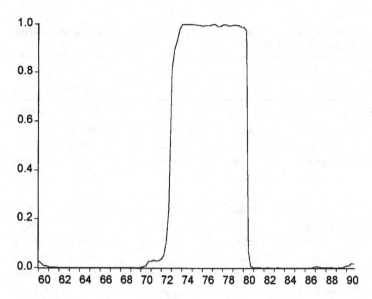

Figure 9.5a
Probability of a low-interest rate state (Gibbs-sampling)

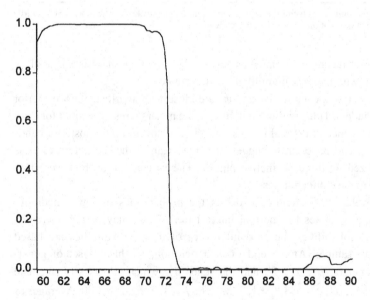

Figure 9.5b
Probability of a medium-interest rate state (Gibbs-sampling)

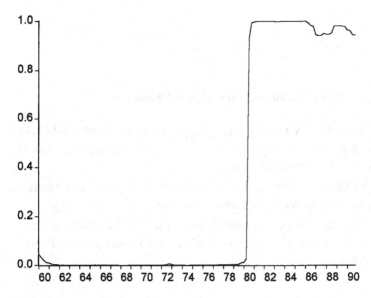

Figure 9.5c
Probability of a high-interest rate state (Gibbs-sampling)

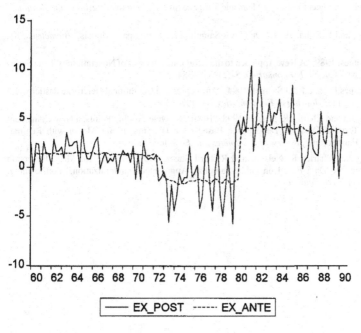

EX_POST ------ EX_ANTE

Figure 9.6
Ex post real interest rates and estimated ex ante real interest rates (three-state Markov-switching mean-variance model: Gibbs-sampling)

Appendix: GAUSS Programs to Accompany Chapter 9

1. GIBS_MS0.PRG: A Gibbs-sampling approach to an AR(0) model with a two-state Markov-switching mean, homoskedastic disturbances: multimove Gibbs-sampling (for real GDP data).

2. GIBS_S3.PRG: A Gibbs-sampling approach to a three-state Markov-switching variance model of stock returns: multimove Gibbs-sampling.

3. G_INT_S3.PRG: A Gibbs-sampling approach to a three-State Markov-switching mean-variance AR(2) model of the real interest rate: multimove Gibbs-sampling.

References

Albert, James H., and Siddhartha Chib. 1993. "Bayes Inference via Gibbs Sampling of Autoregressive Time Series Subject to Markov Mean and Variance Shifts." *Journal of Business and Economic Statistics,* 11(1), 1–15.

Carter, C. K., and P. Kohn. 1994. "On Gibbs Sampling for State Space Models." *Biometrica,* 81, 541–553.

Hamilton, James. 1989. "A New Approach to the Economic Analysis of Nonstationary Time Series and the Business Cycle." *Econometrica,* 57(2), 357–384.

Hamilton, James D., and Raul Susmel. 1994. "Autoregressive Conditional Heteroske dasticity and Changes in Regime." *Journal of Econometrics,* 64, 307–333.

Kim, Chang-Jin and Charles R. Nelson. 1998. "Business Cycle Turning Points, a New Coincident Index, and Tests of Duration Dependence Based on a Dynamic Factor Model with Regime-Switching." Forthcoming, *Review of Economics and Economic Statistics.*

Kim, Chang-Jin, Charles R. Nelson, and Richard Startz. 1998. "Testing for Mean Reversion in Heteroskedastic Data Based on Gibbs-Sampling-Augmented Randomization." Forthcoming, *Journal of Empirical Finance.*

10 State-Space Models with Markov Switching and Gibbs-Sampling

This chapter provides a Bayesian counterpart to chapters 5 and 6, which considered classical inferences for state-space models with some of the hyperparameters being subject to Markov switching. Alternatively, this chapter may be viewed as combining the ideas in chapters 8 and 9, which considered Bayesian inferences for linear state-space models and Markov-switching regression models. Section 10.1 presents the general framework, and the subsequent sections deal with the following specific applications: a new experimental coincident index for the economy, including tests for duration dependence, based on Kim and Nelson 1998, and unobserved components in the U.S./U.K. real exchange rate with heteroskedasticity, based on Engel and Kim 1996. As usual, throughout this chapter, the notation $\tilde{\alpha}_t$ (with a ˜ above α and a subscript t) is used to denote a vector containing $\alpha_1, \alpha_2, \ldots, \alpha_t$.

10.1 General Framework

We first consider the following state-space model with Markov switching, introduced in chapter 5:

Model 1

$$y_t = H_{S_t}\beta_t + A_{S_t}z_t + e_t, \quad e_t \sim \text{i.i.d.}N(0, R_{S_t}), \tag{10.1}$$

$$\beta_t = \tilde{\mu}_{S_t} + F_{S_t}\beta_{t-1} + v_t, \quad v_t \sim \text{i.i.d.}N(0, Q_{S_t}), \tag{10.2}$$

$$E(e_t v_t' | S_t) = 0, \tag{10.3}$$

where H_{S_t}, A_{S_t}, R_{S_t}, $\tilde{\mu}_{S_t}$, F_{S_t}, and Q_{S_t} denote that some of the hyperparameters in the model are dependent on an unobserved variable S_t. As usual, S_t is a discrete-valued, unobserved Markov-switching variables with appropriate transition probabilities.

The conditioning features of the above model make inferences via Bayesian Gibbs-sampling a straightforward application of the methods presented in chapters 8 and 9. Conditional on all the parameters of the model including the transition probabilities, the problem in this section reduces to making inferences on $2T$ unobserved variates, $\tilde{S}_T = [\ S_1 \quad S_2 \quad \ldots \quad S_T\ ]'$ and $\tilde{\beta}_T = [\ \beta_1 \quad \beta_2 \quad \ldots \quad \beta_T\ ]'$. Conditional on $\tilde{S}_T$, the above model is a linear state-space model as in chapter 8, with S_t playing the role of a dummy variable that accounts for known structural break points. Conditional on $\tilde{\beta}_T$, equations

(10.1) and (10.2) form a bivariate regression model with a common Markov-switching variable, S_t, which can easily be dealt with using the procedures presented in chapter 9. In this case, the $\tilde{\beta}_T$ vector is treated as data. Thus, for given arbitrary starting values of the hyperparameters, Gibbs-sampling consists of the following steps:

STEP 1 (an application of chapter 8) Conditional on hyperparameters of the model, $\tilde{S}_T$, and the observed data, generate $\tilde{\beta}_T$ from

$$p(\tilde{\beta}_T | \tilde{y}_T, \tilde{S}_T) = p(\beta_T | \tilde{y}_T, \tilde{S}_T) \prod_{t=1}^{T-1} p(\beta_t | \tilde{y}_t, \tilde{S}_t, \beta_{t+1}), \qquad (10.4)$$

where $\tilde{y}_t = [\, y_1 \quad y_2 \quad y_3 \quad \ldots \quad y_t \,]'$.

STEP 2 (an application of chapter 9) Conditional on hyperparameters of the model, $\tilde{\beta}_T$, and the observed data, generate $\tilde{S}_T$ from

$$p(\tilde{S}_T | \tilde{y}_T, \tilde{\beta}_T) = p(S_T | \tilde{y}_T, \tilde{\beta}_T) \prod_{t=1}^{T-1} p(S_t | \tilde{y}_t, \tilde{\beta}_t, S_{t+1}), \qquad (10.5)$$

where the above density is derived based on a bivariate regression model with a common Markov-switching variable.

STEP 3 Conditional on $\tilde{\beta}_T$, $\tilde{S}_T$, and the observed data, generate hyperparameters of the model from appropriate conditional distributions.

The model can easily be extended to include more than one Markov-switching variable, as in chapter 6. For example, the measurement and the transition equations may not necessarily be dependent on a common Markov-switching variable. Consider the following state-space model with two independent Markov-switching variables:

Model 2

$$y_t = H_{S_{1t}} \beta_t + A_{S_{1t}} z_t + e_t, \quad e_t \sim \text{i.i.d.} N(0, R_{S_{1t}}), \qquad (10.6)$$

$$\beta_t = \tilde{\mu}_{S_{2t}} + F_{S_{2t}} \beta_{t-1} + v_t, \quad v_t \sim \text{i.i.d.} N(0, Q_{S_{2t}}), \qquad (10.7)$$

$$E(e_t v_t') = 0, \qquad (10.8)$$

$$E(S_{1t} S_{2t}) = 0, \qquad (10.9)$$

where some of the hyperparameters in the measurement equation are dependent on an unobserved variable S_{1t}, and some of the hyperparameters in the transition equation are dependent on an unobserved variable S_{2t}. Both S_{1t} and S_{2t} are discrete-valued, unobserved Markov-switching variables with appropriate transition probabilities. S_{1t} and S_{2t} are assumed to be independent of each other.

The procedure for Gibbs-sampling for model 2 is actually simpler than that for model 1, except that we have $3T$ variates to draw ($\tilde{\beta}_T$, $\tilde{S}_{1T}$, and $\tilde{S}_{2T}$), conditional on the model's parameters. For given arbitrary starting values for the hyperparameters, Gibbs-sampling consists of the following steps:

STEP 1 (an application of chapter 8)   Conditional on hyperparameters of the model, $\tilde{S}_{1T}$, $\tilde{S}_{2T}$, and the observed data, generate $\tilde{\beta}_T$ from

$$p(\tilde{\beta}_T|\tilde{y}_T, \tilde{S}_{1T}, \tilde{S}_{2T}) = p(\beta_T|\tilde{y}_T, \tilde{S}_{1T}, \tilde{S}_{2T}) \prod_{t=1}^{T-1} p(\beta_t|\tilde{y}_t, \tilde{S}_{1T}, \tilde{S}_{2T}, \beta_{t+1}) (10.10)$$

STEP 2 (an application of chapter 9)   Conditional on hyperparameters of the model, $\tilde{\beta}_T$, and the observed data, generate $\tilde{S}_{1T}$ from

$$p(\tilde{S}_{1T}|\tilde{y}_T, \tilde{\beta}_T) = p(S_{1T}|\tilde{y}_T, \tilde{\beta}_T) \prod_{t=1}^{T-1} p(S_{1t}|\tilde{y}_t, \tilde{\beta}_t, S_{1,t+1}), \qquad (10.11)$$

where the above density is derived from the measurement equation (10.6) independently of the transition equation (10.7).

STEP 3 (an application of chapter 9)   Conditional on hyperparameters of the model and $\tilde{\beta}_T$, generate $\tilde{S}_{2T}$ from

$$p(\tilde{S}_{2T}|\tilde{\beta}_T) = p(S_{2T}|\tilde{\beta}_T) \prod_{t=1}^{T-1} p(S_{2t}|\tilde{\beta}_t, S_{2,t+1}), \qquad (10.12)$$

where the above density is derived from the transition equation (10.7) independently of the measurement equation (10.6). Conditional on $\tilde{\beta}_T$, the observed data $\tilde{y}_T$ does not contain information on $\tilde{S}_{tT}$ beyond that contained in $\tilde{\beta}_T$.

STEP 4   Conditional on $\tilde{\beta}_T$, $\tilde{S}_{1T}$, $\tilde{S}_{2T}$, and the observed data, generate hyperparameters of the model from appropriate conditional distributions.

As an example of model 1, one might consider the following unobserved component model of the ex ante real interest rate:

$$y_t = r_t + e_t, \quad e_t \sim N(0, \sigma_{e,s_t}^2), \tag{10.13}$$

$$\phi(L)(r_t - \mu_{s_t}) = w_t, \quad w_t \sim N(0, \sigma_{w,s_t}^2), \tag{10.14}$$

$$E(e_t w_t | S_t) = 0, \tag{10.15}$$

$$Pr[S_t = j | S_{t-1} = i] = p_{ij}, \quad \sum_{j=1}^{M} p_{ij} = 1, \tag{10.16}$$

where y_t is the ex post real interest rate and r_t is the unobserved ex ante real interest rate. Some literature has suggested that the ex ante real interest rate might contain a unit root. However, Garcia and Perron (1996) have shown that ignoring regime shifts in a series like the real interest rate results in spurious unit roots for the series. Of particular interest in the above model would be an inference on the largest eigenvalue of the ex ante real interest rate. The proposed model may be considered an alternative to Garcia and Perron's 1996 model of the ex post real interest rate with regime switching. Whereas Garcia and Perron's is a reduced-form model, the above is a structural model.

In the preceding example, it can be shown that the shock e_t in (10.13) is the negative of the inflation forecast error under rational expectations. There is no reason to believe that variance of the inflation forecast errors switches its regime whenever the ex ante real interest rate in (10.14) switches its regime. A more general assumption would be that the ex ante real interest rate and the inflation forecast error are subject to two independent Markov-switching variables, S_{1t} and S_{2t}. We then get the following model of the ex ante real interest rate as an example of model 2:

$$y_t = r_t + e_t, \quad e_t \sim N(0, \sigma_{e,s_{1t}}^2), \tag{10.17}$$

$$\phi(L)(r_t - \mu_{s_{2t}}) = w_t, \quad w_t \sim N(0, \sigma_{w,s_{2t}}^2), \tag{10.18}$$

$$E(e_t w_s) = 0, \tag{10.19}$$

$$Pr[S_{\gamma,t} = j | S_{\gamma,t-1} = i] = p_{\gamma ij}, \quad \sum_{j=1}^{M} p_{\gamma ij} = 1, \quad \gamma = 1, 2. \tag{10.20}$$

10.2 Application 1: Business Cycle Turning Points and a New Coincident Index

Consider the following dynamic factor model with Markov switching of coincident indicators suggested by Diebold and Rudebusch (1996) and introduced in section 5.7:

$$\Delta Y_{it} = \gamma_i(L)\Delta C_t + D_i + e_{it}; \quad i = 1, 2, 3, 4, \tag{10.21}$$

$$\psi_i(L)e_{it} = \epsilon_{it}, \quad \epsilon_{it} \sim \text{i.i.d.}N(0, \sigma_i^2), \tag{10.22}$$

$$\phi(L)(\Delta C_t - \mu_{s_t} - \delta) = w_t, \quad w_t \sim \text{i.i.d.}N(0, 1), \tag{10.23}$$

$$\mu_{s_t} = \mu_0 + \mu_1 S_t, \quad \mu_1 > 0, \quad S_t = \{0, 1\}, \tag{10.24}$$

$$Pr[S_t = 1 | S_{t-1} = 1] = p, \quad Pr[S_t = 0 | S_{t-1} = 0] = q, \tag{10.25}$$

where ΔY_{it} represents the first difference of the log of the i-th indicator, $i = 1, \ldots, 4$; $\gamma_i(L)$ is the polynomial in the lag operator; ΔC_t is the growth rate of the new composite index; μ_{S_t} refers to a Markov-switching deviation of the growth of the common unobserved component from its long-run growth δ; and w_t and ϵ_{it} are independent of one another for all t and i. For expositional purposes, we assume $\gamma_i(L) = \gamma_i$, $\psi_i(L) = 1 - \phi_{i1}L - \phi_{i2}L^2, i = 1, 2, 3, 4,$ and $\phi(L) = 1 - \phi_1 L - \phi_2 L^2$.

As noted in section 5.7, the above model is not identified, as the mean of each series ($E[\Delta Y_{it}] = D_i + \gamma_i(1)\delta$) is overparameterized. Thus we consider the model in deviation from mean form, in which equations (10.21) and (10.23) are replaced by

$$\Delta y_{it} = \gamma_i(L)\Delta c_t + e_{it}, \quad i = 1, 2, 3, 4, \tag{10.21'}$$

$$\phi(L)(\Delta c_t - \mu_{s_t}) = w_t, \quad w_t \sim \text{i.i.d.}N(0, 1), \tag{10.23'}$$

where $\Delta y_{it} = \Delta Y_{it} - \Delta \bar{Y}_i$ and $\Delta c_t = \Delta C_t - \delta$.

Although maximum likelihood estimation of the parameters of the model and inferences on $\Delta \tilde{c}_T = [\Delta c_1 \ \Delta c_2 \ldots \Delta c_T]'$ and $\tilde{S}_T = [\ S_1 \ \ S_2 \ \ \ldots \ \ S_T\ ]'$ based on approximations to the Kalman filter are straightforward to implement, as presented in chapter 5, it is difficult to judge the effects of the approximations on the parameter estimates and on inferences pertaining to the unobserved common component, Δc_t, and the unobserved state, S_t. The effects of the approximation on the steady-state Kalman gain are also unknown, and this uncertainty complicates the task of decomposing $\Delta \bar{Y}_i$ into D_i and δ, which is necessary to extract the composite coincident index, $C_t = \Delta c_t + C_{t-1} + \delta$. In addition, because inferences about S_t and Δc_t are based on final parameter estimates of the model, effects of parameter uncertainty are unknown in the classical approach.

In contrast, the Bayesian Gibbs-sampling approach of Kim and Nelson (1998) incorporates parameter uncertainty by making inferences on unknown parameters, $\Delta \tilde{c}_T$ and $\tilde{S}_T$, using their joint distribution; and it avoids using approximations. (It may not be entirely accurate to say that the Gibbs-sampling framework makes no approximations. The key approximation in the Gibbs-framework is associated with declaring the Gibbs chain to have converged to its steady state. It is in the limit, as the length of the chain goes to infinity, that the approximation error vanishes.) In addition, Gibbs-sampling provides us with information that cannot be extracted from an approximate maximum likelihood estimation of the model in section 5.7. For example, posterior distributions of the parameters and other variates contain important information that we exploit in section 10.3.

The following steps explain details of the Gibbs-sampling procedure, given arbitrary starting values for the parameters of the model:

STEP 1   Conditional on $\tilde{S}_T$, all parameters of the model, and data, $\Delta \tilde{y}_{iT}$, $i = 1, 2, 3, 4$, generate $\Delta \tilde{c}_T$ from a state-space representation of the model in deviation from mean form.

STEP 2   Conditional on $\Delta \tilde{c}_T$ and data on the i-th indicator, Δy_{iT}, generate the parameters associated with the i-th equation in (10.21′) and (10.22), $i = 1, 2, 3, 4$.

STEP 3   Conditional on $\Delta \tilde{c}_T$, generate $\tilde{S}_T$ and parameters associated with equation (10.23′), (10.24), and (10.25).

STEP 4   Conditional on data and the generated parameters of the model, calculate δ, the long-run mean of ΔC_t, and using the generated Δc_t, calculate $C_t = C_{t-1} + \Delta c_t + \delta$, $t = 1, 2, \ldots, T$, given C_0.

The following sections describe each of the above steps in detail. Each of the sections, shows that generating appropriate variates for each of the above steps is an application or a review of previous chapters, because of the conditioning features of the model and Gibbs-sampling. (The results in this section originally appeared in Kim and Nelson 1998.)

10.2.1 Generating $\Delta \tilde{c}_T$, Conditional on $\Delta \tilde{y}_{iT}$, $i = 1, 2, 3, 4$, All Parameters of the model, and $\tilde{S}_T$

If we multiply both sides of (10.21$'$) by $\psi_i(L)$, $i = 1, 2, 3, 4$, we have

$$\Delta y_{it}^* = \gamma_i(L)\psi_i(L)\Delta c_t + \epsilon_{it}, \quad \epsilon_{it} \sim \text{i.i.d.}N(0, \sigma_i^2), \quad i = 1, 2, 3, 4, \quad (10.26)$$

where $\Delta y_{it}^* = \psi_i(L)\Delta y_{it}$. Assuming $\gamma_i(L) = \gamma_i$, $\psi_i(L) = 1 - \psi_{i1}L - \psi_{i2}L^2$, $i = 1, 2, 3, 4$, and $\phi(L) = 1 - \phi L - \phi L^2$, equations (10.26) and (10.23$'$) can be written in the following state-space representation form:

$$\begin{bmatrix} \Delta y_{1t}^* \\ \Delta y_{2t}^* \\ \Delta y_{3t}^* \\ \Delta y_{4t}^* \end{bmatrix} = \begin{bmatrix} \gamma_1 & -\gamma_1\psi_{11} & -\gamma_1\psi_{12} \\ \gamma_2 & -\gamma_2\psi_{21} & -\gamma_2\psi_{22} \\ \gamma_3 & -\gamma_3\psi_{31} & -\gamma_3\psi_{32} \\ \gamma_4 & -\gamma_4\psi_{41} & -\gamma_4\psi_{42} \end{bmatrix} \begin{bmatrix} \Delta c_t \\ \Delta c_{t-1} \\ \Delta c_{t-2} \end{bmatrix} + \begin{bmatrix} \epsilon_{1t} \\ \epsilon_{2t} \\ \epsilon_{3t} \\ \epsilon_{4t} \end{bmatrix}, \quad (10.27)$$

$(\Delta y_t^* = H\beta_t + e_t)$,

$$E(e_t e_t') = R = \begin{bmatrix} \sigma_1^2 & 0 & 0 & 0 \\ 0 & \sigma_2^2 & 0 & 0 \\ 0 & 0 & \sigma_3^2 & 0 \\ 0 & 0 & 0 & \sigma_4^2 \end{bmatrix}, \quad (10.28)$$

where $\Delta y_{it}^* = \Delta y_{it} - \psi_{i1}\Delta y_{i,t-1} - \psi_{i2}\Delta y_{i,t-2}$, $i = 1, 2, 3, 4$;

$$\begin{bmatrix} \Delta c_t \\ \Delta c_{t-1} \\ \Delta c_{t-2} \end{bmatrix} = \begin{bmatrix} \phi(L)\mu_{S_t} \\ 0 \\ 0 \end{bmatrix} + \begin{bmatrix} \phi_1 & \phi_2 & 0 \\ 1 & 0 & 0 \\ 0 & 1 & 0 \end{bmatrix} \begin{bmatrix} \Delta c_{t-1} \\ \Delta c_{t-2} \\ \Delta c_{t-3} \end{bmatrix} + \begin{bmatrix} w_t \\ 0 \\ 0 \end{bmatrix}, \quad (10.29)$$

$(\beta_t = \tilde{M}_{S_t} + F\beta_{t-1} + v_t)$,

$$E(v_t v_t') = Q = \begin{bmatrix} 1 & 0 & 0 \\ 0 & 0 & 0 \\ 0 & 0 & 0 \end{bmatrix}. \quad (10.30)$$

In the above state-space representation, the second and third rows of the transition equation describe identities, and all the elements of the Q matrix are 0 except for the (1,1) element. Thus we have a case where $J = 1$ in section 8.2. The only difference from the state-space representation in section 8.3.1 is that we have the $\tilde{M}_{S_t}$ term in the transition equation. The following reviews the procedure for generating $\tilde{\beta}_T$, and thus, $\Delta \tilde{c}_T$.

Consider the following joint distribution of $\tilde{\beta}_T = [\, \beta_1 \quad \beta_2 \quad \ldots \quad \beta_T \,]'$, given data, $\Delta \tilde{y}_T^* = [\, \Delta \tilde{y}_{1T}^{*}{}' \quad \ldots \quad \Delta \tilde{y}_{4T}^{*}{}' \,]'$, and given the prior distribution of β_0:

$$p(\tilde{\beta}_T | \Delta \tilde{y}_T^*) = p(\beta_T | \Delta \tilde{y}_T^*) \prod_{t=1}^{T-1} p(\beta_t | \Delta \tilde{y}_t^*, \beta_{t+1}), \tag{10.31}$$

where $\Delta \tilde{y}_t^*$ refers to data up to time t. Applying the procedure in chapter 8, generation of $\tilde{\beta}_T$ can be generated from $p(\tilde{\beta}_T | \Delta \tilde{y}_T^*)$ in the following sequence: first, we can generate β_T from $p(\beta_T | \Delta \tilde{y}_T^*)$; then, for $t = T - 1, T - 2, \ldots, 1$, we can generate β_t from $p(\beta_t | \Delta \tilde{y}_t^*, \beta_{t+1})$. Because the state-space model in (10.27) and (10.29) is linear and Gaussian conditional on $\tilde{S}_T$, we can take advantage of the Gaussian Kalman filter to obtain $p(\beta_T | \Delta \tilde{y}_T^*)$ and $p(\beta_t | \Delta \tilde{y}_t^*, \beta_{t+1})$. The fact that the model is linear and Gaussian conditional on $\tilde{S}_T$ allows us to employ the procedures in chapter 8 and is the reason why no approximation of the kind in chapter 5 need be employed.

Also notice that all elements of β_t, except for the first element, Δc_t, are associated with elements of β_{t-1} by the identity matrix. The joint conditional density in (10.31) can therefore alternatively be rewritten in terms of the first element of β_t, that is, Δc_t:

$$p(\tilde{\beta}_T | \Delta \tilde{y}_T^*) = p(\Delta \tilde{c}_T | \Delta \tilde{y}_T^*) = p(\Delta c_T | \Delta \tilde{y}_T^*) \prod_{t=1}^{T-1} p(\Delta c_t | \Delta \tilde{y}_t^*, \Delta c_{t+1}). \tag{10.32}$$

Keeping these relationships in mind, we can proceed to generate Δc_t, $t = 1, 2, \ldots, T$, as follows:

STEP 1   Run the Kalman filter algorithm to calculate $\beta_{t|t} = E(\beta_t | \Delta \tilde{y}_t^*)$ and $P_{t|t} = var(\beta_t | \Delta \tilde{y}_t^*)$ for $t = 1, 2, \ldots, T$ and save the values. The last iteration of the Kalman filter provides us with $\beta_{T|T}$ and $P_{T|T}$, and Δc_T can be generated from

$$\Delta c_T \sim N(\beta_{T|T}(1), P_{T|T}(1, 1)) \tag{10.33}$$

where $\beta_{T|T}(1)$ is the first element of $\beta_{T|T}$ and $P_{T|T}(1, 1)$ is the $(1,1)$ element of $P_{T|T}$.

STEP 2   For $t = T - 1, T - 2, \ldots, 1$, given $\beta_{t|t}$ and $P_{t|t}$, if we treat the generated Δc_{t+1} as an additional observation to the system, the distribution $p(\beta_t | \Delta \tilde{y}_t^*, \Delta c_{t+1})$ is easily derived by applying the updating equations of the

Kalman filter. Because Δc_{t+1}, the first element of β_{t+1}, is given by

$$\Delta c_{t+1} = (1 - \phi_1 L - \phi_2 L^2)\mu_{s_{t+1}} + \phi_1 \Delta c_t + \phi_2 \Delta c_{t-1} + w_{t+1}, \qquad (10.34)$$

or

$$\Delta c_{t+1} = \phi(L)\mu_{s_{t+1}} + F(1)\beta_t + v^*_{t+1}(1), \qquad (10.35)$$

where $F(1)$ is the first row of F and $v_{t+1}(1)$ is the first element of v_{t+1} in equation (10.29), the updating equations are derived as follows:

$$\beta_{t|t,\Delta c_{t+1}} = \beta_{t|t} + P_{t|t}F(1)'f^{*-1}_{t+1|t}\eta^*_{t+1}, \qquad (10.36)$$

$$P_{t|t,\Delta c_{t+1}} = P_{t|t} - P_{t|t}F(1)'f^{*-1}_{t+1|t}F(1)P_{t|t}, \qquad (10.37)$$

where $\eta^*_{t+1} = \Delta c_{t+1} - \phi(L)\mu_{s_{t+1}} - F(1)\beta_{t|t}$ is the forecast error for Δc_{t+1} given information up to time t, $f^*_{t+1|t} = F(1)P_{t|t}F(1)' + \text{var}(w_{t+1})$ is the conditional variance of η^*_{t+1}, and $\text{var}(w_{t+1}) = 1$. Then we can generate Δc_t, for $t = T - 1, T - 2, \ldots, 1$, using:

$$\Delta c_t | \Delta \tilde{y}^*_t, \Delta c_{t+1} \sim N(\beta_{t|t,\Delta c_{t+1}}(1), P_{t|t,\Delta c_{t+1}}(1, 1)), \qquad (10.38)$$

where $\beta_{t|t,\Delta c_{t+1}}(1)$ is the first element of $\beta_{t|t,\Delta c_{t+1}}$ and $P_{t|t,\Delta c_{t+1}}(1, 1)$ is the $(1,1)$ element of $P_{t|t,\Delta c_{t+1}}$.

10.2.2 Generating Parameters Associated with the i-th Coincident Indicator, γ_i, $\tilde{\psi}_i = [\,\psi_{i1}\quad \psi_{i2}\,]'$ and σ_i^2, Conditional on $\Delta \tilde{c}_T$ and $\Delta \tilde{y}_{iT}$, $i = 1, 2, 3, 4$

Conditional on $\Delta \tilde{c}_T$, equations (10.23)–(10.25) are irrelevant, and the model collapses to four independent regression equations with autocorrelated disturbances given in (10.21') and (10.22). Thus, the analysis is exactly the same as in section 8.3.3.

10.2.3 Generating $\tilde{S}_T$, ϕ_1, ϕ_2, μ_0, μ_1, p, and q, Conditional on $\Delta \tilde{c}_T$

Conditional on $\Delta \tilde{c}_T$, the observed data $\Delta \tilde{y}_T$ carry no information about $\tilde{S}_T$ and the parameters in equations (10.23'), (10.24), and (10.25) beyond that contained in $\Delta \tilde{c}_T$. This is true because w_t in (10.23) is independent of the shocks in (10.21') and (10.22). Thus to generate $\tilde{S}_T$ and the related parameters, ϕ_1, ϕ_2, μ_0, μ_1, p, and q, we can focus on equtions (10.23'), (10.24), and (10.25), which form an autoregressive model with Markov-switching mean. $\Delta \tilde{c}_T$ is treated as data for the model. The procedure is the same as in chapter 9.

10.2.4   Calculation of the Composite Coincident Index, C_t

The mean of each coincident variable $(\Delta \bar{Y}_i)$ consists of the portion due to the idiosyncratic component (D_i in equation (10.21)) and the portion due to the common component ($\gamma_i(1)\delta$ in equation (10.23)). The procedure for decomposing $\Delta \bar{Y}_i$, $i = 1, 2, 3, 4$, into its two components and calculate δ is the same as that in section 3.5.2 or 8.3.4, conditional on the parameters of the model.

As in section 8.3.4, we employ an alternative state-space representation of the model given in (10.27) and (10.29):

$$
\begin{bmatrix} \Delta y_{1t} \\ \Delta y_{2t} \\ \Delta y_{3t} \\ \Delta y_{4t} \end{bmatrix} = \begin{bmatrix} \gamma_1 & 0 & 1 & 0 & 0 & 0 & 0 & 0 & 0 & 0 \\ \gamma_2 & 0 & 0 & 0 & 1 & 0 & 0 & 0 & 0 & 0 \\ \gamma_3 & 0 & 0 & 0 & 0 & 0 & 1 & 0 & 0 & 0 \\ \gamma_4 & 0 & 0 & 0 & 0 & 0 & 0 & 0 & 1 & 0 \end{bmatrix} \begin{bmatrix} \Delta c_t \\ \Delta c_{t-1} \\ e_{1t} \\ e_{1,t-1} \\ e_{2t} \\ e_{2,t-1} \\ e_{3t} \\ e_{3,t-1} \\ e_{4t} \\ e_{4,t-1} \end{bmatrix}, \quad (10.39)
$$

$(\Delta y_t = H^* \beta_t^*),$

$$
\begin{bmatrix} \Delta c_t \\ \Delta c_{t-1} \\ e_{1t} \\ e_{1,t-1} \\ \vdots \\ e_{4t} \\ e_{4,t-1} \end{bmatrix} = \begin{bmatrix} \phi(L)\mu_{s_t} \\ 0 \\ 0 \\ 0 \\ \vdots \\ 0 \\ 0 \end{bmatrix}
$$

$$
+ \begin{bmatrix} \phi_1 & \phi_2 & 0 & 0 & \dots & 0 & 0 \\ 1 & 0 & 0 & 0 & \dots & 0 & 0 \\ 0 & 0 & \psi_{11} & \psi_{12} & \dots & 0 & 0 \\ 0 & 0 & 1 & 0 & \dots & 0 & 0 \\ \vdots & \vdots & \vdots & \vdots & \ddots & \vdots & \vdots \\ 0 & 0 & 0 & 0 & \dots & \psi_{41} & \psi_{42} \\ 0 & 0 & 0 & 0 & \dots & 1 & 0 \end{bmatrix} \begin{bmatrix} \Delta c_{t-1} \\ \Delta c_{t-2} \\ e_{1,t-1} \\ e_{1,t-2} \\ \vdots \\ e_{4,t-1} \\ e_{4,t-2} \end{bmatrix} + \begin{bmatrix} w_t \\ 0 \\ \epsilon_{1t} \\ 0 \\ \vdots \\ \epsilon_{4t} \\ 0 \end{bmatrix}, \quad (10.40)
$$

$$(\beta_t^* = M_{S_t}^* + F^* \beta_{t-1}^* + v_t^*),$$

where $\phi(L)\mu_{S_t} = \mu_{S_t} - \phi_1 \mu_{S_{t-1}} - \phi_2 \mu_{S_{t-2}}$.

Denoting K^* as the steady-state Kalman gain obtained from applying the Kalman filter to the above state-space model, the long-run mean of the common component, given the parameters of the model, is provided by

$$\delta = E_1'(I_k - (I_k - K^* H)F)^{-1} K^* \Delta \bar{Y}, \tag{10.41}$$

where $E_1' = [\,1 \quad 0 \quad 0 \quad \ldots \quad 0\,]$, k is the dimension of the β_t^* vector, and $\Delta \bar{Y}$ is a 4×1 vector that contains means of individual ΔY_i. Once δ is identified, for given $\Delta \tilde{c}_T$, and an initial value of C_0, we are able to generate our new composite coincident index as $C_t = \Delta c_t + C_{t-1} + \delta$, $t = 1, 2, \ldots, T$.

10.2.5 Empirical Results

As in section 5.7, the four monthly series for the United States used in this study are those used by the Department of Commerce to construct its composite index of coincident indicators: industrial production (IP), total personal income less transfer payments in 1987 dollars (GMYXPQ), total manufacturing and trade sales in 1987 dollars (MTQ), and employees on nonagricultural payrolls (LPNAG). The time period is 1960.1 through 1995.1. In addition, assuming $\gamma_i(L) = \gamma_i$, $i = 1, 2, 3$, in (10.21′), to account for the fact that the employment variable, Δy_{4t}, may be somewhat lagging the unobserved common component, the fourth equation in (10.21′) is specified as follows:

$$\Delta y_{4t} = \gamma_{40}\Delta c_t + \gamma_{41}\Delta c_{t-1} + \gamma_{42}\Delta c_{t-2} + \gamma_{43}\Delta c_{t-3} + e_{4t}. \tag{10.42}$$

Then the two state-space representations of the model employed are modified as

State-Space Representation 1

$$
\begin{bmatrix} \Delta y_{1t}^* \\ \Delta y_{2t}^* \\ \Delta y_{3t}^* \\ \Delta y_{4t}^* \end{bmatrix}
=
\begin{bmatrix}
\gamma_1 & -\gamma_1\psi_{11} & -\gamma_1\psi_{12} & 0 & 0 & 0 \\
\gamma_2 & -\gamma_2\psi_{21} & -\gamma_2\psi_{22} & 0 & 0 & 0 \\
\gamma_3 & -\gamma_3\psi_{31} & -\gamma_3\psi_{32} & 0 & 0 & 0 \\
\gamma_{40} & \gamma_{41}^* & \gamma_{42}^* & \gamma_{43}^* & \gamma_{44}^* & \gamma_{45}^*
\end{bmatrix}
\begin{bmatrix} \Delta c_t \\ \Delta c_{t-1} \\ \Delta c_{t-2} \\ \Delta c_{t-3} \\ \Delta c_{t-4} \\ \Delta c_{t-5} \end{bmatrix}
+
\begin{bmatrix} \epsilon_{1t} \\ \epsilon_{2t} \\ \epsilon_{3t} \\ \epsilon_{4t} \end{bmatrix},
$$

$$\tag{10.27′}$$

where $y_{it}^* = y_{it} - \psi_{i1}y_{i,t-1} - \psi_{i2}y_{i,t-2}$, $i = 1, 2, 3, 4$; $\gamma_{41}^* = -\gamma_{40}\psi_{41} + \gamma_{41}$;
$\gamma_{42}^* = -\gamma_{40}\psi_{42} - \gamma_{41}\psi_{41} + \gamma_{42}$; $\quad \gamma_{43}^* = -\gamma_{41}\psi_{42} - \gamma_{42}\psi_{41} + \gamma_{43}$; $\quad \gamma_{44}^* = -\gamma_{42}\psi_{42} - \gamma_{43}\psi_{41}$; and $\gamma_{45}^* = -\gamma_{43}\psi_{42}$,

$$
\begin{bmatrix} \Delta c_t \\ \Delta c_{t-1} \\ \Delta c_{t-2} \\ \Delta c_{t-3} \\ \Delta c_{t-4} \\ \Delta c_{t-5} \end{bmatrix} = \begin{bmatrix} \phi(L)\mu_{s_t} \\ 0 \\ 0 \\ 0 \\ 0 \\ 0 \end{bmatrix} + \begin{bmatrix} \phi_1 & \phi_2 & 0 & 0 & 0 & 0 \\ 1 & 0 & 0 & 0 & 0 & 0 \\ 0 & 1 & 0 & 0 & 0 & 0 \\ 0 & 0 & 1 & 0 & 0 & 0 \\ 0 & 0 & 0 & 1 & 0 & 0 \\ 0 & 0 & 0 & 0 & 1 & 0 \end{bmatrix} \begin{bmatrix} \Delta c_{t-1} \\ \Delta c_{t-2} \\ \Delta c_{t-3} \\ \Delta c_{t-4} \\ \Delta c_{t-5} \\ \Delta c_{t-6} \end{bmatrix} + \begin{bmatrix} w_t \\ 0 \\ 0 \\ 0 \\ 0 \\ 0 \end{bmatrix},
$$

$$(10.29')$$

where $\phi(L)\mu_{s_t} = \mu_{s_t} - \phi_1\mu_{s_{t-1}} - \phi_2\mu_{s_{t-2}}$. The above representation is used in generating Δc_t.

State-Space Representation 2

$$
\begin{bmatrix} \Delta y_{1t} \\ \Delta y_{2t} \\ \Delta y_{3t} \\ \Delta y_{4t} \end{bmatrix} = \begin{bmatrix} \gamma_1 & 0 & 0 & 0 & 1 & 0 & 0 & 0 & 0 & 0 & 0 & 0 \\ \gamma_2 & 0 & 0 & 0 & 0 & 0 & 1 & 0 & 0 & 0 & 0 & 0 \\ \gamma_3 & 0 & 0 & 0 & 0 & 0 & 0 & 0 & 1 & 0 & 0 & 0 \\ \gamma_{40} & \gamma_{41} & \gamma_{42} & \gamma_{43} & 0 & 0 & 0 & 0 & 0 & 0 & 1 & 0 \end{bmatrix} \begin{bmatrix} \Delta c_t \\ \Delta c_{t-1} \\ \Delta c_{t-2} \\ \Delta c_{t-3} \\ e_{1t} \\ e_{1,t-1} \\ e_{2t} \\ e_{2,t-1} \\ e_{3t} \\ e_{3,t-1} \\ e_{4t} \\ e_{4,t-1} \end{bmatrix},
$$

$$(10.39')$$

$$
\begin{bmatrix} \Delta c_t \\ \Delta c_{t-1} \\ \Delta c_{t-2} \\ \Delta c_{t-3} \\ e_{1t} \\ e_{1,t-1} \\ \vdots \\ e_{4t} \\ e_{4,t-1} \end{bmatrix} = \begin{bmatrix} \phi(L)\mu_{s_t} \\ 0 \\ 0 \\ 0 \\ 0 \\ 0 \\ \vdots \\ 0 \\ 0 \end{bmatrix} +
$$

$$
\begin{bmatrix}
\phi_1 & \phi_2 & 0 & 0 & 0 & 0 & \cdots & 0 & 0 \\
1 & 0 & 0 & 0 & 0 & 0 & \cdots & 0 & 0 \\
0 & 1 & 0 & 0 & 0 & 0 & \cdots & 0 & 0 \\
0 & 0 & 1 & 0 & 0 & 0 & \cdots & 0 & 0 \\
0 & 0 & 0 & 0 & \psi_{11} & \psi_{12} & \cdots & 0 & 0 \\
0 & 0 & 0 & 0 & 1 & 0 & \cdots & 0 & 0 \\
\vdots & \vdots & \vdots & \vdots & \vdots & \vdots & \ddots & \vdots & \vdots \\
0 & 0 & 0 & 0 & 0 & 0 & \cdots & \psi_{41} & \psi_{42} \\
0 & 0 & 0 & 0 & 0 & 0 & \cdots & 1 & 0
\end{bmatrix}
\begin{bmatrix}
\Delta c_{t-1} \\
\Delta c_{t-2} \\
\Delta c_{t-3} \\
\Delta c_{t-4} \\
e_{1,t-1} \\
e_{1,t-2} \\
\vdots \\
e_{4,t-1} \\
e_{4,t-2}
\end{bmatrix}
+
\begin{bmatrix}
w_t \\
0 \\
0 \\
0 \\
\epsilon_{1t} \\
0 \\
\vdots \\
\epsilon_{4t} \\
0
\end{bmatrix},
$$

$$(10.40')$$

where $\phi(L)\mu_{s_t} = \mu_{s_t} - \phi_1 \mu_{s_{t-1}} - \phi_2 \mu_{s_{t-2}}$. The above representation is used in deriving the mean of ΔC_t based on the steady-state Kalman gain.

Gibbs-sampling is implemented such that the first 2,000 draws in the Gibbs simulation process are discarded, then the next 8,000 draws are saved and used to calculate moments of the posterior distribution. This procedure ensures that the results are not simply an artifact of the initial values. Gelman and Rubin (1992) suggest that a single sequence of samples may give a false impression of convergence no matter how many draws are chosen. Thus, we also try various different initial values. The posterior distributions are robust with respect to different initial values. The 95% posterior probability bands are based on the 2.5th and the 97.5th percentiles of the 8,000 simulated draws.

Table 10.1 presents the Bayesian prior and posterior distributions of the parameters. For each parameter, the prior distribution is specified by mean and standard deviation, and the posterior by mean, standard deviation, median, and the 95% posterior probability bands. Rather tight prior distributions for p and q are designed to incorporate what was known or believed about the average duration of business cycle phases by the beginning of the sample period. The average duration of recessions and booms implied by the means of these priors are 10 months and 33.3 months, respectively. As the model is estimated with data expressed in deviation from means, under the hypothesis of no regime switching, we have $\mu_0 = 0$ and $\mu_0 + \mu_1 = 0$. Standard errors and the 95% posterior probability bands for these parameters seem to provide evidence in favor of Burns and Mitchell's (1946) concept of the division of the business cycle into two separate phases.

Figure 10.1 depicts the posterior probability that the economy was in the recession regime each month as implied by Gibbs-sampling. The shaded areas

Table 10.1
Bayesian prior and posterior distributions: informative priors on fixed transition probabilities

	Prior			Posterior			
	Mean	SD	Mean	SD	MD	95% bands	
q	0.9	0.066	0.875	0.044	0.881	(0.775,	0.945)
p	0.967	0.032	0.976	0.009	0.977	(0.954,	0.991)
ϕ_1	0.0	1	0.313	0.076	0.313	(0.165,	0.471)
ϕ_2	0.0	1	−0.002	0.067	−0.002	(−0.134,	0.131)
μ_0	0.0	1	−1.777	0.294	−1.779	(−2.346,	−1.193)
μ_1	0.0	1	2.110	0.302	2.117	(1.500,	2.686)
δ	−	−	0.568	0.038	0.565	(0.500,	0.650)
$\mu_0 + \mu_1$	−	−	0.333	0.104	0.336	(0.114,	0.526)
γ_1	0.0	1	0.568	0.036	0.568	(0.497,	0.641)
ψ_{11}	0.0	1	−0.003	0.066	−0.005	(−0.132,	0.125)
ψ_{12}	0.0	1	−0.030	0.064	−0.030	(−0.154,	0.096)
σ_1^2	−	−	0.238	0.033	0.237	(0.175,	0.309)
γ_2	0.0	1	0.213	0.021	0.212	(0.173,	0.254)
ψ_{21}	0.0	1	−0.302	0.050	−0.302	(−0.404,	−0.204)
ψ_{22}	0.0	1	−0.070	0.050	−0.069	(−0.167,	0.031)
σ_2^2	−	−	0.317	0.024	0.316	(0.273,	0.366)
γ_3	0.0	1	0.442	0.034	0.441	(0.377,	0.512)
ψ_{31}	0.0	1	−0.354	0.053	−0.353	(−0.458,	−0.244)
ψ_{32}	0.0	1	−0.154	0.052	−0.154	(−0.258,	−0.048)
σ_3^2	−	−	0.660	0.051	0.658	(0.565,	0.767)
γ_{40}	0.0	1	0.120	0.010	0.120	(0.102,	0.140)
γ_{41}	0.0	1	0.006	0.009	0.006	(−0.011,	0.024)
γ_{42}	0.0	1	0.023	0.009	0.023	(0.006,	0.040)
γ_{43}	0.0	1	0.026	0.008	0.026	(0.012,	0.041)
ψ_{41}	0.0	1	−0.022	0.060	−0.021	(−0.141,	0.092)
ψ_{42}	0.0	1	0.277	0.061	0.280	(0.155,	0.390)
σ_4^2	−	−	0.021	0.002	0.021	(0.017,	0.025)

Note: Prior distribution of σ_i^2 is improper. SD and MD refer to standard deviation and median, respectively. 95% Bands refers to 95% posterior probability bands.

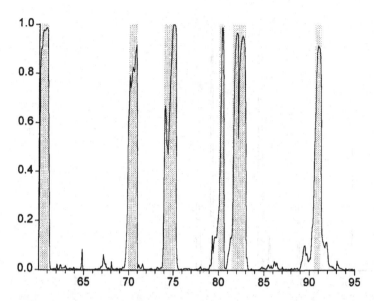

Figure 10.1
Probability of a recession (multivariate model; Gibbs-sampling; informative priors)

represent the periods of NBER recessions (from peak to trough). The posterior probabilities are in close agreement with the NBER reference cycle. However, an important question is: To what extent do the results reflect the ability of the model to extract Burns and Mitchell's (1946) "comovement of economic variables" over the business cycle, or do the results depend on the use of tight priors for transition probabilities?

To evaluate the marginal contribution of going from univariate analysis to a multivariate, common-factor approach, we re-estimate the posterior regime probabilities from a univariate regime-switching model of the industrial production (IP) series, one of the four series employed in this section. The same tight priors as in the multivariate case are given for the transition probabilities of the univariate model. Figure 10.2 shows the results. Univariate analysis results in significantly lower correlation between posterior regime probabilities and the NBER reference cycle. Filardo (1994) and Kim (1996) also report similar findings for individual monthly data, based on maximum likelihood estimation of the univariate regime-switching model.

To evaluate the marginal contribution of the use of tight priors for p and q, the multivariate model is reestimated using noninformative priors for these

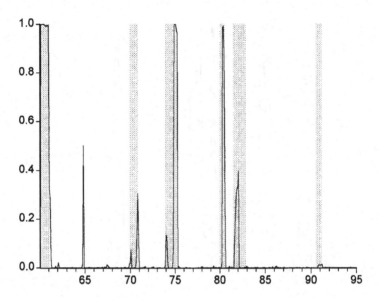

Figure 10.2
Probability of a recession (univariate model; Gibbs-sampling; informative priors)

parameters. Priors are chosen such that expected durations for booms and recessions are both two months (i.e., expected values of the priors on p and q
were both specified as 0.5). Except that the 95% posterior probability bands are
somewhat larger than before, results reported in Table 10.2 are almost the same
as in the case of tight priors. Figure 10.3 depicts posterior recession probabilities from the non-informative priors. One can hardly distinguish figure 10.3
from figure 10.1. Thus, prior information about transition probabilities does
not play an important role in implying whether or not the economy is in the
recession regime. This, along with the substantially weaker results from the
univariate model, suggests that it is the ability of the coincident index to capture 'comovement among economic variables' that accounts for the model's
success in identifying the NBER turning points.

Figure 10.4 plots the composite coincident index implied by the model,
together with the DOC's coincident index. The coincident index derived with
noninformative priors is almost identical to the one with tight priors and thus
is not shown here. Contemporaneous correlation between the first differences
of the two series is 0.9825. Though the model-based index agrees closely with
the DOC index, during recessions the decline in the growth rate of the model-

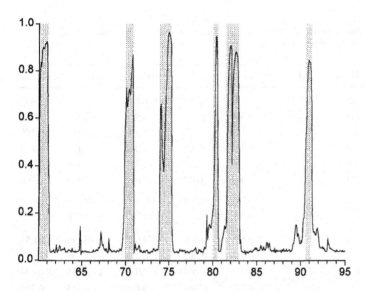

Figure 10.3
Probability of a recession (multivariate model; Gibbs-sampling; noninformative priors)

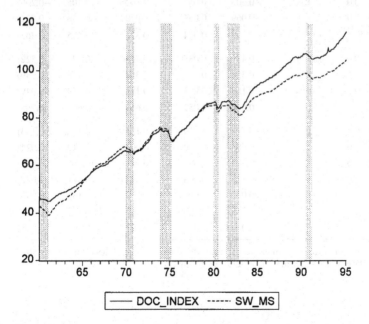

Figure 10.4
New coincident index (from Gibbs-sampling) versus DOC's coincident index

Table 10.2
Bayesian prior and posterior distributions: noninformative priors on transition probabilities

	Prior		Posterior				
	Mean	SD	Mean	SD	MD	95% bands	
q	0.5	0.289	0.808	0.133	0.841	(0.325,	0.938)
p	0.5	0.289	0.946	0.108	0.972	(0.568,	0.989)
ϕ_1	0.0	1	0.341	0.102	0.328	(0.170,	0.575)
ϕ_2	0.0	1	0.001	0.069	0.002	(−0.129,	0.138)
μ_0	0.0	1	−1.659	0.563	−1.779	(−2.435,	−0.044)
μ_1	0.0	1	1.968	0.612	2.097	(0.105,	2.740)
δ	−	−	0.569	0.039	0.566	(0.501,	0.650)
$\mu_0 + \mu_1$	−	−	0.308	0.192	0.316	(−0.029,	0.529)
γ_1	0.0	1	0.571	0.040	0.569	(0.498,	0.654)
ψ_{11}	0.0	1	−0.012	0.066	−0.011	(−0.139,	0.121)
ψ_{12}	0.0	1	−0.033	0.064	−0.033	(−0.158,	0.094)
σ_1^2	−	−	0.237	0.033	0.236	(0.175,	0.305)
γ_2	0.0	1	0.215	0.022	0.214	(0.174,	0.259)
ψ_{21}	0.0	1	−0.303	0.052	−0.302	(−0.405,	−0.206)
ψ_{22}	0.0	1	−0.069	0.051	−0.070	(−0.168,	0.031)
σ_2^2	−	−	0.317	0.024	0.316	(0.275,	0.365)
γ_3	0.0	1	0.445	0.037	0.445	(0.376,	0.522)
ψ_{31}	0.0	1	−0.354	0.053	−0.354	(−0.458,	−0.249)
ψ_{32}	0.0	1	−0.153	0.053	−0.153	(−0.257,	−0.049)
σ_3^2	−	−	0.660	0.052	0.659	(0.567,	0.768)
γ_{40}	0.0	1	0.121	0.010	0.121	(0.102,	0.143)
γ_{41}	0.0	1	0.006	0.009	0.006	(−0.012,	0.024)
γ_{42}	0.0	1	0.023	0.009	0.024	(0.006,	0.040)
γ_{43}	0.0	1	0.026	0.008	0.026	(0.011,	0.042)
ψ_{41}	0.0	1	−0.020	0.058	−0.019	(−0.136,	0.096)
ψ_{42}	0.0	1	0.282	0.060	0.283	(0.162,	0.394)
σ_4^2	−	−	0.021	0.002	0.021	(0.017,	0.025)

Note: Prior distribution of σ_i^2 is improper. SD and MD refer to standard deviation and median, respectively. 95% Bands refers to 95% posterior probability bands.

State-Space Models with Markov Switching and Gibbs-Sampling   255

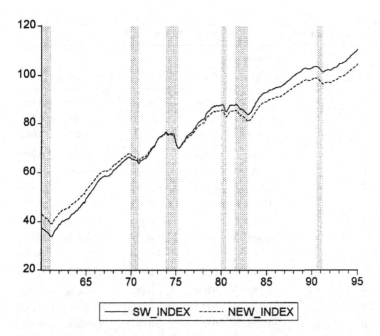

Figure 10.5
New coincident index (from Gibbs-sampling) versus Stock and Watson coincident index (from Gibbs-sampling)

based index is much sharper than that of the DOC index. In the early portion of the sample, the growth rate of the model-based index during booms seems to be higher than that of the DOC index, but in the more recent portion of the sample, the pattern in the growth rates during booms seems to be reversed. After the 1982 recession, the model-based index seems to show slower growth than the DOC coincident index.

It might also be useful to compare the new coincident index with the one based on Stock and Watson's (1991) linear dynamic factor model. Table 10.3 is taken from section 8.3 and presents the Bayesian prior and posterior distributions of the parameters for the Stock and Watson model without the feature of regime switching.

The posterior distributions of parameters are quite close to those from the model with regime switching. One exception is that the sum of the AR coefficients ($\phi_1 + \phi_2$) for the common component is higher for the Stock and Watson model. Figure 10.5, plots and compares the composite coincident indices

Table 10.3
Bayesian prior and posterior distributions: the Stock and Watson model

	Prior		Posterior				
	Mean	SD	Mean	SD	MD	95% Bands	
ϕ_1	0.0	1	0.533	0.069	0.534	(0.395,	0.669)
ϕ_2	0.0	1	0.029	0.062	0.029	(−0.091,	0.153)
δ	−	−	0.567	0.046	0.566	(0.483,	0.662)
γ_1	0.0	1	0.621	0.041	0.619	(0.544,	0.705)
ψ_{11}	0.0	1	−0.032	0.065	−0.036	(−0.163,	0.095)
ψ_{12}	0.0	1	−0.054	0.065	−0.055	(−0.176,	0.074)
σ_1^2	−	−	0.236	0.034	0.235	(0.173,	0.303)
γ_2	0.0	1	0.231	0.023	0.231	(0.188,	0.278)
ψ_{21}	0.0	1	−0.302	0.052	−0.303	(−0.402,	−0.202)
ψ_{22}	0.0	1	−0.065	0.051	−0.066	(−0.163,	0.033)
σ_2^2	−	−	0.316	0.023	0.315	(0.274,	0.363)
γ_3	0.0	1	0.479	0.038	0.477	(0.406,	0.556)
ψ_{31}	0.0	1	−0.358	0.053	−0.356	(−0.460,	−0.253)
ψ_{32}	0.0	1	−0.153	0.053	−0.153	(−0.256,	−0.051)
σ_3^2	−	−	0.668	0.052	0.666	(0.571,	0.775)
γ_{40}	0.0	1	0.133	0.010	0.133	(0.113,	0.153)
γ_{41}	0.0	1	0.003	0.011	0.003	(−0.018,	0.024)
γ_{42}	0.0	1	0.024	0.010	0.024	(0.004,	0.043)
γ_{43}	0.0	1	0.028	0.008	0.028	(0.011,	0.045)
ψ_{41}	0.0	1	−0.003	0.060	−0.002	(−0.120,	0.110)
ψ_{42}	0.0	1	0.293	0.060	0.294	(0.170,	0.410)
σ_4^2	−	−	0.021	0.002	0.021	(0.017,	0.026)

Note: This table is taken from section 8.3. y_{1t}, y_{2t}, y_{3t}, y_{4t} represent IP, GMYXPQ, MTQ, and LPNAG, respectively. Prior distribution of σ_i^2 is improper. SD and MD refer to standard deviation and median, respectively. 95% Bands refers to 95% posterior probability bands.

implied by the two models, with and without regime switching. The two in-dices are almost identical, except that since the 1970s, the Stock and Watson index seems to show higher growth than the new experimental index from a dynamic factor model with regime switching. Overall, the Stock and Watson index agrees more closely with the DOC index than our experimental index, which allows for state switching.

10.3 Application 2: Business Cycle Duration Dependence within a Dynamic Factor Model: An Advantage of the Gibbs-Sampling Approach over the Classical Approach

The Bayesian Gibbs-sampling approach in the previous section provides us with more information than may be extracted from maximum likelihood esti-mation of the model. In particular, as in Kim and Nelson 1998, a straightfor-ward extension of the base model leads naturally to Bayesian tests of business cycle duration dependence.

Duration dependence in the business cycle and time-varying transition prob-abilities are related but not identical concepts. Duration dependence asks whether recessions or booms "age," that is, are they more likely to end the longer they last? It is a special form of time-varying transition probabilities in a regime-switching model of the business cycle. Diebold and Rudebusch (1990) and Diebold, Rudebusch, and Sichel (1993) found evidence that post-war recessions tend to have positive duration dependence, although booms do not. More recently, Durland and McCurdy (1994), using Hamilton's (1989) univariate Markov-switching model of the business cycle, reached the same conclusion. Diebold, Lee, and Weinbach (1994), Filardo (1994), and Filardo and Gordon (1993) dealt with another form of time-varying transition probabil-ities, specifying them as functions of an exogenous variable such as the index of leading indicators. None of these studies, however, specifically deals with duration dependence in a multivariate context. We investigate the hypothesis of duration dependence by extending the dynamic factor model in the previ-ous section to incorporate nonzero probabilities of duration dependence in the transition probabilities. The results in this section originally appeared in Kim and Nelson 1998.

10.3.1 An Extension of the Dynamic Factor Model with Markov Switching to Allow for Nonzero Probabilities of Business Cycle Duration Dependence

To construct a formal test of business cycle duration dependence, the transition probabilities in equation (10.25) are replaced by the following probit specification of the evolution of the business cycle regime variable, S_t:

$$Pr[S_t = 1] = Pr[S_t^* \geq 0], \tag{10.43}$$

where S_t^* is a latent variable defined as

$$S_t^* = \gamma_0 + \gamma_1 S_{t-1} + \gamma_{2,d_2}(1 - S_{t-1})N_{0,t-1} + \gamma_{3,d_3}S_{t-1}N_{1,t-1} + u_t, \tag{10.44}$$

$$d_2 = 0 \text{ or } 1, \quad d_3 = 0 \text{ or } 1 \tag{10.45}$$

$$u_t \sim \text{i.i.d.} N(0, 1), \tag{10.46}$$

where $N_{j,t-1}$, $j = 0, 1$, are the durations up to time $t - 1$ of a recession or boom, respectively; and the parameters γ_{2,d_2} and γ_{3,d_3}, which will be discussed in detail later, determine the nature of business cycle duration dependence. In the above probit specification, the transition probabilities are given by

$$Pr[S_t = 1 \mid S_{t-1} = 1, N_{1,t-1}] = Pr[S_t^* \geq 0 \mid S_{t-1} = 1, N_{1,t-1}]$$
$$= Pr[u_t \geq -\gamma_0 - \gamma_1 - \gamma_{3,d_3}N_{1,t-1})], \tag{10.47}$$

$$Pr[S_t = 0 \mid S_{t-1} = 0, N_{0,t-1}] = Pr[S_t^* < 0 \mid S_{t-1} = 0, N_{0,t-1}]$$
$$= Pr[u_t < -\gamma_0 - \gamma_{2,d_2}N_{0,t-1})]. \tag{10.48}$$

When $\gamma_{2,d_2} = 0$ and $\gamma_{3,d_3} = 0$, we have fixed transition probabilities, or no business cycle duration dependence; and when $\gamma_{2,d_2} > 0$ and $\gamma_{3,d_3} < 0$, business cycles are characterized by positive duration dependence. To allow for nonzero probabilities of positive duration dependence, we adopt assumptions similar to those introduced in George and McCulloch 1993 and Geweke 1996 in the context of variable selection in regression. In particular, while we assume γ_0 and γ_1 each are nonzero with prior probability 1, we follow Geweke (1994) in adopting a prior for γ_{2,d_2} and γ_{3,d_3} that is a mixture of a truncated normal and point mass at 0:

$$\gamma_{2,d_2} \begin{cases} = 0, & \text{if } d_2 = 0, \\ \sim N(\underline{\gamma}_2, \underline{\omega}_2^2)_{I[\gamma_{2,d_2} > 0]}, & \text{if } d_2 = 1, \end{cases} \tag{10.49}$$

$$\gamma_{3,d_3} \begin{cases} = 0, & \text{if } d_3 = 0, \\ \sim N(\underline{\gamma}_3, \underline{\omega}_3^2) I_{[\gamma_{3,d_3} < 0]}, & \text{if } d_3 = 1, \end{cases} \tag{10.50}$$

$$Pr[d_2 = 0] = Pr[\gamma_{2,d_2} = 0] \equiv p_2, \tag{10.51}$$

$$Pr[d_3 = 0] = Pr[\gamma_{3,d_3} = 0] \equiv p_3, \tag{10.52}$$

where the subscript $I[.]$ refers to an indicator function introduced to allow for positive business cycle duration dependence under the alternative hypothesis, and p_2 and p_3 are independent prior probabilities of no duration dependence for recessions and booms. Each of these prior distributions includes the possibility that the duration variables $N_{0,t-1}$ and $N_{1,t-1}$ are excluded from the model. Given these priors, a Bayesian test of business cycle duration dependence is to calculate the posterior probabilities of no duration dependence directly from the proportion of posterior simulations in which $d_2 = 0$ and $d_3 = 0$.

10.3.2 Implementation of Gibbs-Sampling

Replacing the fixed transition probabilities in (10.25) with the potentially duration-dependent transition probabilities in (10.47)–(10.48) requires modification of the basic Gibbs-sampler described in section 10.2. Specifically, the procedures for generating $\tilde{S}_T$ and the transition probabilities should be modified.

Because of the time-varying nature of the transition probabilities, $\tilde{S}_T = [S_1 \ \dots \ S_T]'$ cannot be generated as a block using multimove Gibbs-sampling. Each S_t should be generated one at a time, conditional on $S_{j\neq t}$, $j = 1, 2, \dots, T$, and other variates, using single-move Gibbs-sampling. It is straightforward to modify Albert and Chib's (1993) single-move Gibbs-sampling procedure to achieve this goal.

Conditional on $\tilde{S}_T$, we can count the duration of a recession or a boom ($N_{1,t-1}$ or $N_{0,t-1}$) up to month $t - 1$, $t = 2, 3, \dots, T$. Also, given γ_0, γ_1, γ_{2,d_2}, γ_{3,d_3}, each set $\tilde{S}_T$ can be converted to a set of latent variables $\tilde{S}_T^* = [S_1^* \ S_2^* \ \dots \ S_T^*]'$, based on equation (10.44), by generating u_t from an appropriate truncated standard normal distribution. Conditional on $S_t = 1$ and $S_{t-1} = 1$, for example, u_t is generated from

$$u_t \sim N(0, 1) I_{[u_t \geq -(\gamma_0 + \gamma_1 + \gamma_{3,d_3} N_{1,t-1})]}, \tag{10.53}$$

where the subscript $I[.]$ refers to an indicator function.

Conditional on $\tilde{S}_T$, and thus on $\tilde{S}_T^* = [S_1^* \dots S_T^*]'$, $\tilde{N}_{1,T-1} = [N_{1,1} \dots N_{1,T-1}]'$, and $\tilde{N}_{0,T-1} = [N_{0,1} \dots N_{0,T-1}]'$, the variates in equation (10.44) are independent of the data set and other variates in the system. This conditioning feature of Gibbs-sampling allows us to focus on equation (10.44) for generating transition probabilities and other related parameters for tests of business cycle duration dependence. Thus, the transition probabilities can be generated directly from equations (10.47) and (10.48). The following sections describe in detail how d_i, $i = 2, 3$, and γ variables in equation (10.44) can be generated. The approach in these sections is an application of Geweke 1996. The other variates in the system can be generated in exactly the same way as in the case of fixed transition probabilities, as described in section 10.2.

Generating γ_0, γ_1, $\gamma_{2,1}$ and $\gamma_{3,1}$ First, conditional on γ_{2,d_2} and γ_{3,d_3}, we generate $\gamma^* = [\, \gamma_0 \quad \gamma_1 \,]'$. We define $\tilde{Y}_1$ and $\tilde{X}_1$ as the matrices of the left- and right-hand-side variables in a regression, $S_t^* - \gamma_{2,d_2}(1 - S_{t-1})N_{0,t-1} - \gamma_{3,d_3}S_{t-1}N_{1,t-1} = \gamma_0 + \gamma_1 S_{t-1} + u_t$, $t = 2, 3, \ldots, T$. Given the prior distribution $\gamma^* \sim N(\underline{\gamma}^*, \underline{\omega}^*)$, the posterior distribution of γ^* is given by the following multivariate normal distribution:

$$\gamma^* \sim N(\bar{\gamma}^*, \bar{\omega}^*), \tag{10.54}$$

where $\bar{\omega}^* = (\underline{\omega}^{*-1} + \tilde{X}_1'\tilde{X}_1)^{-1}$ and $\bar{\gamma}^* = \bar{\omega}^*(\underline{\omega}^{*-1}\underline{\gamma}^* + \tilde{X}_1'\tilde{Y}_1)$.

Second, conditional on $\tilde{\gamma}^* = [\gamma_0\, \gamma_1]'$, γ_{3,d_3}, and $d_2 = 1$, we generate $\gamma_{2,1}$. We define $\tilde{Y}_2$ and $\tilde{X}_2$ as the matrices of the left- and right-hand-side variables in a regression, $S_t^* - \gamma_0 - \gamma_1 S_{t-1} - \gamma_{3,d_3}S_{t-1}N_{1,t-1} = \gamma_{2,1}(1 - S_{t-1})N_{0,t-1} + u_t$, $t = 2, 3, \ldots, T$. Assuming the prior is given by a truncated normal distribution, $\gamma_{2,1} \sim N(\underline{\gamma}_2, \underline{\omega}_2^2)I_{[\underline{\gamma}_2 > 0]}$, the posterior distribution of $\gamma_{2,1}$ is denoted by the following truncated normal distribution:

$$\gamma_{2,1} \sim N(\bar{\gamma}_2, \bar{\omega}_2)I_{[\gamma_{2,1} > 0]}, \tag{10.55}$$

where the subscript $I[.]$ refers to an indicator function; $\bar{\omega}_2 = (\underline{\omega}_2^{-2} + \tilde{X}_2'\tilde{X}_2)^{-1}$; and $\bar{\gamma}_2 = \bar{\omega}_2(\underline{\omega}_2^{-2}\underline{\gamma}_2 + \tilde{X}_2'\tilde{Y}_2)$.

Finally, conditional on $\tilde{\gamma}^* = [\gamma_0\, \gamma_1]'$, γ_{2,d_2}, and $d_3 = 1$, we generate $\gamma_{3,1}$. We define $\tilde{Y}_3$ and $\tilde{X}_3$ as the matrices of the left- and right-hand-side variables in a regression, $S_t^* - \gamma_0 - \gamma_1 S_{t-1} - \gamma_{2,d_3}(1 - S_{t-1})N_{0,t-1} = \gamma_{3,1}S_{t-1}N_{0,t-1} + u_t$, $t = 2, 3, \ldots, T$. Assuming the prior is given by a truncated normal distribution, $\gamma_{3,1} \sim N(\underline{\gamma}_3, \underline{\omega}_3^2)I_{[\underline{\gamma}_3 < 0]}$, the posterior distribution of $\gamma_{3,1}$ is denoted by the following truncated normal distribution:

$$\gamma_{3,1} \sim N(\bar{\gamma}_3, \bar{\omega}_3)I_{[\gamma_{3,1} < 0]}, \tag{10.56}$$

where the subscript $I[.]$ refers to an indicator function; $\bar{\omega}_3 = (\underline{\omega}_3^{-2} + \tilde{X}_3'\tilde{X}_3)^{-1}$; and $\bar{\gamma}_3 = \bar{\omega}_3(\underline{\omega}_3^{-1}\underline{\gamma}_3 + \tilde{X}_3'\tilde{Y}_3)$.

Generating d_2 and d_3   As in George and McCulloch 1993 and Geweke 1994, d_2 and d_3 are generated component-wise by sampling consecutively from the conditional distribution

$$f(d_i \mid d_{j \neq i}, \tilde{\gamma}, \tilde{S}_T^*, \tilde{S}_T, \tilde{N}_{0,-1}, \tilde{N}_{1,-1}), \quad i = 2, 3. \tag{10.57}$$

We follow the approach in Geweke 1994 in generating d_2 and d_3.

   For example, d_2 can be generated from the conditional distribution

$$f(d_2 \mid \gamma^*, \gamma_{3,d_3}, \tilde{S}_T^*, \tilde{S}_T, \tilde{N}_{0,-1}, \tilde{N}_{1,-1}), \tag{10.58}$$

where distribution (10.58) is Bernoulli with probability

$$Pr[d_2 = 1 \mid \gamma^*, \gamma_{3,d_3}, \tilde{S}_T^*, \tilde{S}_T, \tilde{N}_{0,-1}, \tilde{N}_{1,-1}] = \frac{p_2}{p_2 + (1 - p_2)\frac{a_1}{a_0}}, \tag{10.59}$$

where p_2 is the prior probability, $Pr[d_2 = 0]$, of no duration dependence for recessions and where

$$a_1 = f(\gamma_{2,d_2} \mid \gamma^*, \gamma_{3,d_3}, \tilde{S}_T^*, \tilde{S}_T, \tilde{N}_{0,-1}, \tilde{N}_{1,-1}, d_2 = 1)_{I[\gamma_{2,1} > 0]}, \tag{10.60}$$

$$a_0 = f(\gamma_{2,d_2} \mid \gamma^*, \gamma_{3,d_3}, \tilde{S}_T^*, \tilde{S}_T, \tilde{N}_{0,-1}, \tilde{N}_{1,-1}, d_2 = 0) \tag{10.61}$$

The term a_1/a_0 in the right-hand side of equation (10.59) is the conditional Bayes factor in favor of $d_2 = 1$ ($\gamma_{2,d_2} > 0$) versus $d_2 = 0$ ($\gamma_{2,d_2} = 0$). This conditional Bayes factor, as proven in Geweke 1996, is given by

$$\frac{a_1}{a_0} = 2\exp\{\frac{\bar{\gamma}_2}{2\bar{\omega}_2} - \frac{\gamma_2}{2\underline{\omega}_2^2}\}(\frac{\sqrt{\bar{\omega}_2}}{\underline{\omega}_2})\left[1 - \Phi(-\frac{\bar{\gamma}_2}{\sqrt{\bar{\omega}_2}})\right], \tag{10.62}$$

where $\Phi(.)$ is the c.d.f. of the standard normal distribution. Thus, based on a comparison of a drawing from the uniform distribution on $[0, 1]$ with the probability calculated from (10.59), d_2 is generated as 0 or 1.

   In a similar way, d_3 can be generated using the following posterior probability:

$$Pr[d_3 = 1 \mid \gamma^*, \gamma_{2,d_2}, \tilde{S}_T^*, \tilde{S}_T, \tilde{N}_{0,-1}, \tilde{N}_{1,-1}] = \frac{p_3}{p_3 + (1 - p_3)\frac{b_1}{b_0}}, \tag{10.63}$$

where b_0 and b_1 are appropriately defined in the same way as are a_0 and a_1, respectively, in equations (10.60) and (10.61); p_3 is the prior probability, $Pr[d_3 = 0]$, of no duration dependence for booms; and the conditional Bayes factor in favor of $d_3 = 1$ ($\gamma_{3,d_3} < 0$) versus $d_3 = 0$ ($\gamma_{3,d_3} = 0$) is given by

$$\frac{b_1}{b_0} = 2 \exp\{\frac{\bar{\gamma}_3}{2\bar{\omega}_3} - \frac{\gamma_3}{2\underline{\omega}_3^2}\}(\frac{\sqrt{\bar{\omega}_3}}{\underline{\omega}_3}) \left[\Phi(-\frac{\bar{\gamma}_3}{\sqrt{\bar{\omega}_3}}) \right]. \tag{10.64}$$

10.3.3 Empirical Results

Of particular interest in this section are the proportions of posterior simulations in which (1) $d_2 = 0$, for a test of no duration dependence for recessions; (2) $d_3 = 0$, for a test of no duration dependence for booms; and (3) $d_2 = d_3 = 0$, for a joint test of no business cycle duration dependence. We adopt different prior probabilities ($p_2 = p_3 = 0.3, 0.4, 0.5, 0.6, 0.7, 0.8$) of no duration dependence and investigate the sensitivity of posterior probabilities to these priors. We also adopt different priors for γ_0, γ_1, $\gamma_{2,1}$ and $\gamma_{3,1}$ in equation (10.44) and investigate the sensitivity of the results. As mentioned in George and McCulloch 1993, from a subjectivist Bayesian standpoint, one would want to choose $\underline{\omega}_j^2$, $j = 2, 3$, large enough to give support to values of $\gamma_{j,1}$, $j = 2, 3$, that are substantively different from 0, but not so large that unrealistic values of $\gamma_{j,1}$, $j = 2, 3$, are supported. Prior distributions employed for these parameters are $\gamma_0 \sim N(-1.28, \underline{\omega}_0^2)$, $\gamma_1 \sim N(3.24, \underline{\omega}_1^2)$—these are equivalent to assuming average durations of recessions and booms to be 10 months and 33.3 months, respectively, under the null of no duration dependence, as in section 10.2—$\gamma_{2,1} \sim N(0, \underline{\omega}_2^2)I_{[\gamma_{2,1}>0]}$, and $\gamma_{3,1} \sim N(0, \underline{\omega}_3^2)I_{[\gamma_{3,1}<0]}$. We try the following three different combinations of $\underline{\omega}$s: Case 1: $\underline{\omega}_0 = \underline{\omega}_1 = 0.3$ and $\underline{\omega}_2 = \underline{\omega}_3 = 0.05$; Case 2: $\underline{\omega}_0 = \underline{\omega}_1 = 0.3$ and $\underline{\omega}_2 = \underline{\omega}_3 = 0.1$; Case 3: $\underline{\omega}_0 = \underline{\omega}_1 = 0.1$ and $\underline{\omega}_2 = \underline{\omega}_3 = 0.1$. Throughout these experiments, we maintain the same priors for all the other variates in the system as in section 10.2 (tables 10.1 and 10.2). For each of the above 18 different sets of prior distributions, we run the Gibbs-sampler for 12,000 iterations. For most of the cases the Gibbs-sampler seems to converge in fewer than 3,000 iterations. To be on the safe side, we discard the first 4,000 and base our inferences on the last 8,000 iterations.

Tables 10.4 through 10.6 summarize the sensitivity of posterior probabilities of no duration dependence to different priors. These are also depicted in figures 10.6 through 10.8. In general, smaller values of $\underline{\omega}_j$, the prior standard deviations of the γ parameters, result in lower posterior probabilities for given

Table 10.4
Sensitivity of posterior probabilities of no duration dependence to different priors: $\underline{\omega}_0 = \underline{\omega}_1 = 0.3$; $\underline{\omega}_2 = \underline{\omega}_3 = 0.05$

	$Pr[d_3 = 0]$: for recessions					
Prior ($p_2 = p_3$)	0.300	0.400	0.500	0.600	0.700	0.800
Posterior	0.014	0.023	0.033	0.044	0.070	0.113

	$Pr[d_3 = 0]$: for booms					
Prior ($p_2 = p_3$)	0.300	0.400	0.500	0.600	0.700	0.800
Posterior	0.122	0.196	0.276	0.355	0.460	0.595

	$Pr[d_2 = 0, d_3 = 0]$: for joint tests					
Prior ($p_2 = p_3$)	0.300	0.400	0.500	0.600	0.700	0.800
Posterior	0.001	0.004	0.008	0.015	0.028	0.054

Table 10.5
Sensitivity of posterior probabilities of no duration dependence to different priors: $\underline{\omega}_0 = \underline{\omega}_1 = 0.3$; $\underline{\omega}_2 = \underline{\omega}_3 = 0.1$

	$Pr[d_2 = 0]$: for recession					
Prior ($p_2 = p_3$)	0.300	0.400	0.500	0.600	0.700	0.800
Posterior	0.029	0.042	0.067	0.081	0.114	0.187

	$Pr[d_3 = 0]$: for booms					
Prior ($p_2 = p_3$)	0.300	0.400	0.500	0.600	0.700	0.800
Posterior	0.405	0.533	0.637	0.734	0.767	0.874

	$Pr[d_2 = 0, d_3 = 0]$: for joint tests					
Prior ($p_2 = p_3$)	0.300	0.400	0.500	0.600	0.700	0.800
Posterior	0.010	0.018	0.040	0.056	0.080	0.162

Table 10.6
Sensitivity of posterior probabilities of no duration dependence to different priors: $\underline{\omega}_0 = \underline{\omega}_1 = 0.1$; $\underline{\omega}_2 = \underline{\omega}_3 = 0.1$

	$Pr[d_2 = 0]$: for recessions					
Prior ($p_2 = p_3$)	0.300	0.400	0.500	0.600	0.700	0.800
Posterior	0.020	0.032	0.036	0.049	0.089	0.153
	$Pr[d_3 = 0]$: for booms					
Prior ($p_2 = p_3$)	0.300	0.400	0.500	0.600	0.700	0.800
Posterior	0.482	0.549	0.673	0.802	0.807	0.876
	$Pr[d_2 = 0, d_3 = 0]$: for joint tests					
Prior ($p_2 = p_3$)	0.300	0.400	0.500	0.600	0.700	0.800
Posterior	0.008	0.017	0.021	0.036	0.067	0.123

Posterior Probabilities

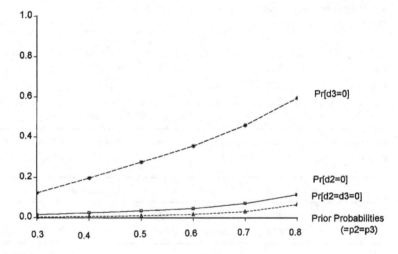

Figure 10.6
Sensitivity of posterior probabilities of no duration dependence to different prior probabilities (p2: Recession; p3: Boom; $\underline{\omega}_0 = \underline{\omega}_1 = 0.3$; $\underline{\omega}_2 = \underline{\omega}_3 = 0.05$)

Posterior Probabilities

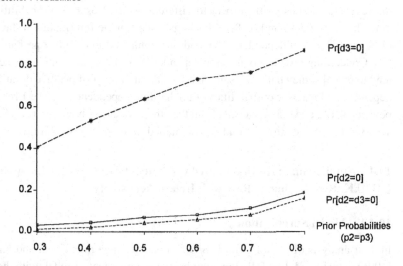

Figure 10.7
Sensitivity of posterior probabilities of no duration dependence to different prior probabilities (p2: Recession; p3: Boom; $\underline{\omega}_0 = \underline{\omega}_1 = 0.3; \underline{\omega}_2 = \underline{\omega}_3 = 0.1$)

Posterior Probabilities

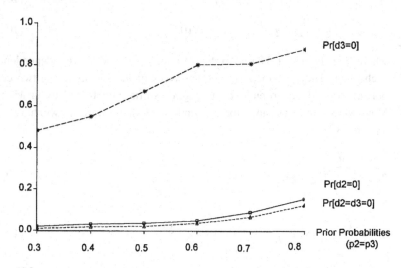

Figure 10.8
Sensitivity of posterior probabilities of no duration dependence to different prior probabilities (p2: Recession; p3: Boom; $\underline{\omega}_0 = \underline{\omega}_1 = 0.1; \underline{\omega}_2 = \underline{\omega}_3 = 0.1$)

prior probabilities. Concerning tests of no duration dependence for recessions, the results are robust with respect to different priors: Posterior probabilities range between 0.014 and 0.187, revealing strong sample information in favor of positive duration dependence beyond that contained in the prior probabilities. Concerning tests of no duration dependence for booms, results for case 1 tend to reveal somewhat weak sample information in favor of positive duration dependence: Posterior probabilities of no duration dependence in case 1 range between 0.122 and 0.595. Results from the other two cases, however, reveal no such sample information beyond that contained in the prior probabilities.

10.4   Application 3: An Unobserved Components Model of the Long-Run U.S./U.K. Real Exchange Rate with Heteroskedasticity

10.4.1   Model Specification

In their analysis of the long-run U.S/U.K. real exchange rate, Engel and Kim (1996) considered the following unobserved-components model with heteroskedastic permanent and transitory components:

$$y_t = z_t + x_t, \tag{10.65}$$

$$z_t = z_{t-1} + w_t, \quad w_t \sim N(0, \sigma_{w,t}^2) \tag{10.66}$$

$$x_t = \phi_1 x_{t-1} + \phi_2 x_{t-2} + u_t, \quad u_t \sim N(0, \sigma_{u,t}^2), \tag{10.67}$$

where y_t is the log of the real exchange rate and w_t and u_t are independent of each other. They assumed that the variances of the shocks to the two components are subject to endogenous regime shifts, which lead to an M-state Markov-switching variance for $\sigma_{w,t}^2$ and an M'-state Markov-switching variance for $\sigma_{u,t}^2$:

$$\sigma_{w,t}^2 = \sum_{j=1}^{M} \sigma_{w,j}^2 S_{1,jt}, \tag{10.68}$$

$$\sigma_{u,t}^2 = \sum_{j=1}^{M'} \sigma_{u,j}^2 S_{2,jt}, \tag{10.69}$$

where

$S_{1,mt} = 1$ if $S_{1t} = m$; $S_{1,mt} = 0$ otherwise, $m = 1, 2, \ldots, M$,   (10.70)

$S_{2,m't} = 1$ if $S_{2t} = m'$; $S_{2,m't} = 0$ otherwise, $m' = 1, 2, \ldots, M'$,   (10.71)

and S_{1t} and S_{2t} are two independent first-order Markov-switching variables with the following transition probabilities:

$$p_{1,ij} = Pr[S_{1t} = j \mid S_{1,t-1} = i], \quad \sum_{j=1}^{M} p_{1,ij} = 1, \qquad (10.72)$$

$$p_{2,ij} = Pr[S_{2t} = j \mid S_{2,t-1} = i], \quad \sum_{j=1}^{M'} p_{2,ij} = 1. \qquad (10.73)$$

For economic rationale of the underlying assumptions such as independence of the shocks to the permanent and transitiory components and the driftless permanent component, refer to Engel and Kim 1996. Engel and Kim estimated different versions of the above model using the Bayesian Gibbs-sampling methodology, and as results they proposed a model with homoskedastic shocks to the permanent component and a three-state Markov-switching variance for the transitory shocks:

$$\sigma_{w,t}^2 = \sigma_w^2, \qquad (10.68')$$

$$\sigma_{u,t}^2 = \sigma_{u,1}^2 S_{2,1t} + \sigma_{u,2}^2 S_{2,2t} + \sigma_{u,3}^2 S_{2,3t}. \qquad (10.69')$$

Writing the model in state-space form, we have

$$y_t = [\, 1 \quad 1 \quad 0 \,] \begin{bmatrix} z_t \\ x_t \\ x_{t-1} \end{bmatrix}, \qquad (10.74)$$

$(y_t = H\beta)$,

$$\begin{bmatrix} z_t \\ x_t \\ x_{t-1} \end{bmatrix} = \begin{bmatrix} 1 & 0 & 0 \\ 0 & \phi_1 & \phi_2 \\ 0 & 1 & 0 \end{bmatrix} \begin{bmatrix} z_{t-1} \\ x_{t-1} \\ x_{t-2} \end{bmatrix} + \begin{bmatrix} w_t \\ u_t \\ 0 \end{bmatrix}, \qquad (10.75)$$

$(\beta_t = F\beta_{t-1} + v_t)$,

$$E(v_t v_t') = Q_t = \begin{bmatrix} \sigma_w^2 & 0 & 0 \\ 0 & \sigma_{u,t}^2 & 0 \\ 0 & 0 & 0 \end{bmatrix}. \qquad (10.76)$$

10.4.2 The Gibbs-Sampling Procedure

For homoskedastic shocks to the permanent component and a three-state Markov-switching variance for shocks to the transitory component, the parameters of interest, along with $\tilde{\beta}_T = \begin{bmatrix} \beta_1 \ldots \beta_T \end{bmatrix}'$ and $\tilde{S}_{2,T} = \begin{bmatrix} S_{2,1} \ldots S_{2,T} \end{bmatrix}'$, are $\tilde{\theta} = \{\sigma_w^2, \phi_1, \phi_2, \sigma_{u1}^2, \sigma_{u2}^2, \sigma_{u3}^2, p_{11}, p_{12}, p_{21}, p_{22}, p_{31}, p_{32}\}$. The following explains briefly how Gibbs sampling is implemented:

STEP 1   Conditional on $\tilde{S}_{2,T}$, parameters of the model, and data, generate $\tilde{\beta}_T$, or equivalently, generate $\tilde{z}_T = \begin{bmatrix} z_1 & \ldots & z_T \end{bmatrix}'$ and $\tilde{x}_T = \begin{bmatrix} x_1 & \ldots & x_T \end{bmatrix}'$.

STEP 2   Conditional on $\tilde{z}_T$, generate σ_w^2 by focusing on equation (10.66). $\tilde{z}_T$ from step 1 is treated as data.

STEP 3   Conditional on $\tilde{x}_T$, generate $\{\phi_1, \phi_2, \sigma_{u1}^2, \sigma_{u2}^2, \sigma_{u3}^2, p_{11}, p_{12}, p_{21}, p_{22}, p_{31}, p_{32}\}$ by focusing on equation (10.67). $\tilde{x}_T$ from step 1 is treated as data.

The state-space representation of the model in (10.75)–(10.77) suggests that generating $\tilde{\beta}_T$ in step 1 is an example of the case in section 8.2 with $J = 2$. In addition, conditional on $\tilde{\beta}_T$, or equivalently, $\tilde{z}_T$ and $\tilde{x}_T$, (10.66) and (10.67) can be treated as two independent equations, because the shocks to the two equations are independent. Thus, steps 2 and 3 are valid. Notice also that step 3 is an example of the regression with a three-state Markov-switching variance presented in chapter 9.

10.4.3 Empirical Results

On purely statistical grounds, Engel and Kim (1996) reported the following empirical results:

1. The real shocks that drive the permanent component are relatively small compared to the nominal shocks that cause temporary deviations in the real exchange rate from its permanent component.

2. The transitory component itself is highly persistent, with the sum of ϕ_1 and ϕ_2 equal to 0.987. (The half-life of a transitory shock is 55 months.).

3. All of the periods of medium and high volatility in the real exchange rate appear to be linked to nominal events—either periods in which the nominal exchange rate floated, or periods of extraordinary inflation that can be linked to monetary events. (Refer to figures 10.9a–10.9c, in which probabilities of low-, medium-, and high-variance states are depicted, respectively.)

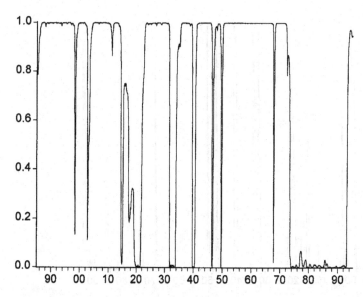

Figure 10.9a
Probability of a low-variance state for transitory component of real exchange rate

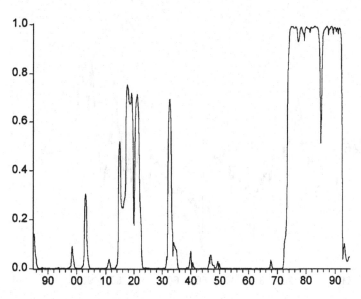

Figure 10.9b
Probability of a medium-variance state for transitory component of real exchange rate

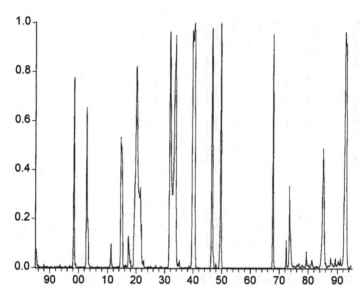

Figure 10.9c
Probability of a high-variance state for transitory component of real exchange rate

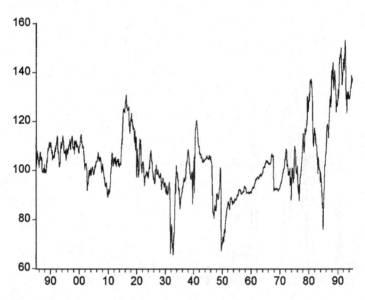

Figure 10.10
Log of U.S./U.K. real exchange rates, 1885–1995

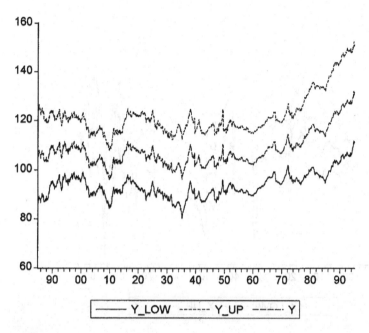

Figure 10.11
Permanent components (y_t) and their 95% confidence bands

   Figure 10.10 shows the log of the U.S./U.K. real exchange rate. The permanent and transitory components estimated from the model are depicted along their 95% confidence bands in figures 10.11 and 10.12. For an economic interpretation of the permanent component, Engel and Kim (1996) relate it to an alternative, theory-based permanent component from Mark and Choi 1996 and Engel 1995. They conclude that relative per capita output levels may be important in understanding the behavior of the long-run real exchange rate.

Appendix: GAUSS Program to Accompany Chapter 10

1. SWMSGIBS.PRG: A Gibbs-sampling approach to a dynamic factor Model with Markov-switching (based on Kim and Nelson 1998).

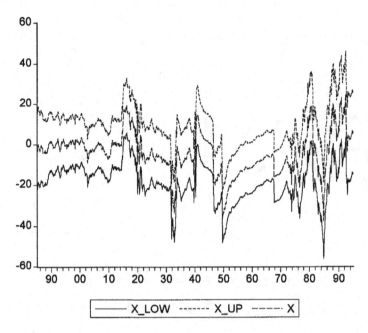

Figure 10.12
Transitory components (x_t) and their 95% confidence bands

References

Albert, James H., and Siddhartha Chib. 1993. "Bayes Inference via Gibbs Sampling of Autoregressive Time Series Subject to Markov Mean and Variance Shifts." *Journal of Business and Economic Statistics,* 11(1), 1–15.

Burns, A. F., and W. C. Mitchell. 1946. *Measuring Business Cycles.* New York: National Bureau of Economic Research.

Diebold, Francis X., J.-H. Lee, and G. C. Weinbach. 1994. "Regime Switching with Time-Varying Transition Probabilities." In *Nonstationary Time Series Analysis and Cointegration,* C. Hargreaves, ed. Oxford: Oxford University Press.

Diebold, Francis X., and Glenn Rudebusch. 1990. "A Nonparametric Investigation of Duration Dependence in the American Business Cycle, *Journal of Political Economy*, 98, 596–616.

Diebold, Francis X., and Glenn D. Rudebusch. 1996. "Measuring Business Cycles: A Modern Perspective." *Review of Economics and Statistics*, 78, 67–77.

Diebold, Francis X., Glenn Rudebusch, and D. E. Sichel. 1993, "Further Evidence on Business-Cycle Duration Dependence." In *Business Cycles, Indicators and Forecasting,* ed. : James Stock and Mark Watson, 255–284. Chicago: University of Chicago Press for the National Bureau of Economic Research.

Durland, J. Michael, and Thomas H. McCurdy. 1994, "Duration-Dependent Transitions in a Markov Model of U.S. GNP Growth." *Journal of Business and Economic Statistics,* 12(3), 279–288.

Engel, Charles. 1995. "Accounting for U.S. Real Exchange Rate Changes." Working paper No. 5646, National Bureau of Economic Research, Cambridge, MA.

Engel, Charles and Chang-Jin Kim. 1998. "The Long-Run U.S/U.K Real Exchange Rate." Forthcoming, *Journal of Money, Credit, and Banking*.

Filardo, Andrew. 1994. "Business Cycle Phases and Their Transitional Dynamics." *Journal of Business and Economic Statistics*, 12, 299–308.

Filardo, Andrew J., and Stephen F. Gordon. 1993. "Business Cycle Durations." Working paper, Federal Reserve Bank, Kansas City, MO.

Garcia, Rene, and Pierre Perron. 1996. "An Analysis of Real Interest Under Regime Shift." *Review of Economics and Statistics*, 78, 111–125.

Gelman, A., and D. B. Rubin. 1992. "A Single Sequence from the Gibbs Sampler Gives a False Sense of Security." In *Bayesian Statistics*, ed. J. M. Bernardo, J. O. Berger, A. P. Dawid, and A. F. M. Smith, pp. 625–631.

George, Edward I., and Robert E. McCulloch. 1993. "Variable Selection via Gibbs Sampling." *Journal of the American Statistical Association*, 88(423), Theory and Methods, 881–889.

Geweke, John. 1996. "Variable Selection and Model Comparison in Regression." In *Bayesian Statistics 5*, ed. J. O. Berger, J. M. Bernardo, A. P. Dawid, and A. F. M. Smith. Oxford: Oxford University Press.

Hamilton, James. 1989. "A New Approach to the Economic Analysis of Nonstationary Time Series and the Business Cycle." *Econometrica*, 57(2), 357–384.

Kim, Chang-Jin. 1996. "Predicting Business Cycle Phases with Indexes of Leading and Coincident Indicators: A Multivariate Regime-Shift Approach." *Journal of Economic Theory and Ecomometrics*, 2(2), 1–27.

Kim, Chang-Jin, and Charles R. Nelson. 1998. "Business Cycle Turning Points, a New Coincident Index, and Tests of Duration Dependence Based on a Dynamic Factor Model with Regime-Switching." Forthcoming, *Review of Economics and Economic Statistics*.

Mark, Nelson C., and Doo-Yull Choi. 1996. "Real Exchange-Rate Prediction over Long Horizons." *Journal of International Economics*, 1, 4, 229–250.

Stock, James H., and Mark W. Watson. 1991. "A Probability Model of the Coincident Economic Indicators." In *Leading Economic Indicators: New Approaches and Forecasting Records*, ed. K. Lahiri and G. H. Moore. Cambridge: Cambridge University Press, 63–89.

11 Gibbs-Sampling and Parameter Uncertainty: Testing for Mean Reversion in Heteroskedastic Data

In the classical approach to a state-space model or a Markov-switching model, inference on the unobserved state vector (β_t) or the Markov-switching variable (S_t) is made conditional on the parameter estimates of the model. This approach ignores uncertainty or the sampling variation associated with the parameter estimates of the model. As discussed in earlier chapters, an advantage of the Bayesian Gibbs-sampling approach is that inferences are made from the joint distribution of the variates of interest and the unknown parameters of the model. Thus, the inference via Bayesian Gibbs-sampling incorporates uncertainty associated with the underlying paramters of the model.

In section 11.1, we discuss two alternative ways of incorporating parameter uncertainty in making inference: one based on the asymptotic normality of the MLE in the classical approach and the other based on the Gibbs-sampling approach. The two methods are compared within the context of a three-state Markov-switching variance model of U.S. monthly stock returns. Section 11.2 reviews variance ratio tests of mean reversion in stock prices. Section 11.3 motivates new tests of mean reversion in the presence of heteroskedasticity. It is shown that the sampling distribution of the variance ratio test statistic could be biased if the historical pattern of heteroskedasticity is not explicitly taken into account. Section 11.4 presents new tests of mean reversion in heteroskedastic data, with a focus on the role of Gibbs-sampling in incorporating the effects of parameter uncertainty on the sampling distribution of the test statistic. Most of the results in this chapter originally appeared in Kim, Nelson, and Startz 1998.

11.1 Alternative Ways of Incorporating Parameter Uncertainty

In sections 4.5 and 9.2, we considered both the classical and the Bayesian Gibbs-sampling approaches to making inference on the following three-state Markov-switching variance model of U.S. stock returns:

$$y_t \sim N(0, \sigma_t^2), \tag{11.1}$$

$$\sigma_t^2 = \sigma_1^2 S_{1t} + \sigma_2^2 S_{2t} + \sigma_3^2 S_{3t}, \tag{11.2}$$

$$S_{kt} = 1 \text{ if } S_t = k, \quad \text{and } S_{kt} = 0, \text{ otherwise}, \quad k = 1, 2, 3, \tag{11.3}$$

$$Pr[S_t = j | S_{t-1} = i] = p_{ij}, \quad i, j = 1, 2, 3, \tag{11.4}$$

$$\sum_{j=1}^{3} p_{ij} = 1 \tag{11.5}$$

$$\sigma_1^2 < \sigma_2^2 < \sigma_3^2, \tag{11.6}$$

where y_t is the demeaned stock return and S_t is an unobserved state variable that evolves according to a first-order Markov process with transition probabilities given in (11.4).

Conditional on the data, suppose that we want to estimate the 95% confidence bands for σ_t^2, $t = 1, 2, \ldots, T$, by taking into account the uncertainty associated with underlying parameters that describe the dynamics of σ_t^2. The following sections explain two alternative ways of achieving this goal.

11.1.1   Utilizing the Asymptotic Normality of MLE

If we let $\theta = \{\sigma_1^2, \sigma_2^2, \sigma_3^2, p_{11}, p_{12}, p_{21}, p_{22}, p_{31}, p_{32}\}$, the usual inference on σ_t^2, $t = 1, 2, \ldots, T$, is made as follows: First, we estimate the parameters of the model, $\hat{\theta}_{MLE}$, using data $\tilde{y}_T = [y_1 \ y_2 \ldots y_T]'$ and the maximum likelihood estimation method; second, we run the basic filter (or smoother) to make inference on $Pr[S_{kt} = 1|\tilde{y}_{t-1}]$ (or $Pr[S_{kt} = 1|\tilde{y}_T]$), $t = 1, 2, \ldots, T$. We then calculate $\hat{\sigma}_t^2|\tilde{y}_\tau, t = 1, 2, \ldots, T$:

$$\hat{\sigma}_t^2 \mid \tilde{y}_\tau, \hat{\theta}_{ML}$$
$$= \hat{\sigma}_{1,ML}^2 Pr[S_{1t}|\hat{\theta}_{ML}, \tilde{y}_\tau] + \hat{\sigma}_{2,ML}^2 Pr[S_{2t}|\hat{\theta}_{ML}, \tilde{y}_\tau] + \hat{\sigma}_{3,ML}^2 Pr[S_{3t}|\hat{\theta}_{ML}, \tilde{y}_\tau], \tag{11.7}$$

where $\tilde{y}_\tau = [y_1 \ y_2 \ldots y_\tau]'$. (In this section, we focus on the case in which $\tau = T$ to directly compare the results from the MLE approach with the results from the Gibbs-sampling approach.) This provides us with a point estimate of $\hat{\sigma}_t^2 \mid \tilde{y}_\tau, \hat{\theta}_{ML}$ for each $t = 1, 2, \ldots, T$.

In estimating the 95% confidence bands for σ_t^2, $t = 1, 2, \ldots, T$, by incorporating uncertainty associated with parameter estimates, we can employ the asymptotic-normality property of the maximum likelihood estimators:

$$\hat{\theta}_{ML} \xrightarrow{a} N(\theta, \text{Cov}(\hat{\theta}_{ML})). \tag{11.8}$$

Once $\hat{\theta}_{ML}$ and $\text{Cov}(\hat{\theta}_{ML})$ are obtained, we can, using the above asymptotic normality, generate J potentially large sets of θ parameters, $\{\theta^1, \theta^2, \theta^2, \ldots \theta^J\}$, from the following multivariate normal distribution:

$$N(\hat{\theta}_{ML}, \text{Cov}(\hat{\theta}_{ML})), \tag{11.9}$$

so that the mean of the J generated sets of parameters is equal to $\hat{\theta}_{ML}$ and the mean of the covariance matrices of the J generated parameters is equal to $\text{Cov}(\hat{\theta}_{ML})$, as $J \to \infty$. Then, conditional on each generated set θ^j of parameters and the data set $\tilde{y}_T$, we calculate the smoothed probability, $Pr[S_{kt} \mid \tilde{y}_T, \theta^j]$, $k = 1, 2, 3$, $j = 1, 2, \ldots, J$, $t = 1, 2, \ldots, T$. For each $t = 1, 2, \ldots, T$, this allows us to calculate J potential realizations of $\sigma_t^2 \mid \tilde{y}_T, \theta^j$, each realization being associated with a particular realization of the parameters from the multivariate normal distribution in (11.9):

$$(\sigma_t^2)^j \mid \tilde{y}_T, \theta^j = (\sigma_1^2)^j Pr[S_{1t}|\theta^j, \tilde{y}_T] + (\sigma_2^2)^j Pr[S_{2t}|\theta^j, \tilde{y}_T]$$

$$+ (\sigma_3^2)^j Pr[S_{3t}|\theta^j, \tilde{y}_T], j = 1, 2, \ldots, J; \quad t = 1, 2, \ldots, T. \tag{11.10}$$

These J realizations of $(\sigma_t^2)^j$, $j = 1, 2, \ldots, J$, are the basis for determining the confidence bands. When $J = 10,000$, for example, after ordering the realizations in an ascending order, the 95% confidence bands are given by $\{(\sigma_t^2)^{250}, (\sigma_t^2)^{9750}\}$, for $t = 1, 2, \ldots, T$.

11.1.2 Utilizing Bayesian Gibbs-Sampling

The above approach, based on the asymptotic normality of the MLE, may not be valid when the sample size is not large enough. In addition, it is difficult to determine how large the sample size should be in order for asymptotic normality to hold.

In making inference on σ_t^2 within the Gibbs-sampling framework, however, asymptotic normality need not be assumed, and the incorporation of parameter uncertainty is built in. Let us review how inferences are made within the Gibbs-sampling framework on the unknown parameters of the model and the unobserved state variables S_t, $t = 1, 2, \ldots, T$, and thus on σ_t^2, $t = 1, 2, \ldots, T$. In the j-th iteration of the Gibbs-sampling, we perform the following steps:

STEP 1   Conditional on data $(\tilde{y}_T)$ and on $\theta^{j-1} = \{\sigma_1^2, \sigma_2^2, \sigma_3^2, p_{11}, p_{12}, p_{21}, p_{22}, p_{31}, p_{32}\}^{j-1}$, generate S_t^j, $t = 1, 2, \ldots, T$.

STEP 2   Conditional on data $(\tilde{y}_T)$ and S_t^j, $t = 1, 2, \ldots, T$, generate θ^j.

STEP 3   Conditional on generated S_t^j, $t = 1, 2, \ldots, T$, and generated θ^j, calculate $(\sigma_t^2)^j$ in the following way:

$$(\sigma_t^2)^j \mid \tilde{y}_T, \theta^j = (\sigma_{1t}^2)^j S_{1t}^j + (\sigma_{2t}^2)^j S_{2t}^j + (\sigma_{3t}^2)^j S_{3t}^j,$$

$$j = 1, 2, \ldots, J, \quad t = 1, 2, \ldots, T. \tag{11.11}$$

Note that equation (11.11) is directly comparable to equation (11.10). The J realizations of $(\sigma_t^2)^j$, $j = 1, 2, \ldots, J$, from (11.11) represent the posterior distribution of σ_t^2, and these are the basis for inference. The posterior mean of σ_t^2 is comparable to $\hat{\sigma}_t^2 \mid \tilde{y}_T, \hat{\theta}_{ML}$ from equation (11.7). When $J = 10,000$, for example, after ordering the realizations in an ascending order, the 95% confidence bands are given by $\{(\sigma_t^2)^{250}, (\sigma_t^2)^{9750}\}$, for $t = 1, 2, \ldots, T$.

11.2 Variance Ratio Tests of Mean Reversion: A Review

The variance ratio (VR) statistic was introduced by Cochrane (1988) to measure the relative importance of the random walk component in real GDP. In using the VR to test the null hypothesis that a series is a random walk against the alternative that it is mean reverting, one makes use of the fact that the variance of the K-period difference of a random walk is simply proportional to K. In the asset return context, let V_t denote the log of the market value of a risky portfolio so that the K-period difference is the K-period return

$$R_t^K = V_t - V_{t-K}. \tag{11.12}$$

If V_t is a random walk, or equivalently, one-period returns are serially random, then we have

$$V_t - V_{t-1} = u_t; \quad u_t \sim \text{i.i.d.}(\mu, \sigma^2), \tag{11.13}$$

and because the K-period return is the accumulation of K successive u_ts,

$$\text{Var}(R_t^K) = K\sigma^2. \tag{11.14}$$

The VR statistic is defined in the asset context as

$$VR(K) = \frac{\text{Var}(R^K)}{\text{Var}(R^1)} \frac{1}{K}, \tag{11.15}$$

which is unity under the random walk hypothesis.

If the series exhibits mean reversion, so that changes in either direction tend to be offset over time by movement back toward the starting point, then $\text{Var}(R^K)$ is less than K times as large as $\text{Var}(R^1)$, so the VR will be less than unity. One explanation for mean reversion would be the presence of a transitory component in asset prices. However, to judge whether or not a sample VR is significantly below unity, one needs to know the sampling distribution of the VR under the null hypothesis.

Poterba and Summers (1988), hereafter PS, and Lo and MacKinlay (1988) used the VR to test for mean reversion in stock prices and concluded that a transitory component accounts for a substantial fraction of the variance in stock returns over horizons of several years. Inference is based on Monte Carlo simulation of the sampling distribution of the VR under the null hypothesis of serially random returns. Recognizing the well-documented heteroskedasticity in stock returns over their sample period, PS compared sampling distributions of the VR for homoskedastic and heteroskedastic data-generating processes and found no meaningful difference. Their data-generating process is intended to preserve the persistence of heteroskedasticity that is observed in historical returns but not the specific pattern. M. Kim, Nelson, and Startz (1991), hereafter KNS91, estimated the sampling distribution of the VR by randomizing actual returns. They also suggested a "stratified randomization" that preserves the historical pattern of high- and low-volatility periods. The fact that the latter revealed substantially weaker evidence of mean reversion than the former suggests that the specific pattern of heteroskedasticity in the sample period may play an important role in inference. However, the approach of KNS91 assumes that the econometrician has certain knowledge of the pattern and does not exploit any information from the pattern of heteroskedasticity in the estimation of the VR. Furthermore, resampling of returns is limited by segregation into subperiods according to volatility.

11.3   Historical Pattern of Heteroskedasticity and the Sampling Distribution of the Variance Ratio Statistic

In measuring the statistical significance of the VR statistic, PS used an estimate of the standard error based on Monte Carlo simulations assuming independently and normally distributed returns. However, as noted above, stock returns are unconditionally non-normal and heteroskedastic with high persistence. As a justification for their use of the estimate of the standard error based on Monte Carlo simulations of i.i.d. normal returns, PS showed that the empirical distribution of the VR statistic with heteroskedasticity is no different from that with homoskedasticity.

Instead of employing Monte Carlo experiments, which require a distributional assumption, KNS91 employed randomization methods to estimate the unknown distribution of the VR. Randomization focuses on the null hypothesis that one variable is distributed independently of another. To estimate the distribution of the VR statistic under the null, KNS91 first shuffled the data to destroy any time dependence, then recalculated the test statistic for each reshuffling. In the presence of persistent heteroskedasticity, however, the usual randomization method may fail because the errors are not interchangeable, since randomization also destroys any time dependence in variance. KNS91 also presented results for a "stratified randomization" that preserves the historical pattern of heteroskedasticity. Their stratified randomization provides a way to retain information in historical heteroskedasticity in returns. However, their division of the sample into low- and high-variance states is arbitrary and limited.

PS reported a Monte Carlo experiment that mimics the actual persistence of volatility but does not preserve the historical pattern. This may be valid when the particular historical pattern of heteroskedasticity does not affect the sampling distribution of the VR statistic.

In this section, we reexamine the effects of heteroskedasticity on the sampling distribution of the VR statistic, as in Kim, Nelson, and Startz 1998, hereafter, KNS98. In particular, we look at the effects of the persistence or specific pattern of heteroskedasticity.

KNS98 experimented by incorporating different amounts of information about heteroskedasticity in historical returns when generating artificial histories, and the empirical distribution of the VR for each case was compared to that of the homoskedastic case. All the results below are based on 10,000 sets of generated monthly returns with 732 observations.

Monte Carlo Experiment 1: No Persistence in Heteroskedasticity

Data-Generating Process

$y_t \sim N(0, \sigma_t^2),$

$\sigma_t^2 = \sigma_1^2 S_{1t} + \sigma_2^2 S_{2t} + \sigma_3^2 S_{3t},$

S_{kt} if $S_t = k,$ and $S_{kt} = 0,$ otherwise; $k = 1, 2, 3,$

$Pr[S_t = j] = p_j,$ $j = 1, 2, 3,$

where the unobserved state variable, S_t, at time t evolves independently of past realizations. The values of p_1, p_2, and p_3 used for data generation are the steady-state probabilities calculated from estimates of the transition probabilities in the three-state Markov-switching variance model of section 11.1, based on historical data. (The parameter estimates are reported in section 9.2.) Values for the other parameters, σ_1^2, σ_2^2, and σ_3^2 are also taken from estimation of the same model based on historical data.

In the above data-generating process, we allow the variance of the returns to be heteroskedastic and regime switching, but switches between regimes are independent of the previous regime. The generated returns contain part of the information in historical returns: that is, proportionally to the frequency with which each regime occurs out of the whole sample. They do not retain information on either the persistence or the pattern of heteroskedasticity in historical returns.

Figure 11.1 shows the empirical distribution function for the 96-month VR statistic in both the homoskedastic and heteroskedastic cases. When returns are independent, heteroskedasticity does not seem to affect the empirical distribution function of the VR.

Monte Carlo Experiment 2: Heteroskedasticity with Historical Persistence

Data-Generating Process

$y_t \sim N(0, \sigma_t^2)$,

$\sigma_t^2 = \sigma_1^2 S_{1t} + \sigma_2^2 S_{2t} + \sigma_3^2 S_{3t}$,

$S_{kt} = 1$ if $S_t = k$, and $S_{kt} = 0$, otherwise; $k = 1, 2, 3$,

$Pr[S_t = j | S_{t-1} = i] = p_{ij}$, $i, j = 1, 2, 3$,

$$\sum_{j=1}^{3} p_{ij} = 1,$$

$\sigma_1^2 < \sigma_2^2 < \sigma_3^2$,

which is the model described in section 11.1. All the parameters that are needed to generate returns are from the Gibbs-sampling estimates based on historical data. Using the estimates of transition probabilities, $\{S_t, t = 1, 2, \ldots, T\}$ is

Density

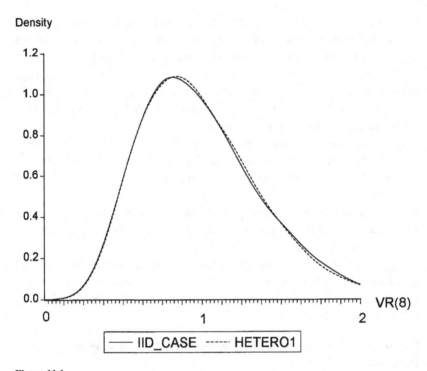

Figure 11.1
Empirical distribution of 96-month variance ratio statistic with homoskedastic returns and heteroskedastic returns from Monte Carlo experiment 1

generated first. Then along with estimates of σ_k^2, $k = 1, 2, 3$, we can easily calculate, using (11.2) and (11.3), $\{\sigma_t^2, t = 1, 2, \ldots, T\}$, which is in turn used to generate returns. In this way, information in historical returns is conveyed to generated returns only through the parameter estimates of the model used for return generation. Returns generated in this way retain information in historical returns beyond that in experiment 1. The additional information is the persistence of historical-return variance. However, they do not retain the specific pattern of heteroskedasticity in historical returns.

Figure 11.2 shows the results. Even when we incorporate persistent heteroskedasticity in our data-generating process, the empirical distribution of the VR statistic does not seem to be affected very much. The results in figures 11.1 and 11.2 are consistent with those of PS. They seem to suggest that the degree of persistence in heteroskedasticity does not affect the distribution of the VR

Density

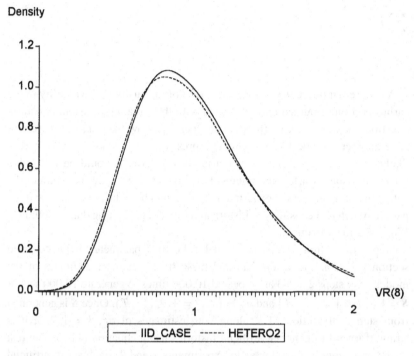

Figure 11.2
Empirical distribution of 96-month variance ratio statistic with homoskedastic returns and heteroskedastic returns from Monte Carlo experiment 2

statistic very much; at least not when the pattern of heteroskedasticity is not fixed when data are generated.

Monte Carlo Experiment 3: Heteroskedasticity with Historical Persistence and Pattern

Data-Generating Process

$$y_t \sim N(0, \sigma_t^2),$$

$$\sigma_t^2 = \sigma_1^2 S_{1t} + \sigma_2^2 S_{2t} + \sigma_3^2 S_{3t},$$

$$S_{kt} = 1 \text{ if } S_t = k, \quad \text{and } S_{kt} = 0, \text{ otherwise;} \quad k = 1, 2, 3,$$

$$Pr[S_t = j | S_{t-1} = i] = p_{ij}, \quad i, j = 1, 2, 3,$$

$$\sum_{j=1}^{3} p_{ij} = 1,$$

$$\sigma_1^2 < \sigma_2^2 < \sigma_3^2.$$

As we see in figure 9.3, we have a period of unusually high volatility in the earlier portion of our sample associated with the Great Depression. A natural question one might ask is: If the history persists, how likely is it that we will have another episode like the Great Depression? If the answer is "not very likely," it may suggest that such unusually rare events should be controlled for in our Monte Carlo experiments. For this purpose, while maintaining the data-generating process in experiment 2, we retain both the persistence and the pattern of heteroskedasticity in historical returns in generating data for our new Monte Carlo experiments.

Step 1 of section 11.1 is replaced by the final parameter estimates from section 9.2. Conditional on data and these final parameter estimates of the model, only steps 2 and 3 are repeated 10,000 times to generate 10,000 sets of $\tilde{S} = \{S_t, \ t = 1, 2, \ldots, T\}$ and $\tilde{\sigma}_T^2 = \{\sigma_t^2, t = 1, 2, \ldots, T\}$. Once $\tilde{S}$ is generated from step 2 of section 11.1, along with estimates of σ_k^2, $k = 1, 2, 3$, it is straightforward to generate artificial histories using equation (11.2). The rest of the procedure is the same as in experiments 1 and 2. Each set of artificial returns generated in this way retains, on average, the same historical pattern of heteroskedasticity plotted in figure 9.3.

Figure 11.3 shows the results. Unlike the previous two cases, the empirical distribution of the VR is much different from that in the homoskedastic case, when the pattern of heteroskedasticity is the historical one. The distribution has wider variance and is more skewed than in the homoskedastic case. This suggests that the VR tests of PS based on Monte Carlo experiments and those of KNS91 based on the usual randomization method had the wrong size, rejecting the null of random returns in favor of mean reversion too often.

11.4   New Tests of Mean Reversion in the Presence of Heteroskedasticity

In this section, we consider two new VR tests of mean reversion proposed by KNS98 that condition on the information that the data contain the historical pattern of heteroskedasticity. For new autoregression tests of mean reversion in heteroskedastic data, refer to Kim and Nelson 1998. KNS91 carried out a stratified randomization of the data in which returns from the high-variance period

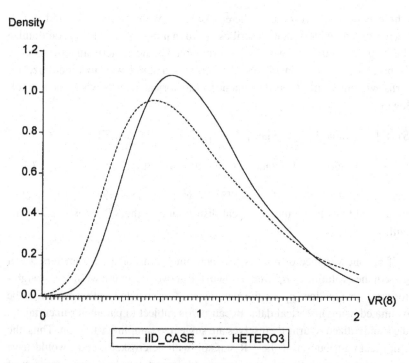

Figure 11.3
Empirical distribution of 96-month variance ratio statistic with homoskedastic returns and heteroskedastic returns from Monte Carlo experiment 3

1930–1939 were placed in a separate urn when generating artificial histories. Their division of the whole sample into only high-variance and low-variance periods, however, is arbitrary and limited, and fails to reflect the uncertainty inherent in estimating state changes. The Gibbs-sampling approach, however, allows us to obtain valid significance levels. Then we consider a potentially more efficient test for mean reversion based on the VR of appropriately standardized returns. Randomization methods, instead of Monte Carlo experiments, are employed to allow for stock returns to be non-normal within a state.

11.4.1   Tests Based on the Variance Ratio of Historical Returns

Assume that

$$y_t \sim (0, \sigma_t^2(\theta)),$$

$$\theta = \{\sigma_1^2, \sigma_2^2, \sigma_3^2, p_{11}, p_{12}, p_{21}, p_{22}, p_{31}, p_{32}\},$$

where demeaned return y_t is heteroskedastic with variance σ_t^2 and θ is a vector of parameters that describes the dynamics of σ_t^2. If we randomize the original return y_t, we lose information on the pattern and persistence of heteroskedasticity in historical returns. A natural way to randomize returns without losing time dependence in historical returns would be the following:

STEP 1   Standardize y_t to get $\{y_t^* = y_t/\sigma_t,\ t = 1, 2, \ldots, T\}$.

STEP 2   Randomize the standardized returns to get $\{y_t^{**},\ t = 1, 2, \ldots, T\}$.

STEP 3   Destandardize y_t^{**} to get $\{\tilde{y}_t^{**} = y_t^{**} \times \sigma_t,\ t = 1, 2, \ldots, T\}$, which is to be used to estimate the empirical distribution of the VR statistic under the null.

If σ_t^2, the variance of returns for each time point, or the parameters θ that govern the evolution of σ_t^2 were known, the above procedure would be straightforward. In practice, σ_t^2 or the parameters θ associated with σ_t^2 have to be estimated using historical data. Because θ is subject to parameter uncertainty, the standardized returns themselves are subject to sampling variation. Thus, the empirical distribution of the VR statistic with heteroskedasticity would have to account for both the effect of parameter uncertainty in θ and the effect of randomization.

To incorporate the effect of uncertainty in the parameters associated with variance of returns, we augment the Gibbs-sampling approach introduced in section 9.2 with the standardizing step of the above procedure. As in section 9.2, each run of Gibbs sampling based on historical returns provides us with particular realizations of the set $\{S_t, t = 1, 2, \ldots, T\}$ and $\{\sigma_1^2, \sigma_2^2, \sigma_3^2\}$, which are used to calculate σ_t^2 according to equation (11.2). Using σ_t^2, $t = 1, 2, \ldots, T$, simulated in this way, we can proceed with steps 1 through 3. If the above procedure is repeated, say, 10,000 times, with each iteration augmented by simulations of σ_t^2 from each run of Gibbs-sampling, we have 10,000 sets of randomized returns. These artificial histories condition on the information about the pattern of heteroskedasticity contained in the historical returns, incorporate parameter uncertainty, and are consistent with the null of mean reversion due to randomization. For each of these 10,000 sets of artificial histories, the VR statistic is calculated and can be used to estimate the empirical distribution of the VR statistic. To estimate the significance level, we count how many times the VRs for the artificial histories fall below the VRs for original historical returns.

11.4.2   New Tests Based on the Variance Ratio of Standardized Returns

This section suggests a modification of the VR statistic to make more efficient use of the information in the data about mean reversion by weighting observations appropriately based on the information in the data about the timing and magnitude of volatility changes.

By standardizing historical returns before calculating the VR test statistic, appropriate weights can be assigned to observations depending on their volatility. An additional complication of this approach is that unlike the test based on original returns, the test statistic itself is subject to sampling variation due to uncertainty in the parameters that describe the dynamics of heteroskedasticity. Thus we compare two distributions: the distribution (due to parameter uncertainty) of the VR test statistic for standardized historical returns and the distribution of the VR test statistic under the null hypothesis estimated from randomizing the standardized returns. As before, in standardizing historical returns, we employ the Gibbs-sampling described in section 9.2.

As in section 11.4.1, at the end of each run of the Gibbs-sampling, we have the simulated set $\{\sigma_t^2, \ t = 1, 2, \ldots, T\}$. We conduct the following steps to perform tests based on the VR of standardized returns:

STEP 1   Standardize y_t to get $\{y_t^* = y_t \times \frac{1}{\sigma_t}, \ t = 1, 2, \ldots, T\}$, which is a particular realization of standardized historical returns.

STEP 2   Calculate VRs for standardized historical returns y_t^*, denoted by $VR^*(k), k = 1, 2, \ldots, K$.

STEP 3   Randomize the standardized returns from step 1 to get $\{y_t^{**}, \ t = 1, 2, \ldots, T\}$.

STEP 4   Calculate VRs for randomized returns y_t^{**} from step 3, denoted by $VR^{**}(k), k = 1, 2, \ldots, K$.

STEP 5   Compare $VR^*(k)$ and $VR^{**}(k)$.

These steps are repeated, say, 10,000 times to get the posterior distribution of the VR for standardized historical returns, $VR^*(k)$, and the empirical distribution of the VR under the null of no mean reversion, $VR^{**}(k)$. To estimate the significance level for the test of mean reversion, we count how many times the VR for the standardized and randomized returns ($VR^{**}(k)$) from Gibbs-sampling-augmented randomization falls below the VR for standardized historical returns ($VR^{*}(k)$) from Gibbs-sampling.

11.4.3 Empirical Results and Comparison with Prior Literature

The data set consists of monthly total returns on NYSE stocks from the CRSP files for both value-weighted (VW) and equal-weighted (EW) portfolios. The one-month T-bill return from Ibbotson Associates is subtracted to obtain the excess return. For comparability with PS and KNS91, the sample period is 1926–1986.

The sample values of the VRs for historical returns reported in table 11.1 are necessarily the same as those reported by KNS91 in their tables I and II for the same sample period, and essentially the same as those reported by PS in their table 1 for 1926–1985. The sample estimates point to mean reversion at a horizon of seven years for VW returns and nine years for EW returns. What differs in this chapter is the method of obtaining p-values.

Based on Monte Carlo methods, PS reported a smallest p-value of .08 for VW excess returns and .005 for EW excess returns. They found that heteroskedasticity that mimicked the persistence but not the specific pattern of volatility had no impact on the sampling distribution of the VR. KNS91 reported results of a stratified randomization that preserves the apparent historical pattern of volatility but does not recognize uncertainty in dating the change. The smallest p-values they reported are .135 at lag seven years for VW excess returns and .059 at lag eight years for EW excess returns. In table 11.1, the smallest p-values reported are .255 at lag seven years for VW excess returns and .074 at eight years for EW excess returns. Thus when we use the Gibbs-sampling procedure of section 11.4.1 to account for parameter uncertainty and to allow resampling of the whole data series rather than only subsamples, we find little, if any, evidence of mean reversion for VW excess returns and weaker evidence for mean reversion for EW excess returns.

In section 11.4.2 and in KNS98, it was proposed that the VR be computed after weighting the returns appropriately based on information contained in the data about the pattern of heteroskedasticity. These results are reported in table 11.2. We can no longer report a single number for the sample VR statistic; rather, the evidence from the data is summarized in the form of a posterior distribution. Looking at the results for VW excess returns first,

Table 11.1
Variance ratios for historical monthly CRSP excess returns, 1926–1986

	Lag K (years)							
	2	3	4	5	6	7	8	9
	Sample VR for value-weighted portfolio returns							
	1.035	0.980	0.919	0.849	0.775	0.682	0.671	0.709
	Sampling distribution based on Gibbs-sampling-augmented randomization							
Mean	0.999	1.006	1.012	1.011	1.004	0.994	0.982	0.971
Median	0.992	0.987	0.978	0.961	0.939	0.920	0.899	0.879
SD	0.142	0.227	0.293	0.348	0.392	0.427	0.454	0.476
p-value	0.614	0.489	0.419	0.365	0.316	0.255	0.273	0.332
	Sample VR for equal-weighted portfolio returns							
	1.009	0.923	0.877	0.783	0.646	0.487	0.427	0.421
	Sampling distribution based on Gibbs-sampling-augmented randomization							
Mean	0.998	1.004	1.008	1.005	0.996	0.985	0.972	0.959
Median	0.996	0.984	0.974	0.952	0.926	0.901	0.878	0.860
SD	0.149	0.236	0.302	0.356	0.402	0.439	0.468	0.490
p-value	0.532	0.396	0.373	0.300	0.197	0.091	0.074	0.088

Note: p-value is the frequency with which simulated VR's smaller than the historical sample value were observed in the Gibbs-sampling-augmented randomization under the null hypothesis.

note that the departure of the VR from 1 is no longer greatest at lag eight years; rather, the smallest posterior mean is observed at lag five years. The p-values are obtained as described in section 11.4.2; briefly, at each iteration of Gibbs-sampling, the VRs for standardized returns are compared with the corresponding VRs for standardized and randomized ruturns. The strongest evidence of mean reversion in VW returns, corresponding to the smallest p-values, is actually at a lag of only four years. Thus, the standardized-returns approach to estimating the VR suggests that mean reversion, if it is present, occurs at much shorter lags than has previously been reported. It also suggests that the evidence for mean reversion is weaker than previously reported; the smallest p-value in table 11.2 is .248 for VW returns, compared with the smallest p-value of .135 reported by KNS91 and .08 by PS.

Corresponding results for the EW excess returns are reported in the lower panel of table 11.2. Again, we have a posterior distribution for the historical

Table 11.2
Posterior and sampling distributions of variance ratios of standardized monthly CRSP excess returns, 1926–1986

	Lag K (years)							
	2	3	4	5	6	7	8	9
	Posterior distribution of the VR for standardized VW returns							
Mean	0.962	0.883	0.829	0.826	0.848	0.843	0.901	1.002
Median	0.961	0.882	0.826	0.824	0.848	0.844	0.902	1.004
SD	0.024	0.036	0.042	0.051	0.064	0.078	0.092	0.106
	Sampling distribution of the VR for standardized and randomized returns (based on Gibbs-sampling-augmented randomization)							
Mean	0.994	0.993	0.992	0.992	0.992	0.993	0.994	0.995
Median	0.993	0.985	0.975	0.964	0.954	0.945	0.931	0.921
SD	0.107	0.174	0.228	0.275	0.316	0.354	0.390	0.424
p-value	0.385	0.278	0.248	0.298	0.361	0.380	0.460	0.571
	Posterior distribution of the VR for standardized EW returns							
Mean	0.916	0.819	0.769	0.763	0.755	0.706	0.710	0.742
Median	0.916	0.818	0.768	0.760	0.749	0.700	0.701	0.733
SD	0.034	0.053	0.067	0.078	0.091	0.106	0.121	0.137
	Sampling distribution of the VR for standardized and randomized returns based on Gibbs-sampling-augmented randomization							
Mean	0.995	0.994	0.993	0.992	0.992	0.992	0.993	0.995
Median	0.993	0.987	0.976	0.965	0.954	0.945	0.936	0.923
SD	0.108	0.177	0.230	0.276	0.317	0.355	0.391	0.424
p-value	0.243	0.174	0.179	0.218	0.247	0.229	0.263	0.313

Note: p-value is the frequency with which realizations of the Gibbs sampling of the posterior distribution were smaller than the corresponding realization under the null hypothesis.

sample VR, and its mean departs farthest from 1, at lag seven years. However, the departure from 1 is not nearly as large as in the case of the original VR. The p-values tell an even more different story. The smallest occur at a lag of three years, with a value of .174. That compares with a smallest p-value of .059 at lag eight years reported by KNS91 and .005 by PS. Thus, the Gibbs-sampling approach to estimating the VR both shortens the lag at which evidence of mean reversion is apparent and suggests that the evidence for mean reversion is weaker than previously reported. It seems clear from these results that making

VR(K)

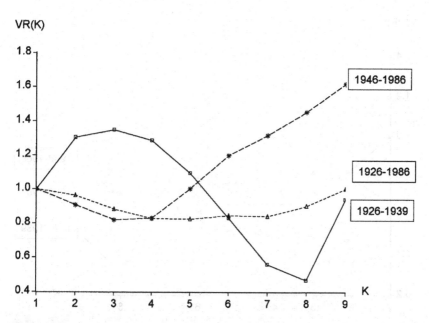

Figure 11.4
Mean of VR for standardized EW returns (1926–1986; 1926–1939; 1946–1986)

use of the information in the data about the pattern of heteroskedasticity, both in estimating the VR and in obtaining p-values, can substantially affect the inferences that are drawn from the data about the degree and lag dynamics of mean reversion. In addition, by comparing the standard deviations (SDs) of the sampling distributions of VRs reported in tables 11.1 and 11.2, one may argue that the tests in section 11.4.2 based on standardized returns are in general more efficient than those in section 11.4.1 based on original returns.

In figures 11.4 and 11.5, posterior means of the VRs for the standardized returns for two subperiods (1926–1939 and 1946–1986) are plotted against those for the full sample (1926–1986). Focusing, for example, on the equal-weighted portfolio, for the subsample that includes Great Depression, the p-value was lowest with 0.06 at lag eight years. For the post–World War II subsample, the p-value was lowest with 0.103 at lag three years. The VRs for the full sample look like some kind of weighted average of those for the two subsamples. If the period of highly volatile returns tends to show stronger evidence of mean reversion, and if the period of far less volatile returns shows less evidence of mean reversion, the VR test results based on historical returns

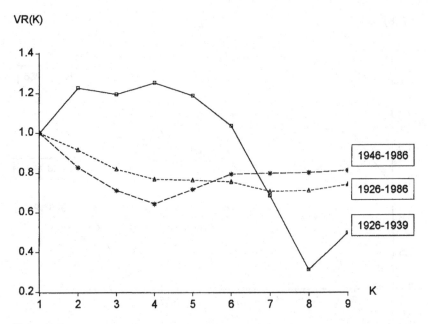

Figure 11.5
Mean of VR for standardized VW returns (1926–1986; 1926–1939; 1946–1986)

may be dominated by the period of highly volatile returns, even though the length of such period is short relative to the full sample. Our test results based on the VR of historical returns tend to confirm this. The information content of returns during the period of high volatility may be small, and using the standardized returns in the VR tests is analogous to assigning less weight on returns during the period of high volatility. Then the test results tend to be dominated by the relatively longer period of low volatility. Test results based on the VR of standardized returns tend to confirm this.

Appendix: GAUSS Programs to Accompany Chapter 11

1. VR_HT_OR.PRG: VR test based on Gibbs-sampling-augmented randomization, original returns (based on Kim, Nelson, and Startz 1998).

2. VR_HT_ST.PRG: VR test based on Gibbs-sampling-augmented randomization, standardized returns (based on Kim, Nelson, and Startz 1998).

References

Cochrane, J. H. 1988. "How Big Is the Random Walk in GNP?" *Journal of Political Economy*, 96, 893–920.

Kim, Chang-Jin and Charles R. Nelson. 1998. "Testing for Mean Reversion in Heteroskedastic Data II: Autoregression Tests Based on Gibbs-Sampling-Augmented Randomization." Forthcoming, *Journal of Empirical Finance*.

Kim, Chang-Jin, Charles R. Nelson, and Richard Startz. 1998a. "Testing for Mean Reversion in Heteroskedastic Data Based on Gibbs-Sampling-Augmented Randomization." *Journal of Empirical Finance*, 5(2), 131–154.

Kim, Myung J., Charles R. Nelson, and Richard Startz. 1991. "Mean Reversion in Stock Prices? A Reappraisal of the Empirical Evidence." *Review of Economic Studies*, 58, 515–528.

Lo, Andrew W., and A. Craig MacKinlay. 1989. "The Size and Power of the Variance Ratio Test in Finite Samples: A Monte Carlo Investigation." *Journal of Econometrics*, 40, 203–238.

Poterba, James M., and Lawrence H. Summers. 1988. "Mean Reversion in Stock Prices: Evidence and Implications."*Journal of Financial Economics*, 22, 27–59.

Index

Printed in the United States
by Baker & Taylor Publisher Services